Know you what it is to be a child?

. . . it is to turn pumpkins into coaches,
and mice into horses, lowness into loftiness,
and nothing into everything.

Francis Thompson, "Shelley"

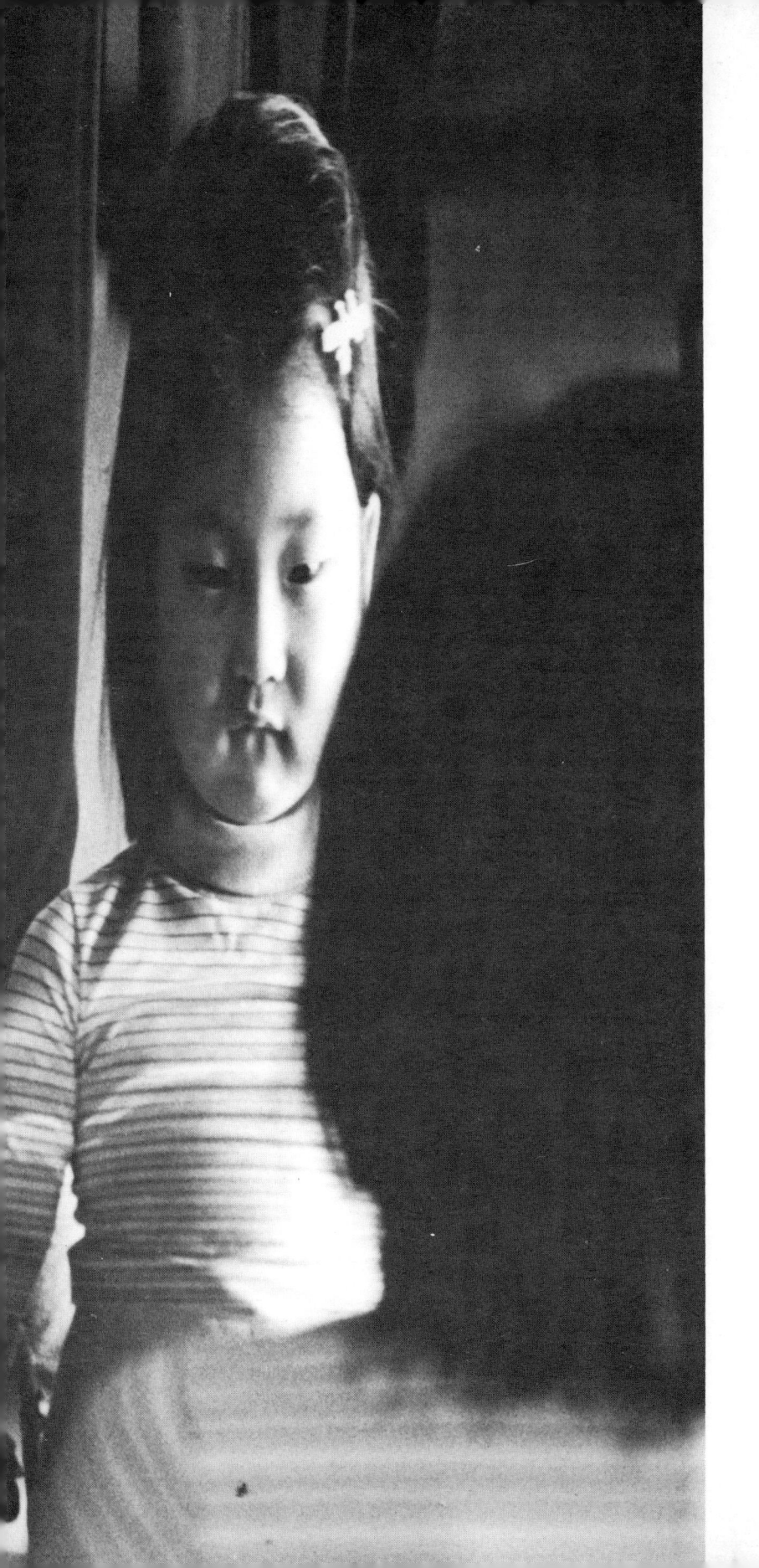

MUSEUMS MAGIC & CHILDREN

Youth Education in Museums

Bonnie Pitman-Gelles

with an Editorial Committee of the American Association of Youth Museums.

Edited by
Carol Bannerman
and
Aubyn Kendall

Published by the Association of Science-Technology Centers, Washington, D.C., with support from the WISEDA Foundation, Fort Worth, Texas. Compiled with support from the National Museum Act, administered by the Smithsonian Institution.

AMERICAN ASSOCIATION OF YOUTH MUSEUMS EDITORIAL COMMITTEE

Mildred Compton, The Children's Museum, Indianapolis, Indiana

Jane Glaser, Office of Museum Programs, Smithsonian Institution, Washington, D.C.

Aalbert Heine, The Corpus Christi Museum, Corpus Christi, Texas

Helmuth J. Naumer, San Antonio Museum Association, San Antonio, Texas

Russell Peithman, Los Angeles Children's Museum, Los Angeles, California

Bonnie Pitman-Gelles, The Seattle Art Museum, Seattle, Washington

Michael Spock, Children's Museum, Boston, Massachusetts

© 1981 by the Association of Science-Technology Centers. All rights reserved. Printed in the United States of America. Designed by Grafik Communications, Ltd., Judy Kirpich and Andrea Legg DeRose.

Cover and Title Page photographs by Bruce Stromberg

Additional copies may be purchased from the Association of Science-Technology Centers, 1413 K St., NW, Tenth Floor, Washington, D.C. 20005.

CONTENTS

Acknowledgements 2
Foreword 3
Introduction 5

Youth Education in Museums
1. Planning a Youth Museum of Exhibits and Programs 7
2. Exhibits and the Museum Experience 23
3. Exhibits Involving the Museum Visitor 35
4. Teaching in the Museum 47
5. Museums and Schools 79
6. Museums and the Classroom Teacher 97
7. The Museum and the Community 111
8. Volunteers in the Museum 131

Program Descriptions
9. Single Visit Programs 145
10. In-Depth and Series Programs 157
11. Courses for Credit 171
12. In-School Programs 179
13. Kits and Loan Materials 187
14. Workshops and Classes 199
15. Junior Curators, Interns and Clubs 213
16. Festivals and Special Events 219

Reference Materials
17. Resources From Museums 229
18. Resource Organizations 234
19. Film Producers and Distributors 236
20. Selected Periodicals 238
21. Bibliographies 240

About AAYM/About ASTC 260

ACKNOWLEDGEMENTS

In 1975, the American Association of Youth Museums (AAYM) received a grant from the National Museum Act, administered by the Smithsonian Institution, to research and write a publication on youth education programs in museums. The initial research for this publication was conducted through questionnaires sent to thousands of art, history, natural history and youth museums, as well as natural science centers, science-technology centers, aquariums, zoos, and botanical gardens. Over the course of several years, additional requests for information were placed in museum journals and letters were sent to individuals identified by members of the editorial committee as well as museum professionals in the above listed types of institutions.

As in all research endeavors, the responses varied. Some museums provided an abundance of materials, while others selected a few programs they felt would be most representative. The members of the editorial committee and I are grateful to the many museum professionals at the hundreds of institutions represented in this publication who had faith in this book. They acknowledged my many letters, returned materials and provided continued guidance regarding developments in their programs. In most cases, the museums had an opportunity to approve a description of their programs; in other instances, the text has been drawn directly from information provided by the institution.

Work on this project fell into two distinct phases. The first part was undertaken with a grant from the National Museum Act and included the research, preparation and editing of a manuscript with the assistance of the AAYM editorial committee and Aubyn Kendall from the Fort Worth Museum of Science and History. Bob Fields and Jane Perkins helped in the first months of the research phase of this project. Russell Peithman, former director of the Charlotte Nature Museum, was the administrator of the National Museum Act grant, and assisted in countless ways.

Once the manuscript was completed, funds were needed for its publication. The Association of Science-Technology Centers obtained a grant from the Wiseda Foundation of Fort Worth, Texas. Because of the time that had passed, many of the programs needed updating. Therefore, over the past year new information has been added and much of the original text rewritten. Dale Zaklad assisted with this phase of research and was a source of continued enthusiasm. I am deeply grateful to Carol Bannerman for her support and enthusiasm. The directors of ASTC, Michael Templeton and Sheila Grinell, both endorsed this project, and their patience and vision must be acknowledged.

There are other people who contributed immeasurably. Several friends—Bonnie Baskin, Ann Bay, Alice Carnes, Priscilla Dunhill, Dan Goldwater, Elaine Gurian, and Ken Yellis—read the manuscript in various stages and offered invaluable suggestions. Susan Smith and Barbara Burnum labored endlessly typing the hundreds of pages of text to prepare the final manuscript. Aubyn Kendall did an outstanding job of editing the original manuscript and taught me a great deal about writing. Without her assistance and guidance, this publication would never have been completed in its initial form.

The editorial committee of the AAYM was a tower of strength and support throughout this project, from their initial planning sessions to the final revisions and recommendations. I thank each member of the committee for his or her encouragement and support.

In addition, there are two other people I would like to acknowledge. Dr. Ferdinand Eckhardt, former director of the Winnipeg Art Gallery, gave me my first job in a museum. He created within me a passionate feeling about the importance of communicating through original artifacts. His belief in the importance of helping the museum visitor to learn *how* to see, rather than lecturing to them, has been a source of continued inspiration to me. He taught me how to look at works of art and how to listen to museum visitors. Dr. Eckhardt always required the best of me and the challenge of meeting his standards forced me to set new ones for myself.

The second person who has been equally important to me through this period has been my husband George. He has carried boxes of files and reams of papers across the country several times. While patiently awaiting the completion of this book, he has been a support to me throughout its various phases.

I would like to dedicate this book to Dr. Eckhardt for introducing me to this field, and to George for helping me to make a contribution to it.

Bonnie Pitman-Gelles
Education Director
Seattle Art Museum

FOREWORD

To those of us involved in youth museums and science centers, *Museums, Magic and Children* is a very important work. Not only is it important for the museum education field, it is also important to educators everywhere, whose work can be enriched by cooperation with museums. Indeed, the book was created in response to hundreds of inquiries received by museums from individuals and organizations wanting to expand their communities' educational offerings through "hands-on" learning activities and exhibitions.

This is a book about children's museums: what they are, how to start one, and how to design "hands-on" programs and exhibits. Beyond that, however, it is about programs for young people in many museums across the nation: More than 200 program descriptions are included representing art, history, and natural history museums, nature centers, science-technology centers, zoos, and others.

Museum professionals generally agree that museums offer a unique and rich learning experience, different from that available in schools. The museum experience is made possible with exhibits, programs, and objects that involve the visitor. Most important are displays and programs that are participatory or experimental in nature. Participatory experiences are offered not only by children's museums, but by many others as well.

As Alma Wittlin has written, children's museums have played a special role in contemporary education by encouraging the use of many senses in the exploration of our environment:

> Long before manipulative activities and the process of discovery were acclaimed by psychologists as motivations to learning, . . . junior museums kept children in rapt attention while handling rocks, calling forth rhythms from African drums, and conducting simple experiments with magnets or inoffensive chemicals.

Todd Pulliam, writing in *Museum News*, raised an important point often overlooked:

> *In a museum sense, there are some differences between children and adults. There are many more similarities. We have confused the differences and failed to note the similarities. . . . I am invariably asked whether children get something special from the tactile experiences provided in many children's museums. And who doesn't? Could you possibly believe that I want only to look at a piece of pumice?*

Children's museums and science-technology centers put Pulliam's ideas about similarities into practice. Some people characterize science-technology centers as museums primarily for children, in the same way that many dismiss children's museums as not relevant to people over the age of 15. In fact, both of these kinds of museums offer unique learning experiences that serve the universal needs of visitors at widely varying educational, age, and cultural levels. Visitors are able to study topics of their own choosing and to advance at their own pace, without fear of failure. By communicating in nonverbal ways, as well as through the written word in labels and catalogues, museums can eliminate many of the barriers found in traditional educational institutions.

Youth museums, science-technology centers, and many other institutions are increasingly basing programs and exhibits on the understanding that all people—young and old alike—learn readily through multisensory experiences. Obviously, this need not mean that all objects in a museum's collection should be accessible to touching. At least five senses can be appealed to in the programs and exhibits of museums in all disciplines. The text and program descriptions that follow offer suggestions for what can be attempted.

Years in preparation, *Museums, Magic and Children* was written all over America. It had its beginning with eight museum professionals speeding across Texas highways in a travel home, brainstorming what the book should be about and outlining examples of success and failure, case studies, and programs. Program ideas were contributed by museums across the country to create this representational—though not complete—view of what is going on for young people in museums.

This volume offers guidance to groups interested in starting youth museums or programs in their own communities. Both as a beginning point and a continuing resource, it covers most essential steps and the important questions to be asked— and answered carefully—before making a total commitment.

Author/compiler Bonnie Pitman-Gelles has, in this book, given us a landmark work in museum education, for both the advanced professional and the beginner, which can give new meaning to museum programs for children and adults. Not something to be read and put back on a shelf, it will be used over and over.

Russell I. Peithman
Executive Director
Los Angeles Children's Museum

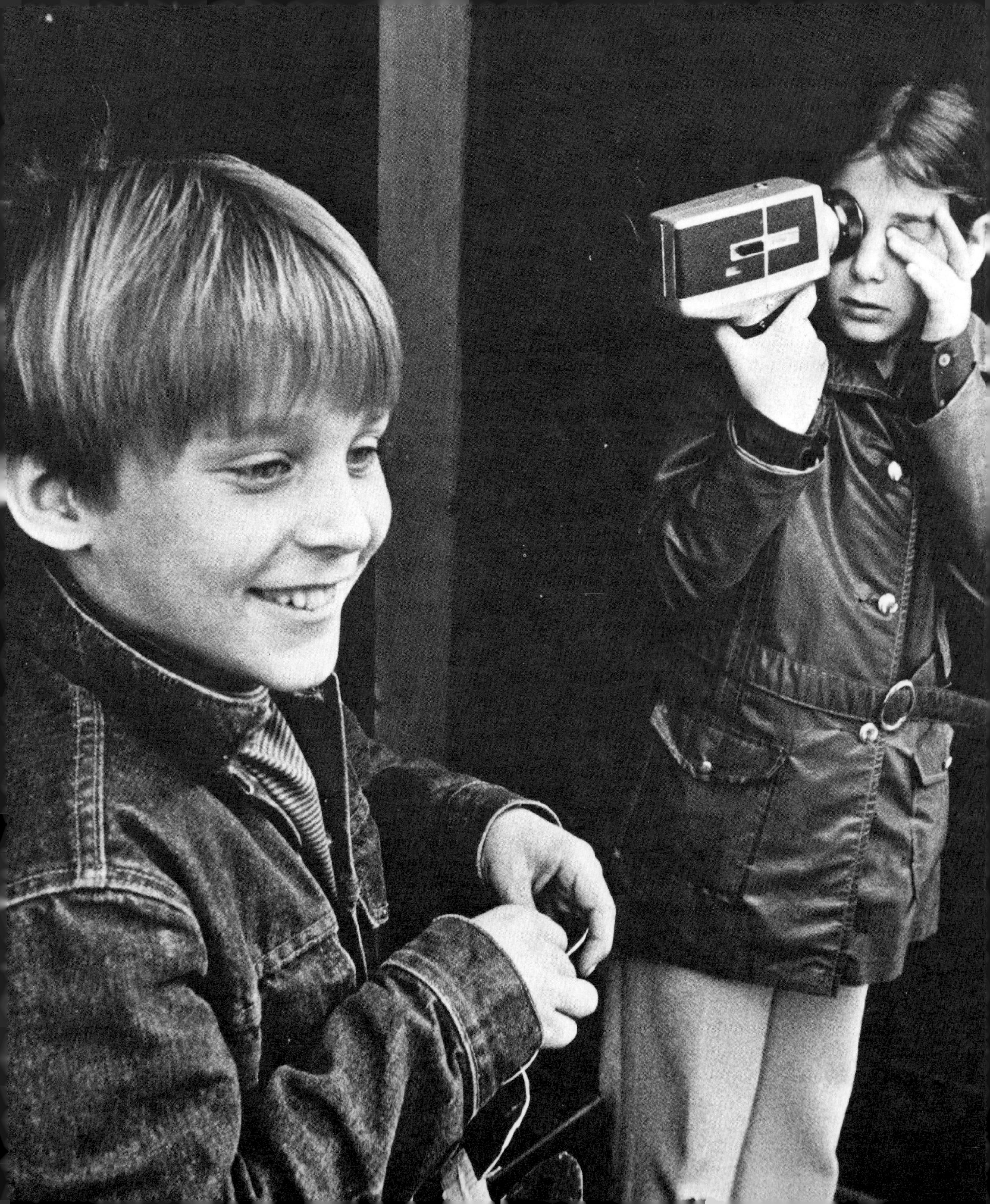

INTRODUCTION

The American Association of Youth Museums had a dream for a number of years: that a publication would document how to establish a youth museum and provide examples of the excellent programs throughout the country that museums present to children, parents and teachers. This publication aims to accomplish this goal. As the title suggests, *Museums, Magic and Children: Youth Education in Museums* deals with the magic transformation that occurs when children learn from exhibitions and objects in the collections of museums.

Museums, Magic and Children is a representative sampling of the exhibitions, programs and approaches to teaching that have been found to be effective with young people. The book is not intended as a directory or listing of all the institutions in the country offering programs to young people, nor does it list every type of program. Rather, the book presents an abundance of examples so that the readers can learn, compare, contract, and select what is appropriate for their own institutions.

The book is in three sections: first, a series of chapters describing methods for developing programs and exhibits; second, more than 200 descriptions of children's programs; and third, a resource section that lists useful organizations, distributors and books. Throughout the text, examples of programs, exhibits and techniques are used to present different points of view. The reader should note that the museums used as illustrations in the text are "examples" rather than the "epitomes" of this type of program or exhibit.

Eight chapters provide information on how to design, implement and evaluate exhibits and programs for children, their parents and teachers. The value of planning and the importance of evaluating are continually stressed. Making changes, modifications, and learning from mistakes is mentioned, though because there are no "case studies" the reader may not realize how many museums work in this way to continually improve their exhibits and programs. When starting a new museum program or exhibit, there are many options to be considered. These chapters illustrate how museums have approached a particular audience, developed a particular theme, or used a particular technique in teaching.

The program descriptions present a sampling of the wealth of ideas, formats and methods for designing tours, workshops, festivals and much more. Although there is almost no repetition between the museums mentioned in the chapters and those in the program descriptions, there are still hundreds of activities that are not represented.

The resource section of the book provides lists of where to go next to contact professional organizations or funding sources; to obtain films, periodicals or the catalogues of materials published by other museums. At the conclusion of each chapter, books that have been quoted are cited. The bibliography expands on these references to include the volumes, articles and other documents that were used to research this book.

Museums, Magic and Children: Youth Education in Museums illustrates the range of ideas and the exciting opportunities museums have developed for children. New chapters should be added as technologies are introduced and as new formats and approaches to reaching children are conceived and tested. The book reveals the commitment museums have to educating children today and hints at the many new things we will be doing with them in the future.

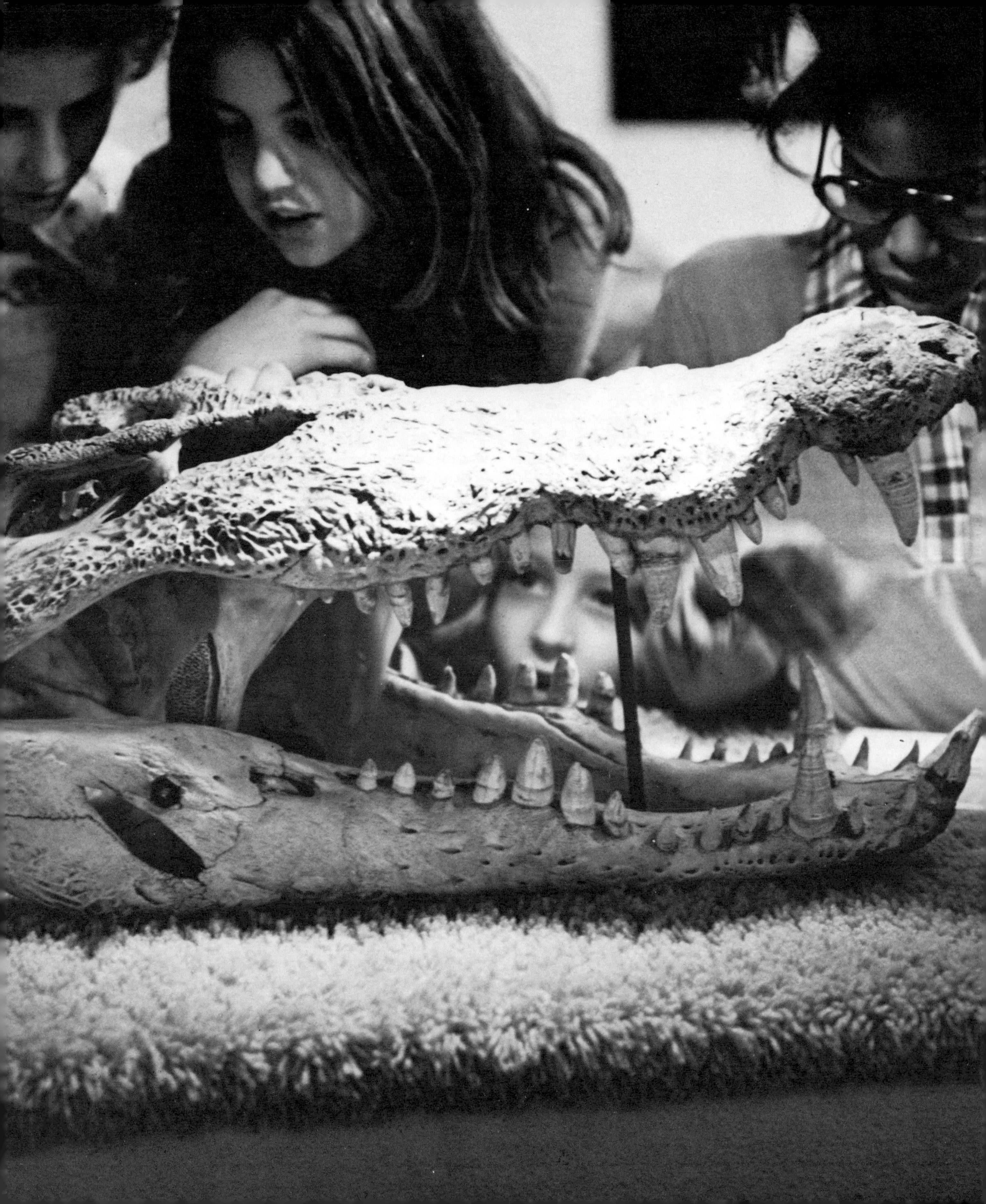

1. PLANNING A YOUTH MUSEUM OF EXHIBITS AND PROGRAMS

As vibrant institutions, museums house the wonders of the natural and man-made world and reflect the creativity of artists, scientists, craftsmen, and writers. They are, first of all, collections of objects and specimens: butterflies, lace, dinosaur bones, Indian pottery, suits of armor, Western paintings, wooden houses, light sculptures, Civil War documents, Greek sculptures, reptiles, lions—the list is endless. People come individually, collectively in family units, and in school classes to see the exhibitions and collections of museums. In whatever grouping, they come to look, to learn, and often to participate.

If the basic function of a museum is to collect, preserve and publicly display these objects and specimens, then a major reason for doing so is to enlighten the public. Museums provide innovative programs and exhibitions, unique contributions to the cultural life of a community. Further, a museum acts as a catalyst, introducing people to new ideas and interests and motivating people to seek further knowledge through study and return visits. Through educational programs and interactive exhibits, a museum helps visitors develop perceptual skills so they can look and discover new relationships on their own. Exhibits provide visitors not only an opportunity to look, but to think, to explore, to wonder, and to investigate.

Today, museum buildings include exhibition halls, auditoriums, classrooms, and libraries, as well as scientific laboratories, participatory galleries, art studios, gardens, nature trails, research centers, planetariums, insect zoos, and media production facilities. Museums are open to the public. People may browse, ask questions, study, and often even borrow or rent such things as paintings or fossils to take home or to the classroom. People come for diverse reasons: to observe the curiosities in the turn-of-the-century blacksmith shop, to examine the infinite variety of color in butterfly wings, or to observe the habitat of a mountain lion. No longer are museums simply cabinets of curiosity, but places providing unique educational resources and opportunities. They are environments, where one can study objects of an ancient civilizations, grow a garden, paint, write poetry, or operate a computer. According to Alma Wittlin, children's museums "have a niche among the pioneers of contemporary education. For decades, they have been appealing to the child's otherwise neglected tactile sense in exploring his environment."

This chapter is divided into two sections. The first section, "How to Start a Youth Museum," was developed in response to numerous requests received by the American Association of Youth Museums from community groups interested in starting and developing youth museums. The second section, "Designing Exhibits and Programs," outlines ways to develop exhibits or programs for children, parents, or teachers. Exhibits and programs are the museum's primary forms of communication with the visitor. The exhibitions, whether temporary or permanent, must relate to the museum's goals and communicate in a meaningful way. The museum's programs should be designed to relate to its exhibitions or collections and provide well-structured and provocative learning opportunities. The range of potential activities vary in format, length, topic, and goals.

Whether designing an exhibition, program, or entire institution, the involvement of the staff at all levels is important. Plans should be flexible enough to accommodate revisions and changes since courage is often needed to drop favorite ideas that will not really be effective.

HOW TO START A YOUTH MUSEUM

Historically, youth museums have been established by many different groups of people—parents, teachers, scientists and artists—interested in children and the ways in which they learn. The Brooklyn Children's Museum was established in 1899 when the curator of fine arts at the Brooklyn Central Museum suggested turning a mansion leased by the Brooklyn Institute of Arts and Sciences into a museum for children. The Brooklyn Children's Museum became the country's first children's museum.

In 1913 the Children's Museum, Boston was founded by a group of science teachers interested in supplementing natural science programs in the schools with real specimens and objects that children could examine and touch. The nation's third youth museum was organized by the Art Institute of Detroit and the Detroit Board of Education as a joint venture. In 1925 the Board of Education assumed responsibility for the museum, making it the first children's museum to be owned and operated by a school system. In the same year the Indianapolis Children's Museum was founded by a core group representing several sectors of the community including a school principal, a director of art instruction and a city librarian.

Today many groups throughout the country entertain the idea of starting a youth museum. Generally, their success is in direct proportion to the support provided by a large segment of the community.

Any group wishing to start a youth museum must be realistic. Museums are expensive; they can not be run on love alone. The expenses of purchasing and maintaining the building, equipment, exhibitions and collections are rising. Some established museums are curtailing activities and increasing fees, because they lack funds to pay staff, maintain the building, and offer programs.

According to one definition set by the American Association of Museums,

> . . . a museum is an organized and permanent nonprofit institution, essentially educational or aesthetic in purpose, with a professional staff, which owns and/or utilizes tangible objects, cares for them, and exhibits them to the public on some regular schedule.

A museum—particularly one for young people—does not fit snugly into a formal definition. It is a magical place filled with people, ideas, and activities. Its audience includes visitors from infants to adults. Its activities are myriad: school tours, festivals, field trips, clubs, classes, loan kits, junior volunteer programs, and much more. The exhibitions can include crawling through a tactile dome, experimenting with electricity, working with computers or analyzing the construction of a Victorian house. It is a place for quiet reflection as well as shared experiences. It is a place that can arouse curiosity as well as satisfy it. Objects and specimens can be brought to the museum for identification since it is a resource center and a caretaker of collections. Exhibiting and caring for its collections and involving the community are daily concerns of these institutions.

Different groups may begin at different points of the following steps because their goals and objectives differ. Some orderly procedure, however, is as necessary for museum planners as a blueprint is for a builder.

Initial Inquiries

Very often the idea of establishing a youth museum originates with a relatively small group of dedicated people. In order to achieve their goals, they first must:
1. Enlist the support of representative people in the community who are enthusiastic about exploring the idea of a youth museum.
2. Study museums and read relevant publications.
3. Determine what museums do (e.g., exhibit, collect, preserve, offer programs, maintain and operate a facility).
4. Visit other museums, especially children's museums.
5. Set up informal meetings with professionals from related organizations in the community.
6. Hold open meetings to learn what other people in the community think.
7. Make plans to have a study done to test support for the idea.
8. Ask such hard questions as: does this idea make sense for our community? is there sufficient interest and support to go on to the next phase?

The Steering Committee

If the questions are answered affirmatively, the initiators should formally organize a steering committee, which will continue to research the idea of a youth museum, establish objectives, explore funding sources, and incorporate the organization with the state. Some of the people who initiated the idea should be included,

as well as representative members of the community whose expertise may be required along the way. Members of the steering committee should be ready to:
- work seven days a week
- raise money
- change, amend, or alter the steering committee membership in order to accomplish the developing objectives
- approach governing authorities (schools, county, municipal and civic leaders) for support in money or services
- turn the day-to-day operations over to a paid professional director.

In addition to seeking advice from individual museum professionals, the committee should contact such organizations as the American Association of Youth Museums, American Association for State and Local History, Association of Science-Technology Centers, the American Association of Museums, and the regional and state museum associations. Locally, the committee should:
- find out what is already available for children in the community
- check with the existing museums, zoos, botanical gardens, science centers, resource centers, health facilities, and universities
- ask about programs, facilities, budgets, audiences, funding sources
- keep a list of the talents and resources of interested people
- visit all types of museums and science-technology centers
- keep asking people and themselves if there is a need for a youth museum.

Goals and Objectives

A youth museum should not duplicate services and programs already available in the community. The museum should provide unique learning opportunities well suited for its collections. There are times when it is appropriate not to start a youth museum, but rather to work with the existing institutions in the community to effect changes in exhibits and programs.

Some youth museums do not deal with certain topics or collections because this is the responsibility of another organization or museum. For example, the New England Aquarium, a neighbor of the Children's Museum of Boston, provides extensive programs to children on New England marine life.
Consequently, the Children's Museum programs, exhibits and collections do not concentrate on this marine life, but appropriate specimens are available in the study collections and loan kits.

Hammering out goals and objectives is a difficult but essential task for the steering committee. These goals will define the purpose, audience, and scope of the youth museum. Once completed, they should indicate whether the museum will be duplicating the work done by other institutions. Valid goals are based on a thorough knowledge of the community and its resources and on an understanding of the support systems and needs of the community. While these goals and objectives will serve as the foundation for future planning and developments, they can be altered at anytime. Some questions to consider while developing goals and objectives are:
- who is the museum's audience? (age group, geographic region, ethnic groups)
- what subject area(s) will the museum focus on? (natural sciences, history, art, science-technology)
- how will learning take place in the youth museum? (participation, study collections, exhibitions)
- what will be the youth museum's role within the community? (school, resource, youth center, library)
- how big will the museum be?
- how many visitors might come?

The goals and objectives of youth museums are all different but each of them defines the purposes of the museum and its relationship to its community.

Examples drawn up by two museums' follow:

Dedicated to developing among children and adults an awareness and appreciation of nature and man through interpretive exhibits and innovative programs during both school and after school hours. Museum collections, dynamic exhibits, and special equipment become tools to communicate ideas and interpret basic concepts and interrelationships in science and ecology.
—The Charlotte Nature Museum

To offer provocative and useful experiences with real materials to children, parents, and teachers . . . currently the museum consists of two major program divisions: The Exhibit Center providing participatory exhibits, informal and group activities,

and public services; and a Resource Center offering training and resource development assistance to schools, community organizations, and parents, as well as circulating educational materials and a Recycle Center.
—The Children's Museum, Boston

A written statement of goals not only serves as a basis for the collection, exhibition, and program policies, but provides the community with a clear understanding of the role and purposes of the proposed youth museum. Clearly defined goals and objectives are essential to proceeding with the planning and development of the museum.

Having cleared the philosophical hurdles, the steering committee must turn its attention to methods of funding a new youth museum, keeping paramount in their plans the need for operating funds (e.g., rent, salaries, utilities, programs, exhibits) as well as building funds. In addition, the committee should investigate the possibility of financial support from:
- local foundations, individuals, business establishments, and civic organizations (e.g., Junior League, Lions Clubs, Council of Jewish Women)
- United Fund or Arts Council campaign
- municipal, county, or state taxes
- the city or school system (in the form of such services as building maintenance, staff salaries)
- federal or state grants from specific agencies
- self-support (through the sale of products and services).

If after this amount of planning and testing the members of the steering committee agree that the youth museum is needed and that there is support for the idea, they should present a prospectus to those interested in the project. The prospectus should include recommendations to incorporate according to the laws of the state, to write bylaws and a constitution, to obtain a planning grant for a feasibility study, and to bring in museum consultants.

It is of the utmost importance for a museum to register its corporation charter as a nonprofit institution with the state. The laws in each state differ and should be followed accordingly. Therefore, legal advice is essential. In addition, the steering committee should also send the 501 (c)(3) application for tax-exempt status to the Internal Revenue Service. Approval takes anywhere from six months to two years, but once the museum qualifies, in some states it will be able to purchase supplies and equipment without paying taxes. With 501(c)(3) status, the museum may also be exempt from local taxes on assets. Gifts and contributions may also be tax-deductible according to present IRS rulings.

The charter or constitution and the bylaws must be prepared by the steering committee under the guidance of an attorney familiar with the state codes. These documents define the purpose of the organization, the obligation and structure of the board of trustees and its committees, the duties of the director of the museum, and the relationship of the director to the board.

The Board of Trustees

Upon incorporation, a board of trustees is legally responsible for maintaining the museum's financial base of support and for establishing the policies governing the institution. Daily operation and administration of the museum, however is the responsibility of a director, not the board. The relationship between the board of trustees and the director is best summarized by the following statement from *Of Mutual Respect and Other Things:* "The board establishes policy and the director oversees operations." (See Figure 1)

The museum bylaws should define the responsibilities and methods of operations that will govern the board. They should also specify the number of trustees, their terms of office and the number of meetings that should be attended each year. An understanding of their responsibilities, the consequences of absenteeism, and the goals and programs of the museum are critical to the successful operation of a board of trustees. Orientation sessions and manuals are useful ways to ensure that this information is provided to each new board member.

Civic-minded, able members of the business, professional, and cultural community comprise a potential reservoir of talent for museum boards. Probably the most important single trait necessary to make a good board member is a selfless willingness to pitch in and work on behalf of the museum. The board of trustees is responsible for:
- upholding the constitution and bylaws
- developing and approving long-range operating plans and policies

Figure 1.
Board of Trustees/Director/Staff Responsibilities

TRUSTEE	DIRECTOR (Link)	STAFF

Establishes Policy
—Collections: acquisitions, maintenance, deaccession;
—Relationship of the Director-Staff-Board;
—Use of museum and its services by the public;
—Staff positions;
—Volunteer organizations
	Carries out policies
	  Proposes
	  Originates
	  Implements
	  Informs staff
		Operates within policies

Financial responsibility —Approves budget and audit —Secures funds for operating —Establishes endowment	Prepares budget to submit to board Secures funds for programs and projects	Assists in preparing budget
Authorizes acquisitions	Recommends acquisitions and deaccessioning	Suggests acquisitions
Hires Director —Approves new staff positions	Accountable to Board (as a whole, not to individual trustees) —Reports to Board —Hires and terminates staff —Recommends new positions —Supervises staff	Accountable to Director —Relationship to Board—informal and through the Director —Grievance procedures —Clear understanding of positions —Training
Advise and counsel —Knowledge of goals —Understanding of institution and all legal aspects	Management —Professionalism —Specialized body of knowledge —Strength to lead trustees —Communication to staff —Operate and administrate —Legal implications —Member of each committee	Informed —Legal aspects
Functional committees —Finances —Membership —Staff promotions and appointment —Building —Recommends to total Board	Member of each committee	Informed
Approves planning	Initiates plans	Suggests plans
Responsibility —To institution —To community	Same and to Board	Same and to Director

Prepared by Jane Glaser, Office of Museum Programs, Smithsonian Institution, Washington, D.C.

○ approving the annual budget, audit, and major expenditures
○ developing long-range plans for financial support,
○ securing funds for operational and capital improvement funds
○ hiring a director.

One of the first responsibilities of the board will be to prepare a master plan delineating the development phases for the youth museum. These might include:

Phase I. A feasibility study: (to determine *types* of exhibits and programs, space requirements and fundraising potential)
Cost: $10,000-$25,000

Phase II. First three years of operation (hire a director, issue publications, implement programs, develop plans for renovations)
Cost: $100,000+, depending on the staff and size of the museum

Phase III: Opening the museum (complete renovations, install exhibitions, hire staff)
Cost: to be determined.

The president of the board will appoint several committees to assist with fundraising, building or site procurement, employment of a director. The first priority will be to raise funds for a feasibility study conducted by a professional firm. Funding for this venture should be sought from local foundations, businesses, or organizations interested in the youth museum project.

A good feasibility study is essential to developing the plans for a new children's museum. With the data obtained from the study, dreams can be made into concrete plans, sketches and slide presentations. The feasibility study can become a cornerstone in the museum's long-range plans, outlining the space, staff and financial needs of the museum. Almost immediately the feasibility study results can be used to help prepare fundraising materials and press releases, recruit volunteers, and assist with the continuing promotion of the concept for a children's museum.

The following points were part of a study completed for the Capitol Children's Museum, Washington, D.C.:
○ assessment of the feasibility of the concept and the need within the community
○ assessment of the potential of the community to financially support the youth museum

Figure 2.
Hard Questions to Ask When Considering a Youth Museum

Why does your community need a youth museum?
Who will be the audience for the museum? preschoolers? school children? teenagers? the disabled? teachers? families?
What subject areas will be covered in the museum?
Why will visitors come to the museum?
Who will support the youth museum?
 Who will pay to develop it? buy the building? set up exhibits?
 Who will pay operating costs from year to year?
What will the museum's role be in the community?
Can an existing institution change to meet this need?
Are you prepared to raise one-quarter to one-half million dollars over a five-year period in your community?
Are you willing to work day and night for five years to develop and support the youth museum?
Are you prepared to work with all elements in the community?
Are you willing to change the membership of the planning group or board of trustees in order to meet your objectives?
If a survey or feasibility study shows that the museum is not needed or that the goals are being achieved by another group, can you give up the plans?
Are you prepared to turn down a building if it does not meet your needs?
Are you prepared to turn down donations of objects that do not fit with the objectives of the museum?
Are you prepared to turn down funds that are too restrictive?
Do the proposed facilities allow for expansion?
Have you developed long-range goals for the museum, for five and ten years?

○ development of plans for museum programs, exhibits, and staff job descriptions
○ outline of facility needs
○ estimation of costs to be incurred for operations and development
○ compilation of reports, data, and graphics to be used for future fundraising requests.

If a building has already been offered to the board, the feasibility study should contain a review of the structure. If no building is under consideration the feasibility study should include recommendations regarding possible sites and buildings.

If after careful examination of the report the board feels that there is both community need and support for a youth museum, the president should instruct the appropriate committees to proceed with a fundraising program in order to hire a director and secure facilities. (See Figure 2.)

Hiring a Director

Meanwhile another committee of the board should actively conduct a search for a paid professional director, who should be a person with a deep commitment to educating young people through museum experiences. In addition to administering the institution and hiring the staff, the director will develop the professional policies for the collections (acquisition and recording of objects), the educational programs, and the exhibition plans. The director is responsible as well for initiation of long-range plans for the museum, preparation of the annual budget and financial expenditures within the approved budget, employing and discharging museum personnel as well as determining their duties and salaries, selection and acquisition of collections with the approval of the board, and participation in board deliberations as a nonvoting member.

The salary of a youth museum director should be commensurate with that of the directors of other cultural and educational organizations in the community and should depend on the professional experience of the individual and size of the staff to be managed. A contract between the director and museum can clearly delineate the responsibilities of the position and the relationship between the board of trustees and the director. Members of the board should realize that the director is responsible to the whole board, not to individual trustees.

With the arrival of the director, the museum enters a new stage of growth. The director will work closely with the president of the board and the various committees in selecting and equipping proper facilities, raising money, establishing community support and developing programs.

Financial policies developed by the board should clearly define the:
- limit of unauthorized expenditures by the director;
- presentation of financial statements
- policy regarding gifts of property, objects, and money
- types of funds to be used by the museum, the purposes and mechanisms for gaining approval for spending the funds.

Seeking Funds

Until a professional director is hired, the board's development and finance committee is directly responsible for soliciting and securing operating funds, preparing budgets, and laying out plans for future developments. Funds to initiate a new youth museum are often easier to locate than the capital essential to operate the museum in the years ahead. Serious consideration must be given to the community's ability to provide operating support over a prolonged period. Without operating funds there would be no money for:
- salaries and benefits for the staff
- maintenance and rent of the building
- exhibit and program design
- building renovations and expansion
- insurance (building, collections, equipment, liability).

Budgets for youth museums vary according to the goals, amount of space, number of staff, energy costs, requirements of the collections, exhibits and programs. In general the annual budgets of youth museums range between $100,000 and $400,000 per year, with some having budgets in excess of $1 million. Figure 3 provides basic statistics from youth museums around the country.

Although small grants for specific projects may be obtained, the museum cannot survive on grants alone. A slide show should be prepared for use in the fundraising campaign on the proposed youth museum explaining its purpose, role within the community, long- and short-range funding requirements, and plans for facilities, staff, and programs. The slide show can be used for presentations before civic groups as well as to corporations, foundations and private donors to raise

Figure 3.
Six Youth Museums—Basic Statistics

MUSEUM	ANNUAL BUDGET (in $1,000s)	TOTAL SQUARE FOOTAGE (IN 1,000s)	SQUARE FOOTAGE OF EXHIBITS (in 1,000s)	ATTENDANCE (in 1,000s)	FULL TIME EMPLOYEES	VOLUNTEERS	MEMBERSHIP
A	1,600	30	17	500	94	10	4,350
B	480	30	12	250	23	60	800
C	400	50	25	160	16	25	360
D	300	15	5	300	12	175	1,100
F	120	11	7	36	8	85	400
G	50	11	7	102	7	30	350

public awareness and financial support for the new museum. Public awareness of the project and a broad base of financial support are essential for the museum's future survival.

Searching For The Building

Before beginning the search for a building, the director and the facilities committee of the board should be familiar with the research compiled by the steering committee, the feasibility study results, and the stated goals of the youth museum. Since the building will have to house ideas, people, exhibits, and objects, it would be wise to compile a list of possible space and activity needs:

reception or admissions
exhibitions
orientation
offices
classrooms
theater/auditorium
lecture rooms or halls
meeting rooms
garden/nature trails
computer
open spaces for receptions
media production facilities
library
laboratories
collections—storage and conservation
shipping and receiving area
general storage
planetarium
recycle center
aquariums
exhibit design and construction shop
lounge for staff and volunteers
mobile units
gift shop and/or restaurant

The committee should also consider the availability of parking facilities and proximity to a main road and public transit systems. Accessibility to the handicapped and safety, security and potential for future expansion are important considerations. Renovation costs—fire prevention equipment, security, lighting, electricity, and temperature/humidity controls—are important considerations for recycled buildings. *Museums News* prepared an entire issue in 1980 on museums and adaptive reuse, which presents a series of case studies on how museums have adapted older structures.

Realizing that one-third to one-half of the total space required for a museum will be used for exhibits, the American Association of Youth Museums' editorial committee listed the following pros and cons regarding suitability of space for a prospective youth museum:

Good Bets
loft spaces
department stores
old theaters
warehouses
garages
storage buildings
fire houses
small train stations
a new building

Bad Bets
old houses (size, construction, too many windows, walls, radiators, zoning codes)
schools (small spaces, often lacking flexibility)
big train stations (too large, renovation problems, expensive to operate and maintain)

If a building seems to be suitable:
- get an architect and contractor to look at it to help make an estimate for the renovation costs
- have a professional museum consultant review the facility and proposed plans
- prepare budget estimates on the cost of renovations and rehabilitation
- prepare budget estimates on the costs of operating the building including fuel for heating, repairs, etc.

The costs for renovation and operations should be within the means of the museum's fundraising capability.

Hiring Professional Staff and Opening the Youth Museum

In assembling a staff (curators, exhibit designers, educational specialists, maintenance), a director should seek energetic, talented, enthusiastic people with a sense of humor and dedication to the goals of a youth museum. The number of staff members employed vary according to the size and needs of each institution. Some museums have full time staffs of almost 100 while others employ as few as three professionals.

Specific job descriptions should be established for each position to prevent misunderstandings. Yet, these guidelines can be implemented in such a way that individual freedom and creativity is not denied. Further, a director should organize departmental policies that clearly define areas of responsibility and authority. Appropriate guidelines and organizational charts can prevent the kind of departmental infighting that is negative at best and destructive at worst.

The professional staff will continue to need leadership and training. The staff should attend professional workshops and meetings and, when needed, seek the help and advice of consultants, at the expense of the institution.

Volunteer Staff

Volunteers will have already played an important role in establishing the youth museum. A vital link with the community, they provide talents, resources, and time that can be invaluable to the professional staff. Without their assistance most museums would have to reduce their services to the public. Although training and supervising a volunteer program takes money and time, the rewards are bountiful.

Volunteers need to feel a sense of accomplishment and that the work they are doing is important to the museum, the community, and themselves. They should be made to feel like staff members and, by the same token, should be expected to assume responsibilities and to make a commitment to the museum.

With the appropriate training, volunteers can work in almost any area of the museum: education, exhibitions, collections, fundraising, sales desk, hospitality, front office, or clerical. Like the staff, they should be provided with clearly defined job descriptions and a carefully developed training program. Periodically, their performance should be reviewed by the staff, and appropriate recognition should be given for meritorious service and special talents. One museum recently rewarded a 15-year veteran with the title of adjunct curator of dolls and toys.

Some standards for selection and training must be established in order to protect the integrity of any volunteer program. It must not become a clique for one social group, nor should anyone be denied admission to the group because of age, race, sex, or creed.

Collections

The collections are the core of most museums, providing the resources and ideas for exhibits and programs. Although a new youth museum could be involved with natural science, history, science-technology, art, or a combination of these subjects, it must be remembered that a museum is a treasure house, not a warehouse, for objects. Therefore, the director and board must establish a policy regarding the acquisition of collections before any objects are accepted by the museum. If the facilities are limited, irrelevant objects, though attractive, probably should not be accepted unless they can be sold or traded in order to fill other needs. Useful guidelines for the development of a collection's policy are available from museum publications.

Ideally, all objects in the collections should belong to the museum. Occasionally, however, new museums will accept short-term loans to fill specific needs for certain exhibitions. Many museums have teaching collections that include objects that can be handled and are therefore considered expendable. Some youth museums give small rocks, minerals, or fossils to children as a reminder of their visit. Naturally these items should not be catalogued, but should be accepted as expendable gifts.

A practical system of accurately identifying and cataloguing objects must be established and maintained, not only as a service to students and scholars but as an orderly inventory of the collections. Specific information on assessing collections, registration methods, and insurance can be obtained from other publications.

A further responsibility of museums is preservation and conservation of objects. Proper lighting, humidity, temperature, and storage facilities are of paramount importance. Collections require space for storage and records as well as special climate controls. These things must be considered during the renovation or construction stages of the museum. The restoration or treatment of any object should be undertaken only by a specialist.

Some museums—art centers and science-technology centers, for example—are defined somewhat differently than museums *per se*. They may not own the objects on exhibit themselves, or maintain exhibits for the presentation on interpretation of knowledge.

Long-Range Planning

"What *should* the museum be?" is the question to be addressed as part of the long-range planning process. Too often long-range plans focus on "What is the museum?" or "What will it be?" While it is not feasible to review the many different strategies for developing long-range and master plans, their importance to an institution's growth must be stressed. A museum should select a planning process that is suitable for its management capabilities, size and budget.

A museum must plan for the future. Institutional goals and program objectives for exhibitions, programs, facilities, collections, staff, budgets, fundraising, and the board should be established and reviewed for three, five, seven or ten years. The specific time period can vary. Staff and trustees should participate in various stages of the planning. Their roles and responsibilities must be defined and their contributions should assist the processes, not delay it. Among other things, the long-range plans should include:

○ the development of institutional goals
○ the development of program objectives for each department
○ a timetable for achieving short- and long-range goals
○ a realistic budget for implementing the goals and objectives with identified revenue needs and sources.

While many people will contribute in the planning process, the final writing will be the responsibility of one or two people. Once defined, the long-range plans should be approved by the Board of Directors. The staff and the trustees need a clear understanding of who is responsible for implementing the program objectives and raising the funds. Both should have a commitment to review and change the proposed plans as needed. Developing and accepting long-range plans often means accepting recommendations for change.

The value of long-range planning is that the trustees and the staff learn to plan, compromise, anticipate and revise their institutional goals and objectives. Individual areas of responsibility are seen as contributing to the entire museum and its future. The planning process must be controlled so that it does not degenerate into endless meeting, memos, indecisions and disappointment. Decisions must be made, and action, through the implementation of the program objectives, must take place.

DESIGNING EXHIBITS AND PROGRAMS

A museum is a laboratory for teaching and learning from collections and exhibitions. Key staff members—curators, educators, exhibit designers, administrators—should all participate in developing plans and assessing the ultimate effectiveness of the programs and exhibitions that reach the public. Planning, developing, implementing, evaluating, and following up exhibitions and programs is an important process, and varies in the number of tasks, time, and sequence of events. The goals, however, are always the same: to consider all of the issues and to make decisions based on the information available. Planning and designing programs requires the establishment of priorities, sometimes causing the museum to move in new directions, and recognizing that some of its work has not been as successful as it might have been. Planning and developing programs requires time, money, and a commitment by the staff to work together for a common goal. Within each of its stages, there is a continuous process of proposing, testing, doing, and revising.

The process of planning and developing exhibitions in museums is frequently misunderstood. People are concerned that they will be caught in a web of meetings and paper work that will bring little or no results. The real value of an effective planning process is in the improved product, which is a result of the ideas and recommendations of the many people in the museum. Curators can provide helpful insight into the development of a written text or select materials for a suitcase exhibition, just as educators can suggest the public's response to an exhibit installation. This process of sharing information and respecting the ideas and recommendations that come forth in the planning phase will help to improve the quality of the exhibits and programs in a museum.

There are many formats for planning and developing exhibits and programs. While particular steps in the process may vary in length or in sequence, there are several stages that seem to form a pattern. These are:

- **Planning Phase:** includes identification of the planning committee and determination of their roles and responsibilities; development of a statement of purpose or goals; identification of audience; determination of objectives based on available space and time; determination of a budget; and development of a preliminary design or plan.
- **Design Phase:** includes research; selection of objects and interpretation techniques; identification of needed resources; development of a detailed plan or script; selection of evaluation techniques.
- **Implementation Phase:** includes the process of doing; such as construction, fabrication, installation and opening an exhibit; or testing, announcing and doing a program with the actual audience.
- **Evaluation and Revision Phase:** assesses the effectiveness of the exhibit or program, based on the user's involvement and needs, and makes decisions on how to change and improve the product.

Planning Phase

1. Statement of Purpose A well-thought-out statement of purpose determines the reason for a program or exhibition and indicates the concepts to be covered. It is a basic rationale for the exhibit or program, and illustrates the main ideas that will be communicated to the audience. In formulating such a statement, the staff should ask focusing questions: What is the reason for doing the exhibit or program? What ideas will be covered? Are people interested in the topic? Why will this program or exhibition be important or useful to the potential learner? Consider the following statements of purpose which define the scope of these museums:

- To make known the world of water.
  New England Aquarium, Boston, Massachusetts
- To use the museum as a resource to stimulate children to compare, and analyze, evaluate and interpret historical concepts.
  Western Reserve Historical Society, Cleveland, Ohio
- To provide exhibits, centering on the theme of perception, which are designed to be manipulated and appreciated at a variety of levels by children and adults.
  The Exploratorium, San Francisco, California

A clearly defined statement of purpose will guide the development of programs and exhibits as well as influence the type of evaluation that is used. Because the above statements define the entire focus of a museum, each institution has carefully created a series of programs and exhibits that meet these purposes. As just one component in an entire institution, a program or exhibit cannot be considered in isolation. Other considerations will be the amount of space, money, staff and resources that can be potentially committed to the project.

2. The Audience One reason that youth museums are effective is that they have clearly identified their audience: children, their families, and teachers. In general, museum education programs are developed for a specific age group. Exhibits or festivals, on the other hand, are for the general public, and because this audience is so broad, project design is difficult. Some questions that need to be asked when determining the audience for programs or exhibits are: Who are they? How old are they? What do they do with their leisure time? Why do they come to the museum? What interests them? Are they disabled? What do they want to learn? How often do they come? Who are the nonvisitors of the museum? Which of these groups does the museum want to reach?

How learning will take place is another important factor in considering the audience, for learning with parents or teachers is entirely different than self-exploration. In addition, different types of experiences need to be provided in any program or exhibit so that the visitor can undertake several roles as an active or passive participant in group situations or as a single observer.

Understanding how adults and children learn must also be considered. Museum professionals need to be familiar with the developmental processes of children, and especially the writings of Jean Piaget and Eric Erikson, and Jerome Bruner among others. Programming for adults—teachers and parents—should consider the writings of Allen Knox, Malcolm Knowles, and others. It is important to know what can be expected of children, their ability to understand the concepts of time and distance as well as to learn to do problem-solving, identification, or classification. For example, to most first graders, Africa and Maine are "far away," meaning not here, because they do not understand the concepts of distance and time. Sixth graders, on the other hand, who have studied history and geography, will comprehend geographical and historical differences, even if they do not have all of the specific facts before them.

When developing new materials or programs, museum professionals should consult with members of the intended audience—students, teachers, and families. Joint planning inevitably results in long-range commitments, not only on the part of the museum, but participants as well. Some museums have community, ethnic, special-needs and student advisory groups that offer recommendations to the staff on subject matter, level of presentation, and types of resource materials that might be designed or provided. An advisory committee must understand their role: they are not programmers or developers, but advisors to a project. Without a clearly defined relationship to the museum, they might misunderstand their responsibilities.

3. Program Objectives Although the statement of purpose is basically philosophical, the objectives of a program or exhibit must be hammered out in a very specific fashion. The objectives help in the selection of materials, methods of interpretation, development of budget and evaluation for a project. Again, questions need to be asked and answered, such as: What kinds of information should the visitors learn? What learning strategies should be used? What changes should result from participating in the program or exhibit? The clearer the objectives, the more helpful they will be to the planning team in the development of the project. Creating objectives also requires determining priorities.

There are many types of objectives that can be established, and not all objectives are useful ones, for they can be too narrow or too broad in scope and purpose. For example, objectives can be used to establish a sequence of events, to define the type of visitor behavior that should be achieved, or define the information or content to be acquired as a result of this participation. There are a number of books listed in the bibliography that are helpful in planning a program or exhibit and establishing objectives. Determining objectives requires decisions because the objectives will effect both the immediate and long-range plans of the museum and the project under consideration.

The following are illustrations of two types of objectives that can be developed; these are only part of the listing that might accompany a full program or exhibit.

Objectives can illustrate a sequence of activities:
- to provide the visitor an opportunity to observe a variety of animals from the African veldt
- to conduct a short demonstration with one animal from the veldt
- to engage students in a discussion of the characteristics of animals who live in this habitat.

Objectives can also indicate the results expected from a learning experience, including the type of learning

that should be achieved, or a change in behavior:
- after studying the ecology of Louisiana, the students will construct and maintain a suitable habitat for an animal from the bayou
- after looking at an exhibit on pre-Columbian art, students will be more willing to look at this art form and have increased their understanding of the aesthetic sensibilities of the pre-Columbian Indians.

Objectives should not be considered as final statements, but as guide codes to be assessed and reviewed throughout the development and implementation of the program. They may change because the research altered the concept, or because the audience responded to the project differently than expected. In such cases, flexibility is the key.

4. Staff Responsibilities and Timetables With increased understanding of what the program or exhibition will be, it is important for the staff to know their responsibilities and determine the amount of time it will take to complete the required tasks. Reviewing the timetables and responsibilities of individual departments, staff members, and placing these in the context of the entire operations of the museum is an important part of the planning phase. Overlapping schedules and resultant periods of pressure should be modified if at all possible. Cooperation and the commitment of the entire program staff should be a central goal of the planning team.

5. The Budget A budget is commonly thought of as a financial process. In actuality, it involves a great deal of program responsibility. The amount of space, number of sessions, length of time, number of staff required, maintenance, security, equipment and many other factors must be considered in developing a budget. How much the project costs in the planning, implementation and evaluation stages must all be determined at this point.

If the project is dependent upon grant funds, a schedule must be outlined that will accommodate grant cycles from the foundation or federal agency. If fees are to be charged, a careful analysis of the cost-effectiveness of the program and the amount of publicity required to secure this kind of programming must also be undertaken.

Costs for public relations, marketing, production, fabrication, and installation must all be estimated with increases for inflation. Part of the effectiveness of budgeting is that it will help to further determine staff priorities, because there are no formulas for making these decisions. As in all other phases of the planning of a project, budgets often need revision.

Design Phase

The design phase includes research, developing a design or script, and all aspects of the actual implementation of a project.

1. Research and Location of Materials Museums are responsible for providing accurate information about the objects and materials they use. For an effective and informative presentation, the staff needs adequate time for research, review, and analysis. During the research phase, additional information may be uncovered that may alter the goals and objectives of the project.

Programs and exhibits require materials and research information. A great deal of information is collected during this phase, not all of which will be used. It is better to have too much than to go into the design phase without the resources in hand. In acquiring information, keep in mind the selection of the objects to be used, the type of publications to be produced, and the preliminary drafts of the labels, workbooks, and catalogues. The more detailed the examination of information, artifacts, and objects, the more effective the use of time will be during the design phase.

2. The Design Based on the goals and objectives of the project and using the information collected during the research phase, outline in detail the methods of interpretation and layout of the exhibit or formats for the program. Then, determine the final selection of the major concepts to be presented and the points that will illustrate these ideas through the collections and resources. The resources collected during the research phase (such as maps, slides, objects, diaries, clothing, program formats, etc.) help develop the final script or program format.

Other considerations include the number of people that will participate, the number of times the visitor will be involved in the project, and the accessibility of the program to the handicapped and to people of different ages and backgrounds. The sequencing of events or objects must include an orientation phase, presentation of the main ideas, and conclusion. Time should be allowed for both active and passive involvement, so that all types of people will feel comfortable in the environment and participate in learning.

Among other considerations during the design phase are public relations, scheduling, durability, conservation, security, maintenance, and availability consumable materials.

3. Evaluation Evaluation will occur on many levels, and it is useful to structure the collection of information in an early phase of the program rather than try to reassemble this information at its conclusion. Some of the tools used to collect and document a program are:

- **Records of attendance** or types of materials that have been borrowed; if possible, records should include who, when, and what was used.
- **Observations** by guards, docents, and staff can assist in understanding more clearly the visitor's behavior; training should be provided so these anecdotal records or systematized charts record the visitor's attention or lack of it, the speed with which they move through the galleries, or how many left the program before its completion. Further, they should note the level of interaction and interest that was shown by the visitor. Teachers and parents can also be used when observing special case studies of an individual child, noting their attention level, type of participation, and comparing this to the home or school activities that they usually participate in.
- **Interviews** can be conducted with participants in a program or with visitors at an exhibit. This trick is to persuade those interviewed to speak honestly and for the interviewer to listen carefully to their comments. A selection of children, teachers, principals, parents, volunteers and staff who have worked with a program should all be considered.
- **Questionnaires** record the audience's response to a program or exhibit, and can determine its effectiveness, the amount of information that has been learned, or the immediate reactions to it. Questionnaires can be helpful in determining why people come and whether they will come again. As with interviewing, developing a questionnaire requires skill from consultants who know how to phrase and organize the questionnaire.
- **Pre-and post-tests** can be administered either in the museum or the classroom, to measure the specific gains of information and knowledge, changes in attitude or acquisition of skills that have resulted from the children's experiences.

It is useful to combine these methods in order to accumulate the data needed to evaluate an exhibit or program properly. Evaluations provide a system of quality control, a process for determining whether or not something is effective, and if it is not, what changes can be made to achieve the desired objectives. Some view evaluation as a threat; others consider it costly, expensive item in the budget. Properly executed, however, evaluation is an important key to the effective planning of an exhibition or program.

Again, the budget and schedules for the program need to be reviewed so that sufficient funds and time are provided for the installation or implementation of the project. With everything in place, the staff and planning team can now move into the implementation phase for their project.

Implementation Phase

Implementation, very simply, is the process of doing. For an exhibit, this means construction, fabrication, installation and adjustments. For a program, it might include training, piloting and revision. The entire staff usually comes together at this time to participate in the final installation and opening of an exhibit or testing out of a specific program. During this process, many small changes occur as the staff realizes problems with scheduling, label content and/or size, or other areas of concern.

Once the exhibit or program is in use, observations of visitors reactions should be undertaken. Determining the success or failure of the project needs to occur so that appropriate changes can take place. Sometimes revisions are too costly or time-consuming, and staff is wise to note the difficulties to be avoided in the future. The implementation phase also includes documentation and evaluation.

A successful implementation phase often occurs when the staff of a museum has worked together successfully during the planning and design phases.

Evaluation and Revision Phase

Evaluation is a process of assessing or measuring the effectiveness of the museum experience. Whether the evaluation is a formal or informal process, it is a useful way for the museum staff to understand whether or not the original goals have been accomplished, and to see what has actually occurred through the public's use of the exhibit or program.

Evaluation should be a continuing process. It should not begin after the project is completed if relevant questions are to be answered properly. Such questions include: the right direction? Do we still want to achieve the original goals, or do we want to set new ones? Can we improve the presentation without altering the basic concepts?

It is essential for an evaluation to have commitment from the staff to revise and change the exhibit or program based on its findings. If the evaluation process has occured throughout the planning, design, and implementation phases, then the product produced is fairly effective, and will need little revision.

The purpose of an evaluation is to assist in the decision-making process. Therefore, it should produce useful and relevant information for the staff, so that it can learn if the original goals and objectives have been obtained. The evaluation should also distinguish between the intended results and the actual results of the audience's participation. Clues are essential, and information from various sorts should be collected, such as breakage, questions asked of the guards, the number of people that visit or attend the lecture, and length of their stay. Evaluations can look for many things, including the effectiveness of a program's sequence of events, costs of services, or amount of learning that has taken place.

While the evaluation is being planned, the following issues should have been considered: What is being evaluated? How will it be evaluated (what kinds of documents will be collected, by whom)? What evaluation strategies will be used? Who will conduct the evaluation? Who is the evaluation for? In addition to budgeting funds to undertake an evaluation, money should also be available to make necessary revisions.

There are several philosophies and approaches to designing and conducting an evaluation of museum exhibits and programs. The reader is directed to the writings of Drs. Chandler Screven, Harris Shettle, George Heine, and Robert Woolf, all of whom are referred to in the bibliography.

The information gathered during the evaluation phase should be presented to the appropriate staff members or administrators in a readable, and usable format, so that after careful analysis, recommendations can be made to add, discard, or redesign the exhibit or program and for assistance in planning future programs.

Part of the planning process includes an understanding of how a specific exhibit or program fits into the overall plan of the museum and its future. One person alone cannot provide all of these answers. However, interaction among all of the staff can assist in determining how all of the pieces will fit together. Part of the goal of any exhibit or program is to accomplish this job with a minimum expenditure of financial funds, materials, personnel and resources. The project must also be effective with the visitor.

The previous discussion about planning, design, implementation and evaluation should be considered as a schematic development of each of these steps. There are numerous articles and books that should be referred to, regarding specific content of each planning phase. However, it is hoped that the previous will be a useful overview of the various steps in a process that is important to any successful museum project.

ACCOUNTABILITY

Museums in the 1980's are becoming increasingly more aware of the need to be accountable to their public, their private and public funding sources, and to themselves and their ability to achieve their own goals and objectives. Accountability issues reach into many different areas including stewardship of the museum and its collections, financial and programmatic concerns, and ability to respond to the community needs.

It should be noted that as not-for-profit organizations, museums have a public responsibility to periodically report on their activities and financial management. Usually these financial reports are part of the museum's annual report. Accounting guidelines, approved by the American Institute of Certified Accountants and published by the Association of Science-Technology Centers and American Association of Museums should be carefully studied by any new museum.

Museums have become increasingly aware of their responsibility for evaluating the effectiveness of an exhibit or program in achieving its goals and reaching its audience. Often evaluations are a required part of receiving a grant. Evaluations can be very useful to the museum's staff producing relevant information in a timely and cost effective manner.

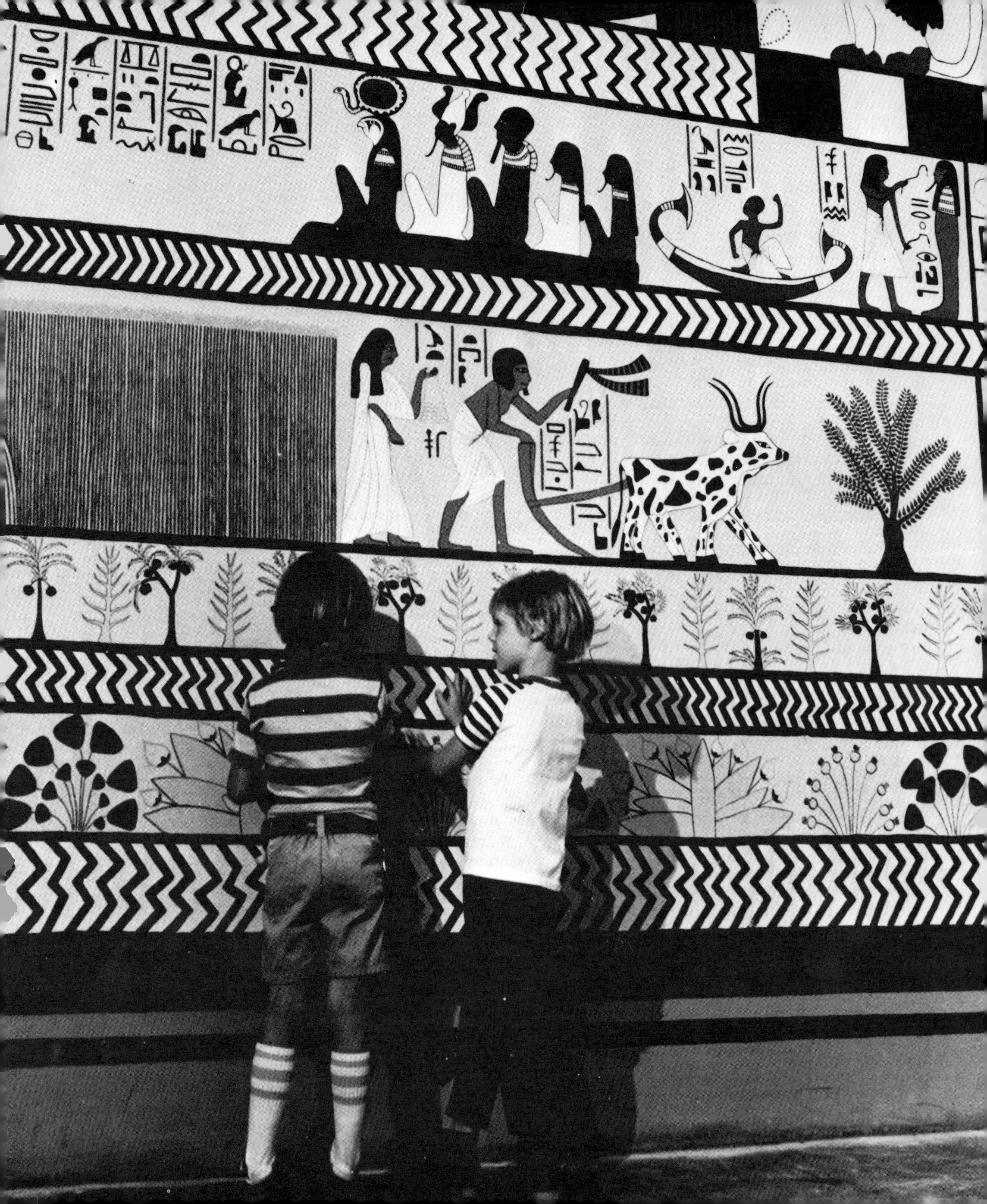

2.
EXHIBITS AND THE MUSEUM EXPERIENCE

Exhibits are the heart of the museum experience, furnishing both entertainment and information. Ranging from simulated environments—such as a limestone cove or a pioneer home—to displays or demonstrations, exhibits often use sensory and participatory techniques to involve the public in learning. In addition to simply looking at the objects, visitors work with computers, draw a buffalo skull, make a collage, listen to the sounds of the ocean, handle stone tools used by prehistoric Indians, feel a skunk's fur, or smell the scent of exotic herbs.

Much of the learning that takes place in the museum is nonstructured and difficult to test, since visitors generally select objects that are of interest to them. They may store information for later use or they may make immediate relationships, connecting one idea to another. Each visitor brings to the museum a unique set of skills, knowledge, and life experiences that are hard to test in advance of a visit to an exhibition. Museums are characterized by informal learning: visitors come by choice; there are no prerequisites for touring the galleries; there is no prescribed route or amount of learning that must take place; and the social interaction and conversation that takes place is important in the learning process.

As museums have become concerned with the need to validate their exhibit presentations, however, behavioral scientists have developed methods to validate exhibit learning. Of course, not everyone comes to the museum specifically to learn. Their motivations vary widely, as do their interpretations of the exhibit. Some people come to museums to wander through the collections, looking at objects at random, and perhaps storing up images, ideas, and information for future use. Their visit may be a solitary experience in a public space. Another group of people perceive the museum visit as a social activity, an opportunity for shared experiences that will be entertaining and informative in an educational setting. Still other groups, such as collectors or school children, come to study the collections, desiring to obtain specific information.

Exploratory behavior in the museum is essential. Museums with collections and equipment that communicate the ideas and phenomenon as well as the products and processes of the natural and man-made world should also accommodate the "itch to explore," which is a most human experience. Museums should increase curiosity, motivate learning, and provide answers to the visitors as they make their own discoveries by observing, recording, comparing, contrasting, and reading.

This does not mean that an exhibition should be a collection of randomly placed objects. Nor should an exhibit be a book with the label text outweighing the objects on view. Adults do not like to read long labels and children cannot. Nor should museums be only an audiovisual center, for visitors have not just come to see movies or slides. Displaying objects in a meaningful way can incorporate labels, audiovisual resources, films, self-guided brochures and other things that help to enhance the visitor's understanding of the objects and their relationships.

TYPES OF EXHIBITS

The objects, colors, shapes, and materials used in museum exhibits cover the full range of the natural and manufactured world, from historically recreated areas like Greenfield Village in Dearborn, Michigan or the

San Diego Zoo with its lush foliage and exotic animals, to a survey of textiles, their styles, and manufacturing processes at the Seattle Art Museum.

Numerous books and articles have been written about designing and installing museum exhibitions. In some respects, exhibits are like store windows, designed to attract and to entice an audience into looking more closely for a period of time.

There are many techniques for displaying and interpreting the collections or subject area of a museum, and the following summarizes some of the methods that museums use for presenting their artifacts and ideas in ways that actively involve the visitor.

A taxonomic and historical survey combines related or unrelated objects in a systematic arrangement. Examples of this type of exhibit include a taxonomic collection of butterflies or an array of prehistoric projectile points, samples of weaving techniques in the 19th century, or children's games for the past hundred years. Taxonomic exhibits allow visitors to study variations and to compare and contrast the objects, and often emphasize a visual storage approach to design by the abundance of objects on view. Numerous objects can enhance the display in this type of exhibit.

Creating a context or organizing objects by their relationships to each other to tell a story is successfully done in period rooms or habitat dioramas, which bring together a number of different objects to show the relationships between them. Another way of creating a context or relationship can be through the organization of exhibits based on themes or concepts. Here, diverse objects are brought together to illustrate a particular point, such as life and death, the cycles of nature, the space age, 20th-century print making, or the animals of the African veldt.

Interactive exhibits involve visitors in experiencing, handling, experimenting, manipulating, and performing tasks in an effort to help them understand processes, ideas, or periods of time. Operating models or original apparatus and demonstrations by staff, as well as the use of audiovisual and interactive exhibit techniques are the core of these exhibits.

Total environments surround the visitors with the sights, sounds, smells, or tastes of simulated, recreated, or real places. People can walk to a cave in Southern Florida at the Florida State Museum, wander down a gaslit street at the turn of the century at the Grand Rapids Public Museum in Michigan, or discuss colonial problems and eat in a colonial tavern at Williamsburg. Environmental exhibits are often supplemented by audiovisual materials and trained interpretors, a considerable amount of information is conveyed via the sensory factors.

DESIGNING AN EXHIBIT

Orderly, effective exhibit planning requires the services of people with different types of expertise, including a specialist on the objects or subject, the curator or scientist; specialists in the area of transforming visual forms and ideas into exhibits, the designer; and, a specialist on communicating with the public, the educator. Not every museum will have staff members with all these skills or responsibilities, in which case volunteer help or professional consultants may be needed. Many museums are recognizing the need for staff collaboration on many levels, to design, develop, and evaluate their exhibits.

Exhibits may develop either because the curator has an idea based on the availability of objects or excitement about an idea, or because the museum wants to present certain ideas or experiences to the community. Although thousands of decisions must be made between the conception of an exhibition idea and the dismantling of the exhibit many months or years later, perhaps the most important is the first decision: whether the idea for the exhibit would be better as a book or film.

If the decision is to prepare an exhibition, then the time frame must be considered that considers potential funding sources and staff availability. An exhibit planning team of appropriate members from various divisions should work with the curator to define what the exhibit is about and to organize its content. It may be useful to produce a list of concepts and ideas with possible design solutions for the technicians. The exhibit planning team should prescribe the goals and objectives; the type of presentation the exhibit will make, including interpretive techniques to support visitor learning such as labels, cassettes, films, demonstration areas, and interactive devices; the amount of space the exhibit shall take up; and a budget that covers the cost of preparing the exhibition, maintaining it, and providing security.

A second phase of the planning and development process for an exhibit includes preparing a script for the exhibit, developing a model that can illustrate the relationship of the object or exhibit unit to the programmatic functions to be accommodated in the exhibit such as tours, seating, or audiovisual presentations. Again, the time frame, budgets, and staff requirements need to be reviewed. The final script prepared by the exhibit team generally receives approval from the director. The script will include a final selection of the artifacts or units to be prepared; the photos, maps, models to be used; and an indication of the graphics, draft copy or final copy for the labels. At this stage, preliminary thought should be given to the public relations and promotion campaign.

Designing an exhibit requires skill, a feeling for the objects, for the need to conserve them, and a commitment to making the exhibits accessible to all. Barrier-free designs have been successfully installed at the Kimbell Art Museum of Fort Worth, the National Air and Space Museum in Washington, D.C., and the Children's Museum of Indianapolis. At the National Air and Space Museum raised-line drawings, available at the information desk to help direct the visitors with sight problems, indicate articles that may be touched and the locations of restrooms and telephones. Audio-taped tours can serve as a guided tour for the blind visitor or scripts for audiovisual presentations can make a visit more meaningful for deaf visitors. Museums should consider the needs of the handicapped visitor while planning exhibits: the height of the cases and paintings, the size of the label text, and the ability to move easily through the gallery space.

The next exhibit development phase includes the fabrication and installation of the exhibit, during which materials for construction are selected and blueprints receive final approval. The construction phase for exhibit units, cases, lighting and label copy should be carefully programmed. The actual installation is often one of the most exciting projects that the staff can participate in. This should be followed by an immediate critique of the galleries. Corrections should be made and modifications noted. Staff who have not previously participated in the exhibit might walk through and comment on the ability of the exhibit to clearly communicate the main ideas and to serve the needs of the various visitors—the scholar, parents, children, and teachers.

Once the exhibit has opened to the public, the staff should continually observe visitors moving through the galleries, noting places that might be redesigned, either in this exhibit or for future times: traffic flow, lighting effectiveness, length or complexity of labels, or variations in pacing. Maintenance of the exhibit should also be carefully noted. Physical damage, mechanical repairs, security, and safety should be noted. Changes, when possible, should be made so that the exhibit continually improves itself. Though this is often a difficult process, it can help to increase the usefulness of the exhibit for the visitors.

Each exhibit inevitably has its own unique character and objectives, which have been determined by the museum staff, the objects or topics, and the intended audience. The core of a good exhibit design is a clear understanding of the exhibit concept and audience. The exhibit need not be a purely linear manner, directing the visitor from one object or place to the next, but the visitor needs a clear understanding of the organization of the exhibit, so that he can make decisions about looking, reading, pausing, and learning. These cues can be given in a number of ways, such as maps, headline labels, or the organizational plan of the exhibit (whether it is taxonomic, chronological, or thematic). In a report prepared for the Royal Ontario Museum, Robert Lakota observed the need for communicating the exhibit plan directly to the visitor at the outset:

> *Keeping this information from the visitor forces them to conceptualize and organize the exhibit themselves, a time-consuming process that only a few visitors attempt successfully. By holding onto the romantic notion that everything must be dis*covered *by visitors to have any "real" impact, we are not only assuring that fewer visitors will profit from their visit, but are also avoiding the necessity of being specific about our intentions. Certainly any exhibit contains information, objects, and relationships to be discovered by visitors, however, to assure that more visitors will make those discoveries and understand what it is they discovered, tell the visitors as clearly as possible:*

- *what the exhibit is about;*
- *what it has to do with them;*
- *how it is organized, and*
- *what they can expect to learn from it.*

Then, restate these points at appropriate locations within the exhibit, and provide an active review at the end.

Many tools have been developed by museums to help orient visitors, direct attention to important aspects of the collection or exhibit, and to structure the visit and learning experience. Often, the visitor spends too much time at the beginning of the exhibit trying to determine what it is that they will be looking at. Care should be given in designing the exhibit to avoid "museum fatigue" as the visitor moves through a succession of exhibits units and experiences. Museum fatigue is created by the lack of contrast between objects and environments, noise, heat, crowding, and a sense of disorientation. The objects on display should create relationships, combine the unfamiliar with the familiar, and help to direct the visitor's viewing patterns. Diversity in the presentation should include consideration for such things as lighting, labels, background colors, ceiling heights, and much more.

There are many ways of designing exhibits to involve the visitors in learning activities. One thing is certain: there is no formula that will guarantee the success of an exhibit. Each technique has merit. Because of the diversity within the audience, it is probably best to use a variety of approaches: labels, self-guides, audio tours, orientation galleries, and demonstrations all supplement the visitor's museum experience.

Some studies indicate that only three to ten percent of the visitors in a museum receive guided tours. Therefore, it is essential that the exhibition plans include a place for orientation, helpful labels, demonstrations and/or self-guides. The varied levels of the audience should be considered and while not all of these interpretive tools need to be in a single exhibit, it is useful to plan on them from the early stages of the design process.

EXHIBIT INTERPRETATION AIDS

Orientation Galleries

Orientation or interpretation theaters and galleries can fulfill many different functions. They introduce the visitor to the museum, to a specific collection, or to a single object, or provide background information about the collection, artist, scientist, or historical event. These galleries can set the tone for the museum visit and stimulate the excitement of discovery. Activities, printed materials or audiovisual presentations can orient the visitor. Their general goals are to tell visitors where they are and what they will be seeing, to provide them information that is not readily apparent through the objects or labels, or help them to make good use of their time. There are two types of orientation galleries: those that orient the visitor to the entire museum's collections or resources, and those that relate to the orientation of a specific exhibition.

1. Orientation to the Museum The Carnegie Museum of Natural History in Pittsburgh has an information and orientation center at its main entrance. Staffed by volunteers and sometimes professional staff, this room includes an information desk where groups can inquire about the collections of the museum, register for tours, or pick up brochures about the collections or special exhibitions. Ten orientation stations around the room include small displays of slides, tapes, pictures and a phone pick-up, which describe the work that goes on behind the scenes at the museum. In one- to five-minute tapes, curators describe the collections, how they are stored, what research goes on, and the field work the museum undertakes. There are from one to four tapes at each station, and topics include all the major divisions of the museum's work.

The New Orleans Museum of Art has created a series of didactic exhibitions entitled *Asterisk,* designed to assist the visitors in understanding and appreciating works in the permanent collection. For example, the exhibit "Casting" illustrates metal paper, clay castings and others through text, illustrations, photomurals, and actual objects from the collection. The exhibit includes information on the aesthetics, processes, social context, and historical subject matter related to the objects and methods involved in casting. A hand-out is available to guide visitors to artworks in galleries, which are not directly dealt with in the *Asterisk* exhibition, but which reflect principles examined and challenge the visitor to transfer this new information. Visitors can go into the permanent collection and look for objects with an *Asterisk* label. Interpretative labeling includes information on how the object was made, why it was made, and aesthetic principles that it illustrates. *The Big Apple*, a special multimedia exhibition at the Museum of the City of New York, incorporates objects from the permanent collection in a special theater gallery and in an audiovisual show. *The Big Apple* traces the history of New York from 1574 to the present. The multiscreen computerized slide show includes objects from the permanent collection and music from the museum's archives to tell the story of the city's founding, growth and diversity. In addition, a spotlight illuminates pertinent historical objects from the museum's collections, such as a hand-pumped fire engine used in a city fire of 1835 or a Broadway horse cart from 1853. *The Big Apple* is more than an orientation exhibition, although it works effectively in that role: It is an exciting experience, which readies visitors for the ideas and objects presented in galleries throughout the museum.

Discovery rooms, such as those at the Field Museum of Natural History, the National Museum of Natural History, or Zoo Lab at the National Zoological Park, play an effective role in orienting visitors. Learning boxes and other resources allow children and adults to investigate, focus their attention, handle objects, and have their questions answered, playing a special role in the learning and orientation of the museum visitor. The discovery rooms also include resource information, which provide the visitor with additional learning opportunities.

2. Orientation to an Exhibition Many museums have found that slide tapes, films and video fulfilled a special role in providing orientation to special exhibits. These audiovisual resources can bring time, cultures and ideas together into one succinct unit.

The Aqua Theater, which accompanies an exhibition on water at the California Museum of Science and Industry, is a multimedia presentation that discusses the need for water in Southern California and acquaints the visitor with the problems of that area. In another approach at the Virginia Museum of Fine Arts, audiovisual slide shows adjacent to the galleries provide background information on the different collections. For example, Faberge's role in the society of the Russian Czar might accompany a display of Faberge jewels, or French architecture in the Middle Ages might augment a medieval collection. These brief, focused presentations provide a cultural frame of reference for artwork on display.

At the Philadelphia Museum of Art, videotapes located outside of the Arensberg Collection may be used before or after viewing the collection. The viewer can select from 11 program tapes in three categories: information about the general context of the collection, such as the Arensbergs as collectors, or World War I; the individual artist, or selected works of art by each of the artists such as *The Bride Stripped Bare*, by Duchamp, and *The Cry*, by Brancusi. The tapes last one-half to eight minutes, with an average length of five minutes.

Orientation exhibitions and media presentations play a special role in the museum. Scripts can be extracted so the hearing-impaired visitor can make use of audiovisual resources. They can be a place where the visually handicapped visitor can learn which objects can be handled and how to get around the museum. Orientation centers or resources can help alleviate the fear or discomfort of a new environment that may be felt by some first-time visitors and can help regular visitors make better use of the museum.

Labels

Labels are museums' most traditional form of communication. Customarily, museums carefully identify each object in a case, listing its name, date, place of origin, and sometimes its accession number. Labels can do more than simply identify an object in a museum. They can give directions on how to operate equipment, describe an historical event, or introduce background information. Effectively prepared, labels can lead the visitor to understand or appreciate an object or discover ideas.

It is generally believed that people do not read museum labels because they are in motion, conversing with others, and interested in the next area of exploration. Therefore, to attract the reader's attention requires skill. Labels must be attractive, but should not overpower the objects. The size, shape, and amount of type must be carefully considered.

Research has proven that serif letters are read more easily than sanserif, and that mixed upper and lower case letters work more effectively than letters that are all the same size. Many studies about the museum visitor's use of labels are cited in the bibliography.

Labels can provide information and are especially effective when they explain what the visitor is looking at, how it was used, how it was made, and similar questions. Labels can also be effective when they ask questions, therefore directing the visitor's attention. At the Corpus Christi Museum in Texas, two labels form the core of an exhibit of 20 objects. The question, "What is it?" is followed by the challenge, "Go to the museum and try to find the names of these objects." Whole families work together trying to determine the identities of the various objects, and answers are provided at the museum's information desk. The exhibit is effective because it allows voluntary education through voluntary activity.

Many museums have several different types of labels for single exhibitions. Introductory labels outline the theme and provide background information. Topical information labels are illustrated through headlines or state questions. Explanatory labels provide specific information on individual objects or on how to operate a piece of equipment. Obviously, the size of type or reading difficulty can vary accordingly. An exhibition using three or more levels of signs should carefully coordinate the signage so that it will work using any one level or none of them at all.

For example, in the exhibition *What If I Couldn't?* at the Boston Children's Museum, labels were prepared for children and adults. The information in the smaller print size label allowed adults to feel comfortable reading and interpreting for their children at appropriate levels. The following labels were used:

Titles (Large print):
What If You . . . Couldn't Hear as Well as Everyone Else?

Labels for Children (Medium Size Print with Illustrations):
People might say that you were hearing impaired, hard of hearing, or deaf. The kind of sounds you could hear would depend on how much and what kind of hearing you had lost.

Labels for Adults (Small Print):
A person who is hearing impaired can have a loss that makes all sounds fainter, (listen to tape 1) but it is more likely that that person hears some kinds of sounds better than others (tape 2, 3, 4). Much of the time the loss involves higher pitched sounds, and, therefore, amplification or shouting may not help much. Speech might be heard, but not understood without a lot of concentration and visual cues, because some of the sounds are left out.

The basic purpose of labels is to help visitors look more closely at the objects or use the exhibit unit. In the process, the label perhaps may expand their store of knowledge and stimulate their imagination. Janet Kamien of The Children's Museum, Boston, suggests that improving museum accessibility for the handicapped

improves conditions for the other visitors as well,
- "Good sightlines for wheelchair users will usually be good sightlines for children.
- Simplified language for deaf visitors will be better language for children, and in fact, your general audience as well.
- Large lettering for visually impaired people will be great for children and for many older people too.
- Tactile components you put in will definitely excite your entire audience."

Demonstrations

In many exhibit areas, museums have incorporated demonstration facilities designed to illustrate processes not easily understood by looking at a tool or reading a label. One advantage of demonstrations, which tend to combine showmanship with teaching, is that they can effectively present information to a large number of people at one time.

In developing demonstration areas, museums must consider whether the space will contain wet or dry experiments, the length of the program and the level of information to be presented, the number of times per day that it will be scheduled, the type of personnel who will do the presentations (volunteers or staff), the ability of the demonstration to be interpreted to handicapped visitors, and the needs for equipment and storage.

At the New England Aquarium, "Animal Interviews" is a formal, live animal presentation given by education volunteers that allows visitors to take a closer look at the variety of aquarium inhabitants. Featured animals include beavers, penguins, sea stars, lobsters, and horseshoe crabs, as well as other reptiles and amphibians. The audience is invited to carefully examine the animals and in some cases to touch them. For example, they may pet a live beaver and examine a beaver skull, or watch a hungry penguin carefully position his fish so it is swallowed head first. Information about the animal's natural environment and adaptations for survival is emphasized through the use of props. Questions from the audience are a central part of these animal interviews.

Science museums offer visitors both exhibit hall demonstrations and auditorium demonstrations. For example, at the Science Museum of Minnesota interpreters in the anthropology hall illustrate musical instruments, spin and weave, cook flat breads at a hearth area, or use tools of the past and present in the hunters and gatherers section. Other demonstrators in science museums make nylon, illustrate electrical principles, dissect a cow's eye to reveal the crystalline lenses, or handle materials too dangerous or delicate for the general public.

Auditorium demonstrations, usually longer, allow the audience to be seated, involve more props, and are generally scripted. For example, at the Maryland Science Center in Baltimore, a demonstrator explains the laws of motion using a cart built for a stage demonstration, and at the Des Moines Center of Science and Industry, children in the audience can participate in electricity demonstrations. At the Center for Science and Industry in Columbus, young children meet "Mr. Peanut," dressed in costume, in a botany demonstration. At its conclusion, children receive kits so that they can plant their own peanuts in the classroom or at home.

In history museums, and especially in the living history communities such as Virginia's Colonial Williamsburg or Greenfield Village in Michigan, costumed interpreters explain the tasks necessary for living in such villages. Boat repairing is seen at Mystic Seaport in Connecticut, blacksmithing is done at Plimoth Plantation, and candles are dipped at Old Sturbridge Village. Visitors observe traditional crafts and sometimes participate in the activities of farming, cleaning, cooking, repairing tools, or splitting shingles. Here demonstrations are a central part of the exhibition technique and interpretation of the collections.

Art museums frequently combine demonstrations designed to explain artistic processes and techniques with exhibits that use the process. The Seattle Art Museum, for example, scheduled almost daily demonstrations of spinning, weaving, dying and embroidery techniques in conjunction with an exhibit on textiles. The Experiencenter is part of the educational program at the Dayton Art Institute. The visitor can contrast the art of the Samurai class shown in exhibits with the folk art of the Edo period experienced in the Experiencenter, in which workshops and demonstrations allow visitors to construct fans, try calligraphy and observe sumi brush painting techniques.

The Cincinnati Zoo and the New England Aquarium are among those science museums that offer demonstrations in which visitors touch animals such as lion cubs, elephants, turtles and starfish. Bringing the animals closer to the children can often dispel myths and help to create a deeper appreciation about living things.

Demonstrations are appealing because they provide answers that are not apparent through the objects. How is it made, what do you use? How long does it take to make it? What does it eat? Museums usually present the viewer with the products and forget that neither children nor adults understand how it was made. Demonstrations can also focus visitors' attention and enhance their abilities to learn.

Exhibit Guides

Ideally, a museum will have at least two types of guides for individual use: a map indicating the names, subjects, and locations of exhibition galleries, telephones, restrooms and other facilities; and a guide to specific collections or exhibits designed to direct the visitor's attention to certain objects and to stimulate imaginative observation. At some museums, including The Metropolitan Museum of Art, these guides are available in braille and large print. Basic tools for visitors, such as guides, help visitors to feel at ease in an environment,

Above is a sketch of the painting on the right. A sketch can be a quick, rough, undetailed drawing or early study.

Can you find the painting in the exhibition that was done from this sketch?

and assist those with limited time to locate key points of interest in the museum.

Self-guides come in hundreds of shapes, lengths and levels of information. Consideration must be given to providing the reader with text that is readable, informative and encourages looking at the exhibits. Clarity of design and ease of reading, while in the museum are also important. Illustrations are helpful if they assist the visitor in identifying the objects or animals on the tour. Self-guides should be fun, not hard work. Care should be given to the route the visitor will be following. If possible, activities should engage both parents and children: listing or classifying animal behaviors, colors in a painting, or the cycle of life in a habitat. When possible, the self-guide should provide ideas on sources of more information about the exhibit, but the references should be accessible in public libraries and book stores. Obviously, self-guides can be written for many audiences: for different languages, the handicapped, school groups, adults, children and families. Although not every self-guide needs to be written at each of these levels, several different self-guides for different audiences should be prepared if possible.

The Museum of Fine Arts in Boston has developed a series of visitor guides for adults and children designed to increase their visual awareness and to give them a context for understanding and enjoying the particular works of art, by supplying historical information or comparisons with everyday life. Guides developed for children focus on observational activities (listing or drawing) to maximize the learning that can take place in the galleries. In addition, the museum adapted adult guides for use with deaf audiences: these give attention to reading levels, art historical content, and use of illustrations.

The Delaware Art Museum has developed several different self-guided discovery tours for families and school groups. The "Discovery Sketch Book" for the exhibition *Artists in Wilmington, 1890-1940* is typical. The sketch book text encourages children to explore not only the exhibition but also the city, noting changes that have occurred in the past 50 years. Answering riddles, drawing sketches, and visiting locations the artists used, are among the experiences that are encouraged.

Journey, published three times a year by the Field Museum, are free self-guides geared to children and families. Topics for each year represent the four scientific disciplines of the museum: anthropology, botany, geology, and zoology. Each pamphlet, designed to sharpen the visitor's observational skills, channels attention to characteristics, objects, and their unique qualities. Some *Journeys* are arranged as series of questions and answers, keyed to specimens in exhibits. For example, in the "Adventures of the Canada Goose:"

> *Begin your journey in hall 21, located just off Stanley Field Hall in the south end of the museum. Here you will meet the Canada Goose. As you enter the hall, find the Canada Goose in the third case to your right. . . . Look carefully at the foot of the Canada goose. . . . How many toes do you see on its foot? Are all its toes attached to a web of skin? Now study the beak, a handy, strong tool. . . . Such a break can pick up grain, strip off grass and other seeds and neatly snip small leaves and seedlings for mealtime.*
> *Draw the beak of a Canada goose.*

The Museum of Science and Industry in Chicago has developed a series of *3-2-1-Contact* folders, which coordinate museum tours with the weekly topics in the science television programs produced by Children's Television Workshop. The family-oriented self-guided tours coordinate gallery visits and particular exhibits to the ideas from each television segment, such as "Hot/Cold" or "Noisy/Quiet." For "Hot/Cold," the guide

31

refers to exhibits that expand on such ideas as "heat energy can do work" and "properties of materials change with temperatures." After helping locate exhibits, the folder poses questions and problems that encourage children to explore and examine their everyday world as well as the exhibits. They also contain action activities such as treasure hunts, activities that can assure the most complete use of the exhibits, and suggest questions that may be answered by the family at the museum or at home. (See above.)

When the family has finished with the folder, it can be returned to the information desk and exchanged for a "Save It For A Brainy Day" page, which suggests activities and experiments to be done at home.

The National Zoological Park of the Smithsonian Institution in Washington, D.C. has experimented with several different formats for self-guides that can be used with families and school groups. All encourage the visitor to look more closely and to record what they have seen. "Search Cards" are self-guides for school groups in a number of areas including birds, animals, and reptiles. Each card in the package refers to one bird or area where birds can be observed. On the front of the card is an illustration so they will know what to look at and questions to help direct their observation. (See above.) Visitors using the "Search Cards" receive conclusion questions at the end, and a list of bibliographical references for further study.

Another of the Zoo's self-guided tour, "Draw a Bill," is a fold-out brochure that allows the visitor to compare and contrast the size and shape of birds' beaks and relate this information to the kinds of food they eat. Each panel contains a graphic illustration of the bird minus its beak, with text about the beak's function. Visitors can draw the beaks of several birds including the Northern Oriole, woodcock, toucan, Bald Eagle and duck. (See above, next page.)

Bird Lab, one of the zoo's discovery rooms, contains discovery boxes on nests, feathers, bills, eating habits; books with information on each of the species; self-guided tours; and binoculars that can be rented. The

Bald Eagle

The eagle is a hunter and a meat-eater. It feeds on fish and rodents.

Strong claws help it catch its prey. Its hook-like beak tears bites out of its large meal.

(If the eagles are hard to see, look at the beak of the stone eagle statue near the duck ponds.)

Ibis

The ibis lives in marshy places or near water. Its long beak probes through mud and water to find food. Its long legs make wading easier.

zoo is developing self-guided materials for family visitors that will accommodate the random nature of the visitor's exploration of the zoo.

Audio Tours

Audio-guided tours usually provide more information than is available in the labels or self-guided brochures. There are a variety of systems to choose from: cassettes, wands or teleguides to name but a few. It is important to know what type of message is to be delivered, and to carefully select the technology best suited for the delivery. In general, the most effective audio tours are those which can be visitor-activated—stopped and started at the visitor's command. A good narrator is essential: the director or curator may not be the best to perform this function. Like labels, audio guides can be interactive and conversational in tone. They can also present different points of view with different levels of information. In considering an audio guide system, costs for production and maintenance must be considered in the budget.

At the Milwaukee Art Center and Boston's Museum of Science, random access systems let the visitor pick up a telephone in the gallery and listen to a four- to six-minute audio presentation about a particular exhibit or artwork. In developing the teleguide system scripts at the Milwaukee Art Center, the staff selected a particular exhibit and defined the main points about the artist's life and style. The scripts (such as the following one about Toulouse-Lautrec) balanced the information about the artist and art works with questions that involved the visitor in observing and comparing the styles of painting.

There are several other posters in this collection in which Lautrec created effects by drawing large white forms with a few simple lines. This also attracts the eye to the poster. After all, a poster's primary function is to attract attention:

> Lautrec's use of a few well chosen colors, and high contrast, were other attention getting techniques. Sometimes a large black area was used instead of white. Look at the poster titled *Le Divan Japonais* on the same wall as the May Milton poster. It's the second one from the left.
> No details in Jane Avril's dress—but are they needed to get over the personality and style of this woman?
> How many colors do you count in this poster? There are only two real colors. But what an effect! Look around the room at just the posters. Don't all of them have the characteristics I've mentioned—simple basic lines, just a few colors, and high contrast?

The Denver Museum of Natural History is one of the many museums that use taped messages with habitats. Usually lasting from one-half to two minutes, the messages provide information on the species and scene or exhibit. Useful supplements to a guided tour, any audio tours or taped message can be difficult to hear if the gallery is noisy. Also, because the visitor can decide not to listen to the whole message, the tape must complete its cycle before it can start again. The heavy usage stationary tapes receive often result in maintenance problems.

References

Arts and the Handicapped: An Issue of Access. New York: Educational Facilities Laboratories, 1975.

Borun, Minda. *Measuring the Immeasurable: A Pilot Study of Museum Effectiveness.* Washington, D.C.: Association of Science-Technology Centers, 1977.

Draper, Linda, ed. *The Visitor and the Museum.* Berkeley: Lowrie Museum of Anthropology, 1977.

Kamien, Janet. *Is There Life After 504?: A Guide to Building and Program Accessibility from The Children's Museum, Boston.* Boston: Children's Museum, 1980.

LaKota, Robert. *Communication with the Museum Visitor: Guidelines for Planning.* Toronto: Royal Ontario Museum, 1976.

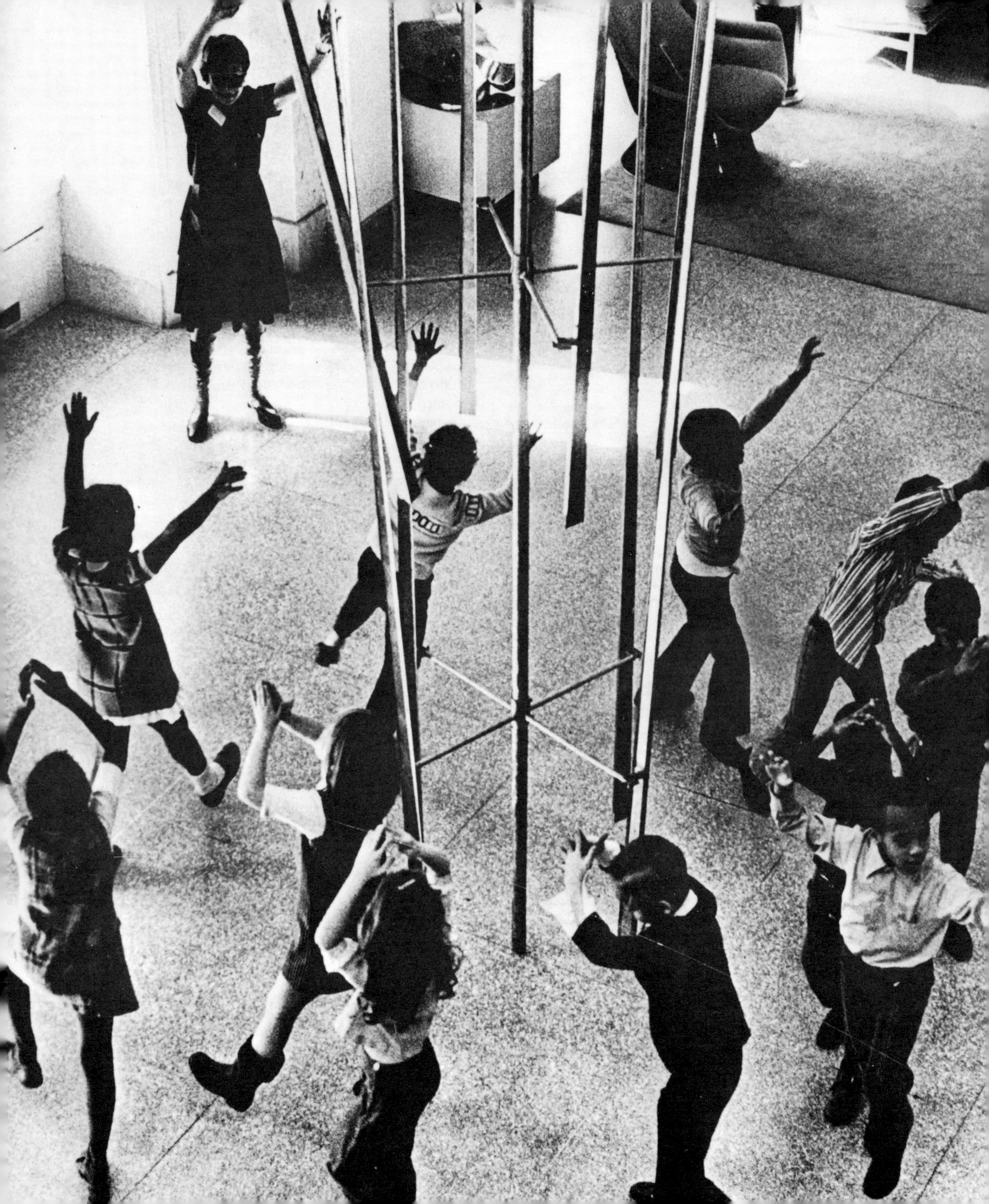

3.
EXHIBITS INVOLVING THE MUSEUM VISITOR

Exhibit techniques such as dioramas, habitats, display cases, and chronological or thematic surveys are vital resources for learning in museums. Interactive exhibit techniques, which provide a sense of discovery or direct experiences with objects, play a vital role in the informal educational institution's ability to let visitors learn by themselves. They appeal to a variety of senses and generally require the adult or child to handle materials, play roles, day dream, operate equipment and participate in play or work. An interactive exhibit can be a single station involving push buttons or computer terminals, more complex visitor-activated units, or entire environments such as those at Colonial Williamsburg and the Florida State Museum's caves.

These exhibitions respect the child's spontaneous drive to learn and adults' desires to both learn and share in children's discoveries. Interactive exhibits take into account the diversity of people's capacities to learn and the variety of needs that exist in different human beings. Although some dioramas may create a certain level of participation through imagination (children may imagine themselves living in a Navajo hogan), interactive exhibits foster learning through sensory involvement.

Interactive exhibits provide direct experiences with objects or exhibits. Some are temporary installations, while others are permanent. Discovery rooms, computer areas, total environments, and exhibit units are among the interactive exhibit techniques found in natural history, science, art, history, and children's museums around the country.

Experiences alone, such as trying on an astronaut's helmet or cooking corn bread, are only part of a successful interactive experience. Museums should carefully construct the pacing and content of interactive exhibitions and programs to avoid "push-the-button-and-run" behavior. The objective of interactive exhibits is to arouse curiosity and help visitors answer questions themselves, rather than passively learning answers via labeling.

In *Experience and Education,* John Dewey observed, "The quality of the experience has two aspects. There is an immediate aspect of agreeableness or disagreeableness, and there is its influence upon later experiences." In some cases, museums have designed experiences to provide a continuity and interrelationship as the visitor moves from one exhibit to another. In preparing these exhibits, the museums recognize the value of placing objects in a context that allows for individual decision-making, interaction, self-directed experiments, communication, and exploration.

Science-technology centers have concentrated on using interactive exhibitry because of their subject matter. Science, itself, is a process of establishing hypotheses, conducting experiments, making relationships, and ultimately discovering an answer. The interactive exhibits of science centers follow a similar pattern: a hypothesis is offered in the form of a single exhibit or series of exhibit units; the visitor uses the exhibit in a variety of ways to test possible answers; and, eventually, may discover a reasonable explanation. Sometimes full understanding occurs while using the exhibit; other times, complete understanding happens weeks or months later when a similar situation occurs in daily life.

Children's museums and science-technology centers have created many successful exhibitions because they recognize that discovery is an essential ingredient for all learning, even though people learn at different levels and in varied ways. These museums create opportunities for both child and adult to say, "Now I understand how that works, . . . now I want to learn more. . . ."

The following review of interactive and environmental exhibits in natural history, history, art, children's, and science museums illustrates the range of exhibit formats, techniques, and styles. Only a few of the hundreds of excellent examples were selected to show the differences in style and approach in each type of museum.

NATURAL HISTORY MUSEUMS

The advantage of discovery rooms or environmental spaces, which are common to natural history museums, is that they provide an excellent orientation to natural objects, allowing people to handle real specimens and to investigate questions they have about exhibits. They may be integral areas of main exhibit halls or small, separate locations.

Characteristically, they require a great deal of volunteer or staff time, supervising activities and maintaining the area's materials. Because their format often limits attendance, ticket systems may be necessary for admittance. Their operation requires careful scheduling and skilled personnel.

At the North Carolina State Museum [of Natural History], museum learning centers—self-contained areas that can accommodate 25 students—are scattered among the major exhibits. Each learning center contains specimens, teaching units, and audiovisual materials, emphasizing one group of organisms such as reptiles and amphibians. An object gallery approach is used: 64 drawers of reference specimens help the nonscientist learn to identify reptiles and amphibians, and how these animals reproduce, communicate, and eat. Some specimens may be handled, while others are only to be viewed. A small reference library, materials, and study areas are available. When not in use by scheduled groups, the casual visitor may use this area, which is adjacent to a display of live animals and the dioramas of the North Carolina environment.

The Object Gallery of the Florida State Museum in Gainesville complements the museum's major exhibits, which are concept-oriented rather than taxonomically oriented. The purpose of the Object Gallery is to help the visitor better understand the collections and their value as teaching and resource tools. It contains some traditional exhibit cases, as well as vertical files with information on how to identify snakes and other specimens; study carrels; aquariums and terrariums; and more than 200 drawers of objects (including projectile points, Kachina dolls, pine cones, land snails). The Object Gallery, a resource library, provides visitors with continuing opportunities to study and explore at their own pace and to relate their findings to the museum's collection.

The Discovery Room, located in a corner of the Smithsonian's National Museum of Natural History, gives visitors the opportunity to touch such things as whale vertebrae, sea urchins, fossils, coral, and plant seeds. The room's informal atmosphere encourages looking and exploring. Large "stumpers" are scattered throughout the room: an elephant tusk, a plankton net, a fossil footprint, to name just a few. Label cards near most "stumpers" pose questions, give information, or refer to the objects in the room. Smaller objects, such as shells and minerals, are arranged in a series of boxes with titles such as, "What is a fossil?" "Colors and Shells" and "Minerals." A box may be taken anywhere in the room, and the contents carefully examined.

Carrying the discovery concept one step further, the museum has developed a Naturalist Center where collections of specimens may be studied, examined with scientific equipment, or photographed. A comprehensive library of natural history reference books, as well as tools, and equipment for the study of specimens assist the research of individual students, collectors, and naturalists using the center. Students, aged 12 and up, use the center's collections and study tools for school-related projects and their own interests. Classes in bird-skinning, mammal preparation, rocks, and minerals use the center's facilities.

Three different educational spaces at the American Museum of Natural History in New York City have been specifically designed to involve the visitor and to complement information presented in exhibits. A discovery room, open during the weekend, contains objects in boxes that may be examined and explored by parents and children. The Alexander M. White Natural Science Center, a teaching exhibit space, describes the nature of New York City for young people. Designed to teach ecology to city children, the exhibit begins with concrete and asphalt and moves on to familiar street scenes, such as a sidewalk excavation, a tree growing on the street, a store window, and others. In each of the 13 units, a built-in activity enables the visitor to participate rather than to view passively. Children become involved in an electric quiz board to identify common minerals, peepholes to observe a vacant lot, and earphones to reveal the sounds of New York City's wildlife. Staff members are available to answer questions.

The museum's People Center provides intimate contact with performers or teachers. The interpretive facility serves as a weekend teaching space, demonstration center, and performance area. Stage areas and informal seating arrangements allow visitors to observe and participate in learning about other cultures and the values of different societies, sometimes juxtaposing contemporary Western forms with those from other times and places. Music or dance from New York and Thailand may occur simultaneously, chamber music may alternate with Ghanian drumming. A Monopoly game or a contemporary American ceramic may be placed with games and pottery from other cultures to point up cultural similarities and differences.

The Place for Wonder at the Field Museum of Natural History introduces children to the infinite variety in the natural world and provides experiences related to the museum's exhibits. This discovery room includes five different types of material: animal, plant, rock, fossil, and cultural artifacts. Dinosaur bones, animal fur, feathers, and skin are placed openly, and drawers contain collections of small items such as insects and shells. Topics are changed periodically in the anthropology area, which features clothes, household items, and school supplies as well as slide and tape presentations.

A discovery room and total environment at the Field allows children to learn what life was like in a Pawnee Earth Lodge. A lodge, like those built by Nebraska's Pawnee Indians from 1250 until the 1870s, has been reconstructed in the museum. Built of poles, thatch, and earth, the circular, high-domed lodge is filled with religious meaning for the Pawnee. A visit to the earth lodge is a total experience explaining the seasonal alterations in Pawnee life as well as the significance of the lodge's construction. Children sit inside the lodge on buffalo robes, examine exact replicas of utensils and clothing, and listen to an explanation of their use.

ART MUSEUMS

Art museums and centers have developed many techniques to involve the visitor in learning about objects and artistic processes. Often special or permanent exhibits focus on looking at and touching original art works, participating in the artistic process, or investigating an entire environment. Many interactive art museum exhibits have proven equally accessible to handicapped visitors.

Discovery spaces in art museums are quite different than those in natural history museums. Here, reproductions or original art works are available for touching, but often without the drawers and reference materials that are intrinsic in the discovery rooms of natural history museums. The El Paso Museum of Art in Texas originally designed its Sensorium for handicapped visitors. The area contains reproductions of art works from major art periods and labels in large type and braille. Sighted visitors may put on blindfolds or semi-opaque masks and partially experience the effects of vision difficulty. Exploring the different textures of the available works, and coming to recognize their reliance on the visual sense is a central part in this display. The visitor can feel resource materials such as water color paper, oil paint, and an etching plate, which can help make the exhibitions more understandable.

At the National Collection of Fine Arts, in Washington, D.C., the Explore Gallery is designed to be an integral part of elementary-aged children's experience at the museum, and relates directly to many of the works on view. Young visitors can touch and look at quality art, enjoy a sensory sculpture garden, ring chimes, listen to music, and watch slide shows.

The Lion's Gallery of the Senses at the Wadsworth Atheneum in Hartford, Connecticut, was opened in 1972 as a gallery for visually impaired and sighted visitors. Popular with people of all ages, it works especially well with children who have physical handicaps and learning disabilities. It emphasizes the imaginative use of all senses to increase the appreciation of visual arts. Visitors are introduced to many forms of artistic expression through a series of changing exhibitions, which are planned to offer a diversified program, including studies of artistic processes, experiments in sound and other media, or examinations of art as cultural expression. Both local and national artists participate in the exhibitions, which often include workshops and demonstrations. Care is given to making exhibitions accessible to disabled visitors: braille labels are used and special training helps staff and volunteers meet the needs of all types of handicapped visitors. Recent exhibits have included *Soundings,* which were sound sculptures and concerts exploring the use of unusual instruments and sound-making techniques; and *Passage,* an environment with tactile and auditory as well as visual components.

The Yellow Space Place, a small gallery in Little Rock's Arkansas Art Center set aside for children, features pieces drawn from the permanent collection. Works of art for each temporary exhibit are related to such single themes or concepts as texture, trees, and the city, thus providing children with an opportunity to see how different artists perceive the same subject in different ways. Children have free access to a well-stocked work area any time during the gallery hours or at weekly supervised "Make-a-Thing" sessions, during which docents improvise with the children. A catalogue workbook is also available with each exhibit.

Computers and environmental spaces are a part of the *Personal Spaces, Special Places* exhibit at the Delaware Art Museum in Wilmington. This exhibition in the children's gallery includes four electronic sculptures. "Infinity and You," a two-way voice-sensitive mirror, teaches children about the personal space their voice can create. Lights and colors are activated in direct proportion to the quality of individual voices. "People Energy Painting" uses white, translucent plastic that is electronically sensitized to the energy in a child's hand. A microcomputer controls the colors produced, but the human touch brings the colors to life with varying hues and intensity proportionate to the energy in the hand. Entering a soft, padded "Self-Energy Awareness Cube," visitors sit with their hands on arm rests, which are sensitive to the tension in bodies. Sounds and colors burst forth in direct proportion to the tension, creating a unity between the individual and the sculpture. "Fiber Optics Environment" surrounds visitors with swirling fibers ablaze with colors that resonate as they speak. Tonal qualities in the voice control the colors as the pitch of the voice changes the intensity and frequency of the sounds.

Total environments that involve children are available in two places at the High Museum of Art in Atlanta. The new exhibition in the Junior Gallery, clearly announces its subject: *Spaces and Illusions* in art and the world. The exhibit invites visitors to explore "real" and everyday space, as well as space that is imagined, distorted, recorded, or translated in paintings, photographs, or other things. *Spaces and Illusions* is a maze of spatial effects, using mirrors, lights, colors, unusual dimensions, patterns, sounds, emotions, lenses, shadows, and anomorphic distortions. Art works are installed throughout to illustrate how various artists have used space. An anomorphic painting, by a local artist, appears distorted except when viewed in a special double coned mirror.

Playscapes, a playground conceived as a work of art by the artist Isamu Noguchi, serves as the High Museum of Art's outdoor branch in the nearby Piedmont Park. This open air gallery links everyday life experiences with art. Occupying about one acre of a downtown park, its colorfully designed pieces of equipment openly invite energetic play and movement. Among the objects available are a black and orange triple slide, a tall triangular swing set, and a monolithic gray and blue spiral slide. *Playscapes* presents children with a joyful introduction to art and a new awareness of the visual elements such as line, color, shape, and texture, which define our world.

HISTORY MUSEUMS

Like art museums, history museums face challenges in interactive exhibits due to the delicate nature of their collections. Frequently, trained interpreters operate or demonstrate processes rather than allowing the visitors to interact with original artifacts. The following three examples illustrate ways that history museums have accommodated interactive techniques to their collections.

The National Museum of American History, Smithsonian Institution, operates three discovery corners related to specific exhibits on the American Revolution, rehabilitative medicine, and electricity. Staff or trained volunteers make presentations in which visitors handle objects and ask questions about their use. The Spirit of '76 Discovery Corner shows what everyday life was like for citizen-soldiers during the American Revolution. Displayed and examined are the foot soldier's slender issue of clothing, munitions, food, and knapsack. Early electrical experiments and the work of Benjamin Franklin, Joseph Henry, Thomas Edison, and Alexander Graham Bell are highlighted in the electricity discovery corner. Visitors may handle electrical apparatus and try their hand at experiments demonstrating static electricity and the operation of an electrode magnet. The rehabilitative discovery corner introduces the general public to various handicaps through the demonstration of rehabilitative aids. Visitors try navigating with a cane, learn about sign language, and put on and operate an artificial arm.

Making scholarly, archival materials interesting and understandable to a wide audience has been a major part of the work at the Museum of Our National Heritage in Lexington, Massachusetts. To complement their scholarly exhibition on the voyage of Sir Francis Drake, the museum added an introductory, interpretive exhibit, *The World of Sir Francis Drake*. The interpretive exhibit was intended to stimulate interest and to help visitors look at the exhibit materials on loan from the British Library. It included role-playing and projection so that the visitors would have a more personal view of Drake and the 16th century. Labels were phrased as questions to encourage visitors to form their own conclusions, and two activities helped visitors understand the finery, texture, weight and shape of Elizabethan costumes. Looking through peepholes, the visitors saw their own faces reflected in a mirror with a life-sized photographic picture of Sir Francis Drake or Elizabeth I. They could also try on specially designed costumes that tied in apron-like fashion. A discovery wall panel illustrated what Drake thought he might find on his travels, and what he really did encounter. On a recreated ship environment with slanting poopdeck and rigging, visitors handled reproductions of navigational instruments, and a push-button panel provided information about the ship and activities that occurred in each section.

Some history museums create total environments, which allow children to walk in and experience by sitting, handling, and touching objects. At the Louisiana Arts and Science Center in Baton Rouge, the way of life in America between 1860 and 1900 is represented in the *Country Store* and *Acadian House* exhibits. The original style of both has been meticulously reproduced inside and out, including the use of 120-year-old cypress doors and beams. *The Country Store* includes the pot-bellied stove and an assortment of wares ranging from jelly beans and medicine to clothing and hardware. Students are asked to compare modern types of retail business and selling practices to the country stores. An appreciation of one of America's past institutions is developed as they see how effectively stores of this type functioned at one time. A moss-and-mud chimney highlights the exterior of the one-room *Acadian House*, which is furnished with the articles necessary to prepare food and make clothing. In the *Acadian House*, students are able to relate changing times to changing lifestyles, and often their own family's history.

Outdoor living history museums introduce visitors to an earlier culture, as families visit the 19th-century village grounds at Old Sturbridge Village or the restored 18th-century community of Old Williamsburg. The visitors can try their hands at open-hearth cooking, weaving, carding wool, dipping candles, and other skills that are almost forgotten in today's era of automation. The Living History Farms Museum in Iowa contains three different farms within its 500 acres of rich prairie grassland: an 1840 pioneer farm; an 1870's village of Walnut Hill; and a 1900 horse-powered farm. Under construction is a farm of the future. The three farms and a tiny village are authentic replicas of their eras. Each farm is regularly worked, therefore children watch farmers hitch oxen, plow fields, make shingles and mend fences—working from dawn until dusk in the early pioneer life of the prairie wilderness in Iowa. The recreated town of Walnut Hill illustrates how in 30 years, farm families became dependent upon rural villages for much of their goods and services with its one-room schoolhouse, general store, veterinary infirmary, carpentry shop, and shops for the potter and blacksmith. The 1900 farm shows how the invention of the steam and internal combustion engines replaced the horse as a source of farm power at this time. Visitors not only watch, but participate. On the village green, children play 19th-century games such as hoop rolling. Children board a tractor-drawn cart, help cook ham and beans, gather corn cobs for stoking the kitchen stove, knead and mix bread and cookie dough, wash their hands at a walnut stand, and wipe them on linen roller towels.

Outdoor museums involve the visitors in a total sensory environment. Trained interpreters help bring to life the homes, people, and documents that normally are static and only looked at in a museum. History comes to life as both visitor and interpreter do the chores, work with the tools, and talk about the politics and struggles of earlier times.

SCIENCE-TECHNOLOGY CENTERS

Exhibits that involve the public in learning through participation are widely used by science-technology centers across the country. The primary aim of these museums is to increase the public's understanding of scientific principles and processes and technology—the application of the principles. These museums use the term "science-technology centers" to distinguish themselves from museums with a more traditional approach. Rather than focusing on artifacts and collections, most of these centers emphasize participatory exhibits and education programs that lead visitors to an understanding of science and its contemporary applications and implications.

The interactive exhibits of science-technology centers may involve the visitor on a variety of levels. What is desired is a sense of discovery, or what some have termed an "ah-hah" response. Whether visitors view an exhibit, push a button to activate a model, conduct an experiment, or climb through an environment, they themselves can become the "discoverer" of a natural phenomena.

The type of interactive approach varies with the phenomena being shown. Just as art or history museums may have irreplaceable objects that cannot be handled, some science topics may be too dangerous for many visitors to handle. A chemical experiment may have to occur behind glass, activated by a button, while attaching wires to make an electrical circuit between a low-powered battery and a bell can be completely manipulated by visitors. Science-technology centers, like other museums, must evaluate the subject matter of exhibits, and create methods for increasing the visitor's participation.

Many people characterize science-technology centers as having halls of exhibits with push buttons. In actuality, push buttons represent the most elementary—and least desirable—level of interactive exhibitry. In general, the more variability that can be allowed for the visitor's use of an exhibit, the more successful the interaction and learning. However, push buttons can help. A traditional museum approach to demonstrating the operations of a hot air balloon might show a balloon rising and falling over a jet of air, which a label explains is hot air. An interactive approach using the push-button technique might permit visitors to push a button, which activates a small, but visible, flame below the balloon. This lets visitors make their own connection between heat, air, and the rising balloon. Carrying the approach a step further, handouts might be available showing how model hot air balloons can be constructed at home.

These museums prefer visitor-operated exhibits that move beyond the push button. These might be exhibits in which visitors pedal a bicycle to create electricity to light a bulb, or blow into a plastic bag to test their lung volume. Wherever the subject matter permits or encourages some activity, a variety of techniques can be used. At the Franklin Institute Science Museum in Philadelphia visitors can move a heavy weight using single, double or triple pulleys, demonstrating the extra advantage that pulleys provide. In "Star Tracers," an exhibit of the Ontario Science Centre, visitors try to trace the image of an object reflected in a mirror, thus having to deal with the relationship between visual perception and muscular activity.

"How Clear Is The View," at the Lawrence Hall of Science, lets visitors learn how to use a telescope as well as how telescope magnification and atmospheric turbulence affect the view through a telescope. Visitors look through one of two telescopes, set at different levels to accommodate people of varying heights, focusing on objects in a simulated night sky. The Hall's "Puzzle Table" consists of 20 logic puzzles (sliding square, disappearing cross, etc.) made of wood or plastic. Most of the puzzles have been modified for use by the visually impaired by providing fixed starting points, textural rather than only color differences, and braille instruction.

Interactive audiovisual exhibits allow visitors to make choices and see the consequences of their actions, while viewing slide-tape or video presentations. At the Franklin Institute Science Museum, a presentation using three slide projectors in a small theater was used in conjunction with an exhibition about energy use and lifestyles. The theater presented choices of electricity sources, major food sources, cleaning alternatives, personal transportation, and locale. The composite environment chosen by the audience was given a relative evaluation in terms of dollar, pollution, and energy costs and in personal effort. The audience could revise their choices after the evaluation.

In a permanent exhibition about newspapers at the Museum of Science and Industry in Chicago, visitors can view a videotaped conference of newspaper editors, choose their own version of the daily newspaper's front page layout, and review the editors' choice. They can also call up the headlines of major selected newspapers on historically important days and select videotaped commentaries by public figures about the media.

Computers have gained increased popularity, although they have not yet been widely used to their full potential as interactive devices. Science-technology centers have done much to demystify computers by making them accessible in public spaces, and using them for a variety of purposes. At the Museum of Science, Boston, for example, seven stations or terminals with keyboards and screens can be used by visitors to perform mathematical calculations, to play games, or to learn more about the museum. Computer programs include information about the museum and its exhibits, the museum's history, tour information, and museum restaurant menus.

Computers are being used to explain computer technology itself and as an integral element of exhibits on other subjects. Both the Lawrence Hall of Science and the Pacific Science Center in Seattle have computers available for classes and for individual program writing. The Seattle museum offers a variety of games and simulations on topics as varied as energy use and first aid. The Cranbrook Institute of Science in suburban Detroit uses computer terminals in conjunction with a display-case human anthropology exhibit and with a Foucault pendulum. Other museums are also using computers with other new technologies, such as video discs.

The use of computers as integral elements of interactive exhibitry is, however, still in its infancy. Although computers today largely provide programmed learning terminals in exhibit halls, they offer a vast potential for new participatory exhibit techniques.

Environmental exhibits, such as the thunderstorm simulator at the Museum of Science and Technology in Tampa or a flight simulator, are also popular in science-technology centers. For example, visitors at the Cleveland Health Education Museum can walk through giant models of various body parts, including the ear, eye, tooth or heart. Once inside these structures, the visitor can see how the body works and, sometimes, view audiovisual presentations or graphic illustrations about the organ's function. At the Center of Science and Industry in Columbus, Ohio, visitors can enter the Jeffery Coal Mine #1, which includes representations of mining from distinct historical periods. Visitors are issued a hard hat (in conjunction with safety regulations) and move through the mine to visit with an early pick-and-shovel miner of pioneer days, view a mechanized 1870s mine, and examine modern methods of mining.

Many science-technology centers link their exhibits together, and perhaps one of the best examples of this is the Exploratorium in San Francisco. The Exploratorium identifies itself as a perceptual science museum, inviting the visitor to learn through participation and exploration. The 500 exhibits have been conceived as props in a "pedagological chain," exploring more than 200 phenomena. The Exploratorium offers multiple and contextually different examples of the same concept, which allows visitors to learn in their own way and not from a single example of each effort or process. Exhibits survey the world of light, color, waves, patterns, logic, the third dimension, sound, and electricity. Explainers—trained high school students—are always in the public areas repairing exhibits, answering questions, and demonstrating principles.

The Exploratorium is a library of props that allows the visitor to gain first-hand contact with natural phenomena. Exhibits on sound and waves, for example, include a giant guitar string—a 120-foot long rope that makes waves like a guitar string but at a sound too low to hear—and a wave machine that, when activated, shows waves rippling through a steel spine. A harmonic series wheel can be spun to produce harmonious sounds.

Many exhibit units have multiple themes, and therefore can relate to a variety of other exhibits. Many exhibits combine arts and science.

Rather than writing an elaborate explanation about a process, the staff of the Exploratorium invents an exhibit or modifies an existing one so that the learner can experience first hand through the nature of discovery.

Science-technology centers have one of the largest visitor attendance of any other type of museum. The demands made on them by millions of parents, grandparents, teachers and children have caused them to develop exhibit formats and presentations that are effective and do not require extensive personalized interpretations. Demonstrations, auditorium presentations, puppetry, plays and other techniques complement the interactive and environmental exhibits. Continually seeking ways to explain the processes and to demystify science, these museums offer all types of people a way to learn, to answer questions, to experiment, and to have fun.

CHILDREN'S MUSEUMS

Since the early part of the century, children's museums have been among the leaders in the development of participatory and interactive exhibitions. Designed specifically as educational institutions in which children can have direct experiences with objects that normally are confined to cases, children's museums have developed exhibitions and programs to accommodate this kind of self-directed learning. By nature, their programs and exhibitions are staff-intensive: volunteers, interns, and interpretive staff play a major role in making these exhibitions more accessible to their public. The goal of most children's museums is to provide a learning environment in which children seek to understand themselves in the world in which they live.

The Brooklyn Children's Museum includes its architecture, collections, permanent exhibits, retail shops, children's library, and take-home collections in a single system of interactive exhibits. The construction materials and methods of the building itself are part of the exhibit environment: color-coded pipes and ventilation ducts, laminated wooden beams, concrete walls, nuts, and bolts are exposed throughout. Familiar objects from urban and rural settings are built-in components: a 1907 trolley car kiosk is the main entrance; park benches and lampposts are part of the earth-covered roof; and an oil storage tank is an enclosed, indoor auditorium. The museum's main exhibit area consists of four terraced levels, moving down from the corner entrance of the semi-underground building. A corrugated steel tube forms a ramp extending across all four levels, providing ready access for handicapped visitors.

Large-scale visitor-operated technological artifacts, such as a stream of water with locks, waterfalls, and waterwheels, are interspersed with objects from the museum's permanent collection. Instructors engage visitors in lively participatory activities, helping visitors explore three broad areas of the museum's collections: cultural history, natural history, and technology.

Understanding more about computers and having an opportunity to work with them can happen at the Children's Museum in Indianapolis. Economic principles are examined in fantasy situations at the *Decision Shop* of the Children's Museum in Indianapolis. The computer has three fantasy situations: ruling a medieval kingdom, trading goods among the star systems, and owning a robot store.

In the "Robot Store" simulation, museum visitors temporarily become owners of a store with only one product, robots made from scrap metal parts. The computer gives the visitor the wholesale costs for each robot, and after the visitor sets the retail price, the computer tells the player how many robots were sold at that price, and how much money was earned or lost. Players have five attempts to arrive at an optimal selling price for the robot. One unique factor in the exhibit is that there are no wrong answers or choices in any of the simulations, although players are informed about the consequences of their decisions. For example, if a player chooses to sell robots for less money than it costs to produce them, the computer will advise him that he is losing money on every robot that he sells. Although the simulation appears to be a game, participants are learning real economic concepts. While bartering goods with another planet, for example, players discover the concepts of supply and demand, choice, cost, and scarcity.

Other interactive exhibits take many formats in children's museums. In general, they are partially environmental in their approach, involving the total senses of the child in the learning experience. At the Los Angeles Children's Museum, *Sticky City* is filled with various oversized foam shapes that stick to each other, the walls and ceilings, providing endless construction possibilities. In the *Shadow Box* (a popular exhibit in science-technology centers, too) visitors step into space, jump, dance, bend, and stretch; when they step away, their shadow stays behind, "frozen" on walls of phosphorescent vinyl.

Simple Machines at the Capital Children's Museum in Washington, D.C., allows children to discover basic principles that are the foundation of all machinery around us. Working with isolated machines allows children to see how pulleys and levers enable them to lift a cinder block heavier than they are and how gears can be used to turn other gears. Designed to be accessible at many age levels, the youngest children delight in being able to lift the cinder block and the older children figure out why it can happen. Children can take apart clocks, adding machines, typewriters and other objects to observe the simple machines in practical action. The exhibit also includes transparent, working telephones that can be used to call other areas of the museum.

At the Children's Museum in Boston, many exhibitions deal with the process of making the world more understandable to the child. Through closed-circuit video equipment, visitors operate WKID-TV, a news studio, and using zoetropes, they learn the process of animation. *What If I Couldn't . . . ?*, an exhibit about handicaps, demonstrates what it's like to have physical impairments and how disabilities can be helped with prostheses, braille, glasses, and a wheel chair.

Study Storage is a special system of collection storage that was developed by the Boston museum's staff to provide access to objects while minimizing handling and loss. Much of the collection is visible to the general public through a large glass wall in the *We're Still Here* exhibit. To allow specially interested visitors to study the collection at closer quarters, all objects are packaged in see-through containers and marked with one of three color-coded symbols. While many museums limit access to all objects, the underlying assumption behind the symbol system is that different objects have different protection needs. The red "looking only" symbol is for one-of-a-kind, irreplaceable fragile objects that may not be handled. The yellow "careful touching" symbol is for those objects that can be touched carefully if touching is necessary to understand the object's function or material. The green "handling" symbol is for objects that may be touched, handled, and passed around. They are generally replaceable contemporary objects, extremely durable objects, replicas, or one of several duplicates.

The manipulatory *Giant Desk Top* has everything 12 times normal size, including a telephone and pencil. Working in a factory assembly line that constructs spinning tops, and exploring living things in a natural history discovery corner of urban animals (mice, ants, worms, cockroaches, rocks, and shells) are examples of interactive activities at the Children's Museum in Boston.

Environmental exhibitions can take up an entire room or the full facilities of the museum, and are designed to involve all the senses. For example, *Mexico!* at the Capital Children's Museum in Washington, D.C., includes a Mexico City room, which gives an idea of life in Mexico City today, including its subway system, travel agencies, post offices and gas stations. A slide show introduces Mexico and its people. Adjoining the city room is the provincial (Oaxacan) kitchen, where children learn to grind chocolate on a molcajete and mix it with a molinillo. They taste the difference between Mexican and U.S. chocolates, examine the ceramic decorations on the kitchenware, and try Mexican crafts. Family activities, such as weaving and cooking, can be seen and in some cases children participate in weaving or drawing water from the well. The Plaza Central includes a church, government buildings, business offices, and a market where holiday fiestas and daily social gatherings can occur. Finally, the visitors can see a log cabin, which is another type of house that might be found in rural Mexico, and make some tortillas. Artists from Mexico add new elements to the exhibit, such as paintings in the rural room, folk dancing in the Plaza, and demonstrations of traditional free-form pottery.

The Children's Museum in Boston has an authentic two-story artisan's house and shop from Kyoto, Japan. Rotating shop exhibits demonstrate tasks such as noodle-making, mat-making, paper-screen making and pot making. The house is long and narrow with its storefront facing a replica of a street. The interior house remains graceful and delicate, with panes of rice paper on the sliding doors, religious and decorative artifacts set into alcoves on the wall, and a garden of plants and white rock from Japan in the back. Children quickly notice that there are no refrigerators for the people in Kyoto, who shop daily. The counter and stove appear low to an American child, accommodating Japanese people who are generally shorter.

City Slice is a three-story cross section of a city street and mansard house, with exposed construction, telephone, manhole, pipes, cables, sewer catch basin, soil structure and cut-away subway car, which shows how the systems help to operate the city. "Grandparents House," part of *City Slice*, is the cutaway of a Victorian cottage that has been continuously lived in since the turn of the century. Children can see the construction of the house (including the wiring, and remodeling of the bathrooms), work in a kitchen and parlor, try on clothes in grandmother's attic, and help grandfather in the cellar at his workbench using his old tools. Interpreting this exhibit depends in part on the memories that visitors have about the objects that are on view. For instance, on seeing a radio in the parlor, parents can remember listening to *Fibber McGee and Molly* as a child, and recount aspects of the lifestyle before there was television.

Children's museums have created numerous exhibits that help children to understand more about the world in which they live, how things work, what they are made of and how they relate to the child's world. Answering these and other questions that help children feel more comfortable about their environment is central to the mission of most of these museums. The success of some exhibits in children's museums such as the zoetrope, grandmother's attic, the city have led to the development of "second generation exhibits" in new children's museums. However, a successful children's museum is not a series of unrelated activity centers, but a carefully designed environment that links the various component parts together, allows for all types of learning experiences and makes both the children and adults feel comfortable.

CONCLUSION

There are no absolute formulas for designing an exhibit, much less interactive exhibits. Art, history, natural history, children's museums, zoos and science-technology centers have all succeeded in developing different types of participatory exhibits that are successful with adults and children. Because people enjoy learning, especially when it is fun as well as interesting, interactive exhibits often are "crowd pleasers" drawing large numbers of people to the museum. Interactive exhibits also allow visitors to learn at their own pace, individually or in groups. The flexibility of their formats, styles, and components provide staffs in museums with a wide range of choices.

It is important to remember that not every museum exhibit requires opportunities to push buttons, work computers, make candles, climb through a limestone cave, or manipulate shapes in a velcro room. Some themes or collections cannot be handled, some objects wear out. Some exhibits cause traffic problems. Curators and educators designing participatory exhibits must realize in advance that gimmicks alone will not work.

Successful interactive exhibits require a respect and understanding of the objects and materials to be presented as well as the audience that will view them. They require careful decisions about the appropriateness of a technique and a willingness to change what does not work. While interactive exhibits present enormous challenges to the museum staff, they are also rewarding for both staff and visitor.

References

Arth, Malcolm. "The People Center—Anthropology for the Layman," *Curator*, 18 (September 1975), pp. 315–325.

Dewey, John. *Experience and Education*. New York: Collier Books, 1963.

Franco, Barbara. "Exhibiting Archival Materials: A Method of Interpretation." *Museum News* 58 (September/October 1979), pp. 55–59.

Gabianelli, Vincent J., and Edward Munyer. "A Place to Learn," *Museum News*, 53 (December 1974) pp. 28–33.

Oppenheimer, Frank. "Everyone is You . . . Or Me," *Technology Review*, 79 (June 1976), pp. 2–7.

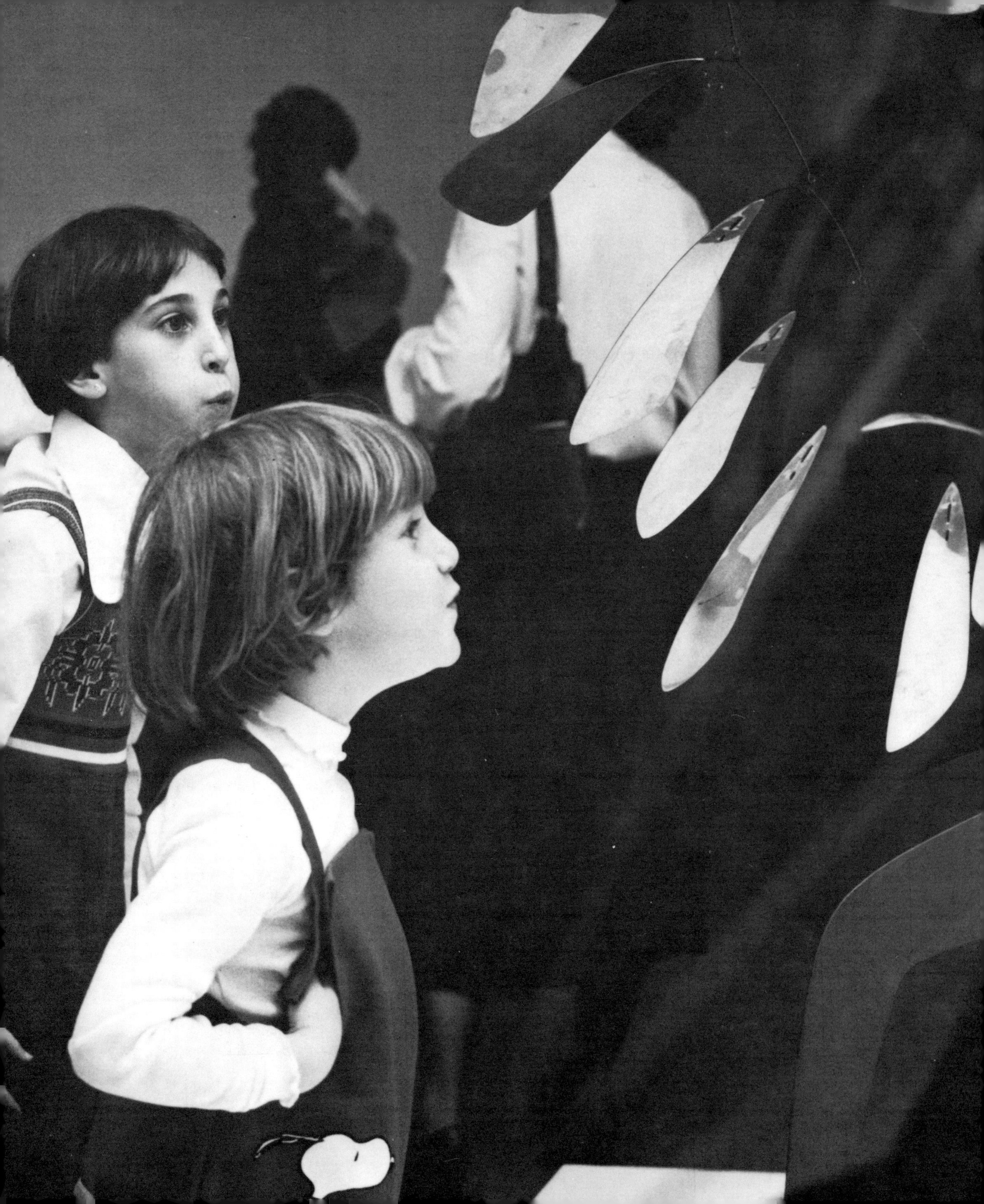

4.
TEACHING IN THE MUSEUM

For the most part, museums have changed. No longer is it accurate to imagine countless numbers of school children being led by harried docents through endless galleries, straining to understand what is being said and hoping to catch a glimpse of the object—a rare seated Buddha, the world's largest elephant, a priceless collection of diamonds. "Sight-seeing" tours and "canned lectures" are beginning to pass out of the repertoire of most museum education departments, to be replaced by experiences that involve and stimulate the learner's interest in acquiring more information. These activities generally relate to the child's understanding of the world and develop their skills for observing, classifying, and generalizing information.

Activities and open-ended questions that encourage creative looking and thoughtful answers are taking the place of simple lectures. For example, not only do children look at the image of Buddha and wonder who he is, but they consider why he is important, how the artist conveyed his importance, and how they might react to the statue if they were to see it in a temple. Children may pose, sitting as a Buddha, carefully arranging their hands to affect the different *mudras*, and holding the position so that they can begin to experience the sensations of becoming a statue. Other children might orchestrate the sounds and music that would take place in a temple setting, or consider more carefully the life story of Buddha as they act it out.

Much of the educational process in a museum consists of introducing people to unknown subjects and objects. The museum's responsibility is to make learning meaningful, and to relate scientific, historical, and aesthetic concepts to the child's world of experience, thereby increasing his ability to learn and to retain the information. A list of the (most popular) aims of museum educational programs include:

1. To develop an awareness of the museum visit as an enjoyable experience
2. To develop the learner's skills for observing and understanding objects in the man-made and natural world
3. To teach concepts about the created and natural world
4. To equip the learner for independent study and observation on return visits.

Children acquire most of their knowledge by observing, classifying, measuring, gathering information, and making inferences. Used almost unconsciously by children, these methods are used consciously by scientists and teachers in the processes of research and discovery. The skills, for example, of a scientist are extensions of the abilities already present in every individual, and which, as they develop, enable each person to understand more about the world in which he lives. The museum's exhibits and classes should provide planned experiences to stimulate curiosity, develop different skills, and enable children to extend their knowledge of specific subjects into other areas. Children's natural curiosity can take root in a museum, as they explore and play, learning from the environment.

Freeman Tilden, in his book *Interpreting our Heritage*, defines the function called "interpretation," which has been effectively used by museums, parks, zoos, and other cultural institutions:

> *An educational activity which aims to reveal meanings and relationships through the use of original objects, by firsthand experience, and by illustrative media, rather than simply to communicate actual information.*

This is an objective definition; interpretation goes far beyond any dictionary relationship of worlds.

Tilden goes on to say, "So, for the consideration of the interpreter, I offer two brief concepts of interpretation, one for his private contemplation, and the other for his contact with the public. First for himself: interpretation is the revelation of a larger truth that lies behind any statement of fact. The other concept is more correctly described as an admonition, perhaps: interpretation should capitalize mere curiosity for the enrichment of the human mind and spirit."

Tilden and other authors that have written about interpretation of cultural resources and collections have noted there is no real methodology or history for this type of education. Museums have adapted existing educational methodologies and processes to the museum's environment rather than inventing their own. Museums are incorporating techniques that have proven to be effective in the classrooms, the theater and creative writing as well as in other areas such as the arts, history, or social studies.

What then, is the essence of the interpretation of a museum's exhibition? It is a difficult question to answer, and organizing interpretive programs requires many components. The exhibition and the objects or collections are essential to an effective interpretive program. The labels, demonstrations, and other interpretive techniques must all be useful for the visitor. This chapter reviews teaching techniques that are used by docents, teachers, and interpreters on museum staffs throughout the country. The techniques illustrate different formats that have been used successfully and are among the options available to museum educators interested in developing direct interpretative programs. As in any interpretation project, the teaching techniques that are used, whether they are questions, role playing, or perception games, must directly relate to what is being displayed. As Tilden has put it, "the chief aim of interpretation is not instruction, but provocation."

DEVELOPING AN INTERPRETIVE PROGRAM

Organizing an interpretative program requires consideration of several elements: the techniques and skills to communicate knowledge about the collections, the ability to organize and pace a tour, and the ability to manage groups.

To be an interpreter in a museum, whether as a docent or a museum teacher, requires knowledge about the subject being taught. Thorough understanding of the topics being presented is essential, so that questions can be asked and relationships made in organizing a discovery process. Knowledge about the physical arrangement of the exhibit's objects or units is also essential, so that connections and transitions can be developed to complement the movement through the galleries. Learning how to ask questions, how to listen to the audience, and observe group interaction are critical skills to be developed. Both in the presentation of information and in the organization of the tour and subject matter, creativity is important. Respect for the audience as well as an understanding of their needs, background, availability of time, and learning skills is essential to make the program an effective one.

In addition, other skills are necessary for any interpreter: the ability to change and adapt a program on short notice, either because children do not understand the information being presented, or because a rearrangement has occurred in the galleries; and the ability to freely admit not knowing an answer to a question. In fact, a skilled interpreter will make the group feel comfortable by showing that he/she is not omnipotent. This may be done by leading the group itself to answer a question, by suggesting sources in which they might find the answer themselves, or by discussing the questions that the museum or researchers have not been able to answer.

An important part of effective interpretation is pacing: arranging and sequencing the activities, concepts, and physical movement of the tour through the galleries. One must consider the attention span of the audience, the organization of space and distance to be covered, and the effects of viewer fatigue. To enhance the learning process, objects and concepts must be carefully selected and organized to fulfill the program's objectives. Museum educators have found it effective to concentrate on a few selected works that allow the learner to develop observational and perceptual skills and judgments rather than to view the visit as a shopping spree. Sometimes compromises must be made in selecting objects to be viewed to provide time to look and concentrate; an opportunity to see how others perceive the object, and time to rest and to refer back to objects that have been studied previously.

A third element for good interpretive programs is a clear understanding of the group interactive processes.

Persons skilled in understanding group communications are good at both listening and observing. They ask questions and encourage the participants to become involved comfortably. The teacher or docent will enthusiastically accept the personal observations made by the learners, recognizing that in most cases there are no right or wrong answers. In addition, the leader will recognize when the group has lost touch with what is being said because of technical terms, dates, low volume from the speaker, or lack of enthusiasm for the subject. Other communication skills include the recognition of each individual in the group, acknowledgements of their questions, and understanding that some individuals may choose to be silent. Numerous other skills in developing a good interpretive program are considered in excellent books on the topic.

A clear understanding of individuals and their various stages of intellectual and physical developments is essential to construction of a good education program.

THE CHILD

Children go through distinct stages of physical and intellectual growth. Just as children learn to walk and talk at different stages in their life, they also learn to identify, reason, hypothesize, and conceptualize at different stages. It would be impossible here to review all of the studies and works in the areas of child development and developmental psychology. Excellent books by Jean Piaget and Erik Erikson, as well as interpretations of their work, should be studied.

Museums sometimes develop excellent programs that are inappropriate for the audience they are trying to reach. Trying to teach abstract concepts of time or culture to children between the ages of two and seven would be inappropriate. At these ages, children should be participating in direct experiences dealing with their egocentric nature and focusing on aspects of their daily lives, rather than trying to understand the historically different cultures of man. Recognize that there is a time and place for everything to happen in a museum and that museums should be a learning resource for an entire lifetime. Museum educators should not "cram it all in" a single session, but should develop sequences of activities for learners of different ages.

Major differences exist between a young and older child's thinking and learning process. Candace Floyd has written an informative article on "Education and Old Economy: Programs Children can Understand," which specifically analyzes the various Piagetian stages of cognitive development in relationship to how Old Economy's programs have been adapted to these stages. A young child, aged one to seven, has no concept of time, and uses the comparative sizes of rocks or paintings to determine their relative ages, a larger rock being the older.

For the younger child, dinosaurs and grandmothers basically lived at the same time. Museums trying to teach children in the first and second grade the various periods of the dinosaur should not teach the historical facts about the dinosaurs and their worlds. Rather they should compare and contrast the size and shape of the dinosaur to contemporary, familiar animals. A museum can capitalize on many young children's fascination with dinosaurs, and develop a program that allows them physically to "become" dinosaurs in a group, understanding the enormous problems of moving when you are that size. Classroom programs should help orient children to the museum and what they will see on the trip.

By the time children are in their middle elementary school years, aged 7 to 11, they have the capacity to reason, based on direct experiences, and have a concept of past and present. However, they are not yet able to deal with totally abstract concepts and complex thinking, which adults take as a matter of course. At this stage, pre-museum visit preparation in classroom activities will have real meaning because the children make direct connections between what they have experienced before and what they are doing in the present. Understanding community life or learning about the African veldt life cycle can occur, as children see the animals in different places within the zoo's complex or museum's galleries.

Children 9 to 12 can deal with abstract concepts and develop a hypothesis about ideas for which they have had no direct experience. For example, they can focus on a philosophy of a religious society, or deal effectively with the concepts of ecology. At this stage, learning through physical manipulation and participation remains important, but learning can happen without these activities.

Because museum teaching can encompass social, political, economic, aesthetic, technological and behavioral concepts, the more relevant learning can be made to everyday life, the less isolated an experience it will be. Museums can bridge the gap between the exhibit and the child's experience with learning activities that require participation.

Concept-oriented programs developed for children at the appropriate ages will increase their awareness of the broad issues, enabling children to learn something applied in the future. It is exciting to attack the collections in this manner: to deal with an artifact or specimen as part of a whole scheme, rather than as a curiosity piece. At a zoo, an understanding of the ecology of an entire area can begin by observing the animal life in a few acres. A museum can display skeletons of prehistoric animals and artifacts from vanishing civilizations as a bridge between the old and the new. Educators working in such environments have the opportunity to go beyond the classroom text and provide unique programs that effectively link the past, present, and future worlds.

The National Park Service's N.E.E.D. Program is based upon concepts such as continuity and change, interaction and interdependence, and variety and similarity. The concepts of interaction and interdependence illustrate that nothing exists in isolation, that each person constantly interacts with living and nonliving things. This concept could provide a focus for exploring the structure of family and community life, systems of communication, the food chain, electricity, and gravity. At Old Sturbridge Village, students who participate in carding wool, spinning flax, threshing wheat, and building a fence begin to understand the concepts of time and change. They can also speculate about the amount of time needed to plow a field or prepare food, and compare methods used in the 19th century to the present.

The use of concepts alone will not guarantee a program's success. The concepts must relate to the holdings or exhibitions of a museum, and be clearly illustrated with examples. Further, the museum educator must select teaching techniques that are most appropriate for interpreting the concepts. Browsing curriculum outlines in textbooks from school systems can help to determine the level of information and types of concepts that are best suited for the children.

When developing programs for children, museums must consider the needs of disabled children. Often minor adjustments can be made in the museum program (increased lighting levels or sound amplification) or in the installation of equipment (the height of tables), to serve children with special needs. Because many states place disabled children in regular classroom situations, the museum's education staff must be prepared to handle these children and adapt programs accordingly. Training programs on disabilities for the museum staff and interpreters may be the first, most important, step.

Programs designed for the handicapped may require slower pacing so that children in wheelchairs can move around or deaf children can first look at the interpreter and then the exhibition. Frequently repetition of questions and comments may be required for disabled children. If slides or films are being used, audiovisual presentations may need to be captioned so a deaf person can understand what is happening on the screen.

Orientation programs can help disabled children understand where they are going, how they will get there, what will occur once they arrive at the museum, and what will happen when they return to their classroom. These questions need answers in advance of the children's arrival so that they will feel more comfortable about what their experiences will be and so less time can be spent during the orientation process on the differences between the museum environment and their classroom. Slide shows are an effective way to help bring the museum into the classroom, especially when they review the activities and objects that will be a part of the museum experience.

A program for handicapped children can be more effective when people who have special needs are involved in the planning phase. Such involvement may be as simple as having a staff which is inexperienced in needs of the deaf or blind, watch a sign interpretation of a tour or a blind person handling objects. This can lead to ideas for adapting regular programs. On a more in-depth level, persons with disabilities can provide advice on topics such as the special needs of their specific disability or the importance of personal sensitivity towards individuals who happen to have disabilities. It is important to remember, however, that just because an individual has a disability he/she may not know everything about special learning needs, and that program adaptations for one disability may not serve others.

Working with children and adults who are handicapped and knowledgeable about people with handicaps can help to develop more effective programs for all visitors. Simple things, such as grouping children in wheelchairs into very small groups to avoid clustering at the elevators or providing photographic enlargements to be studied by children with visual impairments, illustrate ways that a museum can accommodate these children. A museum staff should understand that it will both succeed and fail in initial work with special needs audiences. The process will call upon their talents at perceiving relationships and seeing the museum in an entirely different way and will encourage both staff and docents to want to serve this new constituency.

GEARING TECHNIQUES TO CONCEPTS AND NEEDS

The techniques used to teach in a museum must be carefully selected. Role playing may be more suited to one situation, a didactic presentation or use of data retreival sheets to another. Too much emphasis on games or handling objects can detract from the attention of the learning activity. Above all, teaching methods should not overpower the children.

In developing the program, there are three levels at which relationships can be made. First, a direct relationship should take place with the child, perhaps asking them to describe their daily routines before a program about 18th-century life styles, or asking them to count all the colors they are wearing. This direct association with the children's immediate world will help them to feel more at ease and encourage ideas for further development in the tours.

The next level of relationships should occur between the child and the museum environment: either a gallery, an exhibit unit or an individual object. Make comparisons and contrasts between what they see and how it is different from what they know. For example, by examining what they see in the 18th-century kitchen and how it is different from their own home, they might predict how a person would feel or what they might be concerned with based on what they see in the room. This helps the children to focus directly on the exhibits and provides personalized reasons for thinking and observing. Another way to enhance relationships between the child and the exhibit is through observing: for example, having them look for a bird that has all of the colors they are wearing and then closely examining it. These techniques help create a relationship between the objects being studied and the child.

A third level of relationships can help children make a connection between what has happened in the museum and their everyday life or real world. Thus, by observing and understanding the variations of brown in a bird specimen, they can then learn to examine more closely pebbles or a vacant lot to see how other objects have been camouflaged. Similarly, children can compare lighting technologies of different periods of history seen in the museum tour, to the various methods of lighting and sources of energy in their own homes. Hopefully, the museum will instill a sense of enjoyment about the learning and provoke their curiosity to learn more. Developing the children's perceptual skills will keep these learning experiences from ending when the child leaves the museum and encourage them to come back.

Several types of learning can take place in the museum, ranging from developing awareness of an object's existence to transferring information about it to prior experiences. Old Sturbridge Village has prepared the following useful listing of the learning that can take place in a museum:

Learning	Teachers Can Ask
Observational skills	Look for evidence of . . . List all of the . . .
Comparing and contrasting	How is . . . different from one in your house?
Predicting	Suppose that . . . this house were in New Mexico; . . . the father worked in an office away from home . . .
Generalizing	Now that we have explored your house, too, what are you willing to say about . . . in both houses?
Exploring feelings	What possessions did the family value most highly? How does this room make you feel?
Developing concepts	Which things seem to go together?
Hypothesizing	Based on what we have seen, what are you willing to say about . . . ?

TYPES OF LEARNING ACTIVITIES

The following interpretive techniques actively involve learners in solving problems and in interacting with each other and their leader. Some involve the use of different senses; most involve some of the learning skills described above. They foster learning skills including describing, analyzing relationships, interpreting works, and learning how to relate the familiar with the unfamiliar, thus building knowledge for the future.

These teaching strategies should not overpower the collection's or exhibition's focus, but rather complement and enhance the learners' abilities to see, understand, integrate and use the information they are learning. In addition to identifying and discriminating between objects, children analyze different aesthetic elements or scientific concepts, and develop ways to interpret exhibits and collections.

Questioning Strategies

Seeking alternatives to lecturing, museums may focus on ways to have children discover for themselves, solve problems, indicate preferences, and observe and ponder relationships. Such approaches involve the children's curiosity and encourage them to return to the museum to ask more questions and to seek more answers. The asking and answering of questions is basic to problem solving. In a museum, this approach can be a most effective way to persuade the learner to view an object more closely.

Although the Socratic method of object interpretation is the most frequently used teaching technique, it is also the most often misused. The question may be inappropriate, rhetorical, or require too simple an answer. The ability to ask questions on several different levels and to encourage the viewer to observe the exhibit more closely takes patience and the capacity to analyze one's own thoughts and actions critically. Questions requiring "yes/no" answers can limit the children's observational skills. However, if the teacher is trying to check the student's knowledge of factual information, such as "Do all minerals have a crystal structure?", then this type of question can be effective. There are other ways to ask the same question. It could have been phrased, "What are some of the ways all minerals are alike?" This question requires answers based on observed and learned information, and promotes a dialogue. In addition, more than one answer is correct. Learning how to use questions to promote thinking, stimulate creative ideas and focus attention on details and develop concepts can be accomplished with an understanding of how to use the strategy.

The teacher must know why the question is being asked. Purposeful questions require knowledge of the subject and a response to the students' levels of interest. Effective questioning strategies develop along the students' interests and questions. Questions can help students develop an idea, promote further understanding, change their attitudes, as well as test for learned information.

Memory questions can determine if certain information has been learned. The answers require recall, identification, yes/no answers, and definitions. Memory questions test whether facts and information are in place before moving on to a larger concept or more difficult information. Memory questions include "What kind of a spindle is this?" or "What time of year do the Hopi believe that kachinas leave the San Francisco peaks?".

A second approach for using questions is to see if students can put facts together to solve a particular problem. Through these questions, students learn to apply reason and explain relationships, integrating new information into their previous experiences. Examples of problem-solving questions include "Why does the spindle whirl in that shape?" or "How do you think this clay jar was made?".

A third questioning strategy encourages the stimulation of interest and creativity. There are no right or wrong answers in general, and such questions often involve many different types of answers. Students transfer new information and ideas, and then make judgments. Originality and predicting solutions to a problem are often encouraged through this questioning strategy. Examples of interpretive questions include "What sounds would you hear in this painting?" or "Why do you think this photographer decided to take this picture at this moment?" "What kind of food do you think they would eat, and how do you think they would live?"

A fourth strategy results in children evaluating, making decisions, and defending their selections and observations. Answering such questions requires students to organize information they have acquired, formulate an opinion, and be able to justify it. Often, using a particular perspective as a basis for the answers, evaluative questions require preknowledge and are based on a standard that has been established or can be justified. Evaluative questions include "Why do you think people join religious communities such as Old Harmony?" or "Which of these environments—tropical or antarctic—would you prefer to live in and why?".

When developing a museum tour it is important to use a variety of question formats, as each helps learners to observe in different ways and provokes thinking.

Constructing an effective question takes skill, and requires that the teacher know what learning is desired. Jargon and unfamiliar terms should be avoided and the wording of a question should be clear and direct. Students should be allowed time to answer the question. Questions should be posed one at a time, and not in a series, which could cause confusion as to which should be answered first. Reassurance that their answers are welcomed and correct engenders confidence in students and encourages them to respond more freely. When an answer is only partly correct, a skilled teacher will rephrase the question, using the correct information to create another question. Misinformation in a response can be helpful to docents, suggesting new tour needs.

Answers are as important as questions. Since students may observe things an adult would not see, the docent or teacher must notice the child who responds differently. The exploration of an idea or concept through questions should be designed so that the viewer examines materials more closely and observes the relationships with the objects. Not all questions need to have an answer—there are mysteries in this world and in learning about it.

Carefully developed, questions and answers become a dialogue between the museum teacher and the children, and form the base of an inquiry or discovery program.

Questioning Strategy from the Minneapolis Institute of Arts
HOW PEOPLE LIVED: SAMPLE QUESTIONS
Cranach the Elder, *Portraits of Moritz von Buchner and his wife Anna*

(Fact)	1. What are the different textures you can find in these paintings?
(Fact Follow-Up)	2. How did the artist use line to describe the various textures?
(Interpretive)	3. What kind of people do you think these are?
(Evaluative)	4. Would you like to have lived in those times/be dressed in that way?

Sander, *Circus People*

(Fact)	1. Who are these people?
(Interpretive)	2. Can you think of the jobs each one might have in the circus?
(Interpretive)	3. Why do you think the photographer decided to take his photograph right at that moment?
(Evaluative)	4. Each of you pretend you are going to take a picture. What will be in your picture? Where will you take it? Will you position the people and things in your picture or will you take the picture just as you see it?
(Evaluative Follow-Up)	5. How did you decide what you would include in your photograph?

Inquiry Process

Although based on questioning strategies, inquiry reaches beyond traditional, expository teaching, or lecturing. Questions, which are used as guides in an inquiry process, must be both clear and concise. The inquiry method is based on stating a problem, preparing a hypothesis or answer to the problem, testing the hypothesis, and organizing the evidence around a conclusion. Students participate and interact with each other and the museum exhibits as they search for evidence to solve their problems. Teachers refrain from providing too much information, which is treated as data rather than a final answer or solution. The inquiry process emphasizes how to investigate rather than the facts of the subject being studied. Not an authoritarian process, it permits creative thinking, discovery, and recognizes different view points. *Teaching as a Subversive Activity* states:

> The inquiry method is very much a product of our eclectic age. It makes the syllabus obsolete; students generate their own stories by becoming involved in the methods of learning. Where the older school environment had asked 'Who discovered America?' the inquiry method asks, 'How do you discover who discovered America?' The older school environment stressed that learning is being told what happened.

The inquiry environment stresses that learning is a happening in itself.

Student-centered, rather than teacher-centered, inquiry requires available resource materials and a high level of student participation. The museum teacher or docent is the intermediary between the hypothesis and students. Responsibility is given to the students, usually curious by nature, who seek solutions through this discovery method. In museums, students are often presented with a collection of seemingly unrelated objects and encouraged to determine relationships and classifications. They are urged to document their reasons, ask questions, and to seek answers. The students can work in small groups, undertake study through careful observation and classification, or conduct actual research.

There are four stages to the inquiry process. First, a problem must be stated that requires a solution. The problem must be made clear, meaningful, and manageable. In the second phase, students develop a tentative answer or hypothesis that includes the examination and classification of available information, suggests relationships, and states a tentative answer. The third phase of the inquiry process requires testing the hypothesis or tentative answer. The students, using all the information they have gathered, test to see if their answers make sense. Analysis of positive and negative points is equally important. The students assemble the evidence, arrange it in categories, and analyze their evidence, seeking a conclusion. The fourth stage is developing a conclusion or solution to their problem. Obviously, if the conclusion is the same as the hypothesis proposed by the students, it is valid. If the concluding statement is not the same as the hypothesis, then it is invalid. In testing the hypothesis against the evidence, patterns of relationships are perceived that support, modify, or negate the hypothesis. It is important during the conclusion to make a relationship between the tested evidence before stating the conclusion. The quest for an answer usually leads students beyond a simple conclusion. In the course of learning new information, the students will apply this conclusion to new situations, thus broadening the conclusions. Generalizing and applying the conclusion is what makes the inquiry process meaningful.

In an inquiry process, there is no right or wrong answer and no single interpretation. Everyone may have a different frame of reference and, therefore, a different solution. The historical concepts or facts to be discussed should be limited, because it is impossible to cover the social, economical, political, scientific, and religious concepts of an entire era in American history in a single tour.

Time for interaction during the tour is an important part of the inquiry process. Students should be encouraged to observe and react, and to compare their ideas. Once the problem has been defined and the hypothesis stated, the evidence necessary may be different than what had been planned. It is thus important to be creative and to respond to the interests and enthusiasm of new students.

The Office of Elementary and Secondary Education of the Smithsonian Institution developed the following materials, which illustrate the use of the inquiry process. Using brief biographical sketches of a colonial family, the student must determine in which rooms on view in the museum the family lived. After analyzing the rooms and furnishings, students should be able to generalize about the family's social, economic, and cultural background and the use of various objects. This adjacent step-by-step procedure can be used in the gallery or elsewhere with slides.

The inquiry process is the basis for most of the participatory teaching techniques that will be discussed in the following pages. The opposite of the lecture approach, inquiry develops skills that can be used long after the process is completed, an important function. It is a teaching technique that requires skill to be properly done.

Data Retrieval Sheets

The data retrieval technique helps students form a hypothesis based on evidence in the collection or exhibition. Recorded observations serve as the basis for follow-up discussions either in the museums or classrooms. The data retrieval method gives the students control over the material being covered, because the information they collected becomes the focus of the discussions. The data retrieval format helps students to develop an understanding of what they have observed, to organize and classify material in a systematic way, and to test a hypothesis based on observable information.

Inquiry Strategy from the Smithsonian Institution
Procedure

Present raw data about the Seth Story family and instruct students to make general statements about the family (i.e., education, community and social relationships, type of home, the kind of people they were).

Ask: Do you think this was a typical Colonial family? Why?

Responses
Numerous statements could result. These will be examined further as the lesson proceeds. Remember, there are no wrong guesses . . . only those that need evidence for modification.

Ask: How much education do you think this family had?

What members received education?

How much and what kind of education did they receive?

Ask: What general statements could you make about their position in the community?

Ask: What kind of social activities might they have had?

Present Early Colonial Objects to the Class.

Ask: Which of the objects do you feel the family would have used?

Which objects wouldn't they have been likely to use?

Any selections could be valid. Students must be encouraged to justify their selections. Students may request information on some objects, and teachers should provide this.

Be certain to call for justifications and refer to the list of general statements. Inform them that these are two rooms in two different houses and that the family they are discussing lived in one of them. They are to examine the data, objects, and rooms to determine which one the family lived in.

Ask: Can you see any of the objects which you selected?

They may not be able to do this from slides.

What similarities/differences can be seen in the rooms?

Students should note differences in furnishings, construction, decor. Some similarities in furniture and objects will be noted.

Ask: Which objects would fit into one room rather than the other?

Ask: Which objects would fit into either room?

They may select several objects that could have been used in either house. They should realize that many objects even today are common to families of different social and economic standing.

Ask: What clues can you find in the room that—with the other evidence—help you to determine which room the family would have lived in?

By this time they will have come to some general conclusions and may wish to modify their original statements.

Now ask them what type of family they might expect to find living in the other room?

They should conclude that the Seth Story family lived in the appropriate house because of unfinished walls, rough furnishings, farm implements.

Call for a listing based on the headings used for Seth Story family.

Let them generalize and justify by reference to the room. Then pass out the data on the other family and have them conclude if their generalizations were valid based on the evidence.

Designing a data retrieval sheet requires the careful selection of a concept that will be the focus of students' work. The concept should be interesting and appropriate for the collections and the students' age level. Further, the concept must be answered through direct observations of the objects or exhibits in the museum.

The data retrieval sheet can require students to draw, map patterns or movements, circle words, list, describe, count, compare, categorize, or evaluate. Its design must provide space for the students to record their information. As in all other teaching techniques, vocabulary must be carefully chosen, and the directions and questions must be clearly stated.

Although directions can be presented to a large group *en masse*, students can independently tour the galleries in search of the information needed to complete their forms. Reconvening for concluding discussions, the students can share their discoveries, reactions and observations.

Teachers and docents using the data retrieval method must understand that a certain amount of chaos exists as students set about to make their discoveries. Also, the discussions are usually of vital interest to the students, who have spent 20–30 minutes carefully observing and recording their observations and comparing notes with their friends. Dividing a class of more than 30 students into two areas of the museum allows freedom of movement and avoids clustering of large groups around individual exhibits. Select exhibits that will allow groups of students to gather around to make their observations. The conservation needs of the collection may need to be considered. Often, the use of writing materials in the galleries must be cleared with the conservation or curatorial staff, and attention to this must happen in advance of the class's entry into the gallery.

The data retrieval technique can be a problem for children with limited verbal skills. It can degenerate into a simple "treasure hunt" unless ample time is allowed for analyzing the collected raw data. Some educators feel the technique requires too much time for taking notes and reduces opportunities for questions and interaction with the gallery guide. Data retrieval can be especially effective with middle and high school students, who often enjoy the sense of independence and welcome the opportunity to solve problems and establish relationships.

Gearing the difficulty of sheets to the students' grade levels, the Philadelphia Museum of Art uses data retrieval sheets in a variety of lessons. The Renaissance Painting Lesson, for example, which is presented to grades 5 through 12, concentrates on the development of illusionism from 1300 to 1600 and the methods of Italian painters. Working alone or in groups, students choose their own examples from each century and evaluate the examples in terms of the techniques they observe. The museum teacher helps the group combine the data to achieve some sense of the general trends of the period, including exceptions to the rule.

Data Retrieval Strategy from the Philadelphia Museum of Art
Renaissance Painting: Development of Illusionism

There are four major techniques that painters can use to make a picture (paint on a flat surface) look like the real world (a variety of real things in a three-dimensional space).

In each of these four categories rate your paintings by placing a number in the column:
1 = used very little → 10 = used very much

	Painting #1	Painting #2	Painting #3
Painting Dates			
Artist's Techniques: 1 **Accurate Drawing:** makes objects look life-like; details included, sizes in natural proportions (no one part too large or too small).			
2 **Light** and **Shadow:** makes things look 3-D; for example — No Shadow / With Shadow			
3 **Atmospheric Space:** Colors fade as things get farther away; most distant area is just pale blue.			
4 **Linear** (uses lines) **Perspective**—in other words the "railroad track trick"—parallel lines are made to come together so they look like they are going away:			
Totals			

The Field Museum of Natural History in Chicago uses the data retrieval technique to allow students to collect information that can be used for discussions and study after the field trip. The museum has developed sheets that provide basic concepts in a topic of the museum, such as anthropology, and indicate ways to explore the concept during the museum visit. For example, students are encouraged to carefully examine the three Native American halls, comparing and contrasting the cultures' food, shelter, and clothing. From this the students can consider how these peoples' environments affected the ways they lived and the choices made in living in the varied environments.

Another way to collect data, used by the Worcester Art Museum in Massachusetts, is to have students inventory objects in a painting. Because paintings from some periods, such as Dutch 17th-century art, accurately depict the environments in which they were created, students can learn a great deal about the people of the time and how they lived. Each student is assigned a painting and is given time to examine it, listing all of the items and activities observed in the painting. Following the inventory, students reconvene to compare the lists from all of the paintings and to discuss questions relevant to their inventories and the people of the period.

Data Retrieval Strategy from the Field Museum of Natural History

Visit Hall 5, Woodland Indians. The Indian cultures that once were found in the Chicago area are represented here. Each case tells you something about the many aspects of life: food, clothing, tools, games or ceremonies.

As you look at the exhibits and the models of the summer and winter homes, see how many kinds of animals were used by these people. By visiting other Halls, such as 16 (American Animals) or Hall 20 (Birds) you can see the animals in their natural habitats.

You can compare different Indian cultures by seeing how each group solved the problems of food, shelter, and clothing. Collect the information on the following chart which will help to organize the information and then

After completing the chart discuss the following concept: How people live is influenced by the things they have to work with in their environment.

	Food (What did they eat? How was it prepared?)	Shelter (What kind of houses did they build? What materials did they use?)	Clothing (What materials did they use?)
Woodland Indians			
Plains Indians			
Southwest Indians			

Data Retrieval Strategy from the Worcester Art Museum

Title of Work: *A Village Scene in Winter with a Frozen River*
Date, if known:
Artists: *Aert vander Neer*
Dates, if known: *1603/14–1677*

Inventory

Items
5 trees
3 fences
1 dog
18 people
 (14 men, 4 women)
snow
frozen water
4 boats
golf club
skates
buildings
 stores or taverns
 churches
 houses
canal
walking path
building signs/notices
large gate
wall

Activities
skating
talking
playing golf
carrying wood
walking

Questions to consider:
How would you describe this environment?
What do the people in the city do for work? for play?
What do the people in the country do for work? for play?
What do their homes look like?
What kind of tasks do men perform?
What kinds of tasks do women perform?
What do these people eat?
How do they dress?
What do you think they admire?
What do you think they fear?

Using the data retrieval format, students can take a census in a gallery of paintings, learn about architectural elements on a walk through a neighboring community, or record the methods of locomotion for animals in a zoo. This technique can help students feel at ease and can orient them to the collections because it directs their looking and provides immediate rewards. The collected information can be used in numerous ways: to write a short story, to develop a play, or to organize an exhibit in the museum, classroom, or home. By requiring students to observe items carefully over an extended period, the student not only formulate a clear visual image of the objects or exhibit but also develop techniques of observation that can be used in the future.

Handling Objects

Artifacts and specimens that can be touched are indispensable teaching tools in museums when used properly. African masks, cowrie shells, Indian drums, colonial costumes, 18th-century spectacles, bear claws, dinosaur bones, a live armadillo—the list is endless; the benefits, incalculable.

Touching specimens must not be considered an end in itself, but rather a means of helping children to utilize their senses, to think creatively, and to integrate their experiences into a broader scheme. There is a special magic in putting on high-topped boots or a sunbonnet and in holding a branding iron or butter mold. Such activities can help lead to a better understanding of frontier life.

Young children often learn more easily from three-dimensional objects than from written or spoken words. Handling objects involves many senses and allows children to learn in a number of ways. For example, children can experience the size, weight, texture, smell, and shape of a deer's antler, and compare it to a water buffalo horn. This physical exercise can help explain the similarities of the materials and the differences in functions. Handling objects can make children more at ease and increase their interest in initially foreign concepts and artifacts.

The nature of a museum's exhibits and collections will determine the availability of objects. Many

Handling Objects Strategy from Winterthur Museum
Cataloguing Work Sheet

Object: Puppet (toy)

Material(s): wood, felt, fur, nails

Age: 1800's to present   *Date:* unknown

Size (estimated): length: 10½ in.   *width:* 1½ in.
wooden rod out of back at 15 in.

Condition: good

Construction Process: could be hand carved, or manufactured
finishing touches by hand

Description: (overall form, outstanding details, decorations, color, finish, and texture), write out and draw:

painted
red, blue, yellow, black, white
smooth
hard, soft

Other observations: very flexible, moves freely

This object is used for: entertainment, toy

What other sources would you use to get information on this object? toy maker, toy museums

---

museums purchase collections strictly for educational purposes. Some history and natural history museums use duplicate or undocumented objects and specimens as "touch" materials. If reproductions are used along with original artifacts, make a distinction so that children are not misled. Water buckets were so well-used, that they are simply worn out; fragile Oriental vases are easily broken when handled: explain why some objects can not be handled to help children understand the importance of conservation and preservation of materials for future generations. Demonstrate how to handle artifacts with both hands, to examine them, and to pass them on to the next child.

Handling objects should take place under direct supervision of a trained person, and can occur as part of a larger program in a special space, such as a natural history discovery room. Select a variety of objects with different sizes, weights, textures, colors, functions, and values. Provide adequate time for the children to examine the object, ask questions, and carefully look again following answers to their questions. Part of the magic of handling an object is the freedom to examine it with whatever senses seem appropriate and to process it for a moment. Children should not be rushed to pass the object along, although there is always eagerness to see what else is being circulated. A sufficient number of objects should be available so that each child can examine several, if not all, of the objects in circulation.

An important consideration in handling objects is the space required. Many museums seat children on the floor in a carpeted area that is large enough to allow passing the objects and examining them. After the objects are circulated, the docent or museum teacher must account for them and replace them in storage. To do this quickly and efficiently, a storage box can contain outlines of each object. Once they are returned to the box, any missing items can be readily identified and located.

Many museums have children handle objects as part of the regular tour. For example, at the Museum of History and Science in Louisville, the "Different Beaks for Different Eats" discovery tour lets children closely observe and study a variety of unique bird mouths in a self-directed manner. Students handle bird beaks carefully and complete a pamphlet with a series of questions about different shapes and lengths of the bills, how birds move, and how birds use their beaks to eat. Using tweezers, strainers, and other utensils children compare and contrast ways different animals would pick up and eat foods such as seeds, fish, or berries. Through the use of these utensils and careful examination of the beak specimens, children discover the importance of a strainer-type bill for ducks or a short stout bill for seed eaters.

Seventh and eighth graders involved in the "Curatorial Experience" tour of the Winterthur Museum look at functional and decorative objects to determine their purpose, form, what they say about their users, and how they relate to contemporary objects. In groups of three students, they examine the contents of a special basket and tour in the galleries. Each group has a curatorial basket, which contains related objects in protective padding, a pair of cotton gloves, ruler, pencil, clipboard, and three worksheets. The worksheets direct their examination of the objects and help students understand concepts related to artifact conservation. Using curatorial tools and techniques, the students examine the objects and fill out the worksheet. Children with learning difficulties can draw pictures, rather than write out information. Guides assist the students by asking questions to direct their discovery process. After completing the sheets, the students compare and contrast the objects to discover their relationships and view slides of museum exhibitions to analyze their effectiveness and ways to improve them.

The Museum of the City of New York has a "please touch" reconstruction of a 17th-century Dutch home in New Amsterdam. Children are encouraged to feel and use its butter churn, cooking utensils, spinning wheels, and Queen Anne furniture, and to wear period clothing as a part of the museum tour program. All of the above programs have been equally successful with handicapped children, and provide a special way for them to have access to the museum's collections.

Ferrets, rabbits, skunks, starfish, snakes, and turtles play starring roles in educational programs at zoos, aquaria, natural history museums, nature centers, and children's museums. Special care must be given to the type of animals selected for such programs. Attention must be taken to protect them from mishandling. Stroking and examining a live animal, comparing its protective coverings, nails, or mouth structure to their own, is a unique and exciting way for children to examine and carefully learn about animals. Programs that allow children to handle live animals should go beyond simple identification: What is it? Questions should seek a fuller understanding of the animal and its relationship to its environment: Where does it live? What foods does it eat? How does it get its food? How does it protect itself from other animals and from the climate? How is it like me?

Many museums, however, do not have sufficient teaching collections or staff to enable a full-scale object handling program such as those described above. A provocative alternative is the "Touch Cart" program of the Denver Museum of Natural History, which operates only during the month of May. Designed to deal with the problem of overcrowding due to spring tour groups, the "Touch Carts" provide a more informal approach than tours, as well as an opportunity for children to handle materials without special arrangements. Each cart contains materials related to the exhibit area in which it is located. For example, a cart with fossils would be located in the prehistoric hall near the dinosaurs. Visitors handle items under the supervision of a docent, who works as a facilitator, encouraging the children to question and relate their observations of the objects to the exhibition. Using inquiry strategies, docents ask the children to look closely "Does it look familiar?" "What do you think it was used for?" "Where would you find such a specimen?" Docents with touch carts in a lobby or orientation area are used by some museums to handle weekend crowds.

Reading Primary Resource Materials

Examining primary source documents can personalize the experiences of history and illustrate the effects of events, dates, and people on other people. Using original documents—birth and death certificates, a letter to the U.S. President from a person suffering through the Depression, or the diary of a young Civil War soldier—has an immediate effect on students, who not only develop analytical and research skills but also realize that history has been written by people who have analyzed such documents and developed their own point of view.

Through primary sources, students confront two essential facts about history. First, the historical record reflects the personal, social, political, and economic perspective of the participants. Second, the users—scholars or the students themselves—bring to the sources their own biases, created by their own personal situations and environments. As students use primary sources, they realize that history exists through tentative interpretation.

There are several advantages to working with primary resource documents, including diaries, drawings, memoirs, letters, photographs, ledgers, and floor plans of homes. The resources can be reproduced for careful examination by the students. Not only does examining materials prepared by a real person who lived at another time create an aura of immediacy and personality, it also permits students to focus on details according to their own interests and needs. It encourages comparisons with contemporary events and materials. Additionally, primary sources can be used by museums in a variety of programs and formats.

Reproductions can be used in the museum, in outreach programs, and for pre- or post-visit classroom activities. Original documents displayed in exhibit cases may be reproduced and distributed to tour groups. This permits the students to analyze the message, language, and sentence structure, and to see other pages of the document not presented in the exhibit case. Reproductions can be contrasted with contemporary, readily available documents; for example, a handwritten census ledger of the 1800s can be compared with computerized modern census.

In preparation for the Mission Houses Museum tour in Honolulu, teachers receive a pre-visit package, which includes drawings and illustrations of the mission houses area in 1822 and in 1844. Students compare and contrast the architecture or styles and differences in landscape layouts. The package includes reproductions of the "Outfit for the Sandwich Islands," prepared in 1834 by the mission, supplies needed by missionaries for a three-year stay and their 150-day voyage. The outfit lists not only the clothing, but crockery, furniture, ironware and other necessary items. It encourages students to consider the way of life that the missionaries felt they would be undertaking on the voyage and during their tour of duty. Students can develop their own conclusions about the effects of the voyage based on the types of clothing that the missionaries needed to take

Primary Resource from Mission Houses Museum

Gentleman's Outfit for the Voyage, of 150 days.

1 sea cap and hat,
1 stock or black cravat,
25 old shirts,
25 collars,
2 vests, dark,
2 spencers, dark,
3 pr. pantaloons, dark,
14 pr. stockings,
2 pr. shoes,
1 cloak,
1 woollen suit,
5 pocket handkerchiefs,
11 changes of sheets,
21 towels,
3 lbs. soap,
2 flannel shirts,
10 pr. pillow cases,
2 blankets,
1 washbason, tin,
1 looking glass,
1 lamp.

---

with them, and can understand more clearly the preparation the missionaries undertook to prepare for their work in the islands.

Students who attend the National Archives' "Introduction to Research" program are given specific guidance on research methods for using the materials in the National Archives. Small groups are guided on a search for information from documents relating to Dr. A. T. Augusta, a black surgeon in the Union Army, who was forced off a Washington, D.C. streetcar when he refused the conductor's order to ride on the car's platform in the rain. Students handle and discuss such documents as an 1880 Washington, D.C. census, Dr. Augusta's service record, and his correspondence with President Lincoln. By analyzing these documents, students understand more clearly how individuals involved in the incident present their own point of view.

The education division of the National Archives promotes teaching with primary sources in a variety of ways, including regular features in social education journals and a series of publications for classroom teachers on units to supplement social studies curricula. Such units contain 30-40 facsimiles of documents from the National Archives and a variety of student exercises.

Old Sturbridge Village uses primary resources to help students understand how people lived in the 19th century. Through an estate inventory of a farmer who died in 1837, students learn about a farm family's patterns of life and work. The inventory shows the acreage and value of the farm, as well as the quantity and value of its livestock, tools, equipment, household furnishings, and utensils. From the inventory students can speculate on the work environment, the farmer's skills, and other sources of employment. Students can also inventory their own home and compare it to the estate's holding, and by comparing the prices of materials can consider the differences of economic value in the past and present.

A similar activity at Old Sturbridge utilizes the seasonal work outline drawn up by the farm manager of the Pliny Freeman farm, as recreated at the historical village museum. The month-by-month outline illustrates the effect of the seasons on work activities. While students are at the village, they focus on the activities being performed. From their own observations and contact with interpreters, they compare their experience with that of a 19th-century farmer. They are encouraged to list their parents' work tasks for comparison with that of the Freeman farm, to consider how 19th-century and modern workers are variously affected by the seasons.

An excellent illustration of the various stages of an inquiry process using primary source materials and artifacts is presented in the January/February 1981 issue of *Art to Zoo*, a publication of the Smithsonian's Office of Elementary and Secondary Education. The issue presents, for use by individual students or a whole class, a person through reproductions of primary sources. In addition to suggesting discussion ideas for this particular person, the issue offers guidelines for developing similar lessons. One idea is to present a living person through primary source materials and classroom discussion, and to then have that person visit the class in person.

Discussions among students, and between the class and (museum or classroom) teacher, are an important part of the interpretive process. To challenge each other's conclusions, students must look more carefully for details and make relationships between facts, evidence, and the person or event.

Primary Resource from Old Sturbridge Village

A FARM FAMILY'S POSSESSIONS

The inventory of the Estate of Seth Dunham of Brimfield, Massachusetts, 1837.

REAL ESTATE	
95 acres land and building	$1750.00
LIVESTOCK	
Horse	40.00
2 Oxen	65.00
3 Cows	80.00
4 Two year old Heiffers	40.00
3 Yearlings	18.00
3 Calves	9.00
22 Sheep	25.00
2 Hogs	20.00
TOOLS AND EQUIPMENT	
1 Cart	15.00
1 Grindstone	1.00
1 Old Waggon and Harness	5.00
1 Old Bridle	.25
1 Gimlet-10c. 1 Hand Saw-1.	1.10
3 Baskets	.75
1 Axe	1.00
2 Axes-50c. 1 Shave-33c.	.83
Scythes and 1 Snathe-50c. Flail-25c.	.75
1 Post Axe and 2 Wedges	.75
1 Ox Yoke-75. 2 Yoke-50c.	1.25
1 Chain-100c. 1 Chain-75c.	1.75
1 Manure Fork	.75
2 Hoes-50c. 1 Shovel-25c.	.75
1 Calf Skin	1.25
Stone boat plank	.50
Cradle	.25
4 Pitchforks 1 Rake	.75
14 Dry casks	1.00
Weaving Apparatus	1.00
HOUSEHOLD FURNISHINGS	
1 Clock	6.00
1 Bureau	8.00
1 Chest and Drawers	2.00
1 Light Stand	1.00
1 Easy Chair	1.50
6 Dining Chairs	2.00
1 Dining Table	2.50
1 Kitchen Table	.75
6 Kitchen Chairs	1.50
1 Rocking Chair	.25
2 Old Chests	.25
1 Bellows	.25
1 Lantern	.42
4 Candle Sticks	.40
1 Feather Bed, under Bed Cord & Bed Stead	10.00
2 Old Beds & Bed Stead	4.00
1 Bed, Bed Stead & Bedding	12.00

Participating in an Activity . . . Trying Out a Process

Cooking a meal, spinning some yarn, weeding a garden, passing a bucket in a fire brigade, experimenting with wave motion, creating a mask, or making paper—these are but a few of the activities enjoyed by children at museums all over the country. These activities develop skills and challenge children to think about the museums' collections or exhibits in a purposeful way.

Participating in an activity requires the personal involvement of the learner. Children become motivated to learn and obtain a deeper understanding of the subject matter. New information is retained because of their active involvement. Participating in activities usually occurs as part of an entire museum education program. Inquiry strategies or skills such as organization, summarizing, discovering relationships, making generalizations, and transferring information from one concept to another are incorporated into these activities.

There are several considerations in the design of programs that involve participatory activities. Some can accommodate only small groups. Others, which involve large groups (30 or more), will produce high noise and movement levels. Materials and supplies must be readily available, replaceable, and inexpensive. Activities require set-up and clean-up time, as well as storage space for supplies. Skilled supervision of activities

1 Bed Stead & Under Bed	1.50	2 Deep Plates & 1 Platter	.50
1 Coverlet	3.00	3 Bowls & 1 Creamer	.42
1 Pair Blankets	1.00	9 Spoons	.40
1 ditto ditto	2.00	5 Tumblers	.25
2 Bed Quilts	1.50	Knives & Forks	.50
1 Comfortable	1.00	1 Tea Pot	.25
5 Yds. Flannel	2.50	1 Waiter	.25
5 Flannel Sheets	7.50	Shovel Tongs & Andirons	.75
2 Cotton Sheets	1.00	1 Tea Kettle	.50
1 Bed Quilt	1.50	1 Pail Pot	.75
Tow & Yarn	.50	1 ditto Kettle	.25
Curtains	1.00	2 Bake pans & high pan	1.00
5 Towels	.50	2 Brass Kettles	2.50
2 ditto	.25	1 5 Pail Kettle	1.00
3 Cheese Cloths	1.25	6 Milk Pans (earthen)	.48
2 Yds. Cotton Cloth	.25	2 Pails	.25
2 Yds. Full Cloth	2.00	Tin Ware	2.00
3 Table Spreads	2.25	Stone Ware	.50
12 Pillow Cases	.75	Tin Pails	.33
6 Cotton Sheets	2.00	**OTHER TOOLS AND EQUIPMENT**	
UTENSILS		Spinning Wheels Reel & Swifts	2.00
3 Small measures	.25		
12 Plates	1.00		
Cups & Saucers	.62		
15 Plates	.60		

within the museum is essential. Careful instructions for the students should explain what they are doing and why, as well as how it relates to their entire museum experience.

Hour-long tours of the Museum of Northern Arizona in Flagstaff concentrate on the natural history of the Colorado Plateau and center around concepts, artifacts, and participation. Students might conduct a simulated excavation of a fossil in a paleontology program or might feed a plant and observe its method of insect-entrapment in a program on carnivorous plants. Programs relating to the native people of the area might include use of prehistoric hunting weapons, making pots out of clay, or practicing traditional Hopi musical instruments. Presentations are tailored to a class's curriculum and presentations are given in the museum or classroom, depending on the teacher's wishes. In all cases, children are directly involved in some activity.

"The Book and the Spade: Archeology and the Bible," a four-session program offered by the Jewish Museum of New York City, focuses on the ancient Near East as the source of many ideological, technological, and social developments that are fundamental to the Western world. This mini-course focuses on archeological methods; inventions and technologies pioneered long ago; the development of the alphabet; and ancient market economics. Everyday life is stressed throughout the program, with frequent comparisons between ancient cultures and the modern world. Each session includes a workshop, in which children learn how to make pottery, build ancient style plows from wood and string, or decipher ancient languages. The activity sessions, a central part of the museum's educational program, allow children to bring life to ancient cultures while learning skills.

Programs to help children discover the movement and rhythm of works of art utilize the creative arts—dance, music, sketching, writing poetry. Activities that encourage the children to take a point of view and make decisions in the manner of an artist, help them to develop the skills necessary for looking at works of art. At the Arkansas Arts Center in Little Rock, children use simple materials (colored yarn, paper and string) to make contour drawings; they explore the meaning of abstraction by working with shapes of colored paper as they examine works on display in galleries. Art, music, and dance bring African cultures to life at the Museum of African Art at the Smithsonian Institution. After gallery tours, children try on African clothing, play musical instruments, and participate in craft workshops, all of which help bring African traditions alive in an exciting way. Activity-oriented sessions help children gain a deeper understanding and appreciation of the history, technology, and purposes of such African art forms as masks, textiles, and jewelry. For example, children in pre-school through third grade might examine the concept of a mask in Africa, and then make a Dogon rabbit mask using paper bags, paper, crayons, and beads. Children in the third grade and up examine the historical background and social significance of the Ashanti gold weights and using clay and gold paint, make their own small weights in geometric, animal, and human shapes. African proverbs and their important relationship to gold weights are also explored.

The St. Louis Art Museum and the Delaware Art Museum have both developed programs using film with creative art activities to explain how to look at works of art. For example, one session at the Delaware Museum of Art involved a screening of three films that focus on various types of movement. Following the films, children used their bodies to create noise machines, experiencing motion and rhythm as types of expression, and created a machine with "working parts," attaching their bodies to each other and adding voices to make the machine have sound. Following this activity, the children looked at an Alexander Calder mobile with crescent discs. The combination of events—viewing a sculpture, creating their own machine, and looking at films—helped the children to understand the variables of movement and to perceive subtleties in art. A useful book, *What To Do When the Lights Go On: A Comprehensive Guide to Sixteen MM Films and Related Activities for Children,* describes activities at museums throughout the country that combine film, creative art experiences, objects in collections.

The Holt Planetarium at the Lawrence Hall of Science, Berkeley is among the many small planetariums that offer participatory shows, which illustrate that science is an exciting and understandable endeavor. By taking an active part in the show rather than passively observing an audiovisual presentation, the audience absorbs more about scientific concepts and processes.

For example, instead of pointing out constellations on the dome of the planetarium, the audience uses star charts to locate the stars themselves. Other topics for activities at the planetarium include classical and modern astronomy, navigation, inventions, model rockets, solar energy, and digital electronics. The activities, which complement exhibits in the science center, are developed, tested, and refined through trial classes. Some activities are presented to school groups during a single field trip while others are organized as on-going classes lasting as many as eight sessions. The *Planetarium Educator's Workshop Guide,* prepared by the International Planetarium Society, outlines a number of participatory activities for people interested in teaching astronomy, physics, or working in the planetarium environment.

The pond-life program at the Peninsula Nature and Science Center in Newport News, Virginia, introduces the pond as an ecosystem. During a collecting trip, students wade into the pond to catch aquatic animals, which they later examine under a laboratory microscope.

Many museums have developed activity materials to help students prepare for or follow up their museum tour. In many cases, museums perceive these activities as being as important as the actual museum event. For example, at the Brooklyn Museum of Art, students study the Jan Martense Schenck house, built in 1675, and then partially reconstructed in the museum. A resource kit provides background information about the Schenck family, its emigration from Holland, and maps of the journey and the New World. The students consider how the family might have felt as they undertook their journey, list their favorite possessions which they might have taken in a small chest, and draw pictures of Jan's trip. By comparing the kit's and modern maps, they consider how the journey might have changed in the past 300 years. Other activities include making a tape recording of the sounds that might have been heard inside the Schenck house, discussion of the various activities undertaken by the family, making a floor plan and comparing it to the one at the museum, and making an inventory of the possessions inside the house. All of these can be done in preparation for the museum trip, or following it.

At the Field Museum of Natural History in Chicago, the "Prairies: Plants and Animal Discovery Units," include a series of activities that help children locate and examine prairie remnants left in the Chicago area. In visiting some of these prairie locations in preparation for the museum tour, students are asked to make inventories, categorize their inventories, measure the size of the plants and animals, and record animal and insect life on the prairie as they have found. Additional activities which are encouraged include examination and comparison of the prairie visit to things found in a vacant lot or in the children's backyards; making maps of grasslands, in Illinois, North America, and the world; writing stories about life for the prairie settlers; or drawing a picture of how the prairie once looked and comparing it to today.

Old Sturbridge Village has developed a series of activity cards listing materials and step-by-step illustrated directions for recreating 19th-century objects and crafts processes. Cards can be followed easily by either students or teachers, or can be reproduced and distributed to a group. Patterns and designs are concluded where needed, and introductory notes help place the activities in a historical context.

Participatory museum experiences involve the inquiry process, but go beyond the questioning and research level to involve the students in a variety of activities that help to bring the museums' collections and exhibits to life. Learning activities must have a clear purpose, which must be communicated to the students and their teachers. The learning activities should also help students acquire confidence and increase their knowledge. They should be flexible enough to allow the group to respond in its own way. The activities should be built upon basic principles of learning, and involve the students in active processes that help to increase their abilities, while motivating their interests to learn.

Perception Games

Art museums have adapted theater techniques and other creative activities to an interpretive technique that is usually referred to as perception or gallery games. Recognizing the unique qualities of looking at art and that perception is a selective process, this broad range of interpretive activities combines games techniques, improvisational theater, and certain forms of role playing with questioning processes and the inquiry method to help teach visual perception. Perception games help children involve their mental, physical, and perceptual skills as they become physically involved in observational experiences. Through perception games, objects come to life: individuals in a painting might carry on a dialogue, an abstract painting might come to life by assuming smells and sounds, or a still life of foods might be consumed as children savor the tastes and smells. Perception games are designed to help the students develop an awareness and sensitivity of the varied interpretations that can be applied to a work of art.

The guides at The High Museum of Art present the museum's philosophy about gallery games:

> *One of the most important concepts for a child to grasp is that his perception, his point of view, and his reaction to the world which surrounds him is both important and valid. Games can be used to facilitate the involvement of the child with a work of art on a nonverbal level. Through these games, he can respond, imitate, and identify with the colors, shapes, objects, and spaces—the elements of design in a work of art. He can act out the relationships, formal and otherwise, in a painting or sculpture, thereby analyzing and physically experiencing the work of art, bringing the work to life.*

Perception games must be seen as tools in the interpretive process, rather than as an end in themselves. Games will not work equally well with all docents or museum teachers, nor with all works of art or groups of children. The use of games as a part of a museum tour requires the leader to have a quick imagination and rapport with the children that includes a sense of trust and a willingness to participate in games.

The success of these games depends largely on the wording of directions, the relationship of the directions being given to the work of art, the relevance of the games to the work of art, and the sequence of the objects being explored on the tour. Children need time to respond to the instructions, and the questions, and to participate in activities. Following each game, it is important to review what the children have experienced, to find out what they remember, or to ask how they are different as a result of this activity. Perception games should relate to objects and to the theme of the tour, and should not be introduced at random. Pertinent transitional activities, statements, or questions, which strengthen the activities' relationships, are essential as the children move from one object or gallery to the next.

Games can increase the student's learning potential by developing their skills of analysis, perception, and generalization.

This technique requires a certain amount of understanding of theater, and the work of Viola Spolin has often been used as the basis for the development of many games. Spolin's improvisational theater techniques provides guidelines on how to undertake "side coaching," which helps to guide the students without giving them the answers as they participate in these activities and does not imply approval or disapproval. Side coaching should be short and to the point, providing a directed activity that involves the student's senses. For example, "smell the smoke," "see the color red repeated," "feel the weight of the clothes on your body," etc. These instructions help the students to keep from losing track of themselves while they participate in their perception games and encourage organized examination of a work of art.

Perception games require a docent to both lead and follow the children as they explore the work of art. Not everyone is ready to act out a scene from a 17th-century painting, or become part of a mobile. Docents must quickly ascertain which games will be appropriate for which groups. In addition, the game technique does not revolve around right or wrong answers, but provides opportunities for an infinite variety of experiences based on the children's abilities to become involved in the process. Game techniques may not be the most effective way to look at works of art, but there has been an increasing enthusiasm for this approach in art museums. Some feel that perception games are too much fun, and do not directly relate to the works of art on view. As with any participatory touring techniques, care must be taken to review the material that has been covered, to learn more carefully about what perceptual skills have been developed in the children, and to ascertain if they can come back to the museum and learn on their own.

Children cannot always verbalize their thoughts and feelings, but they can usually illustrate their ideas with physical motion or facial expressions and sounds. These games allow children to explore works of art through physical experiences, while they analyze the artist's colors, lines and shapes and their effects on each other. Effectively used, games can channel the energies of children and help them to see the works of art more clearly and more imaginatively.

Games can be used for many different purposes.
- **Relaxation:** to encourage the children to feel at ease in the new environment of the museum
- **Orientation:** to develop the children's awareness of the looking process and what it will require
- **Socialization:** to help docents meet their groups, and to help the children interact and talk during the museum experience
- **Organization:** to bring children together into one group
- **Participation:** to involve children at their own level of experience in activities that will focus their attention on the works of art

The following selection of perception games illustrates only a very *small* portion of the different types of games that can be developed by museums for use on their tours. There are hundreds more, each inspired by the individual works of art and artists and teachers within the museum setting.

1. Warm-up Games/Learning About Your Group

After a long bus ride, children are often tired, overwhelmed, and a bit anxious. Anything that will make them feel more at ease in the museum and help the docent establish rapport with them is a bonus. The main thing is to make young children realize that they are going to have fun while they are at the museum.

Some elementary school children at the National Collection of Fine Art, in Washington, D.C., are greeted with a game, which is designed to help them think more consciously about the different colors. A docent says, "Stand with your eyes closed and think about your favorite color. Fill your mind with it . . . Feel it cover you all over . . . As I touch you, call out your color name, one at a time." After individually tapping the students, the docent has the group say their colors *en masse*.

A game for older children might emphasize the importance of looking and remembering what has been seen. The students face each other in pairs and looking carefully at one another, from head to toes. Standing back-to-back each student alters his or her own appearance by removing glasses, rolling up sleeves, or changing the part in his or her hair. The pairs faces each other again and try to discover what changes have been made. This short exercise illustrates that details can be easily missed and that seeing requires physical and mental effort. Other concentration or introductory games have children mirror each other's hand or facial movements or have children identify all of the colors they are wearing. Introductory games should set the tone of the museum experience and be appropriate for the group's learning experience.

2. Looking At a Gallery with a Focus

Gallery games provide children with a focus or reason for observing an exhibit or collection on their own. Too often, they are rushed from one art work to the next, without time to look at the full range of the collections. In addition, these games can be used to develop a transition from one gallery or object to the next, thereby relating the various parts of the learning experience and developing the theme of the tour.

At the Denver Museum of Art, students can participate in a "visual walk," which is designed to help them compare their memory of what they saw in a three-to five-minute walk through the museum's galleries. Through this, they realize that no two people saw or remembered exactly the same thing, that personal preferences and walking patterns affect what people remembered, and that it takes a long time to notice all that there is to see in a museum gallery.

For example, the docent tells the students they will walk through three rooms of art in three minutes, and that afterwards a question will be asked about their visual perceptions. Without elaborating, the docent leads the group at a leisurely pace, not talking but letting the students form their own conversations and eavesdropping. Sitting in an area where students can no longer see the art, the docent comments that the group walked the same path past the same objects. The students are asked to describe one thing they remembered vividly from the walk. Following their descriptions, the docent can ask why the students think they noticed different items and how each student might see more if they visited the rooms again. The docent may choose to do the walk again, following the discussion.

Another way to get students to focus on a gallery is to have them explore all the colors, shapes, or textures that they are wearing on themselves (clothes, shoes, hair, nails, etc). The students then spend five minutes exploring the gallery, looking for all of the colors or other items that the artists have used. Once they have found an object with all of these elements in it, they should make a list of what they see and where they find it. Or, each student might stand by the object that most closely resembles them and other students can compare and contrast their observations, seeking a color or shape that is not readily apparent. The goal of this type of game is to help children notice various elements in their everyday dress, and to realize there is much that they did not originally notice about themselves. This exercise should be followed by careful analysis of individual objects in the galleries, which can lead to the development of a very clear image for the children about a single work of art.

Exploring a Single Object

There are hundreds of ways to examine individual objects within a museum's collection. The children could be asked to trace the shapes of repeated lines or to show how these cause the eyes to move through the painting. They might examine a portrait, developing a sense of the personality of the sitter, based on the visual clues provided by the artist. From the examination, the students can construct the feelings that the sitter would have had, assume the position, and carry on a dialogue or complete the action within the painting.

The High Museum, in Atlanta, has developed a number of activities that assist children in understanding their point of view. These activities deal with the children's physical position, opinions, experiences, and observations. An excerpt from the *Handbook for Guides* provides the following illustration:

Point of View

Everyone has a point of view. Your point of view is how you "see" things, and how you feel about things—your opinions, your perspective. What your viewpoint is depends on who you are, what you know, what you have experienced and learned in life, where you are in time (historical context) and in space.

How often do you look at things while standing absolutely still?
Do you walk around?
Cock your head to one side?
Bend down to look at an object from underneath or stand up on something to get a better look?
Have you ever moved yourself closer to an object or moved the object closer to you in order to see it in more detail?

If so, you have changed your "point of view," or way of looking.

For example, position your hand at arm's length, palm-side directly in front of you.
Describe what you see.

Keeping your hand at arm's length, rotate your hand so that the other side is visible.
What do you see now?

Next, position your hand with your fingertips pointing directly at your nose.
Look at your hand closely.
What do you see?
Although you have been looking at the same object throughout this activity, you have seen three different things.

What changed about your hand with each? How did these changes affect what you saw?

Can you think of any other ways to change your point of view?

Have the children experiment briefly . . . leaving the hands stationary and changing the position of their heads instead.

Is changing positions the only thing that can affect your point of view?

During the images tour at the Ringling Museums in Sarasota, Florida, students focus on an individual art work through one of two perception games, one which interprets the work verbally and the other which is silent. In "The Portrait Game," students sit in the gallery and individually choose a painting, which contains people or animals. The docent has the students assume the identity of one character in the painting and think about such questions as "Who are you? How old are you? What do you do? What are you wearing and thinking about?". At a signal, the students assume the position of their character. The students can "come alive," and move into the next gallery in the manner of their character or pantomime their character while the rest of the group guesses the appropriate painting.

In "Create a Story," the group examines a painting and imagines the sounds of the location, what is happening there, and how they (as individuals in the painting) feel about being there. The group then creates a story about the painting and what is happening, following their own imaginations. The docent may start the story, but lets the children provide the details and main story line.

A similar story/game format is used at the Philadelphia Museum of Art with the *Constantine and Lion* tapestry. After viewing the tapestry quietly, the docent asks the students what they see. Usually the students initially answer, "A man, a lion, a sword, and blood." Encouraged by the docent to find anything else, the students begin to notice other characters, objects, designs, and such things as borders. The docent asks each to think about what is happening, and then has individual students tell a story about what is happening based on the visual information in the tapestry. Other students discuss the individual stories, and the teacher or docent encourages them to justify their agreement or objections based on the visual information of the tapestry.

A similar game at the Philadelphia museum focuses on a Calder mobile, and has the students imitate the movement of the mobile with their bodies. Their performance is judged by the similarity to the mobile in speed, circular motion, disparity of movement of the distant parts, and other factors.

Perception games can also be combined with other interpretive techniques to expand the students understanding of a work of art. The Brooklyn Museum successfully uses art activities, role playing and other techniques with perception games. For example using Japanese Ukiyo-e prints, and depicting actors in their roles, students learn some of the similarities between the function of popular Japanese prints and popular collectable posters of today.

The purpose of the perception games activities is not to detract from the work of art, but to provide the students with a number of different ways to look and to think and to respond to these works. Games can introduce students to the idea of actively looking at exhibits in a museum, and can be used on taxonomic displays as well as environmental spaces.

Role Playing

Role playing experiences in museums range from a re-created conversation or meeting between people traveling across the country to an overnight live-in experience at a fort or a two-week program working as a costumed interpretor at Old Sturbridge. In this type of experience, students assume the identity, however briefly, of someone who lived in another age. It may include dressing in costume or following the everyday pursuits of a person who lived 100 years ago.

Sometimes it is difficult for students to assume the identity of their character in a short time; however, advance preparation by the classroom teacher can alleviate much of this problem. When students carry on

```
NAME:      GINNY HOPKINS              OCCUPATION:  Waitress
AGE:       22                         RACE:        Black
                                      RESIDENCE:   New York, N.Y.

- I came to New York from Florida; my husband is down south working
  on a chain gang for stealing which he said he didn't do.

- I have two children staying with my mother.  I plan to send for
  them as soon as I raise enough money.

- At this moment I am working as a waitress and the pay is poor.  After
  my rent and buying food, nothing is left.

- I don't know when I will be able to visit my husband and children.
  I feel so lonely at times.
```

```
NAME:      FATHER THOMAS FARRELL      OCCUPATION:  Priest
AGE:       54                         RACE:        White
                                      RESIDENCE:   Boston, Ma.

- I came to Boston from Ireland with my father in 1880.

- I attended a seminary in Baltimore to become a priest.

- After I was ordained, I moved to Boston where I was made assistant
  pastor of St. Benedict the Moor Roman Catholic Church which at
  that time was half Irish and half black.

- As the number of black members increased, they wanted the church
  to move to a black neighborhood.  The whites refused to go.

- Eventually the church split and I moved to Roxbury with the black
  members.

- I have worked hard to make the church meet the needs of the people,
  but a number of the members would rather have a black pastor.
  I am wondering if I should resign.
```

conversations of people in the 18th century, it might be best to use imagination, rather than asking them to translate their phraseology from the 20th century. The problem of confusing roles with real life has been counteracted in part by in-depth experiences, offered in programs at Old Economy, Old Sturbridge Village, Colonial Williamsburg, and other institutions. Partial or full costumes are often used to help students accept their roles more fully. The role playing experience in these programs usually involves preparation of a meal, dipping candles, churning butter, carrying water, riding in wagons, or working in schoolhouses or farmyards, thus extending the student's involvement beyond the purely verbal level.

An advantage of role-playing activities is the active, direct involvement of an entire class and interaction in discussion sessions. Skill is required by leaders of such activities, who must set the scene, help orchestrate the activities, and keep the students interested and focused on the issues at hand. The characters on the role cards may be individuals who really lived or fictional persons created from available facts. Reading levels of the students must be carefully considered. In general, museums have developed role-playing cards in the first-person singular. Thus, if a class is unprepared, the leader can read the cards allowed and the activity can commence easily.

The National Portrait Gallery in Washington, D.C. has developed a series of educational role-playing programs that combine classroom preparation with a museum visit. Fifty color-coded role cards are provided to teachers who have registered for tours, and students are given identity sheets at least one week before a museum staff member visits their classroom. Each student reads his or her identity sheet aloud to the class, thus establishing a sense of the total community and each individual's place in it. The students write seven brief diary entries, including comments about work, family, social life, or other interests, showing what a week would be like for their character. Students are also encouraged to find or draw a picture of their character. Finally, students are encouraged to work with their teacher on research about the historical period of their program and to compare it to current situations in the same locale. The museum staff attending the class presents a situation, such as a debate or meeting, during which the students practice their roles. The museum visit that follows focuses on the period and the characters involved.

Taking its title from a Langston Hughes poem, "I, Too, Am America" examines the problem confronting

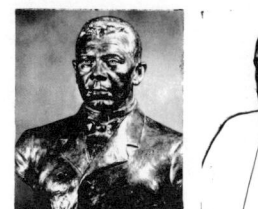

```
NAME:     VICTORIA EARLE MATTHEWS        OCCUPATION: Social Reformer
AGE:      58                             RACE:       Black
                                         RESIDENCE:  New York, N.Y.

- I was the youngest daughter of a former slave and moved to New
  York from Georgia in 1870.

- I attended New York public schools and the City College of New York.

- At college I became interested in social problems and, after gradua-
  tion, I started writing for small newspapers in support of women's
  rights and equality for the black race.

- Several years ago I helped to establish the White Rose Home which
  offered room and board to poor women out of work.

- The Home now has a library, and we have classes in domestic train-
  ing and race history.

- I hope it will provide black women with pride, some independence,
  and security.
```

```
NAME:     BILLIE BURKE                   OCCUPATION: Writer
AGE:      27                             RACE:       Black
                                         RESIDENCE:  New York, N.Y.

- I was born to well-off parents in Boston, Massachusetts.

- After graduation from high school, I attended Columbia University
  on an academic scholarship and got my degree four years ago.

- I now write for Crisis, a magazine run by the National Association
  for the Advancement of Colored People (NAACP).

- One thing that bothers me is that, except for Crisis, there are
  not many magazines which publish black authors.

- Many of my talented friends are working as busboys and waiters.
  To me that's unfair, but what can I do about it?
```

black Americans in the 1920s and the radically different solutions offered to them. Role cards for this program present black residents of Harlem and white reformers interested in helping them. (See above.) In the period before the museum staff-visit, the students read works by Hughes, Jean Toomer, Claude McKay and others, listen to jazz from the era, and collect pictures of city life. In researching life at that time, the students compare and contrast life for black Americans in the 1920s and current times.

In the classroom, the Portrait Gallery staff convene a meeting set in a 1921 Harlem church. The students, in character, respond to appeals made by Booker T. Washington, W. E. B. DuBois, and Marcus Garvey (played by museum staff members) and conclude the session by voting on the best course for black Americans to take. The program continues with a visit to the museum where the students examine portraits of individuals whose lives and achievements relate to the issues explored in the "church" meeting, and focus on the artistic, social, and political contributions the people made to American society.

The "Trailways and Turnpikes" program of the Western Reserve Historical Society in Cleveland, uses a 30-minute role-playing activity as a part of a two-hour tour of the museum. The program focuses on the effect of different forms of transportation on the nation's growth, and the role-playing activity is in the form of a town meeting to reach consensus about whether a proposed railroad will be permitted to pass through the community. Using both inquiry and role-playing techniques, the activity is intended to help students to understand the complexity of the past, to become aware of factors influencing change, and to understand that all changes have positive and negative results.

The role cards given to each student contain biographical details and a description of the character's ideas or attitudes about the railway based on age, occupation, personal philosophy, and social or economic consequences. While some students receive clearly pro- or con-railway characters, others have ambivalent characters:

CANAL LOCK KEEPER
Michael Patrick: 52 years old, married, 6 children.

"My job as lock keeper is important in this community. It provides a fair living for me and my family. I don't want to see a change, I know that the railroad would take away from travel and that would hurt me. At 52, I'm too old to look for a new occupation and afraid to try."

MERCHANT
Nate Fisher: 46 years old, married, 6 children.

"I don't want that railroad if it means people coming to town and opening stores like mine. We've done just fine with the canal, we don't need a railroad."

GENERAL STORE OWNER
Walter Luckett: 52 years old, married, no children living at home, 2 employees.

"Sometimes business is good, especially in the spring and fall. But, in the winter when the canal is frozen, customers are few and my employees do not work at all. The railroad would allow goods to come in year round and would encourage more people to settle here. That would mean more customers. Besides being good for business, it would mean more work for my employees. I would like the railroad very much."

WAGONEER
Joseph Thompson: 26 years old, single, free Black.

"I drive a horse and wagon. I deliver goods and produce to different towns. If we had a railroad here, I could take goods to the station so they could be sent out. I could also pick up the goods coming in. The train will not go to every town, but with my wagon, I can make deliveries to all the towns it skips."

During the debate, students elaborate on their assigned role and may disagree with the conclusions implied on the card. Interaction among the students is encouraged, and discussion is not channeled through the museum instructor. Following a vote at the conclusion of the town meeting, the students consider the process of decision-making historically and currently. While the railroad/canal issue is interesting from an historical perspective, the activity's value is in the inquiry and role-playing process itself.

Using role-playing and inquiry approaches during live-in programs can help students to ask questions and reason out the answers. The National Park Service has designed the "Environmental Living Program," a five-part unit including a teacher workshop, and initial visit by the class to the site, classroom preparation for the visit, an overnight stay at the site, and follow-up activities in the school. In addition to these activities, the program allows the children to assume different roles such as Civil War soldier, a sailor aboard a schooner, or an Indian living in an adobe, depending on which historic park is offering the program. According to their role assignments, the students chop wood, brew coffee, watch the fire, wake the cooks, or discuss the problems that people living on this site would have been considering.

These live-in programs at historic parks, history museums, and children's museums involve intensive preparation and hard work by the museum staff and teachers. However, enthusiastic response and a long waiting list indicate that the idea is an important one, since it utilizes the full resources of the museum and teaches children, through direct experiences, about a way of life that no longer exists. Role-playing activities are also effectively used in several exhibit loan kits.

Theater

Inventions and civilizations come alive when famous people, past and present, talk about their work during theater presentations in museums all over the country. Because artifacts are detached from the living experiences that brought them into creation, many museums in particular science and history museums, have developed theater programs that bring their galleries to life. Living history museums have long known the success a costumed interpreter can bring to their museum. Theater components in museums may involve amateur or professionals performing puppet shows, professional actors in cameo roles in galleries, or full theater productions. The results are that the galleries are transformed into an inviting and intriguing environment, and the audience is motivated to look more closely at the exhibits and collections that form the basis of these presentations.

Perhaps more than any of the previously discussed interpretive techniques, the use of theater requires highly skilled and trained facilitators. Professionals who understand and are skilled in all aspects of theater are necessary to undertake the production of scripts. In most cases, it is best to use primary source material, developing characters and thoughts around autobiographical information obtained from autobiographies or biographies. Secondary source materials can be helpful, and are often used, depending on the type of piece. As in all interpretive techniques, clear objectives must be formulated, so that the actors can make direct relationships between their work and the collections in the galleries and to help the audience understand the purpose of the performance.

Theater pieces can be an excellent way to attract large crowds, or to provide a presentation for two or three classes simultaneously. Skillfully done, there are few things as exciting as live theater, and museums can find that this technique can be a real drawing card for both public audiences and school groups. Several types of theater works can take place in the museum, and although they do not involve the visitor, many of them encourage the visitors to talk, ask questions, or engage in some type of activity.

Museums have used theater techniques in different ways in galleries, including demonstrations, character cameos presented by professional actors, and short plays or puppet performances.

Science and history museums have a long tradition of offering demonstrations to help visitors understand how things are made or how they work. Many demonstration techniques have been discussed in the chapters on exhibitions: demonstrations may be presented in theaters or exhibit areas by staff or volunteers in costume or normal dress. In whatever format or location, demonstrations focus on the skills, methods, and stages of a specific process, whether it is making paper, churning butter, or weaving fabric.

Character cameos are one-person dramatic interpretations, usually performed in galleries, with either a real or fictional figure reliving a particular moment in their lives. At Colonial Williamsburg, for example, during the summer months, different actors have undertaken the roles of an indentured servant in the pillary—complaining about the act that his love of freedom is as valid as that of the patriots'—or a gardener from the governor's palace, who comments on the orderly way in which he keeps the grounds and his concern of the growing disorder in American politics.

Character cameos are researched and scripted in the same manner of regular plays, but allow for variations based on the interests of the audience. They can accommodate large or small audiences, who can become directly involved in the performance. The planter/militia officer at Colonial Williamsburg, for example, rounds up visitors and makes them participate in an 18th-century militia drill. At the Science Museum of Minnesota, visitors are startled out of their reveries as Akh, the Spirit of the Mummy, makes her declaration of innocence. The aura, majesty, and magic of the Egyptian princess, created by the actress in her character cameo, sparks the attention and curiosity of museum visitors, who see that a mummy was once a living human being with pain, pleasure, feelings, and thoughts. The visitors listen intently to her legends, and one is asked to be a model as Akh describes the elaborate and sacred burial rituals of her people and discusses with them how these rituals relate to their lives here and now.

Museums have used theater in a more formal technique through puppet shows, musicals, or plays on specific topics or famous people in science, history or the arts, such as Einstein, Marie Curie or others. Short plays and puppet performances generally require certain types of staging and have a "run" of several weeks or months.

As part of its theater offerings, the Brooklyn Museum presented *Has Anybody Seen the Nile?*, a comedy performed written in collaboration with a local theater group. Staged in the gallery, the play incorporated works on view through verbal or visual references. The play helped the audience to understand the workings of the Nile and its meaning for the ancient Egyptians.

Articles in recent issues of *History News,* the AASLH magazine, illustrate the use of drama as part of the interpretation of historic houses and sites. Professional playwrights have been hired to research and prepare scripts and professional actors are used to present them to the visitors. At the Hermann-Grima Historic House in New Orleans a troupe of professional actors presented a series of scenes recreating 19th-century daily life in the house. Carefully researched from primary materials, the play depicts the events in a day during the cholera epidemic in the city and illustrates its effects on the slaves, freemen of color and owners of the home. They play was offered 10 times a day for six days. Tryon Palace in New Bern, North Carolina hired a professional theater company to write, produce and act out a play that required hundred of hours of research. Tyron Palace served as the royal governors' residence and the center of government prior to the Revolutionary War. Nine scripts are staged in the palace and surrounding areas. Summer visitors may come across a number of different character vignettes during their one-day tour or return in the evening to see one of two historical dramas with five characters created from extensive research.

The Association of Science and Technology Centers has published a book, *A Stage for Science: Dramatic Techniques for Science/Technology Centers*, which provides a useful overview of the range of activities that museums consider to be a part of a theater format. In addition, this book provides examples of dialogue and screenplays that describe the techniques that were used by different science centers.

Some museum theater requires substantial amounts of research, finances, and staff. To make the investment effective for the museum and potential audiences, promotion and public relations efforts are essential.

CONCLUSION

Each of the previous teaching strategies is presented out of context. They are elements of an entire tour, which may include a number of these strategies during the one-hour or full-day program that the museum offers. Perhaps the most important thing for the museum educator to consider is the appropriate selection of teaching techniques for each audience. In developing the tour, the museum staff must be clear about what they want the students to learn—whether it is facts, concepts, generalizations—and must choose an appropriate combination of activity experiences, information, sequence of activities, and objects from the collection.

In developing a museum tour for students, the museum must know what audience they will be serving, the number of people to be accommodated, the length of time that they will be in the museum, and whether it is a single- or multiple-visit program. The tour should make use of the museum's exhibits or collections. Objectives should be clear, teachers must know the most important objectives, the types of activities, and sequence of activities that will take place throughout the program. Museums should provide guidelines regarding the rules for behavior.

Increasingly, museums have been concerned with providing effective interpretive programs to the disabled visitor. Many offer grants to its staff to attend special training programs and seminars that have increased their sensitivity to working with handicapped visitors or presented workshops in cooperation with other local museums. Museums have coordinated sensitivity sessions, held by groups representing different disabled conditions, for all levels of staff and volunteers. Several museums offer tours using total communication techniques, which communicate with hearing impaired visitors. In addition, museums have included on tours artifacts that can be handled and can represent various periods and cultures in the collections. Free audio tours, exhibition brochures in braille and large print, raised-line maps, three-dimensional museum models, and braille and large-print guides all help visually impaired visitors. Numerous articles, books, and journals have reported on effective museum programs for the disabled museum visitor. Of special note are the two issues of *Roundtable Reports: The Journal of Museum Education,* (Volume 6, No. 2 and No. 3); and the materials available from the National Endowment for the Arts and the National Committee on the Arts and the Handicapped.

Interpreting collections is not confined to the previous list of teaching techniques. Interpretation is a combination of labels, printed information, instruction, self-guided tours, electronic guides, and personalized interpretation. Teaching techniques help children to learn how to see, ask questions, make judgments about things that they have never seen. Effectively used, teaching techniques require great sensitivity in the use of voice and gestures, as they increase the students' abilities to think and heighten their perceptual awareness. Effective interpreters must have information, skill at presenting this information, and the patience to work with the audience. They must learn how to create relationships and to encourage the visitors to think rather than simply listen. Skilled interpreters will help the visitor to visualize and participate in different times and places.

Many of the previous teaching techniques illustrate the importance of visitors enjoying their experience in the museum. Fun, play, laughter, and happiness are qualities often desired by museum educators as part of the learning experience. Professionals are becoming aware that a combination of information and enjoyment can lead to a more productive memory about the museum and can make learning that has taken place last longer with more meaning. Anticipating the coming interests in expanding the role of the museum as an institution involved in formal education and aware that learning can be fun, Alma Wittlin made the following observation:

> *No justification seems to exist, or a distinction between 'education' and 'enjoyment' as two separate functions of a museum, especially in connection with the objects of aesthetic quality, which are sources of general education contributing to intellectual and emotional sensitization. It should indeed be one of the tasks of the museum of the future to convince people of the fallacy of a distinction in principle between enjoyment and learning, and of ample possibilities of combining both in one and the same experience.*

References

Alderson, William T., and Shirley Payne Low. *Interpretation of Historic Sites.* Nashville: American Association for State and Local History, 1976.

Alexander, Mary, Byers, CeCe and Freivogel, Elsie. "History in the Raw, A Documentary Approach to Civil Rights." *Social Education* (November/December, 1978) pp. 563–564.

Baldi, Mary Lou. *Environmental Living Program.* Washington, D.C.: Government Printing Office, 1976.

Elder, Betty. "Drama for Interpretation. *History News* 36 (June 81) pp. 8–11.

Floyd, Candace. "Education at Old Economy: Programs Children can Understand," *History News* 35 (March 1980) pp. 12–14.

Friedman, Alan; Lowery, Lawrence; Pulos, Steven, and Sneider, Cary. *Planetarium Educator's Workshop Guide.* Rochester, New York: International Planetarium Society, 1980.

Gaffney, Maureen and Laybourne, Gerry Bond. *What To Do When The Lights Go On: A Comprehensive Guide to 16 mm Films and Related Activities for Children.* Phoenix: The Oryx Press, 1980.

Grinell, Sheila. *A Stage for Science: Dramatic Techniques at Science-Technology Centers.* Washington: The Association of Science/Technology Centers, 1979.

Hancock, Paula and Morris, Kelly. *Handbook for Guides, Part I.* Atlanta: The High Museum of Art, 1978.

Krockover, Gerald, and Hauck, Jeannette. "Training for Docent: How to Talk to Visitors," Technical Leaflet #125, American Association for State and Local History, March 1980.

McGathery, Glenn, and Hartmann, Martha. "Museums as a Teaching Resource; An Inquiry Approach," *Science and Children,* 11 (November 1973) pp. 11–13.

Postman, Neil, and Weingartner, Charles N. *Teaching As a Subversive Activity.* New York: Delacorte, 1969.

Tilden, Freeman. *Interpreting Our Heritage.* Chapel Hill: University of North Carolina Press, 1957.

Wittlin, Alma S. *The History Museum: Its History and Its Task in Education.* London: 1949.

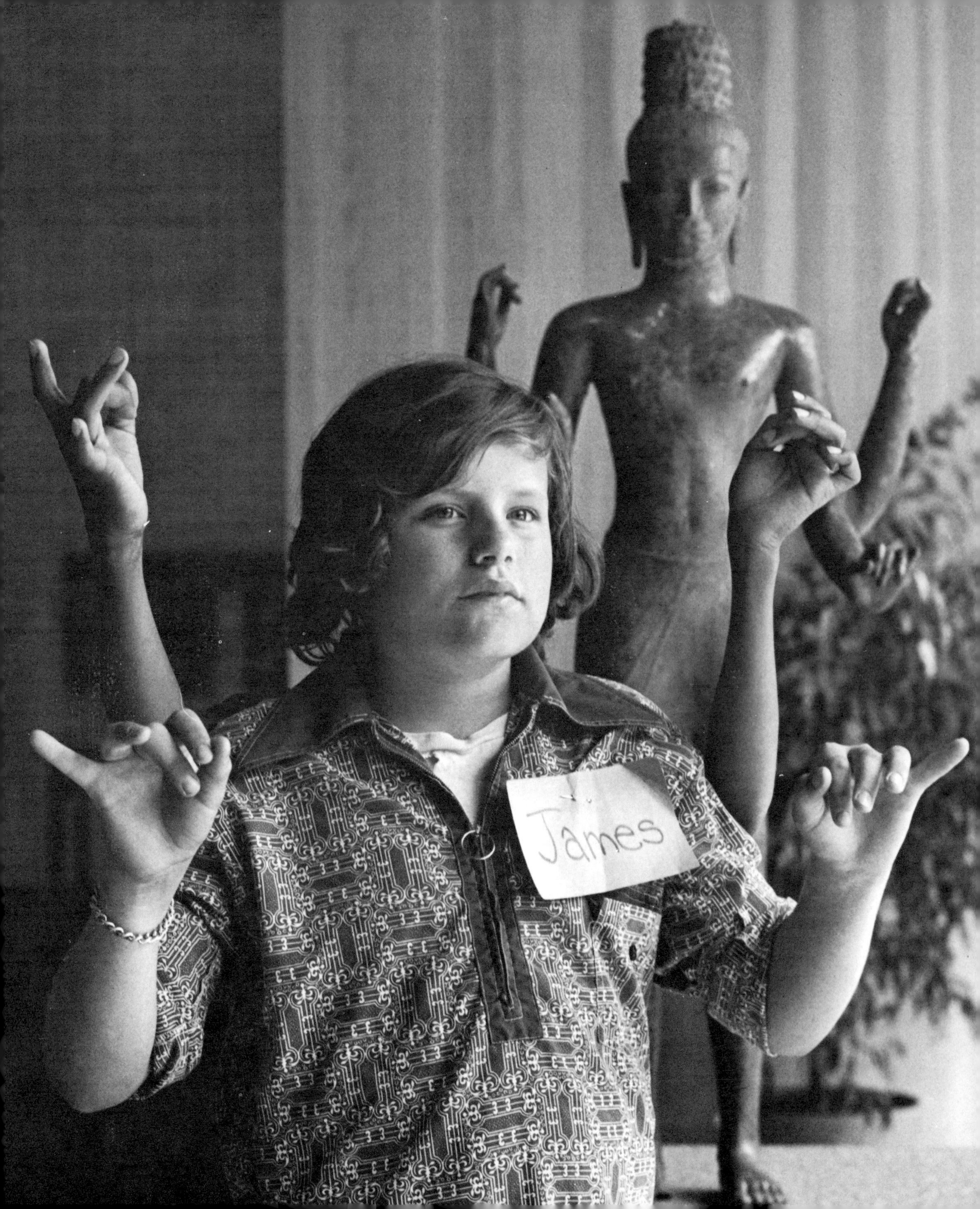
James

5. MUSEUMS AND SCHOOLS

Although as educational institutions museums and schools both educate children, they are fundamentally different in what and how they teach. For example, schools educate using words, while museums educate using objects and exhibits. This difference is important, since some children learn best using concrete object experience, while words, being abstract, do not have the same impact.

Museums are places where informal learning takes place: people come by choice, no credentials or prerequisites are required, and the audience is heterogeneous with diverse ages, interests, and social, economic and educational backgrounds. Social interaction, especially among family groups, is essential and desired. Schools are based on the study of different subject areas and are organized into curricula that require different levels of performance to move forward academically. In schools, schedules are set, days are regulated, goals are met or attempted, and tests are given. Children in a school class generally represent a specific range of social and economic backgrounds although their interest levels may vary tremendously.

Museums house real objects or exhibits available to students and teachers for study. In museums, children can see firsthand objects in art, history, and science that are only described in books. At their best, museums use their collections to build on the learners' interests, needs, and capacities for acquiring more information. The recognition that museums are not schools with a curriculum to be studied, from kindergarten through college, has opened the doors for the development of a tremendous number of different programs, relationships, and accomplishments.

Many articles, studies, and books, most notably *The Art Museum as Educator* and articles in *Roundtable Reports*, have discussed the philosophical and practical issues of museums and schools working together. Some writers caution against programs that are directly related to the curriculum, while others feel this is necessary to ensure success and support from the community. Some feel museums should take their collections or reproductions to the classroom, while others only offer programs in the museum. Some advocate a commitment to single visit tours, while others feel museums should only offer series programs. There have been many successes and failures, and much debate about the appropriate age level and the content of school programs.

The reader should review the literature and make decisions based on the goals of the museum, its collection, staff, and financial resources. The needs of the school system, children, and community, as well as the existing and potential relationships that can be developed, must also be considered. This chapter is based on the assumption that museums and schools need each other, and that by narrowing their differences, effective programs can be developed.

COLLABORATIVE PLANNING

When museums and schools decide to develop programs together, there are two points of view. The school teacher is concerned with curriculum priorities and wants the time in the museum to respond to these issues, enhancing the students' understanding of their studies. The museum educator is concerned with the interpretation and use of the collections that can work effectively within the museum's goals and involve the students. School teachers have had little experience in working directly with real objects, museum educators have had limited experience working in the classroom or with a curriculum.

Bringing the classroom teacher and museum educator together is important. Sometimes this happens gradually because a successful relationship has been developed between the local school system and the museum over the years. Other times, special grants require the two educational institutes to work together for the first time. Joint planning and the implementation of a museum/school program is not an easy task. Working together requires willingness and commitment from both parties. Alberta Sebolt notes:

Collaboration means you are willing to work together to create, develop, design, and implement a program which you both want. Most of all, collaboration means a promise of time spent in learning about and from each other, while planning a program to address learner needs through clearly defined objectives.

Facilitating a collaborative planning process can be the responsibility of the museum, the school, or a separate organization. The Cultural Education Collaborative in Boston and Museums Collaborative of New York City represent two service organizations that help bridge the gap between museums and schools. These organizations facilitate the exchange of ideas and resources between museums and schools.

Because of the important and very special nature of collaborative school/museum planning and programming, some guidelines will be offered, which should be combined with earlier discussions of designing exhibitions and programs.

Basic decisions must be made before the planning process begins: why is the program or service being developed; what problem or need of the school or museum will be addressed; what resources are available, including money; and how much time will be provided for planning. Answers to such questions are necessary if interest and support is to be obtained for a planning phase.

A planning team should be developed and time provided for them to do their work. The size and composition of the planning group will vary with individual programs, but might include curriculum supervisors, resource specialists, principals, teachers, parents, curators, and museum educators. Students, the ultimate audience, should be consulted. A significant advantages of a joint planning effort is that the various individuals involved gain respect for each other's ideas, needs and concerns as they structure the goals and objectives, and implement and revise the program. The resolution of the differences and learning to understand the needs of different constituents will do much to ensure an effective program based on cooperation instead of competition. The added advantage is that a group of individuals will be committed to the museum's program because it also satisfies their needs as teachers.

Planners should define the program, content, goals, objectives, teaching strategies, and scheduling after considering various options. The planning group may change: new people will be added and some will rotate out as the program's requirements are more clearly articulated. Accounts of the meetings and decisions should be kept and agreed upon. The full planning group should review all plans and decisions.

Similar to all planning processes, the group should:
- identify the reasons for developing the program or service
- develop goals and objectives
- identify the resources needed to successfully implement the program
- identify and secure funds for the program
- identify the audience: students' learning level, interests, demands on their time; and teachers' interest, commitment time, background
- develop time tables for publicity, training, implementing, and evaluating
- consider options for resource and program formats for students and teachers
- define the roles and responsibilities of the museum, the student, the classroom teachers and the school administration
- review the logistics of the program with everyone involved, from guards to principals
- involve key administrative persons, i.e., principals, the curriculum supervisor, and director.
- train the museum staff, volunteers and teachers
- try out the program or service and assess its effectiveness
- make changes
- continue to revise and improve, listening to both learners and teachers

- consider the future of the program
- maintain open communications with the planning group and the clients
- generate information about the program, keeping people informed and expanding the base of support and interest in the project.

Careful attention to the program's logistics is essential. Principals and teachers are keenly aware of the school calendar, daily schedule, placement in the curriculum, space, materials distribution and times available for training. Arrangements with libraries, media centers, or the museum for slides, films, records, tapes, or books must be formalized and coordinated in advance. Schedules for school holidays, tests and lunch is essential information. The best of programs will have only minimal impact if the students and teachers are preoccupied with these events.

Realizing the importance of first impressions, the Cultural Education Collaborative of Boston requires that museums and schools share descriptions of the students, curriculum priorities, previous programs, and the museum's resources with each other at the initial meeting. Their representatives discuss learning strategies that each has found effective with students, exchange information and perceptions about each other, and discuss expectations. Agendas for future meetings depend on the project.

Securing the support of key officials is important. Depending on the scope of the project, this could be the curriculum supervisor and/or superintendent, as well as the museum director and curators. Their support and interest can make many things happen, including the time to coordinate schedules and resources. School principals, an essential link in the program, control schedules, allocations of physical space, funds and resources. Help principals to become advocates for utilizing museums. Curriculum supervisors are especially important in the development of curriculum-related programs, and can also assist with training sessions for teachers and arrange for in-service credits. Regular communication with museum and school administrators strengthens commitment to cooperation.

The Wichita Public School's Office of Museum Programs, which is responsible for coordinating the schools' programs with local art, history, and Indian museums, has developed written and signed statements defining the relationship between the museums, the school district, and director of the Office of Museum Programs. These signed documents ensure that the participants recognize the program and are aware of each institution's responsibilities.

FUNDING MUSEUM/SCHOOL PROGRAMS

Adequate funding is essential to the successful implementation of museum/school programs. Early in development, realistic budgets and sources of financial support must be identified and secured. Museums and schools have supported their work together in many ways.

Museums:
- absorb the costs of school programs in their general operating budget
- receive special grants
- receive funds through contracts for services provided from the school
- charge a fee per child or class

Schools:
- assign a staff person to work at the museum
- receive special grants
- allocate resources
- pay fees per class
- pay through contracts for services provided

Museums traditionally have close relationships with local school systems. In fact, some museums were founded by teachers interested in providing additional educational opportunities to students (e.g., The Children's Museum of Boston, the Fort Worth Museum of Science and History, and the Jacksonville Children's Museum). Founded by the DeKalb Board of Education in Atlanta, the Fernbank Science Center is an integral part of the public school system offering numerous classes for credit to the students and teachers. The science center also prepares exhibits and after-school programs in the physical, natural and life sciences. Teachers have found museum programs that travel to the schools effectively provide richer learning environments that allow them to use objects as they relate to the child's experience. Since 1975, the Office of Museum Programs, which operates within the Curriculum

Services Division of the Witchita Public Schools, has been in charge of an interpretive museum education program that designs exhibits and media programs, circulates them in the schools, and coordinates the activities of public school students in the education programs at other local museums.

Some state and local education departments annually contract with museums to pay for students' participation in certain programs. The contract or grant fee reimburses the museum for its educational services: professional time, materials, and facilities. Compared to the cost of doing the program in the classroom—including purchasing supplies, hiring and training the teachers, and buying the textbooks—this arrangement often is a bargain. One disadvantage of "per student" allocations is that the museum may become involved in a "numbers game." Sometimes, as well, a museum must provide services that are not in line with its objectives.

Six different examples of contractual arrangements follow:

1. The school visits program sponsored by the State Department of Education gives Massachusetts public, private and parochial school children a free visit to the Museum of Science, Boston including one major program free. To qualify, students must come in organized school groups during the school year, and teachers must make reservations in advance. The museum permits return visits at no additional charge, including one free program with each visit, for groups in sequential programs. Student passes, good for a return visit, are distributed at the museum or by mail to schools, one pass for every 30 students enrolled.

2. The Pacific Science Center receives funds from the state superintendent of public instruction, who in turn seeks authorization from the state legislature to contract with the museum for the school services. These services include itemized per-capita costs, class visits and teacher training. Evaluations are an integral part of these contracts and the program includes an annual report, which is circulated throughout the state.

3. The Cultural Education Collaborative in Boston has received funding for more than six years from the Bureau of Equal Educational Opportunities of the Massachusetts Department of Education to support schools working with the museums, performing arts organizations, and science and art centers to provide learning experiences in integrated settings.

4. The Cleveland Museum of Art's program with the East Cleveland elementary schools is paid for by the local board of education. The program, in operation since 1971, offers studio projects and classes that use a variety of art forms in the classroom, combined with a full week "residency" at the art museum and other participating cultural institutions. Extensive teacher training opportunities are presented. The school district has obtained funding for this program through different grants from the U.S. Department of Education and state subsidies.

5. The School Voucher program of the Museums Collaborative, which links selected New York City schools and cultural institutions, delivers quality cultural education to students. It stimulates the participating museums to offer new educational services in direct response to the schools' needs. Modeled after the community voucher program, the School Voucher program gives the selected schools "cultural vouchers," or limited lines of credit, which enable each school to buy individualized educational services and programs from participating museums. The museums redeem the vouchers for payment at Museum's Collaborative. In addition to the funds in the form of vouchers, the program provides a training component for teachers and their principals, skills and funds to develop curriculum materials, a newsletter sharing information about exemplary programs, and transportation for student trips.

6. The Charlotte Nature Museum in North Carolina, and the Philadelphia Museum of Art are among the museums that have teachers assigned to the museum from the local school boards. Such an allocation currently may be easier for the school district because it may have more tenured teachers than dispersible cash. On the positive side, the teacher or coordinator can bring to the museum a knowledge of the curriculum and resource materials currently being used by the system and of the types of programs that appeal to both teachers and children. Knowledge of the school system, its schedules, and regulations is also an advantage when developing new programs. However, a school coordinator may insist that everything fit too carefully within particular curricula without recognizing the special qualities of a museum and the uniqueness of its collections.

Numerous programs have been developed by museums with federal grants. These programs require a close working relationship between the museum and the school district to benefit the training of teachers, development of curriculum-related resource materials, and in-depth programming for the children. Federal support has come from many different programs at the Department of Education, National Endowments for the Arts and Humanities, National Science Foundation, and other agencies, including the Departments of Labor, Justice and Commerce. Attention must be given to developing programs that meet the guidelines. Museums should only develop programs that are compatible with their philosophical and program goals, should not design programs that divert their precious resources.

Continuity of funding should be an initial and continuing objective. A united effort can strengthen the appeal to funding sources.

SCHOOLS VISIT MUSEUMS

Group tours are still the most popular organized program between museums and schools. Many programs relate to the curriculum studied at specific grade levels, while others focus solely on the collections and techniques for observing and analyzing. The advantages of joint planning have been outlined; nevertheless, many successful programs are operating that were independently developed. The following section of museum/school programs reviews a range of activities that can be designed to take place in the museum. Arbitrarily, only a few example programs are given in each category. The *Program Descriptions* section provides additional examples in each category.

Self-guided programs have been developed by museums to accommodate school groups when the guided programs are booked or for teachers interested in undertaking programs they have designed. Printed materials, audiovisual resources, loan kits, and teacher-training sessions provide assistance to the teachers.
- The Museum of Science and Industry, Chicago, has a "Teacher's Guide" designed to help teachers develop their own tours, selecting demonstrations and exhibits that relate most effectively to the curriculum. The guide describes all the exhibits and demonstrations, and a subject index helps teachers focus on different curriculum areas. Demonstrations must be reserved in advance.
- The New York Aquarium offers two-hour orientation sessions for teachers who wish to learn how to utilize the aquarium as a teaching resource. The program illustrates they need not be marine biologists to help their children have an exciting and meaningful learning experience at the aquarium. Simulation games, beach walks, behind-the-scenes tours, and audiovisual presentations expose teachers to many pre- and post-visit activities for all grade levels. Any teacher bringing a class between April and June must attend the workshop.
- An historic waterfront neighborhood in the old seaport town of Portsmouth, New Hampshire, Strawberry Banke is site-specific rather than time-specific. Unlike most outdoor museums, it does not limit its interpretation to a given period in the past but rather interprets the entire neighborhood history to the present. The neighborhood is made up of 30 structures ranging in appearance from the 17th to the 20th century. In order to help children understand how and why the neighborhood changed over time, a field trip booklet helps the children to make comparisons among the various museum houses and their own homes.
- The Cleveland Museum of Art's audiovisual center shows slide tapes to school groups unable to obtain a guided tour and before staff-led tours. Averaging five to 15 minutes, the slide/tape programs help the students focus on the works of art they will encounter in the exhibits. There are over 50 slide tapes available: one examines the many details and images on a mummy case, another focuses on a succession of details in a small 15th century painting, while another introduces the African and Asian art collections. After viewing the tapes, the class visits the galleries with an increased interest in looking closely at the objects.

A **Single-visit tour** is one of the most popular program formats. Such programs will introduce children and teachers to the resources of the collection, develop some basic perceptual skills, convey information, and encourage return visits. While a one- or two-hour tour, is, in reality, only a preliminary introduction to the museum, these programs sometimes relate to the curriculum, involve demonstrations, and handling collections, as well as looking at the collections.

- The Museum of Science, Boston, has developed Project Eye-Opener for children in Title I programs. During the 90-minute special introductory tour, they listen to their own voice over the telephone, stand "shoulder-to-toe" with a dinosaur, and watch a baby chick hatch. A highlight is a visit to the Live Animal Room, where everyone gets a chance to pet the animals. The emphasis is on a personal introduction to the museum so that the children feel comfortable in the environment and understand the basic purpose of the institution.
- The Newark Museum in New Jersey offers one-hour single visit programs on topics in history, science, and art for grades one and up. A sample program on Tibet might include a visit to the Buddhist altar and meditation room; examination of displays of Tibetan ritual objects, musical instruments, painting and sculpture; and a film on religion.
- The Hagley Museum in Wilmington, Delaware, offers an energy tour to grades K to 12, which introduces the way water and steam provided industrial power in the 1800s and how they produce electricity to operate the museum today. By observing and operating models of a water-wheel, a water-turbine system, and a steam engine students learn how each provides power and compare these to the operating hydroelectric plant. A pre-visit kit includes a poster of each machine, slides, lesson plans, and study materials from the Department of Energy and the National Science Teachers Association.
- The McAllen International Museum in Texas coordinates all of its school programs with the kindergarten to sixth grade curriculums of its local district. Students come to the museum each year for a program on a different topic. Thus, by the sixth grade, students have been to the museum seven times. The programs vary from a puppet show, *Tale of a Toothache*, and a gallery tour, or an exploration of different ranch communities to man as a symbol maker, which examines symbols in commercial logos, mathematics, music, and gesture.

Series visit programs have become increasingly popular as museums seek to provide more information. Single visit tours can expose children to the resources but the time limitations constrain the amount and level of learning that takes place. Series visits provide opportunities for a more focused look at the collections, more experiences, and more time in the museums. They also let teachers work in training sessions or actually design the program, relating it to the curriculum. The advantages of such programming includes increased information and time in the galleries and opportunities for workshops, studios and demonstrations. The most obvious disadvantage is the reduced number of students that can be served. Successful in-depth programs often include pre- and post-visit materials and teacher workshops, all designed to increase the quality of the museum learning experience.

- The Honolulu Academy of Arts offers a six-session art enrichment program to fifth graders in 16 different schools. The program consists of six gallery tours followed by studio workshops that develop the students' perceptual awareness and understanding of the materials and creative processes used by artists in different cultures. There are two sessions each on painting and printmaking, and one each on sculpture and patterns. Utilizing the full range of the museum's collections, including Oriental, ancient, Renaissance and modern art, students compare and contrast artistic styles, techniques, and materials.

○ The National Museum of Natural History, at the Smithsonian Institution in Washington, offers a three-part program for junior and senior high school students on geology and art. Integrated with the history curriculum of the public schools, the program includes sessions on Potomac geology and building stones, a tour examining the federal buildings for materials, and a final session on the architecture and styles seen around Pennsylvania Avenue. A teacher workshop, which precedes scheduling of the classes, reviews the logistics and content of the program.

○ G.A.M.E., in New York City, works with teachers to design individual theme programs that complement the class curriculum and involve three consecutive two-hour visits. Teachers participate in a pre-visit teacher workshop, and receive or develop pre- and post-visit materials for their students. The themes, developed using the museum exhibit areas, include perception (eye and brain, dimensions, shadows, illusions); culture-neighborhood in transition (a multimedia three-generational study of four ethnic families from the Upper West Side); and natural science (Central Park Pond, horticulture, insects and animals).

Courses for credit, offered by museums in association with school districts, have increased as the philosophy of public education has changed from the traditional structured classes to an expanded use of community organizations and environments. In offering courses for credit to either the elementary or secondary students, the museum must pay close attention to curriculum requirements and must be prepared to meet all the specifications set forth by the board of education. Students who enroll in these programs work at the museum as they would at school. In some communities, such as Boston, the Cultural Education Collaborative serves as a broker for certain types of grants, helps pair the schools and museums, and handles the administrative work with the school department. In other communities, the museum and school work together to plan, administer, implement, and evaluate these programs.

○ The Dallas Museum of Natural History offers courses for credit under the guidance of a biology teacher from the Dallas Independent School District. Curators assist with individual instruction and acquaint students with the museum's resources and collections, which are used as part of the course of study.

○ The Cleveland Health Education Museum provides in-depth programs on health education for six weeks, two hours per day, as part of the school curriculum. Students have produced their own closed-circuit television programs on health care, and learn about careers in health and such specialized topics as preventive medicine and sports medicine.

○ The Blanford Nature Center of the Grand Rapids Public Museum in Michigan has a Museum School Environmental Program. At the end of the fifth grade, 50 to 60 academically talented students who are interested in rugged outdoor activities are selected by their teachers and principals and bussed daily to the Nature Center. There, making use of the entire facility for their course of study, the students are trained as junior interpreter-guides for first and second grade classes on a ratio of one interpreter to two children. They also operate a chicken-egg business with a flock of 150 chickens at the Center's demonstration farm.

○ The Brooks Memorial Art Gallery in Memphis, Tennessee coordinates Arts and the Basic Curriculum, or the ABC Program. Ten fourth grade classes from various schools visit the gallery seven times a year. The program integrates the arts into the child's daily curriculum, stressing and interpreting the curriculum. Lesson plans, written according to the needs of the teacher, involve all areas—social studies, math, science, and language arts. Lessons include classroom preparation by the teacher, a gallery activity that connects the classroom activity with the art works, and follow-up activities, as well as objectives, materials and evaluation for use by the teacher.

Internships provide personal work-related educational experiences for high school students. Careful selection and placement of students can result in a cohesive and vital extension of the museum's permanent staff. Many school districts permit students to earn credit for the successful completion of internships, which take place during a single semester or over a full academic year. The museum staff must be committed to working with the interns to ensure a real understanding of the museum's operations.

- Students from the High School Executive Internship Program and other similar programs work with the executive director and director of education at the Queens Botanical Garden, learning the scope of the museum's administrative and programmatic work.
- The Jewish Museum works with interns for a full semester, during which they are trained to conduct tours and special education programs on a regular basis.
- The Metropolitan Museum of Art apprenticeship program place students in more than 26 departments of the museum, including photography, American art, bookkeeping, special publications, and education. Half of their time is spent on departmental projects, exploring the collections, participating in special activities, and taking guided visits with staff members to gain an overview of this complex institution. The remaining time is spent helping their department with routine work. During the school year, interns receive credit for working either for parttime over 12 weeks, or fulltime for four to six weeks in work-study programs. Summer apprentices receive a small honorarium for their one month of service.

Many variations of each of these program formats exist, dictated by the particular qualities of the museum, the school, and the community. Schools often prefer single-visit programs due to the cost of bussing students and the requirements for reorganizing schedules. Nevertheless, the more time the students spend at the museum, the more likely the program will result in a higher quality learning experience. Teacher training programs and resource materials will help the museum work with teachers in advance of visits and will help tailor programs to their needs.

SCHEDULING A MUSEUM PROGRAM

"We would like to bring the class to the museum, but. . . ." "The place is so big. . . ." "There are 45 children in my class. . . ." "My students are deaf. . . ." "They do not seem to get much out of the experiences. . . ." "Where can we eat lunch?"

How students respond to the museum depends largely upon the orientation provided before the visit. The classroom teacher must, among other things, explain that the museum experience is not just another field trip. Very young children may fear that the animals in natural history exhibits are alive or they may think that they were killed expressly for the display. Students may have been told not to touch anything, a problem to overcome if the museum is providing a "hands-on" participatory experience. Then again, they may be disappointed if this museum is not the one with the mummy.

In the best of circumstances, both the staff and teachers should prepare prior to arrival at the museum's door. Contact between teachers and the museum is important if the children are to get the most out of the experience. A museum can accommodate only so many students at one time because of gallery space and the number of available docents or staff. The schedule, therefore, should include specifics about the numbers of students allowed in each group. Most museums try to keep a ratio of one teacher to 5-15 children. Docents who have to maneuver 25 to 30 children through a museum are at a real disadvantage. Obviously, the children are handicapped too, since it is both difficult to concentrate and to see the cases when the group is too large.

Publicity sent to the school should be lively and colorful. The materials should get off the principal's desk and up on the teachers' bulletin board where teachers will notice it. Facilities and resources for handicapped children should always be indicated.

The museum's scheduling secretary receiving the tour requests, should record the number of students, age or grade level, arrival time, special needs of students, and areas of interest. A staff member or docent calls the teachers a few days before the visit to discuss the

children's needs and interests. A brochure sent to the schools should include general information on the museum: collections, exhibits, hours, telephone number and address. It should also contain:
- appropriate ages for programs and resources
- hours and length of the program
- numbers of students and chaperones per class
- brief, lively, and informative description of the program
- admission rates, if any
- facilities and resources for handicapped visitors
- facilities for lunches, if any
- resource center or library if open to the teacher
- other types of activities or resources available at the museum for children or teachers.

Confirmation procedures are equally important. This can remind the teachers of their roles and responsibilities regarding the visit to the museum, as well as of the programs and resources available to them. The following information should be considered for inclusion:
- times, dates, name of docent or museum staff
- number of chaperones
- contact person at the museum
- the ratio of children to museum staff or volunteers
- check-in procedures—where, how, and parking facilities
- regulations about name tags, cameras, pencils, coats
- review of the *types* of activities in which the students will be involved
- a "free pass" to encourage a prelimary visit by the teacher
- list of resource materials available: slide kits, loan kits, etc.

Necessary museum preparations include:
- ascertain arrival and departure times
- determine entrances and exits; notify guards
- plan tour routes to avoid bottlenecks and noise problems
- discuss methods of handling behavior problems
- arrange for appropriate materials and supplies for demonstrations or participatory activities
- allow time to explain museum policies, introduce the subject, and review the learning experience
- make provisions to accommodate handicapped children
- plan drinking fountain and bathroom stops

Good communication is essential to a well-planned tour. The scheduling secretary or person responsible for touring with the group should discuss specific plans with the teacher and the teacher's reasons for visiting the museum. The programs offered should be sufficiently flexible to interest the teachers and children and to adapt to their individual needs. Accommodating the expectations of the students and teachers, being able to attend to their interests, and encouraging their enthusiasm for the subject matter, will assist the museum in providing high quality educational programs.

OUTREACH PROGRAMS

For more than 100 years, museums have been offering outreach programs to people who would not otherwise have contact with museums. Museums have designed programs that send lecturers, docents, resource boxes, exhibits, slide sets, reproductions, scientific equipment, and original artifacts to classrooms and community groups. Some programs work within a single neighborhood, while others reach out to the entire state. Teaching sets were sent to New York schools by the American Museum of Natural History in the 1890s. The Newark Museum displayed exhibits of paintings and sculpture reproductions in seven branches of the public library in 1929, and the Children's Museum of Boston has circulated loan kits since its founding in 1913.

At the end of the last century, art and natural history museums began loaning lantern slides to teachers; today, slide programs, videotapes, films, and posters are used in their place. Reproductions of paintings and artifacts have been popular throughout the years because they are inexpensive, available in quantity, and allow students to closely examine and handle objects. Study collections have been circulated successfully by some institutions for many years. Art and history museums generally loan reproductions and audiovisual materials, such as slides, films, photographs, and tapes. Science and natural history museums have less difficulty in lending their study collections for classroom use because the specimens or resources are available in greater quantity. Outreach programs also include visits to the classroom by museum staff and volunteers. Live animals, costumes, pioneer household possessions, and scientific equipment travel to classes in station wagons, mobile vans, slide carousels, and suitcase exhibits and trunks.

Outreach programs, usually organized around a theme, may be offered locally or statewide. Whatever the format, outreach programs are designed to further children's understanding of the museum and the topics, and illustrate the sponsoring museum's commitment to reaching schools and the general public.

Developing outreach programs requires the involvement of the clients or users in the development phase and the testing of programs and materials. Unless the programs are useful, informative, attractively packaged, and understandably relevant, they will not be used. Handbooks or user guides should be thoughtfully prepared, and workshops should be given to clarify the teacher's role and to demonstrate how to use the materials. Outreach materials should be tested, revised, and tested again. While in circulation, the materials should be examined regularly so that each user finds them in good order.

The content of an outreach program must be carefully worked out. Using the museum's collections and exhibitions, the program can relate directly to the collections or augment the classroom curriculum. It can precede a museum visit or substitute for one. The program's objectives, content, and activities must be relevant if the program is to be used. Although outreach programs can span a wide variety of topics, resources, and activities, they all should actively involve the student in the learning process and provide ideas for projects that can be undertaken following the program.

In large measure, the relationship between the museum and the users—schools systems or community groups—will determine the success of an outreach program. The school districts and individual teachers can help inform other potential users about the programs and how to use them. Museum staff should observe the programs or kits in classroom use. Respect the teachers' comments about the program's usefulness, relevance, ease of equipment operation, and success with students.

Programs or materials can be designed for use without guidance, although some may require a workshop prior to their use. If materials supplement the curriculum, the teacher must feel confident in their use and know when it is appropriate to schedule them.

Developing and operating loan programs costs money. The staff must have time to plan with the potential users, do research, develop the materials, test them, revise them, and pay attention to them. If the museum operates a vehicle, it needs space to store it and funds to repair it. All loan programs result in a certain amount of wear, damage, and loss of the materials, ranging from a single slide or glass frame to the motor in a van. Development and user costs must be determined in advance. Insurance is an important expense item, the type and amount of insurance depending on the materials in circulation. Determine who pays the costs for what expenses: users' fees can pay for the development and operation of a program or only a portion of these costs. The museum should know the total costs of outreach programs,—planning, research, production, development, scheduling, shipping, evaluating, replacing, and recirculating—so that the user's fees and costs to the museum are acknowledged and accounted for.

Logistics are also important to managing loan programs. The teachers and schools must know in advance what type of equipment, space, lighting, security and other requirements will be needed. Some museums vans or mobile programs require specific electrical and waterline set-ups in addition to parking space. Announcing the arrival of mobile exhibits to the entire community can usefully extend the outreach program. Advance preparations and publicity must be accomplished; generally the museum works with local sponsors.

Careful **scheduling** of the loan programs or visiting resource specialists is critical to the success of the program. Some programs, like the Trip-Out-Trucks of the Fine Arts Museum in San Francisco, make regularly scheduled stops at specified locations in the community and special one-time visits at others.

At some museums, such as the Children's Museum of Indianapolis and the St. Louis Art Museum, resource centers are responsible for coordinating, producing, and scheduling loan programs and for workshops. Numerous systems exist for scheduling, confirming, and collecting materials. Each of those museums has developed a method based on the requirements of the loan materials, number of pieces in circulation, and the museum's ability to administer the program.

The involvement of teachers and curriculum supervisors in the development of programs can improve their quality and usability. Still, the museum's outreach efforts are in large measure dependent on the school system's or individual teacher's desire to use them and ability to pay for them, as well as the museum's logistic and scheduling assistance.

The following programs simply illustrate the range of activities that museums currently offer; a more complete picture of what museums are doing to effectively reach into the classroom and the community is included in the *Program Descriptions* section.

Resource specialists, either staff members or volunteers, visit classrooms taking original art works, live animals, reproductions, scientific equipment or slide programs. The presentations vary in length from 20 minutes to two hours and can reach an unlimited number of children. These programs are often very effective in reaching handicapped and hospitalized audiences. In general, the specialists visit schools located within an hour's driving distance of the museum.

The success of these programs depends on the ability of the resource specialist to communicate effectively and to involve the teachers and students. Care should be taken so that the resource specialists do not arrive when the school is not expecting them. The teacher shall not consider this a "break period," leaving the specialist alone with the students. These programs may exist as self-contained units or as pre-requisites to a museum tour.

- The Maryland Science Center in Baltimore offers a traveling science program for grades five through eight in geology, chemistry, and environmental studies. Equipment and materials are brought to the classroom for lecture/demonstrations or laboratory workshop sessions at the request of the teachers.
- At the Dallas Museum of Natural History in Texas, docents visit grades two through six classrooms with portable exhibit cases containing mounted animal specimens and supplementary materials with follow-up activities. During the 30-minute presentation, the children examine the specimens and ask questions.
- The Siouxland and Heritage Museum in South Dakota takes small, live native animals, birds and reptiles to the classroom for a demonstration and discussion of their habits and habitat. Students handle the animals and observe their behavior. The museum educator uses the inquiry method to elicit responses and to encourage the children, in preschool through the third grade, to look carefully at the animals and to consider where they live, how they eat, and survive.
- The Whitney Museum of American Art in New York City offers a slide/lecture and discussion workshop conducted in the classrooms by a museum teacher. Students are introduced to contemporary art works that relate to their experience of the world. Art exercises, which reinforce the ideas discussed, follow the lecture.
- The National Portrait Gallery in Washington, D.C. offers a series of programs that require a classroom

visit by a staff member or docent, followed by a gallery tour. Topics, such as the trial of John Brown or westward expansion, are available to grades seven to 12. The 45-minute classroom presentation includes written and visual materials that set the stage for role-playing. Students assume specific roles, confront problems, and determine priorities as they might in pioneering a new community or telling a museum director which portraits should be collected.

- The Peabody Museum of Salem, Massachusetts, offers a series of assembly programs for a fee to groups of up to 100. Schools may select from nine topics ranging from ballooning or Pacific volcanoes to New England and the China Trade. The staff members present programs of slides or films, a lecture, and question/answer sessions. Artifacts, such as baleen that is used in demonstrations, may be handled by the audience if time permits.
- The Museum of Modern Art, New York City, organized a special project in which students execute line drawings according to instructions furnished by the artist Sol LeWitt. The artist prepared instructions for eight drawings and students in each school selected the work they would produce on a school wall, which represented collaborative efforts that contributed to a single work. Although removed from direct contact with LeWitt, the students did experience his way of thinking.

Audiovisual resource materials bring collections and special exhibitions to students through slides, films, and, more recently, videotape. Several museums throughout the country, such as the Milwaukee Public Museum, Grand Rapids Public Museum, and the Museum of Science and History in Little Rock, provide public and private schools with extensive collections of audiovisual materials, which include films, filmstrips, and more. The extension service of the National Gallery of Art in Washington circulates audiovisual resources to more than 4,000 communities each year.

Audiovisual programs can combine images, enlarge on details, and focus the viewers' attention. They can examine a single object in detail or place it in its social or historical context. The costs, equipment, and expertise required for audiovisual production often results in collaborative efforts between museums and a television or media group.

Audiovisual materials may be borrowed by the teacher in anticipation of a museum visit or to supplement the regular curriculum. *Art and Human Values,* a slide show of the Minneapolis Art Institute, for example, is a enrichment program for a humanities curriculum for gifted students. Some sites, the Visitor Information Center of the NASA/Lewis Research Center in Cleveland, for example, maintains an extensive library of audiovisual materials that it will copy onto tapes supplied by teachers. Other museums, such as the New York State Historical Society, produces slide/tape programs and resource materials for sale to teachers or school districts.

- The Philadelphia Museum of Art offers a series of framed reproductions from its collection. Available in sets of 10, the reproductions can be rotated among the classes over a three-month period. Each reproduction is accompanied by learning activities, information on the artist and the painting. The loans are designed to encourage the students to react honestly, to reflect on their reaction, and to learn how to focus attention on paintings from medieval to modern times.
- The Conner Museum in Kingsville, Texas circulates bilingual slide/tape series on the museum's collections, Texas history, and specific archeological sites. Available for loan to schools and community groups, these programs can either prepare students for museum visits or supplement the classroom curriculum.
- The Idaho Historical Society prepared a 250-unit slide series and accompanying manuals that illustrate important concepts in geography, the environment, civics, anthropology, and economics as they relate to the state's history. The entire kit, available for purchase, contains 10 sets of slides and a script is coded for presentations to adults and children.
- The Wadsworth Atheneum in Hartford has developed *Insights: The Visual Arts in American History,* a notebook of 200 slides arranged in 10

chronological units. The slides, taken in 21 museums and historic houses in the greater Hartford area, illustrate a variety of objects from paintings to kitchen utensils. Each unit contains a script keyed to the slides, background information, suggestions for teacher use, and information about the participating institutions. An in-service workshop, conducted by the Wadsworth Atheneum, familiarizes user of *Insights* with the different approaches to the materials. *Insights* was developed to integrate the visual arts into various aspects of the school curriculum.

Portable loan kits generally come in two formats: those with artifacts in sealed cases and those with objects that may be handled. Both usually include written and graphic materials. Some exhibits and kits also include a full range of resources: teacher workbooks, film strips and films, books, and artifacts of specimens. Evaluation questionnaires are generally sent out, and sometimes are followed by indepth interviews with the teachers. The loan period ranges from two days to two weeks or more, depending on demand for the material and the complexity of the kit. Consideration must be given to proper packing, security, insurance, and transportation to and from the museum. Objects needed for loan exhibits may be acquired in various ways. The Fort Worth Museum of Science and History obtains some loan kit specimens as a result of its Natural Science Club field work. Docents taking trips, community organizations, stores, merchants, artists, and historians are all potential resources for materials from specific countries. Specimens from the collections for which there is insufficient data, common taxidermied animals and birds in great supply, or specimens removed from exhibits can all be used.

- The Grand Rapids Public Museum in Michigan loans dioramas, specimens in cases, pictures, charts, and slides. Exhibit cases focusing on one topic; dioramas ranging from the city in 1800 to a Pueblo kiva; mounted specimens and cultural artifacts from Africa, Canada and Central America are among the many available items. Formulated as self-contained glass-fronted boxes, which include labels and some teaching materials, they are delivered to teachers by the museum upon request.
- The Minneapolis Art Institute loans schools different types of suitcase exhibitions that include objects from the museum's collections as well as slides, teacher guides, and brochures. A textile sampler, which introduces the history of weaving, contains large weaving sample boards, fabric swatches, raw wool, and cording and spinning tools. A mobile study exhibition of enclosed cases contains objects from the museum's collections ranging from 18th-century tin candle sconces to chrome and plexiglass objects.
- The Oakland Museum in California circulates exhibits in sturdy suitcases that reflect the various museum departments. Each suitcase exhibit consists of artifacts, art work or natural science specimens, definition cards, photographs, maps, and a slide presentation. A User's Manual provides instructions for presentations. Circulating exhibits include *The Ecology of the San Francisco Bay Area*, *Chinese Fisherman: Pioneers of California's Commercial Fishing Industry*, and *California Pottery*.
- The High Museum of Art in Atlanta, Georgia produced a series of suitcase exhibits based on an exhibition in its Junior Gallery. Designed for use in grades five to eight statewide, these *Space and Illusions* traveling exhibitions are integrated into all curriculum areas, from science and math to art. Students explore space in art and the everyday world, as well as distorted, translated, or imagined space. The suitcase exhibits contain two peephole shows, an anamorphic painting, examples of illusions, games, art reproductions, games, and a slide show. A teacher's handbook, mailed in advance of the suitcase, describes the unit and suggests follow-up activities.
- The Children's Museum of Boston circulates a wide range of materials, among them the innovative MATCH (Materials and Activities for Teachers and Children) boxes. Designed to make learning the product of the child's play and actions, they contain objects of all sorts: films, pictures, games, recordings, projectors, objects, and a detailed teacher's guide. Children study film loops to find out what various birds eat; they grind corn to make "nokake," an Algonquin food; they reconstruct life in ancient Greece by "reading" objects found in an

excavated villa; they write, edit, illustrate, and print their own book; and they drill soapstone using a Netsilik Eskimo bow-drill. Delta Education of Nashua, New Hampshire, in partnership with the museum, now markets commercial versions of some MATCH units for sale to school systems, curriculum centers, and teachers' colleges.

Some museums circulate **full-scale traveling exhibits** to schools and community groups. Often state museums, such as the Virginia Museum of Fine Arts, offer these services throughout their state. In general, circulating exhibits are self-contained in shipping crates, are available for three to six weeks, and require varying amounts of space for exhibition in a school hall or library. Rental fees and transportation costs vary from museum to museum. Insurance coverage is essential, and responsibility for insurance, damage, security, and transportation must be clearly defined.

Because circulating exhibitions are basically designed for an adult audience, they will not be reviewed in the same depth as other outreach programs.

- The Milwaukee Art Center has developed a series of circulating exhibits, in addition to its other offerings designed specifically for classrooms. All of the exhibits include, or can be supplemented by, slide resources or films loaned by the museum. The exhibits require up to 100 linear feet, and most include participatory activities. *What is a Painting Made Of?* illustrates the tools and materials used in modern and past paintings, explains the most commonly used painting techniques, and describes the history of water color, oil, tempera and casting. *City Places*, designed for elementary students, contains urban landmarks photographs, and instructions on how the construction of "super cities" using found materials such as boxes, shelf paper, and fabric.
- The Children's Museum of Denver has developed a series of portable participatory exhibits for rental to schools and community groups. *Figure It Out*, designed to help children in grades one through six, contains a variety of games, puzzles, and other activities that let children practice both computation and mathematical thinking, and illustrate that mathematics is part of everyday life. Each exhibition includes pre-and post-visit materials. Other exhibits are available on colors, movie-making and disabilities.

Mobile units and vans have been taking museum resources to distant communities for 25 years. Often seen as roving ambassadors of the museum, they provide a variety of experiences to community and school groups. Ranging from small vans to semitrucks, some mobile units carrying materials for participatory activities, while others are designed as museum galleries on wheels.

One advantage is that experienced museum people travel with the unit to assist the users in learning about a subject or acquiring a new skill. Another is that through repeat visits to one site, the staff can develop a special rapport with the host organization at the school or community site.

Some of the vans, such as the Trip-out-Trucks of the deYoung Art School in San Francisco, bring participatory activities to the classroom or community center. Several science museums such as the Lawrence Hall of Science in Berkeley, California have developed traveling resource centers to help teachers with their science curriculums. Zoos, such as the Staten Island Zoological Society of New York City, bring live animals to schools and community groups in a zoomobile program.

More than forty museums nationwide have mobile units functioning as museums on wheels. These 30-to 50-foot trailers are expensive to operate and maintain. Rental and mileage on the cab, salary of the driver-curator, travel, insurance, and maintenance can run more than $75,000 annually. Additional funds are needed to develop and install new exhibits.

In cooperation with the Red Ball Company, which furnished a 40-foot trailer, the Children's Museum of Indianapolis circulated an exhibition dealing with the concept of movement during the year that the museum was building a new facility. The project was discontinued when the building was completed due to the continuing operating costs of the mobile museum, estimated to be between $50,000 and $70,000 a year.

- The Virginia Museum of Fine Arts in Richmond operates four artmobiles, each staffed by a curator, which take selected original works from the col-

lection to communities throughout the state. These "galleries-on-wheels" have been touring the state since 1953. When the first artmobile was no longer suitable for long-distance travel, it was transformed into a stationary unit to take on the function of a youth gallery.
- The Museum of New Mexico's mobile exhibit, *Pueblo Indian Life in New Mexico*, represents that life style through a recreation of a Pueblo family home. Designed for children grades one through six, with bilingual labeling, the unit covers the entire state over a three-year period.
- The Office of Museum Programs for the Wichita Public Schools operates three mobile museums with exhibits on crafts, history, and science. The Mobile Science Museum provides public school students with exhibits, study collections, and participatory activities on the flora, fauna, geology, and climate of Kansas that enrich and reinforce the elementary classroom science program.
- The Akron Art Institute Artmobile program expands on art programs in elementary schools during the school year and visits city parks and county recreation sites during the summer. This self-contained, 40-foot van is a roving art program, which combines a major exhibition designed specifically for children with related studio art projects. Information about site selection, publicity, electrical connections, security procedures, tour scheduling, and evaluation methods, is sent to the site coordinator prior to the visit. A exhibition catalogue enables teachers to prepare students for the exhibition and to plan follow-up activities.
- The Pacific Science Center uses a portable planetarium, which inflates in minutes, to take sky shows and participatory astronomy activities to schools. Up to 30 students can crawl inside the dome to view the nighttime sky, where they develop a star chart to take home for future use.

Printed resource materials, such as newspapers and journals, are another way of extending the museum's resources and programs into the classroom. These written resource materials, in many formats, are specifically written by museums for students in the elementary and secondary schools. These pamphlets and journals do not relate to specific programs or loan kits, but are designed to stimulate interest in different art, science, and history topics.

Some museums collect and publish the stories, poems, and papers written by children participating in different programs. *The Illinois History Magazine,* published monthly by the Illinois State Historical Society, uses research papers submitted by students in grades seven through 12. The Brockton Art Center in Massachusetts publishes a collection of writing from students in grades five through seven who participate in the Art and Language Arts Program. Such publications help to motivate and involve students in different types of projects. They can serve as documentation of their accomplishments and participation as they are an integral part of the program design.
- The Fernbank Science Center offers two versions of JUST FOR US (JUST FOR Understanding Science): one for primary students, and a simpler version for elementary students. Published five times each year, the four-page pamphlet is simply written and illustrated. Each issue focuses on specific topics. "The Year of the Coast," for example,

introduced what a coast is, how it is used, what causes it to change, and the importance of marshlands. A "Teacher Sheet" provides further information on the topic and lists useful audiovisual and print resources.
- Columbus, Ohio's Center of Science and Industry (COSI) has produced a series of "COSI FIS Kits ("fizz" is Fun In Science), which focus on different aspects of natural and physical sciences. "Seeds," for example, illustrates what seeds are, where they come from, how they scatter, and how to grow such seeds as peanuts. The "FIS Kits" present scientific concepts, such as propagation and adaptation, by using familiar objects, such as peanuts and pine cones. "FIS Kits" printed as a tabloid, contain drawings, riddles, texts, bibliographies, and suggested activities.
- The New Jersey Historical Society in Newark publishes *The Cockpit*, an instructional workbook, for elementary and secondary students throughout the state. This biannual 16-page illustrated resource takes a topical approach to New Jersey studies and places the state's development in the context of national history. These materials, utilized by classroom teachers and leaders of the Junior Historian Clubs throughout the state, reflect archival and material objects in the museum's collection.
- The Children's Museum of Denver is national headquarters for the newspaper *Boing!*, which is distributed free of charge to elementary school children in Denver and other cities in cooperation with participating children's museums throughout the country. *Boing!* published bi-monthly, adapts the familiar adult newspaper format to accomodate the reading needs and interests of younger children. It carries a series of feature articles, regular columns for parents and teachers, and special departments such as "Dr. Duebig," who provides consultation on family and personal problems). Puzzles, riddles, mazes, games and contests deal with topics of importance and interest to children. Museums participating in the *Boing!* network may provide local-interest stories and listings of museum events, and may sell local advertising to be included in newspapers circulated in its own city.
- The National Gallery of Art and Scholastic Magazine cooperatively publish *Art and Man*, bimonthly magazine for secondary students. Available by subscription nationally, it introduces a variety of art forms and artists from the past to contemporary times. Each issue focuses on a different principle or element of art such as color, form, or texture. For example, the issue on color featured Vincent Van Gogh with a four-page background essay on his life and work and a color centerfold of *Starry Night*. An article on other artists examined the way artists in different periods used color in their work. Each issue presents an interview with a student artist, a collaction of studio activities, and a listing of television programs, museum exhibitions, and other ideas of interest to students.

MUSEUM AND SCHOOLS IN THE FUTURE

Students will continuing visiting museums to see the original "evidence" described in art, history, and science textbooks. The unique experiences afforded through programs that involve direct participation in learning will continue to be the highest priority of museums. Undoubtedly, new formats will be added to those described earlier, and, of course, new program topics will enrich each of those formats.

Visits to museums by students focus on the direct observation of exhibits, collections, and, through interpretive programs, on a deeper understanding of the artists, scientists, craftsmen, and others who contribute to the creation of our world. The museum experience should also help students understand how to look at exhibits, thus developing the skills necessary for self study. Because some schools are limiting field trips due to increasing transportation costs, new sources of support for transportation costs must be found.

The commitment of museums to involving schools and their students has meant the development of programs such as mobile vans, resource specialists, and audiovisual and printed resource materials. These outreach programs will continue to serve thousands of students in nearby and distant areas, although increasing costs will also effect the use, availability, and fees of such programs.

New technologies will thrust educational programs and teaching formats in museums and schools into a new era. Cable television, video discs, satellite transmission, computers, and other technologies will affect museum presentations. Museums will be able to compile information on their slide libraries in computers, which will assist with typesetting, labeling, and updating of learning packages and bibliographies. Combinations of technologies will enable resource specialists in museums to interact directly with students in classrooms miles from the museums. New technologies will alter the traditional forms of outreach, helping museums make their resources available to an ever broadening public. In addition, they will provide methods for museums to individualize their learning programs.

Museums, however, will need to experiment and learn from mistakes as they experiment with ways to effectively manage computers, video discs, cable television, and other formats.

The rising costs of shipping, mailing, reproducing, and replacing materials such as those described in this chapter will also cause changes in format and teaching style. This will challenge museums to not only employ new technologies but to be more innovative in the use of traditional techniques. Museums will experiment with new communications technologies and traditional formats in order to identify effective methods for teaching and illustrating their topics and collections. Nevertheless, these programs will never replace the experience of visiting the museum, using the exhibits, and seeing the objects personally.

The supportive relationships that exist between schools and museums will take on new meaning as funds for education programs face an uncertain future. Collaborative program planning and implementation has created excellent programs that accommodate the needs of both institutions and that are suitable and interesting to students. Recognizing the significant role teachers can play in the implementation of museum programs, museums have increased their attention on the needs of the classroom teachers. Increased participation of teachers and school administrators will undoubtedly result in more informed and supportive relationships with the schools.

References

1. Heine, Aalbert. *Museums and Teachers*. Occasional papers No. 3. Corpus Christi, Texas: Corpus Christi Museum, 1977.
2. Jenness, Aylette. *Creating a Partnership: Museums and Schools*. Boston: The Cultural Educationl Collaborative, 1980.
3. Marcus, Stephen. *Designing Programs and Looking Ahead*. Boston: The Cultural Education Collaborative, 1978.
———. *Cultural Organizations in Career Education*. Index. Boston: Cultural Education Collaborative, 1978.
4. Newsom, Barbara Y. and Silver, Adele Z. *The Art Museum as Educator*. Berkeley: University of California Press, 1978.
5. Sebolt, Alberta. *Collaborative Programs: Museums and Schools*. Sturbridge, MA.: Old Sturbridge Village, 1980.

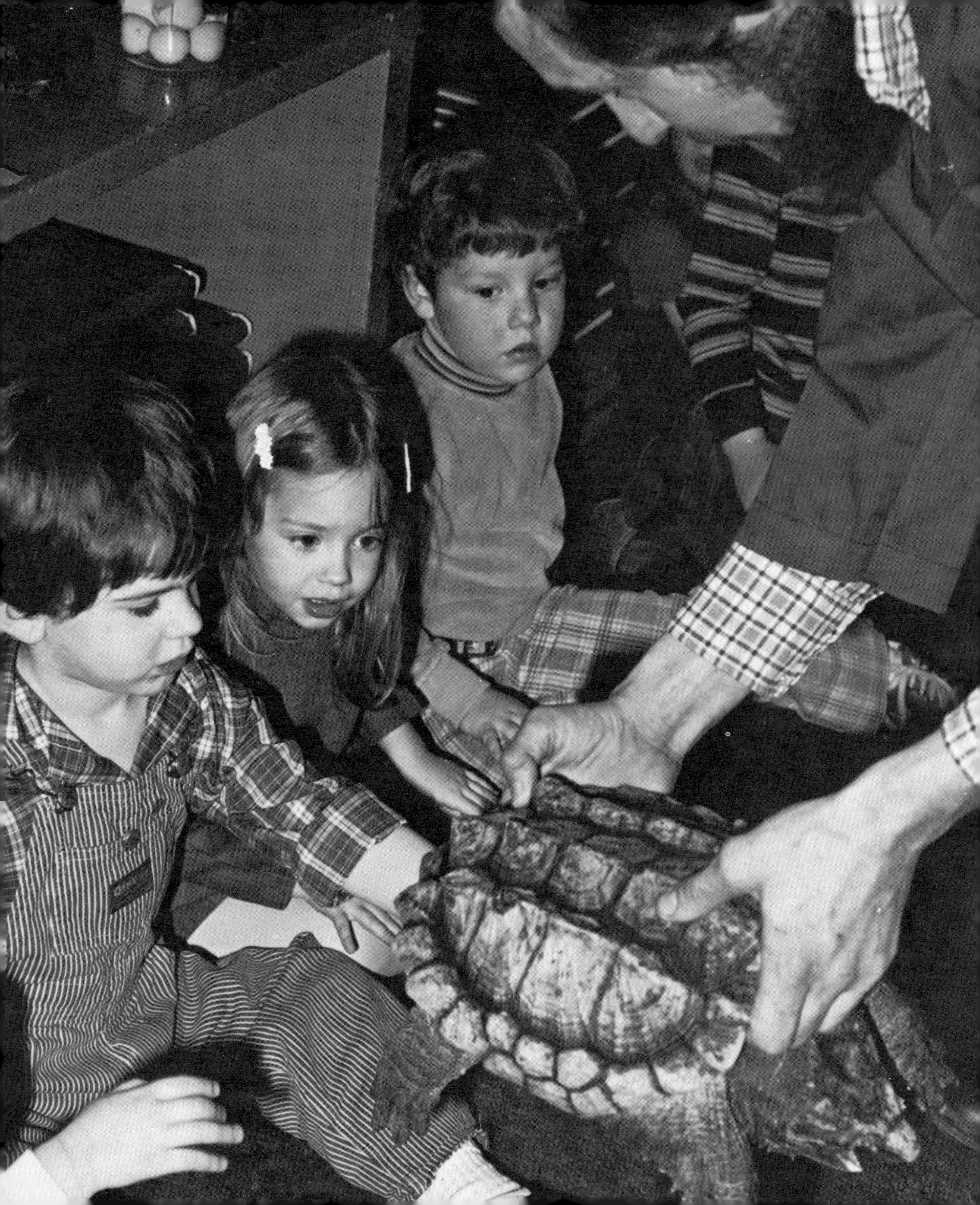

6.
MUSEUMS AND THE CLASSROOM TEACHER

Museum educators have become increasingly aware that classroom teachers play an important role in the effective implementation of museum programs. Teachers who understand how to use museum exhibits and collections can make a difference in the quality of their students' educational experiences in museums. Museums have developed numerous ways to interest school teachers in learning about museums and the variety of programs available to them.

An important reason for the increased focus on working with both elementary and secondary teachers is that the museum education staff and docents may not be able to meet all of the requests for service, due to limited staff size or large demand. Teachers who are trained to use museum exhibits and materials can develop their own programs. Also, teachers are with students for an entire academic year, while the museum program may last only a few hours. Thus, the museum-aware classroom teacher is able to extend the museum's influence for a longer period. Another reason for the focus on reaching teachers is that the teachers who have participated in museum programs can play an effective role in suggesting and developing new programs. Teachers who have a clear understanding of a museum program can more effectively prepare their classes for the program and employ follow-up activities, thus enhancing the learning experience.

An essay in *The Art Museum as Educator* reviews both the reasons for this emphasis and illustrates several different formats used by museums to work with teachers. Among the common formats are teacher training programs, resource centers, and printed materials.

TEACHER TRAINING PROGRAMS

Teacher training programs, from orientation sessions to sabbaticals, are of vital importance to museums. They reach teachers who can bring their enthusiasm, ideas, and children to museums. Teachers who understand how to use a museum as an educational resource, rather than as a holiday from the classroom, can make a significant difference in the quality of museum programs, whether in the classroom or museum.

When designing a training program for teachers, it is important to determine the goals, content, and evaluation methods. Communicating and interpreting through exhibits and objects is usually confined to museums, and many teachers do not feel comfortable or confident about having to teach in galleries on their own. They have had little experience teaching with paintings, historic houses, or physics exhibits. Teachers often attend museum training programs looking for specific ideas and teaching techniques that will be immediately transferable to the classroom. Training programs may focus on the subject matter of the museum or on effective techniques for teaching from exhibits. They also can combine content and technique.

The museum staff must remember that classroom teachers will "teach as they were taught." If a training session is a lecture, the classroom teacher probably will present the materials to their students in the same way. Also, if demonstrations of quilting or inquiry strategies are part of the program, then the schedule should permit the teachers to actually practice these skills. Verbal and physical participation by the teachers is essential to a successful program. In some training programs, teachers design their own curricula or resource materials for classroom use; this requires that the museum be committed to supporting the teachers as they implement their projects.

Getting teachers to participate may not be an easy task. Schedule training programs at times that are convenient to teachers, perhaps during in-service days or in the summer. Workshops should utilize the museum's resources: provide something the teachers can get nowhere else. If museum workshops are of uniformly high quality and approved by school officials, teachers are often eager to participate. In-service or academic credits can be arranged. The museum must be aware of the teachers' needs, interests, and requirements.

Museums often offer **orientation and workshop programs** for teachers in the fall in order to attract the school audience, to provide information on planning museum visits, and to publicize available resources and activities. These workshops may be general introductions to the museum and its services or may focus on a limited number of special programs. In-depth experiences provided by living history programs, for example, require a comprehensive training experience for the teachers so that students can be adequately prepared for the program and offered useful post-visit activities.

- The New Orleans Museum of Art conducts "educator workshops" periodically throughout the academic year, designed especially for teachers and administrators who are interested in making effective use of the museum. Although they focus on varying topics, the workshops are centered on education department services, such as docent-guided tours, the film library, and pre-visit preparations. While orienting the teachers to the museum resources, the workshops also emphasize that the museum's education department is aware of, and willing to work with, the constraints and requirements.
- Environmental Living Programs at such sites as the Petaluma Adobe State Park in California and Turkey Run Farm in Virginia are designed to help teachers prepare for their classes' overnight visit to the site. The teachers examine artifacts, cook meals, make adobe bricks, and dip candles, all the things the children will do later. Staff members serve as resource people providing information on the historic site and ways it can be used. Following the Turkey Run Farm workshop, the teachers are able to help the students prepare for the visit by making costumes and researching the ways that people lived and worked. After training in the skills course, teachers may organize and execute their own encampment at the Environmental Living Center.
- The School in the Exploratorium staff in San Francisco, working in conjunction with Learning Disabilities Centers, offered workshops for parents, teachers, and administrators of disabled children. Workshop participants used Exploratorium exhibits to experience the kinds of visual, auditory, tactile, and vestibular perception problems often encountered by children with learning disabilities. This helps them understand more clearly the problems faced by learning disabled children and teaches them how to use the Exploratorium exhibits with the children.

Teachers participate in **in-service credit programs,** which are required by the state departments of education, to obtain salary increments and to upgrade and maintain certification. The programs provide continued training and develop teachers' expertise. In-service credits, which indicate the amount of work accomplished, can be obtained in three-hour, one-day, or 15-week programs, depending on the number and length of sessions.

The local school board and principals must cooperate with museums that wish to offer programs for credit, and the requirements for school districts, state education departments, and curriculum areas vary tremendously. Museums offering in-service programs for the first time, might want to work with a local university or college to arrange for academic credit to be granted. The endorsement of a college or university generally results in approval from the school districts. Some museums, such as The Lawrence Hall of Science at the University of California, Berkeley, operate vans that travel to schools providing in-service teacher workshops and sharing ideas.

- The Wadsworth Atheneum in Hartford offers half-day in-service workshops to art, humanities, and science teachers. Credit may be arranged for the workshops, which introduce different methods for working with art objects. Art, music, and humanities teachers, for example, attend a session that explores connections between art and music and between the senses of seeing and hearing. Secondary-school science teachers attend sessions that examine misconceptions and assumptions about artists and scientists.
- The North Carolina State Museum (of Natural History) offers a 15-hour service program designed around three classroom-laboratory sessions and one all-day field trip, which gives teachers basic natural history and ecological information about community resource areas. Teachers learn how to handle, identify, and use native wildlife and plants with their students, and how to plan and implement field trips to natural areas or museums. Programs are offered to resource teachers on a county-wide basis, in any North Carolina county. Some counties cover travel costs for the museum staff. Credit is offered for teacher recertification.
- The China House Gallery in New York City offers an in-service accredited course in Chinese history and culture in cooperation with the Board of Education. The 15-week course covers art history, Chinese-American heritage, contemporary China, folklore, geography, literature, philosophy, Sino-American relations, calligraphy, and other topics. A fee is charged for both credit and noncredit versions offered during the spring and fall.
- The Children's Museum of Boston, through a grant from the Bureau of Education for the Handicapped, developed an in-service training program about working with mainstreamed special-needs students for regular classroom teachers. The program not only provides information about disabilities, methods, and materials resources, but also emphasizes the teachers' attitudes about and comfort with special-needs students. Support and intervention is constantly available as the teachers guide handicapped children and adults through the museum on a one-to-one basis. Meetings following that experience allow participants to share their experiences and feelings, and offer guidance from the program supervisor. The program also provides readings about mainstreaming, rudimentary sign language classes, and seminars.

Elementary and secondary teachers frequently work on advanced degrees or earn graduate credits to increase their salaries, maintain accreditation, and acquire skills in new areas of study. Museums have developed **graduate credit courses** in cooperation with graduate programs, extension divisions, and summer schools at colleges and universities. The academic institutions must approve the curriculum for graduate courses and generally list those courses in their catalogues. University faculty may assist in teaching the courses, but this is not a requirement. Fees paid to the university may be split between the museum and college, particularly when the course is held at the museum and taught by museum staff. Collaborative efforts among museums and universities are offered both in the academic and summer sessions.

- The Museum of Science and Industry in Chicago, in cooperation with colleges and the Chicago Board of Education, has developed courses and workshops on philosophies and strategies in teaching science and mathematics, which may be taken for a variety of graduate and undergraduate credit options. The use of informal science education resources, as exemplified by the museum, is emphasized in courses such as "Teaching Elementary School Science" and "Using Instructional Games in the Mathematics Classroom." The classes help teachers understand science principles and improve their abilities to teach them in the classroom. Classes meet during the week and on Saturdays, using faculty from the sponsoring university.
- The Guggenheim Museum's Learning to Read Through the Arts Programs, Inc., presents its methodologies in an intensive three-credit graduate seminar at Rutgers University. The LTRTA approach to reading is presented to teachers who work with gifted, handicapped, and normal children. The seminar helps the teachers develop their skills in the arts and curricula that integrate art activities into teaching strategies.
- The Minnesota Historical Society in St. Paul offers a five-credit graduate-level class each summer, in cooperation with the University of Minnesota history department. The intensive, two-week course for elementary and secondary teachers offers content information, examines teaching resources, and introduces the Historical Society's collection. The class has a different thematic focus each summer.

- The Cultural Educators Roundtable of St. Louis, in cooperation with the University of Missouri-St. Louis, offers a Summer Graduate Institute on utilizing community cultural resources to teachers of grades kindergarten through 12. The three-week course meets daily to acquaint participants with on-site use of educational resources in 15 museums and libraries. The teachers are trained to do research and to design primary and supplementary source materials for classroom use.
- The Cultural Education Collaborative in Boston developed a summer institute that brought together museums and schools to develop programs for the academic year. The principal from the school's planning group and teams of teachers, who may receive graduate credits through a local university or in-service credit from their school districts, are paid for their time through grant funds. The Collaborative, which coordinates the summer institute and the academic programs, pairs each school with a museum based on the applications submitted. Teachers paired with the Plimoth Plantation developed a fifth-grade program about Pilgrims and Wampanoog life; designed resource materials, which included study units, dioramas, and dictionaries; and planned activities, such as visiting Plimoth Plantation. A unique feature of the summer institute is a one-week break between two one-week sessions, which gives teachers time to reflect on the curriculum materials and concepts they want to develop.
- The Teacher Center at Old Sturbridge Village trains teachers from all over New England to develop curricula that make full use of the village's exhibits, environment, artifacts, and other materials on 19th-century New England. The two-week program suggests different approaches to studying modern communities and is available for three graduate credits from the state colleges. While exploring significant social issues (e.g., the American family, or environmental problems), teachers work with primary sources: pictures, objects, and buildings. They also learn effective methods of combining field experiences, museum objects, and classroom activities and begin to design curriculum studies that utilize their own community resources. Each month during the school year, they return to Old Sturbridge to discuss teaching problems they might be experiencing. Because of its emphasis on curriculum development, the State Department of Education accepted the program as part of the certification process for elementary and secondary teachers.

Elementary and secondary teachers in most school systems receive **sabbaticals** for either a full year or one semester. Teachers, inspired to develop additional resources for classroom teaching, have used sabbaticals to work at museums developing new teaching materials. Elementary teachers on sabbaticals have worked at the Pacific Science Center, Seattle, to develop materials and activities in science and mathematics. Through a cooperative program with Western Washington State College, these teachers may use the museum experience for academic credit towards a master's degree. Teachers have taken sabbaticals at the Jefferson National Expansion Memorial in St. Louis to develop learning packets, slide sets, and supplementary handbooks, which can be used to enhance studies of American history.

Some museums have extended their commitment to teachers through their loan programs, which provide materials (from slides to exhibits of specimens and artifacts) and professional staff who are responsible for working with teachers. When a facility is included, teachers can meet in the museum resource centers.

TEACHER RESOURCE CENTERS

Many museums have developed resource centers as a way to make the museums' collections more accessible to teachers, parents, youth group leaders, and students. Resource centers offer materials ranging from slides and mounted owls to models of adobe villages and objects from the collections that can be loaned to the public. There are essentially two types of resource centers. One operates like a library, loaning materials to the community as well as maintaining and designing new materials. The second operates as a loan service and also offers training classes for teachers and members of the community.

Operating a resource center requires a financial as well as philosophical commitment from a museum. Space and staff must be provided to house the resource collections, develop programs, and respond to requests for services. The circulating materials, whether a single slide or entire exhibit, must be checked and sometimes repaired when the loan is returned. New kits and programs must be developed, which requires time and money for designing, researching, collecting, testing, and revising. Resource centers that offer programs must be able to schedule, advertise, teach, and evaluate the sessions.

Responsibilities, goals, and the audience for resource centers vary tremendously. Some centers only provide information. For example, The Arts Resource and Information Center at the Minneapolis Institute of Arts provides teachers and the public with information about all kinds of art events, resource specialists, field trip possibilities, and loan materials. Located in the museum lobby, it is a central point for people to stop by or call with their questions. It also provides easy access to the extensive programs and resources of the museum's education department.

The Culture Connection was the computer-based information and referral service of Boston's Cultural Education Collaborative. Teachers and staff in subscribing schools can dial a toll-free number for information about cultural resources in a particular subject area, for a particular age group, or at a specific location. Almost 350 cultural institutions listed their programs with Culture Connection, which was an important aid for school and community educators who were selecting programs or resource materials. Its staff discussed the caller's particular need, interest, or curriculum area; brainstormed on ideas; retrieved information for discussion, and mailed detailed print-outs of the resources and programs that seemed most appropriate. Funding for the Culture Connection came from school system subscriptions and a grant from the Massachusetts State Department of Education.

Two examples of the many resource centers that provide **materials for loan** include the Children's Museum of Indianapolis and The Los Angeles County Museum of Natural History.
- The Children's Museum of Indianapolis Resource Center circulates more than 800 portable exhibits and loan kits free of charge within the city. Utilizing artifacts from the museum collections, the loans available to schools and other children's service organizations, such as Scout troops, church groups and day care centers. Most study materials relate to the natural sciences, social culture and history in 60 subject areas. Some are glass-fronted mounts and descriptive portable cases containing small artifacts or natural history mounts and descriptive labels on topics such as the Seminole family or African weaving. Other study materials consist mainly of charts, maps, and pictorial materials. Kits include individual artifacts to be placed in showcases, teacher materials, audiovisual materials, and handmade artifacts. The loan period for all materials is from two to four weeks. The Children's Museum began circulating resource materials and exhibits in the early 1930s as a way of bringing the museum to people forced to stay home by the Depression.
- The Los Angeles County Museum of Natural History through its Education Division Lending Service circulates artifacts and specimens, dioramas of historic buildings, 50,000 slides of science and history subjects, maps, posters, and more. In operation for more than 40 years, this circulating collection includes materials from the museum's collection that lack sufficient data, materials gathered by staff and volunteers on their travels, and donations. Any taxpayer in the county may register for the lending service by purchasing a $5 card, which is good for one year. Loans are available for two weeks and are not renewable. In addition to the loan materials that are in constant circulation, the museum has developed "Lending Service Units," which include 300 objects reflecting a cross section of the museum's collections. Many school districts rent units at $500 for the year, retaining the resources in the district for the academic year.

There are numerous examples of museum resource centers designed to loan educational materials to schools. The Milwaukee Public Museum, the Grand Rapids Public Museum, and the Albright Knox Art Gallery are among the museums that offer these services to their communities. Many other museums have loan programs but do not have a resource center.

Two resource centers that not only have extensive **loan materials** and collections, but also offer a wide selection of **programs and services** are at the St. Louis Art Museum and the Children's Museum of Boston.

- The St. Louis Museum of Art Resource Center offers teacher services, workshops and conferences, materials, slide kits, and posters for loan and satellite resource centers at four sites throughout the state. An educational lab of the museum, Resource Center provides free services to teachers and students and serves as an educational "shop" where learning materials (e.g., slides, lesson plans, reproductions) may be purchased or borrowed.

The museum staff offers workshops and consultations to explain to teachers how to use the museum's resources in the curriculum. Graduate credit courses are available during the year and a summer program examines "The Museum as a Learning Resource". The Resource Center's materials for loan or purchase include handbooks on the collections, catalogues of exhibits, and a collection of lesson plans that integrate the arts into the basic curriculum. The slide collection and slide kit programs include more than 45,000 slides, accompanied by written materials. The slides, available for two-week loans, can be used as pre-or post-visit programs, and are mailed to schools throughout the state. Topics include "First Visit to the Museum," specific artistic periods, and special exhibitions. Posters by a number of artists are available for one-month loans. The museum also operates a media center that can do photographing from books and audio-record presentations and circulates carefully selected children's films. The Resource Center publishes *The Museum Newsletter* for teachers about the programs and exhibits at the museum, which provides specific ideas for pre-and post-visit activities.

- The Children's Museum in Boston provides services for teachers, parents, community workers, and adults in a number of areas related to the education of children. The center maintains books, pamphlets, and information on a range of topics; workshop rooms; a recycling center; and a kit-rental department. Educational development is a primary function of the Resource Center, which collaborates with other educational, cultural, and community organizations, publishers, and film-and television-production companies to create materials and programs for local, regional, and national audiences. The Resource Center offers professional development opportunities, runs workshops and courses, provides consulting services to neighborhood organizations and schools, and organizes special events and exhibits on such topics as special education, ethnic awareness, and child development. Introductory tours of the Resource Center are available to groups and individuals.

The Learning Collections of the Resource Center include an extensively catalogued collection of books, audiovisual media, artifacts, equipment, games, and toys related to the principal educational themes of the museum: cultural and ethnic groups, American social history, the urban environment, science, natural history, and child development. The materials are housed by theme in specially designed display, reading, and activity areas called "studies." Museum visitors may explore the resources of the Learning Collection free of charge, and borrowing members of the museum may borrow materials from the collection for home use.

Kits of learning activities on more than 75 topics can be rented from the Kit Rental Department of the Resource Center for two-to three-week periods, at fees of $10 to $40. There are four kinds of kits: 1) activity kits of equipment, objects, and graphic materials such as books and activity instructions on Indian games and shells; 2) study kits of artifacts, graphic materials, books, activities, supplies, and teacher guides on topics such as a specific culture or farm life in different cultures; 3) exhibits kits of artifacts, books, and pictures for display; and 4) curriculum kits of artifacts, models, written materials, supplies, audiovisual resources, teacher guides, and curriculum plans on topics such as the city, or the Japanese family.

How to Read a Fish

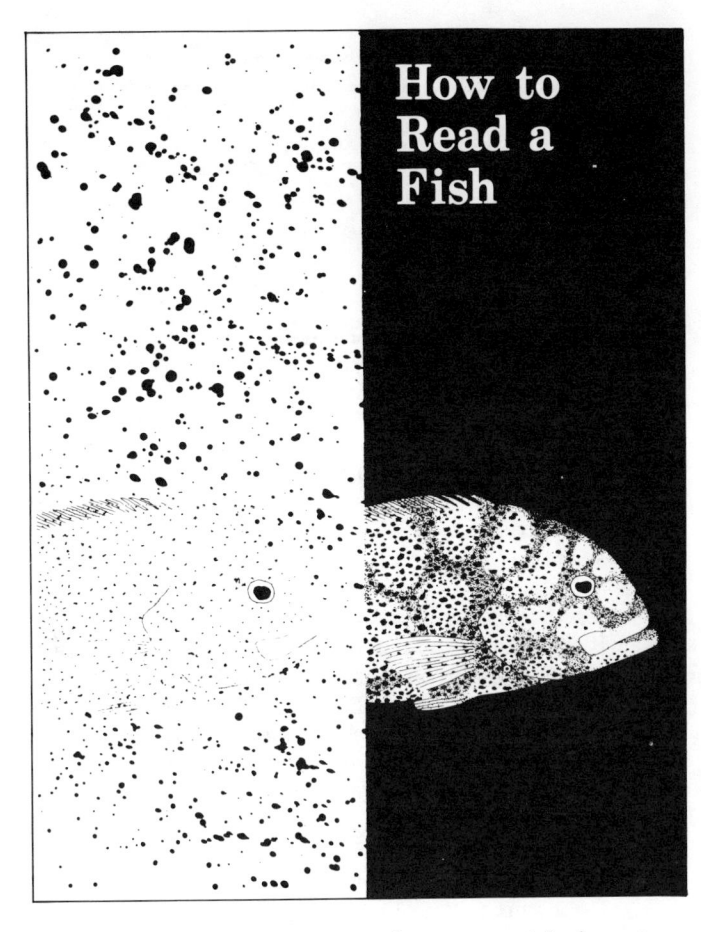

Recycle is a unique source of raw materials for arts, crafts, science and other learning projects. The recycling center collects things factories throw away (rubber, foam, plastic, fabric, boxes) and sells them by volume or weight. The museum has published *Recyclopedia*, a book of creative and educational uses for Recycle materials, printed by Houghton-Mifflin and available in the museum's shop.

Not every museum has the capacity or mandate to operate resource centers for teachers or community groups. The requirements of funding, maintaining, and continually expanding and improving the materials in a resource center are important considerations. Some museums operate shops or books stores that partially fulfill the function of a resource center, selling books, magazines, kits, experiments, small pieces of equipment, and more, so that the motivated teacher or parent can use these materials to develop their own activities. Other museums use vans or museum-on-wheels to take the resources and training programs to teachers. Nevertheless, the importance of working with teachers cannot be underestimated and resource centers provide a viable way of offering technical assistance and personal support to teachers.

PRINTED RESOURCE MATERIALS

Publications developed by museums can fulfill many functions. Information, ideas, and activities can be distributed throughout school systems in the state or even the country, thus bringing the museum's resources and collections to many audiences. The type of resources range from catalogues of the collections or special exhibitions to specific curriculum resources.

Like all materials prepared for a specific audience, the museum should have a clear idea as to who will use the written resources, why they will be used, and how they will be used. The following have been developed primarily for teachers, but many could be adapted for use by parents or other adults who work with children.

Preparing written resource materials for teachers requires that the museum staff be willing to make decisions as well as work with the teachers. The text can be prepared by the museum staff, including curators, and although teachers do not have to write the texts, they must be consulted about their usefulness. Teachers' observations and criticism must be respected and, if possible, incorporated into revisions.

Among the types of written materials the museum might prepare are guides to help teachers select and organize tours; pre-visit guide book a curriculum unit to assist the teacher in their classroom. Other important decisions are: Who will use the material? How much information will the teacher have? Will the material be a part of a workshop program to involve and to prepare the teacher, or will it be used by the teacher independently?

Written resource materials, like programs, require that drafts be prepared, tested and revised. If the teachers do not understand how to pack a suitcase exhibit or if the suggested classroom activities are impractical or uninteresting, then changes should be made. Written resources, whether they are self-guided tours or teacher workbooks, must be well-designed and laid out. A clear design concept with attractive and appropriate format can help to increase the user's interest in reading, following instructions, and implementing ideas. For example, a text that is to be read accompanying slides while the lights are off should be printed in a type face bold enough to be read under these conditions. The museum staff should try out the materials under simulated classroom conditions before giving them to teachers and should observe teachers using the resource.

Updating and revising teacher resource materials is an important consideration. As the goals of a program are modified, the accompanying text should also be changed. New information and research will require revision of materials. A graphic and content format can be developed that eases the addition of new units to the existing documents.

Publications may be produced as part of a grant or with general operating funds. Good publications should be accessible to the broadest possible audience, and may be appropriate for sale in the museum store or teacher resource center.

Good printed resources retain their value when taken away from the museum and, therefore, provide a sense of permanence about the museum experience. The teachers can control the use of the materials, selecting specific activities or an entire unit as it seems appropriate for their students.

Catalogues for the collection and special exhibitions are designed for a general audience. Some museums, like the Santa Barbara Museum of Art have written special catalogues as educational resources. *Iconocom* resulted from a three-part series of exhibits on the museum's permanent collection, which organized the objects into symbols of the spirit, color as symbol, and symbols of time and place. The museum has also organized tours and a slide program on these themes. In its museum shop, the Cleveland Museum of Art offers a series of eight brief introductions to its permanent collections for $.25. These introductory catalogues contain a review of several pieces in the collection, a glossary, and appropriate map.

Deciding which museum to visit and what programs to use is of major importance to teachers. **Catalogues of services for schools** may be published by an individual institution or a consortia of museums. The goal of these various publications, which appear as fliers, newspapers, or books, is to inform teachers and administrators about the programs offered at the museum.

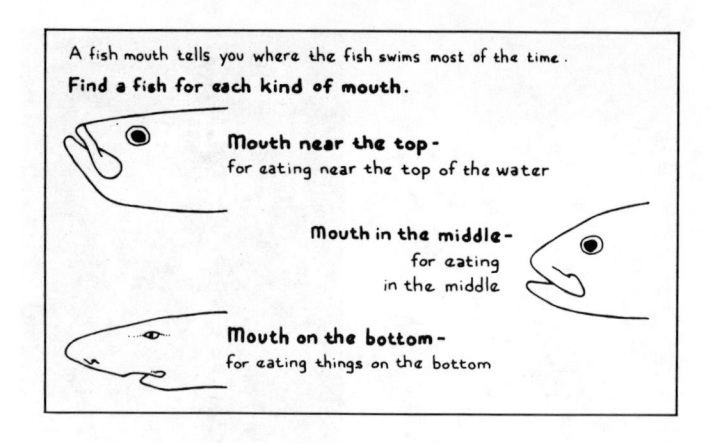

○ The Peabody Museum of Salem, Massachusetts lists its educational services in a flier distributed to all area schools. A brief description of the museum's collections and divisions accompanies the detailed listings of the educational programs offered from kindergarten through high school. Information about fees, location, reservation procedures and group size is also included. Assembly programs, seasonal classes, and specific programs are listed on the brochure along with enough information to assist the teacher in selecting an appropriate program for each class. For example, a listing is available for grades four through six called "Explorer: Captain Cook in the South Seas," which traces the 18th-century voyages of Captain James Cook and asks, "What was it like to meet the island peoples whose lives were so different from our own?".

○ The Museum Consortium of Buffalo, New York publishes the *First and Last—Catalogue of School Services*. The annual newspaper goes to all area schools and outlines tours and services available from seven Buffalo museums. Tours, loan programs, discovery rooms, and mobile vans are listed. Instructions on how to schedule tours, museum rules and basic data about the individual institutions are listed.

○ Museums Collaborative of New York City biannually publishes an *Educational Resources Directory*, a guide to 71 museums, zoos, botanical gardens and historical societies in the city. The directory provides schools, community organizations, and the general public with descriptive listings of the programs, resources, publications, and services for the institutions. It also contains basic data and transportation routes.

○ The Minnesota Historical Society annually publishes a *Catalogue of Educational Services*. Divided into materials and services sections, it lists the available films, slides, video, traveling exhibits, teacher workshops, historic sites tours, and resource packages. Information on ordering these programs and resources is also included.

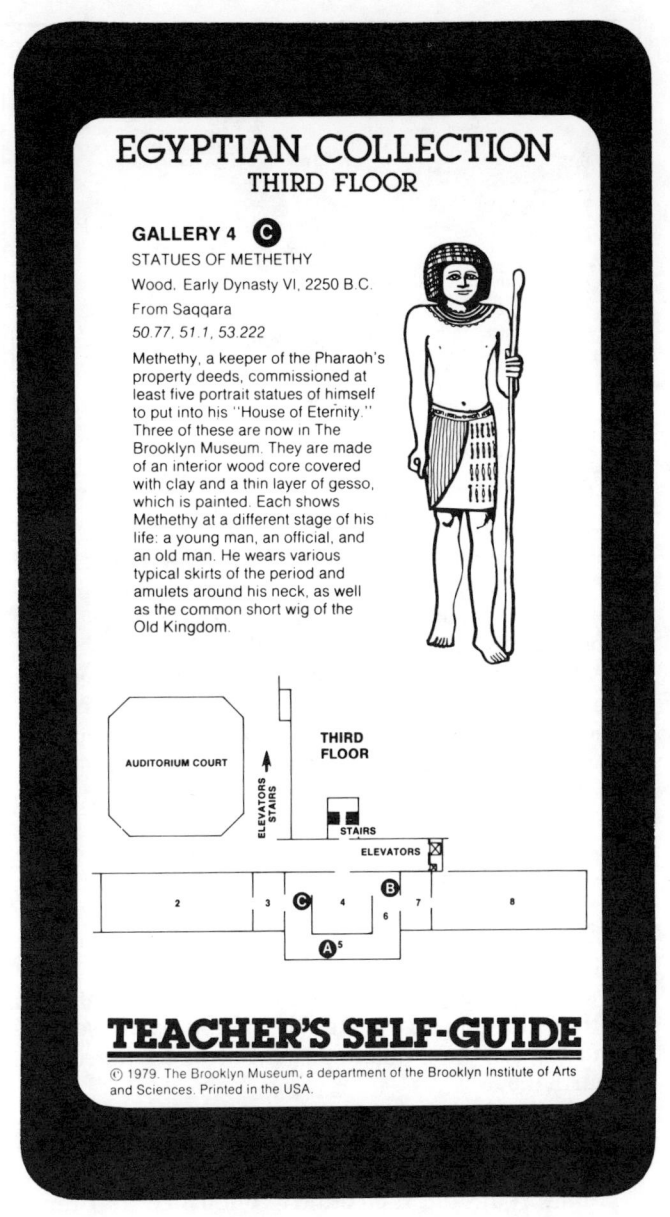

EGYPTIAN COLLECTION
THIRD FLOOR

GALLERY 4 C
STATUES OF METHETHY
Wood. Early Dynasty VI, 2250 B.C.
From Saqqara
50.77, 51.1, 53.222

Methethy, a keeper of the Pharaoh's property deeds, commissioned at least five portrait statues of himself to put into his "House of Eternity." Three of these are now in The Brooklyn Museum. They are made of an interior wood core covered with clay and a thin layer of gesso, which is painted. Each shows Methethy at a different stage of his life: a young man, an official, and an old man. He wears various typical skirts of the period and amulets around his neck, as well as the common short wig of the Old Kingdom.

THIRD FLOOR

TEACHER'S SELF-GUIDE

© 1979. The Brooklyn Museum, a department of the Brooklyn Institute of Arts and Sciences. Printed in the USA.

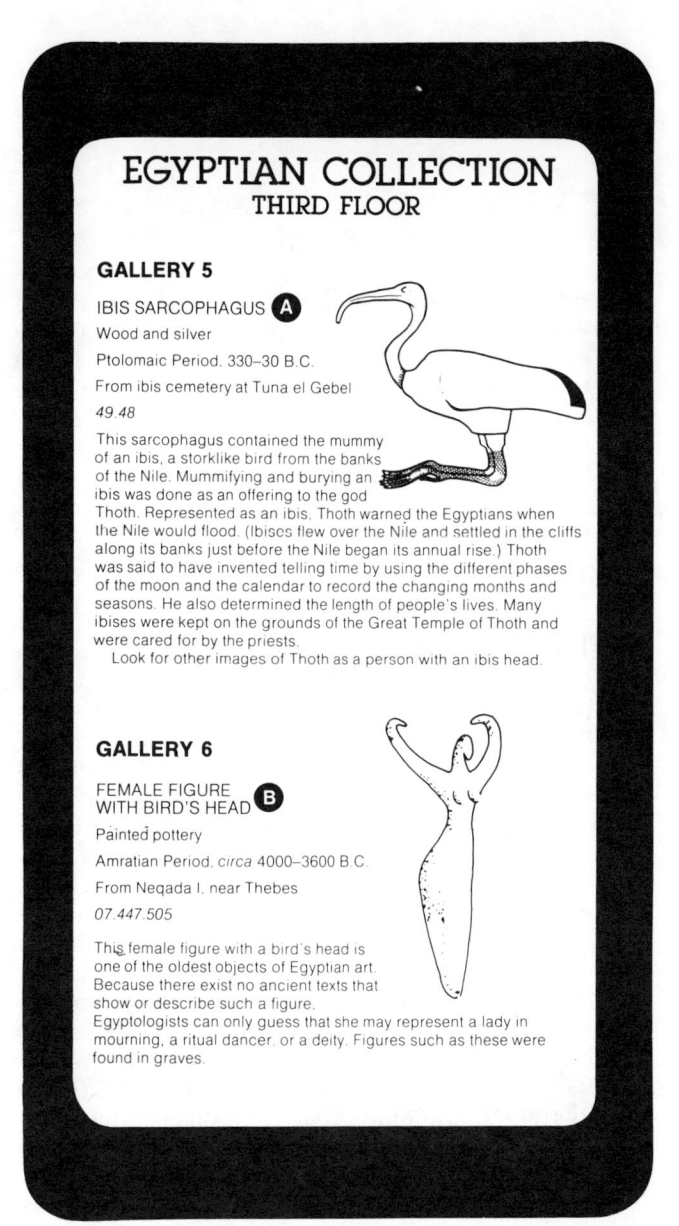

EGYPTIAN COLLECTION
THIRD FLOOR

GALLERY 5
IBIS SARCOPHAGUS A
Wood and silver
Ptolomaic Period, 330–30 B.C.
From ibis cemetery at Tuna el Gebel
49.48

This sarcophagus contained the mummy of an ibis, a storklike bird from the banks of the Nile. Mummifying and burying an ibis was done as an offering to the god Thoth. Represented as an ibis, Thoth warned the Egyptians when the Nile would flood. (Ibises flew over the Nile and settled in the cliffs along its banks just before the Nile began its annual rise.) Thoth was said to have invented telling time by using the different phases of the moon and the calendar to record the changing months and seasons. He also determined the length of people's lives. Many ibises were kept on the grounds of the Great Temple of Thoth and were cared for by the priests.
  Look for other images of Thoth as a person with an ibis head.

GALLERY 6
FEMALE FIGURE
WITH BIRD'S HEAD B
Painted pottery
Amratian Period, circa 4000–3600 B.C.
From Neqada I, near Thebes
07.447.505

This female figure with a bird's head is one of the oldest objects of Egyptian art. Because there exist no ancient texts that show or describe such a figure, Egyptologists can only guess that she may represent a lady in mourning, a ritual dancer, or a deity. Figures such as these were found in graves.

  Having reached capacity enrollments in guided-tour programs, museums have designed **self-guided tour materials** to serve teachers who want to use the museum. These single-visit tours should be thematicaly organized to include a selection of objects rather than be simple walks through the galleries in which students merely identify objects without an understanding of what they are and why they are in the museum. Self-guided tours should be scheduled in advance. Materials for the tour should be sent to the teachers early enough to encourage them to visit the museum and locate and preview the exhibits recommended for the tour. Upon arrival the teachers and classes should be greeted at the museum entrance, and provided with the necessary information and maps. Self-guided visits provide many teachers with the opportunity to develop programs on their own, and make the museum collections accessible to large numbers of students.

○ The Shedd Aquarium in Chicago has developed a participatory tour sheet—*How to Read a Fish*—for use with elementary and secondary students. The guide is an introduction to looking at fish and how they adapted to the environment. Students learn how to "read" a fish by observing, recording, comparing, and contrasting different species of fish. Through illustrations and questions, the students is helped to collect information about the different colors, feeding habits, and shapes fish have and how these help them to survive.

○ The Brooklyn Museum has developed a series of *Teacher Self Guides* on its decorative arts, Oriental,

American Indian and Egyptian collections. Mailed to the teachers in advance of the tour, the package encourages attendance at the museum to locate the objects, select a theme that links with their curriculum, such as daily life activities, ceremonies, work, relationships to nature or contrasts in life styles. Each *Self Guide* contains an activity and an object card, each clearly illustrated and easily managed while touring in the galleries. The object card illustrates and describes the objects, and the activity card gives instructions and ideas for touring the collections.

○ The Washington Park Zoo in Portland, Oregon has designed five *Self-Guiding Tour Packets* to assist teachers of grades K-6 in preparing students for a field trip, conducting the field trip, and following up afterwards. Topics range from similarities and differences, to threatened and endangered species. Every packet emphasizes providing students with activity sheets to be completed during the visit so their visit is task oriented. The activity sheets emphasize observation, recording and inference. For example, the packet on "Animal Similarities and Differences" includes: preparation activities that relate to all areas of the curriculum so students can research and discuss differences between animals and man, or identify ways people use animals; filmography lists with loan sources identified; and student activity sheets which can be reproduced and distributed which include determining sizes, shapes and coverings; and follow-up activities.

○ The Anacostia Neighborhood Museum in Washington, D.C. has written a walking tour of the neighborhood for teachers to use with children in preschool through grade 6. Through comparative pictures and photographs, simple narrative, and activity suggestions, it provides children with a general historical account of Anacostia from the 1600s and specific information about the history of such sites as the Frederick Douglass House and Barry's Farm. Suggested follow-up activities include learning old-time games and songs from a senior citizen in the community or using scraps to build a replica of an Indian village or of a major street in the community.

12 Convex lenses are interesting to study in depth because they are versatile and useful tools. Your school supply of magnifying glasses is a ready source of convex lenses.

They do more than magnify! Let your students experiment with the lenses. Help them find the three examples described below which demonstrate what can happen to light when it is refracted through a convex lens.

a Convex lenses can be used to focus light. Use any light that is far away as the source of light to focus. Hold the lens close to your hand and move the lens around until you have a clear spot of light on your hand. All of the light from the light source is focused at that spot. This is called the focal point. If that point is two inches from the lens, for example, the focal length of the lens is two inches. Find the focal length of your lens.

What are you doing when you use a magnifying glass to burn a leaf?

Teaching resources in the form of handbooks, activity sheets, kits, and curriculums have been developed for the very important tasks of preparing for and following up museum visits. In whatever format, size, or shape the resources take, all of these materials introduce the collections and provide ideas, information and, perhaps, materials for pre-and post-visit classroom activities. Teacher guides, handbooks, and curriculums usually include listings of related resources (slides, films, loan materials) and a bibliography that can further enhance their use. Workshops should not be a prerequisite for their use, but can provide teachers with the skills for such activities as weaving cloth or identifying birds. Teaching resources may also provide ideas for utilizing museums' collections on a daily basis in the classroom.

The following reviews of written resource materials illustrate the range of materials offered by museums, from newspapers with single-visit ideas to full-semester curricula.

○ The Smithsonian Institution, through the Office of Elementary and Secondary Education, publishes *Art to Zoo*, a newspaper distributed to 50,000 teachers throughout the country. Published four times each year, it brings news from the Smithsonian to teachers of grades three to eight, helping them with ideas and information to increase their use of museums in their own community. The paper is designed to help teachers and students learn to use objects as research tools. Each issue is usually devoted to a single topic; information on theme activities, bibliographies, resource suggestions, and a "pull out page" for students are also included. The activities and information suggested in each issue are selected so that they can be used in classrooms throughout the country.

○ The Exploratorium has prepared a series of *Idea and Recipe Sheets* based on the School in the Exploratorium curriculum, designed specifically for

Experiment #1 Your brain will close or fill-in things which your eyes don't see in order to make a complete picture.

How do you describe a scene like this?
Is it two half cars with a tree in between?
Or is it a whole car parked behind a tree?
Your brain fills in the part of the car your eyes don't see because of closure.

It is easy to see that there is a bird in this picture. How many pears are there? How many does your brain fill in because of closure?

Are there other parts of the picture that are not all there but that you recognize because of closure?

How is the bird printed so that your brain will see it as various shades of black, white and gray?

CLOSURE Human eyes are constantly sending sight messages to the brain. The brain constantly tries to organize these messages into pictures that make sense. To make a complete picture, your brain will even close or fill-in things which your eyes don't see — this is called *closure*. Closure seems to have something to do with how you learned to look at things early in life . . . and it's more likely to happen if the pattern is familiar. Scientists don't really know how the brain does this.

Experiment #2 Closure seems to have to do with how you learned to look at things early in life . . . and it's more likely to happen if the pattern is familiar.

In a few words, write a description of each of the patterns above.
Picture 1 is a _____
Picture 2 is a _____
Picture 3 is a _____
Now, use your imagination. Pretend that you don't know what a circle is or a square, and that you never saw a puppy dog. Describe the three figures again. Remember, you can't use the words "circle", "square", or "puppy dog".
Picture 1 _____
Picture 2 _____
Picture 3 _____
What do you think you see first when you look at something?

Experiment #3 Scientists don't really know how the brain fills in pictures that are not complete. Understanding *closure* could help explain a lot about how the brain works.

Draw a simple picture, or print a word, with part of the picture or word left out. See if other people can tell what your picture is. Experiment to see how much you can leave out of a picture before people can't understand what it is.

© 1978 Franklin Institute

teachers. They contain interesting topics to explore with students, experiments and projects using readily available materials, and bibliographies. For example, *Something About Light and Optics* includes an introductory essay on light and a series of simple experiments that illustrate different qualities of light, reflection and mirrors and refraction and lenses. Recipe sheets guide in the construction and experiments of such things as kaleidoscopes, magic wands, floating pennies and a pin hole viewer.

○ The Field Museum of Natural History in Chicago has developed a series of *Discovery Units,* written resource materials designed to complement loan kits and other extension resources. These units provide information on different collections as well as ideas for classroom learning activities. A *Discovery Unit* may be used by teachers who want to develop a self-guided tour or it may be used in conjunction with other extension resources. The museum has illustrated discovery units on many topics including "African Life," "Pioneer Life," and "The Prairie." The units, such as the one on Imperial China, include a series of essays and activites that can be done to enhance the students understanding of each topic. For example, after the essay on the written language of China, students could write a letter to a friend using pictographs for words whenever possible, or compare Egyptian pictographs to the Chinese in the museum's collections. A list of exhibits to visit, resources available through the extension program, and bibliography are also included.

○ The Missouri Historical Society and CEMREL, Inc., have cooperated to develop and test a set of learning materials to accompany artifacts sent to the schools and displayed in the galleries. *Pursuing the Past: Eads Bridge, St. Louis: 1833-1887,* trains teachers and students to work with the inquiry method to develop an hypothesis. The responsibility for learning is placed on the learner. The planning team utilizes all available resources during the research phase of the Eads Bridge project—archives, books, photographs. *The Historian As Detective,* the student's resource book for this program, helps children to understand that it can be fun to investigate and learn about their heritage or region. Student activities include researching, writing, and illustrating their own personal histories and examining historical documents and artifacts.

○ The Cleveland Museum of Natural History has written a manual (available for sale) for teachers and group leaders on "Nature in the City." The manual consists of 17 natural history-oriented activities using urban lots or school grounds as outdoor laboratories for exploration. Programs are multidisciplinary and include projects for science, math, creative writing, vocabulary building, art, and music. The activities are suitable for lower elementary grades.

○ Old Sturbridge Village has published a catalogue of background papers and primary resource materials produced by the Education Department staff in collaboration with teachers at many levels. The resource packets and other materials engage students in learning through contact with historical evidence. By reading first-person accounts or exploring objects of the past, students gain new and valuable perspectives on their own lives. The village has organized its resource materials into three themes: family, work, and community. Within each theme are three types of materials: background papers or essays written by researchers describing the major subthemes, trends, and historical interpretations of the village's period; resource packets, which contain edited primary documents such as diaries, letters, journals, account books, and almanacs; and teacher materials. The last presents an historical background, guide to the documents, and activity suggestions. Other sections of the catalogue include supplementary media, such as study prints, facsimile documents, maps, slides, films, curriculum kits, and reproductions.

- The Museum of the City of New York has written a book, *A Short History of East Harlem*, at the request of the community, because there was no information on the neighborhood in which the museum is located. Designed to be used by school teachers or community groups and students, it is an historical overview of East Harlem, illustrated with maps, documents, prints, dioramas, and photographs from the museum's collection. This informative and unique history book is available for sale to the teachers and community leaders.

- The Franklin Institute Science Museum in Philadelphia has developed the *Science Enrichment Service*, which are kits that teachers can take home to continue investigation of the scientific principles or technological development that students have seen at the museum. Each kit contains a poster that illustrates the concept studied, worksheets for 35 students, and a teacher's guide. Each worksheet contains at least three cumulative experiments, each building on the previous. The teacher's guide suggests added activities on the subject and talks about the subject of the kit in greater detail. As an example, one of the SES series is "Do You See What I See?"—a study on visual perception. In the worksheets, optical illusions are treated as common experiences that teach us something about how the eyes and brain work together—not as "mistakes" the eyes make, or "tricks" the brain plays on us. Students experiment with optical illusions and other visual experiments.

- The St. Louis Art Museum distributed its *Handbook of Museum-Based Lesson Plans*, to teachers throughout the state. The lesson plans integrate works of art into the basic learning processes. Developed as part of a program that involves students in a series of half-day sessions at the museum and follow-up programs in the classroom, specific lesson plans are determined in advance by both local and museum personnel. These lessons use works of art as the focus of investigation through which perceptual awareness necessary for language arts and social studies are developed. The lesson plan formats have nine sections: unit goal; lesson preparation; material; objectives; content and activities; notes; evaluation; follow-up context; and title. For example, of activities from a Language Arts unit on narrative painting and narrative writing includes:

1) **Lesson Objective:** Students will be able to build a story from a narrative painting and structure the story within a given framework, listing events in order;

2) **Lesson Preparation:** Discuss the elements of a good story such as setting, characters, conversation, plot, good ending;

3) **Lesson Content and Activities:** View and discuss paintings that tell a story, in terms of main idea, action, main characters, list events of the story of a narrative painting, write the story that the painting tells, set the scene, describe what is happening, explain the action, include conversations, anticipate what would or could happen to the characters;

4) **Follow-Up Context:** Illustrate the ending of your story or role-play a painting, assigning each child a character and letting them develop the story;

5) **Evaluation:** Can the students build a story from a narrative painting? and

6) **Notes:** resource center slides and materials, slides, paper, crayons, markers and paint.

- The Roger Williams Zoo Park in Providence, Rhode Island, in collaboration with local schools, has developed a comprehensive five-component education project for grades five and six. This program, designed to supplement the existing science curriculum, uses the zoo as an educational resource center. One result of the project was the publication of two texts—*Rhode Island's Water World* and *Zoo Animals and You*—, approximately 50 supplementary worksheets, and two accompanying teachers' editions. Classroom study of *Zoo Animals and You* is recommended at three hours per week, divided between the study of science (biology, zoology, health, nutrition and mathematics) and other disciplines (language arts, social studies, and the creative arts). A teacher's guide complements the student's text, providing objectives, motivational and supplemental activities, worksheets, discussion questions, vocabulary lists and resource listings of books and audiovisual materials for each unit.

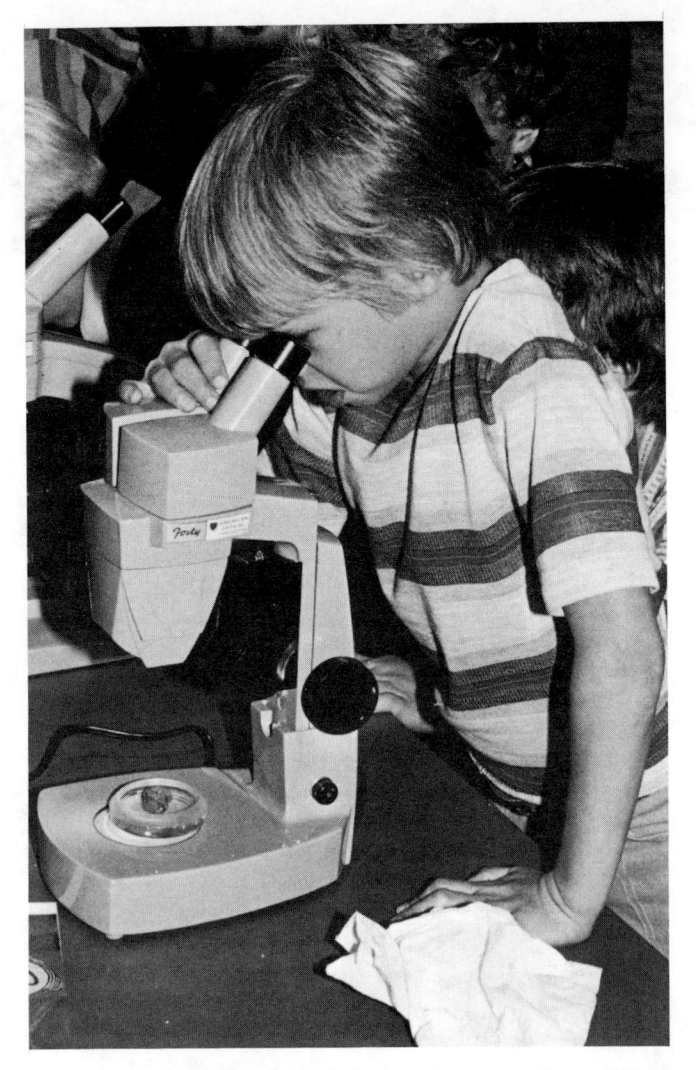

The important role teachers play in museum education programs in the classroom or in the galleries can not be overstressed. How museums work with or assist the teacher can happen in many ways—through workshops and courses, written materials, or the space and materials of a resource center. In developing any of these services, the museum must know why it is doing it and what will it do for the teacher. It must also be sure that it can provide the services. Working with teachers requires a commitment of time, staff, and resources. It also requires a respect for the teacher as a professional and an understanding of the demands made upon his time. Developing successful programs and resources for teachers can and does happen. The following paragraph from *The Art Museum as Educator* summarizes the importance teachers should have to the museum:

> "Museums hold in trust an endless supply of ideas, visions, human mysteries to be unlocked for audiences of all kinds. It may be true that none of the museum's several audiences is more frustrating or more difficult, but it is clear that none is more important than teachers, none more worthy of all the energy, imagination, and intelligence the museum can command. It is not too much to urge that museums put the best people they can find to work on that job." (p. 470)

References

Newsom, Barbara Y., and Silver, Adele Z., Eds. *The Art Museum as Educator.* Berkeley: University of California Press, 1977.

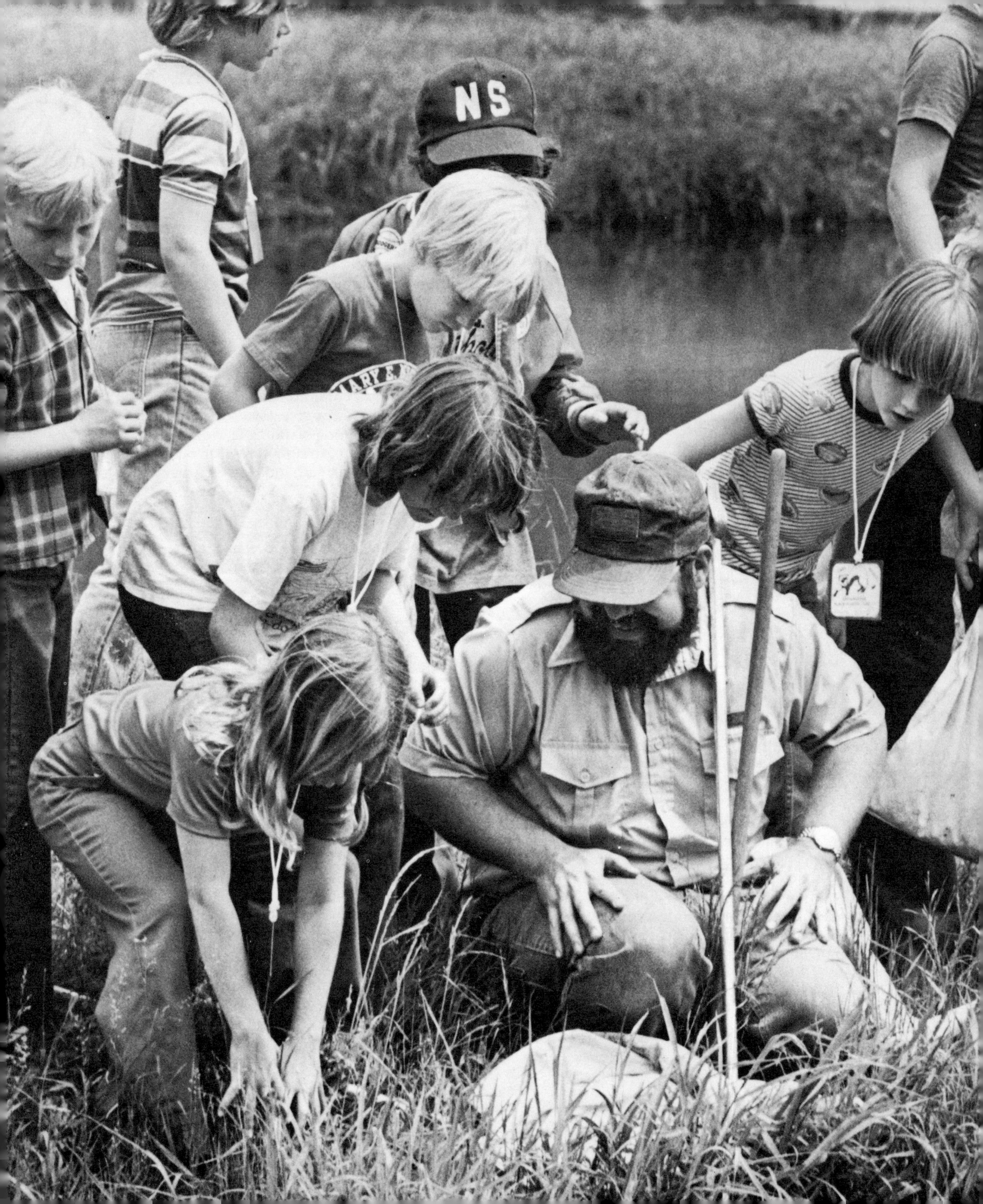
NS

7.
THE MUSEUM AND THE COMMUNITY

The size and make-up of the communities that museums serve have changed radically in the past 20 years. Since most museums are located in cities or small towns, the ways museums serve their communities have been affected by increased urbanization, shifting age distributions in the population, mobility, the energy shortage, inflation, and competition for increased leisure time. The reasons visitors attend museums have, however, remained the same: a desire to share delight, to learn, or to be entertained.

From the mid-1940s to the 1960s, the middle class moved to the suburbs and minority workers became a major segment of the cities. Museum members and suburban school classes had to travel much greater distances to take advantage of programs and educational resources that used to be nearby. Requests for relevance and increasing ethnic identity fostered new kinds of programs in museums. These took a variety of forms, including presentations of bilingual programs to accommodate the increased number of Spanish-speaking citizens in the neighborhoods. Today, it appears that cities' populations are again in flux.

Museums have been examining and expanding their roles as educational institutions providing services to diverse audiences. They have been moving away from the role of a "great house of treasures" primarily for the well-to-do. The staff, collections, and resources have become helpful to people in the community who have been redefining their identities and searching for connections with their past. Some museums also have undertaken an active role in examining social issues such as drug addiction, alcoholism, and other urban problems. The Museum of the City of New York has been a leader in such exhibitions. This type of exhibition format, as well as the tremendous variety of programs that have been offered by museums around the country, have shown that museums are able to increase their services, sometimes by working with community advisory groups. While museums are developing a clearer sense of their responsibility in the community, they are continually refining and redefining their role. In general, the following have been agreed upon as basic strategies for developing community education programs for all types of museums. The museum should:

- make an effort to complement existing community services, rather than duplicate them
- be concerned with broadening the populations that it serves, and with providing them with relevant and informative programs both in the museum and in the community
- bring the community into the museum, helping them to understand how to use its resources, exhibitions, and staff
- continue to be a stimulating and exciting place to involve visitors in learning.

Museums have seen an increase in the number of people who join as members, as well as those who become visitors to exhibitions, programs, and festivals. Millions of people come to museums annually who are not reached through the formal education programs offered to school groups.

The increasing museum attendance suggests that "baby boom" children are now joining museums as adults, and are visiting museums with their own children. People who live in communities surrounding museums—families, single parents, grandparents, disabled children, and many others—are all being encouraged to participate in museums' programs and exhibitions. Visitors generally attend in groups of family or friends. Only a small portion of visitors attend special programs organized for families, community groups, or museum members, and, thus, educational opportunities for the "general public" can not be overstressed. The interaction of such groups affects the behavior patterns generally associated with increased numbers of visitors.

Imagination, dedication, and energy are central qualities of a museum's community programs. The possibilities are endless, and many museums have effectively expanded their programs to reach new groups. Community programs are among the most difficult for museums to develop, because they require extra thought about their substance and public relations aspects.

A museum must define the audience to which the program will be addressed: members, neighborhood residents, tourists, institutionalized individuals, families, or others. The age, economic background, ethnic heritage, disabilities, and other issues that will affect their ability and interest in attending the program should be considered. Among the questions to be asked are:

- What are the interests and age levels of the group? What do they collect? What do they read? What do they do with their free time?
- What times are they available? When can they come? How long can they stay? How often are they willing to come?
- Is public or private transportation available? How long will it take to get to the program, and at what cost?
- Is the program accessible to the disabled visitor? The bilingual visitor?

In an effort to accommodate the needs of the community, museums should consider such differences as intellectual and physical skills. Workshops, classes, and other formal educational programs are only one aspect of community programming. Interpretive materials for large numbers of people—guides for families, labels written on two interest levels, and demonstrations—can permit family groups to benefit at their own varied levels. Resource materials should be developed, and when possible should include activities that can be undertaken at home following the museum visit. Print and broadcast media should be incorporated into the museum's work, enabling it to reach people who may not be able to attend the museum.

In all community programming efforts, the museum should relate the goals of the museum to the lives of the people it is trying to reach.

Two Audiences

It is useful to consider two groups of potential visitors: teenagers and families.

Teenagers represent a small proportion of museum visitors, general 5 to 20 percent of the total student population. Teenagers, however, are able to come to museums by themselves, can deal with intellectually sophisticated topics, and are interested in developing their skills. They are often motivated to join programs in which they can earn high school credit or learn more about career planning.

For museums, this means that independent or group programs should provide concrete goals and a sense of accomplishment. Apprenticeships, internships, summer employment, and work-study programs, which provide an opportunity to meet professionals in different careers, are appealing. Because of the demands of a teenage social life, consideration should be given to the hours the programs are offered and the amount of time required to participate. Some teenagers will prefer assisting on short-term projects, special events, or festivals; others will be more interested in learning skills that will take hours of supervised effort, such as mounting lights or assisting in classes.

Family groups visit a museum for 90 minutes to four hours, using their time in a variety of ways as groups and individuals. If a museum develops a sequence of programs (workshops or field trips), attention should be given to the length of the sessions and number of times the family will have to come together. Transportation costs or distances may make it difficult for a family to attend an eight-week program, whereas a two- to four-week series will be more appealing.

The length of the session must also be considered. Parents may wait for children who are taking a one-hour workshop, especially if they are coming from some distance. While remaining in the museum galleries has its own advantages, parents may rather use their precious weekend hours to attend to chores. Therefore, weekend programs for children might be offered for longer periods of time or might involve both parents and children. Each community has unique characteristics that affect the types of programs offered for children and parents.

COMMUNITIES AND FUNDING

Some museums were created specifically to meet the needs of a community and its children: the Anacostia Neighborhood Museum in Washington, D.C., and the Junior Arts Center in Los Angeles, for example. Other museums offer a variety of festivals and events to honor holiday observances and to bring large numbers of people to the museum. Equally important are the longer-term workshops, clubs, camps, or internships that provide in-depth experiences and training for participants. Museums strengthen their own position in the community by providing carefully designed and implemented programs for people of all ages, either at the museum or a suitable site elsewhere.

A planning committee should include advisory groups made up of individuals from the audience or who understand its needs and concerns. Some museums hire a professional staff member who works solely on community activities and outreach efforts. In some cities, collaboratives—independent, nonprofit organizations—have been formed to bring museum resources together with community groups, facilitating a new kind of community program.

Financing community programs is a challenge. Fees may be charged, with the funds generally used to reimburse the teachers and artists who offer the programs. Sometimes museums can fund scholarships from fees received for other services or from gifts. Museums also receive grants from local foundations or from city governments to provide services for special audiences. Often these grants provide opportunities for museums to reach out to constituents that they might not usually have served.

A provocative alternative to funding community programs was developed by the Museums Collaborative in New York City through their Cultural Voucher Program. Selected community organizations in New York City receive money, in the form of vouchers, from the Collaborative. The community groups control the funds, which enable them to purchase services of their choice from authorized museums. The carefully designed programs resulting from the system has given museums added incentive to respond to the needs of new audiences.

For example, in cooperation with the City Arts Workshop and Martin DuPorres Center, the Museum of American Folk Art helped create colorful murals that now brighten the hall of the DuPorres' Community Service Center, a multiservice agency in a Long Island City housing project that serves blacks and Hispanics. Using art by community youths, professional artists planned the museums and trained participants in painting techniques necessary to execute the finished product. Working with three museums, the Afro-American Ethnic Orientation Society offers classes in African dance, crafts, and music, that culminate three times a year in a performance for parents and the community. The South Bronx auditorium comes alive with African rhythms played on hand-made instruments, to accompany traditional dances. These are just two of the many varied programs designed through a collaborative effort of museums and community groups.

The Children's Museum of Indianapolis has developed a program specifically for the families living in the museum's inner-city neighborhood. Supported by corporate and local neighborhood advisory council grants, the museum presents 20 to 30 free programs each year that are specifically geared to the "neighbors." Developed with advisory council assistance, the activities range from a choir to workshops on such topics as mask-making, pumpkin-carving, reading, and play writing. Seasonal workshops, special events, and festivals are also programmed.

The Children's Museum of Denver has developed a marketing approach to generating income. Rather than request contributions from banks and businesses, the museum presents a business proposition designed to meet the needs of both institutions and to produce income for both. This approach has proven to be extremely successful for the museum and its business partners: the museum now generates 95 percent of its income from marketing its goods and services. A sampling of the educational goods and services that the Children's Museum has produced for revenue purposes follows:

- The Children's Museum produces a variety of educational family publications that are either sold or distributed free of charge. Whenever possible, seed grants are obtained to cover design and production costs. Finished products are sold wholesale to businesses for promotional and advertising use or to merchants for retail sale. Publications are often produced exclusively for a business client and custom packaged to meet its particular needs. The "Safety Snoop" package, for example, helps children find safety hazards in their home, and is being distributed by an insurance company. "Pets and Kids," which provides hints for children about pet care of their pets, is distributed by the Humane Society.

- The museum publishes *Boing!*, a monthly newspaper for families and school children, in cooperation with other museums around the country. It is distributed free to more than 250,000 families in Denver and two million children nationwide. Each issue contains national materials and each museum prepares local information on several pages for its own community. In addition to museum stories and information, the pages can also be sold for local advertising, which the business community has found to be a cost-effective means for soliciting new consumers and promoting products.
- The Children's Museum also produces a series of portable, participatory exhibits that can be rented by schools, shopping malls, or banks. All are hands-on activity centers that bring the excitement, discovery, and learning associated with the museum to the community.
- The Children's Museum has a reputation for creating and implementing successful promotions and events cosponsored by businesses, the media, and the museum. These exclusive, creative events provide sponsors with an effective way to draw new clients and customers, high visibility, free publicity, and association with one of the city's most popular cultural institutions. The museum charges the sponsor the costs, plus the management fee. For example, in "J. C. Penney Pals," children register for pen pals at local Penney stores; through *Boing!* the museum matches pals and distributes identification cards that entitle children to a variety of discounts and free admission to the museum. At the celebrity art auction, local celebrities create original art work that is auctioned off, with proceeds going to the museum.

Financing any type of new program for a museum is a challenge, but community programs provide opportunities to go beyond the traditional grant or foundation route. Unlike a movie, where parents and children sit together quietly for two hours, museums are a place where families can participate in hours of creative experiences that also provide a great deal of learning and fun. Today, museums should charge competitive fees for such services, and not "give them away" or simply break even. Museums need to market their programs more effectively as they reach out to new audiences.

PUBLIC RELATIONS AND THE MUSEUM'S IMAGE

Once community programs are established, the museum must communicate with its membership and the public it is trying to reach. A problem with community programs at many museums is that a single event is spotlighted at a time, without linking programs and the full range of offerings together. A more coordinated effort can clarify to the public the different types of activities and levels of involvement that are possible. A museum should also develop a number of programs—whether for families, the public, or schools—that are offered consistently, thereby building up an audience that becomes regular attendees to the program. A great deal of effort is needed to introduce a new family to a museum as well as to keep a family that has attended.

Publicity for public programs is essential and its importance must be stressed. The image of the museum presented through publicity communicates not only the types of opportunities the museum can offer but illustrates visually and verbally the audience being served.

Public relations can show the museum fun as well as educational. Zoological parks have high attendance because people associate a zoo visit with a family outing that is both fun and educational. Families looking at animals can talk, run, and eat ice cream cones. This freedom to feel at ease has done much to account for zoo's high attendance. The public's image of a museum will affect the museum's ability to involve new audiences. Whenever possible, statistics should be maintained to provide data to the education, public relations, and membership divisions.

Another element of public relations and image is the importance of having professional staff at the museum on weekends. Traditionally, professional staff work five-day weeks, nine to five. A museum might consider giving program and curatorial staff a flexible work week so they can be available to supervise and participate in weekend and evening programs. This will also increase the public's awareness of the staff and its commitment to serving the public.

The following selection of programs that take place in the museum illustrate the range of educational programs currently taking place in museums around the country. They have been arranged by the times at which they are offered, rather than by their audience.

PROGRAMS IN THE MUSEUM

Traditionally, museum galleries and classrooms are filled with the sounds of school groups tumbling through the halls. Recognizing the educational importance of the pre-school years, museums across the country have been diversifying their programs to accommodate the needs of the younger child and their parents or teachers. After-school programs involve neighborhood children, scouts and other groups of children interested in learning through club or internship activities. The scope of weekday activities beyond school tours is illustrated through the following examples.

Pre-School Programs

Reaching children between the ages of three and six has been a challenge to many museums. Educators and psychologists have pointed out that at these ages, children form many of the attitudes they carry throughout their adult years. At the same time, their short attention spans limit the amount of "learning" that can actually take place.

The Fort Worth Museum of Science and History offers an entire pre-school program that provides learning opportunities utilizing scientific and cultural collections at the museum. Children attend the museum's pre-school much the way they would any regular pre-school. Attendance is high with waiting lines on enrollment day. The museum is able to offer a broad spectrum of classes and to utilize the museum's collections, introducing concepts about science and natural history as well as the various cultures represented in the museum. Children participate in a variety of activities and handle live animals and ancient artifacts. An additional advantage for the museum is that the pre-school utilizes classes all day rather than on weekend day afternoons and weekends.

At the Wadsworth Atheneum, parents with children between the ages of four and six attend a three-week gallery-based learning experience in which games, movement, and fantasy encourage them to learn from one another while experiencing art. Themes vary with each instructor. For example, in "Your Body's Art," children look at shapes, spaces, colors, and motion in paintings and sculptures about people. Body tracings, storytelling, and movement are used to explore the body's potential for creating art.

Parents and children share a growing confidence in their abilities to enjoy art materials in various "Parent/Child Workshops" at the Metropolitan Museum of Art. For example, 12 one-hour sessions bring parents and pre-school children together to help them learn to express themselves, to understand the disciplines of artists' endeavors, and to make connections between the art works in the museum's collections and the processes of creation. During classes, the children work with paint, collage materials, and clay; the parents work with one media each week. At the beginning of the class, which emphasizes the creative process and discovery, rather than on the end product, visual materials are shown, and tools and materials are demonstrated.

Science Experiences for Pre-Schoolers is a series of one-hour classes held weekly in the mornings and afternoons at the Museum of Science and Industry, Chicago. The science experiences allow parents and children aged three to five to explore books and materials dealing with light, water, machines, and sound. The children and their parents are involved in programs that combine classroom activities with the museum's exhibits.

With the changes in society, single-family parenting and working mothers become more commonplace, creating a need for more activities and programs for pre-school children. Museums are being called upon to expand their programming ideas and to assist in meeting the challenge of creative learning experiences for the preschooler.

After-School and Evening Programs

Museums have developed a range of after-school and weekend programs to reach children that are interested and enthusiastic in learning more about the museum and its collections. Sometimes such children can be accommodated by free drop-in programs; in other cases, a series of classes, a club, or internship might be designed. After-school programs provide opportunities for children to become involved in specific topics and allow the museum to work with enthusiastic children.

To serve the needs of the neighborhood and many interested people, the Museum of Fine Arts in Boston offers a series of free 90-minute drop-in programs on the weekend and after school. Working with a variety of materials, children investigate specific themes (color, line, or shape) or a particular collection in the museum (Egyptian, for example). Each week, a different museum gallery is explored as the children create their own art works, write poetry, and learn to look more closely at objects in the museum. For example, in the medieval galleries, after working with a professional story-teller, children create their own tale based on the animals and people depicted in the tapestries. This activity may lead ultimately to a weaving project, or a mural.

The Junior Museum of The Metropolitan Museum of Art offers poetry workshops designed for children ages 8 to 13, who have been selected by private and public schools because of their interest in art. The Poetry Workshops provide special opportunities for children to meet artists, work in the galleries, and to write their own poems, which are compiled into an anthology and presented in public readings in the Junior Museum's auditorium. The program lasts for an entire semester, and provides an in-depth exploration of the museum.

Opportunities for independent research in science and technology are provided by the Oregon Museum of Science and Industry (OMSI) Research Center. The OMSI Center makes available equipment, technical assistance, supplies, and laboratory space for project work in biological, physical, computer, and natural sciences. In addition to staff assistance, local and regional researchers and specialists act as expert advisors to lab members who must be at least 12 years old. As an introduction to the program, study groups examine a variety of subjects within the general topic of exploration. The groups are designed for both interested students looking for specific research topics and those who need to acquire a basic skill before tackling an independent project. Students participate in classroom, laboratory, and applied research activities.

A similar program is available at the National Museum of Natural History, through the Naturalist Center, which allows students to work on their own research projects in a variety of topics (mineralogy, biology, etc.) using the collections and equipment available in the center. At Colonial Williamsburg, the Young Researchers Program works with students in grades 4 through 12 who work with the museum staff in exciting, introductory programs, including a simulated archeological dig, object analysis, orientation to Tidewater, Virginia, introduction to plantation life, and historical restoration.

Evening programs provide museums with unique opportunities to reach high school students. For example, the M.A.S.S. (Motivated Astronomy Students Seminar) of the Pacific Science Center, is a group of about 40 high school students interested in astronomy, which meet two evenings per month to hear lectures by astronomers, participate in field trips to astronomy-related events, and host public star parties where they help people use telescopes and binoculars to locate planets and constellations in the nighttime sky. At Colonial Williamsburg, high school students participate in theatrical dramatizations with a Revolutionary perspective: 18th-century singing and games, colonial dancing, and debates in the Hall of the House of Burgesses. These programs can be reserved by individuals or groups interested in learning more about colonial life.

Scout troops and neighborhood youth organizations often plan trips to museums in the form of tours or special programs. At the Florida State Museum, children in such groups study the early Florida Indians, Florida history, the local ecosystem, and Florida geological history. They learn techniques used by paleontologists, study skins of animals, and explore a cave from Northern Florida. Old Sturbridge Village offers afternoon classes for youth groups: shaping leather, crimping tin, cooking without a stove—all activities of children 150 years ago. Participants are at least 12 years old, and organizations join for a three-week craft program to explore the tools, utensils, and skills of early 19th-century artisans and crafts people. Programs like these and others that shall be described in the summer workshop programs at the Fernbank Science Center help children in scout groups to earn their badges.

A special program, designed for youth groups, such as scouts, Indian guides, etc., is offered after school and on weekends by the Carnegie Museum of Natural History. Museum Explorers on Safari (MEOS) is a 90-minute, activity-oriented program that concentrates on a specific topic of the museum. Groups of up to 15 children ages 8 to 12 study specific themes such as animals, botany, or fossils. Completing treasure hunts, making masks, or inventing imaginary mammals are but a few of the activities that, along with selected exhibits and touchable materials and slide presentations, reinforce the theme.

Another after-school format that has been very popular in history and natural history museums are clubs for future scientists and historians. A science club for children 8 to 13 years of age at the Ontario Science Centre, offers programs for five weeks in which members of the staff explore a wide variety of topics, including computers, whales, weather, and information about the museum's exhibitions. The Future Scientist's program at the Cleveland Museum of Natural History, which combines laboratory and field programs in the natural sciences, is designed and managed by science instructors and biologists and assisted by staff scientists, university faculty, and scientists from industry who work with children ages 14 to 17. Recent projects have been a survey for the Ohio Department of Natural Resources, nesting birds records for Cornell, ornithological laboratories, and a series of laboratory sessions on biological and geological microscopy investigation techniques.

Many state historical societies have organized junior historian programs, which coordinate studies of the state's local history for young people in elementary and secondary schools. Often organized through local school districts, chapters of the "Junior Historians" exist throughout the state and undertake special projects designed to expand the children's awareness of their state and to elicit community interest and support.

Young people can also participate after school in junior intern programs, which introduce young people to museum work as a professional career. At the Brockton Art Center during the first month of their three-month internship, students are given a behind-the-scenes look at how the museum functions on a daily basis. The interns talk with the museum staff, including the director, curators, and technicians; they visit the storage rooms, conservation laboratories, and exhibitions in preparation. The second month involves visits to other museums in the area and focuses on collections and questions such as the research and provenance of a piece, acquisitions procedures, and registration. The program culminates in the third month, when the junior interns design activities for students their own age in conjunction with an exhibit presented in the galleries. By developing projects and approaches of interest for their peers, junior interns provide a valuable service to the museum.

The Humanities Training Project of the Museum of Transportation in Boston involves local teenagers in a 10-week series of workshops on local history, transportation history, museum work, curriculum development, oral history, and working with children. At the completion of the workshops, the teenagers run a four-part program for children from their own communities on neighborhood history, local history, and the role of transportation.

At the Virginia Museum of Art in Richmond, a youth guild works with 100 high school students who serve as security aids, museum/theater ushers, and clerical assistants in the museum. Some members of the youth guild have painted decorations for the gallery events. Others give slide talks about the museum for clubs and schools, and several are trained at the Virginia Rehabilitative Center for the Visually Handicapped to provide visits for the museum's blind and visually impaired audiences.

Clubs and junior curator programs allow young volunteers an opportunity, under the guidance of professionals, to work with collections, research projects, collect specimens, dust exhibit cases, feed animals, and, in general, make a substantive contribution to the operations of the museum. Such programming has special appeal to teenagers because it helps them develop new skills through specialized instruction and learn from experts in their fields assisting them in understanding different career opportunities. These programs can also help the students to gain a sense of independence and self worth while earning credits, or, sometimes, money.

Weekend Community Programs

The weekend is a special time for parents and children to get together. Museums can take advantage of this time to have children come to the museum and participate in trading posts, performance programs, art classes, or youth group programs. In addition, families often use this time to tour the galleries or join in festivals, workshops, and other events. The following collection of weekend programs illustrates the range of public, family, and special event activities for children that museums across the country offer.

"Trading posts" at the Milwaukee Public Museum, Corpus Christi Museum, and other museums around the country are wonderful Saturday events for children between the ages of 6 and 16. At the Corpus Christi Museum in Texas, the Trading Post for children under the age of 13 was built with rough planking and hand-hewn beams that create the impression of age. A trader in coonskin cap (the museum director) rings the bell and starts the trading session on Saturday morning. The basic idea of this and all other trading posts, is to interest children in the world around them—be it a rock, fossil, feather, old stamp, coin, squared nail, shell, or any of the other thousands of treasures that children collect. The trader tells them about their own treasures, or the ones they acquire by trading at the post. Children can collect "skins" or the equivalent of museum money and trade for something of greater value. The philosophy behind most of the trading posts that operate so effectively around the country is to stimulate children and to help youngsters with their hobbies, to get them items for school show-and-tell programs, and to complete their collections. Most of all it is to get them to know the museum and public library and to read about their new acquisitions. If there's a problem about an operating trading post, it is perhaps the enthusiasm of the over-the-counter activities, as youngsters crowd around the exhibit or trading post area for the weekend exchange.

Extending the concept of discovery rooms are the "touch-do-discover" programs offered at the Milwaukee Public Museum. Each week a series of participatory learning activities takes place in the museum's youth center for children and adults of all ages. Some days focus on a special theme: for example in one, children and adults learn how to read a rock and touch a dinosaur bone or volcanic rock. In addition, they chip off their own fossil, find beach fossils, conduct rock and mineral tests, and walk in the footprints of a dinosaur. They discover how to use the tools of the American Indian, learn that some rocks float or glow in the dark, and view rocks under a microscope. Other topics of these activity sessions have included survival in the snow, as children learn about the Eskimos and Indians of the far north. Parents and children alike delight in these activities while learning more about the museum's collections as well as the world about them.

Another approach to involving children on the weekends has been the free Saturday art classes available at the Toledo Art Museum and the Akron Art Institute. Free Saturday art classes for children constitute a long-standing tradition at many museums. At the Toledo museum, from September through May, children attend month-long workshops, which meet on Saturday mornings and explore a different theme each month. Members may be given preferential registration. Qualified art teachers are hired to teach and design innovative studio classes that stress the creative process and discovery as well as make use of the museum's collections and special exhibitions.

Saturday workshops can take many formats, and are a popular tradition for children and museums. Available for a fee, sessions usually range from four to six weeks on Saturday mornings, and are designed for specific age groups. For example, at the Los Angeles County Museum of Art, a series of Saturday sessions for gifted and talented early teenagers are designed to help the youth observe and critically assess works of art in light of various cultures and works of literature. Scholars in fields, such as history and archeology, will assist teenagers in developing their own interpretive projects for the museum. At the Valentine Museum in Richmond, Virginia, Saturday workshops focus on the resources of the collection. In covering areas such as Indian pottery, children learn how to make pinch pots, coil pots, and other traditional methods. In addition, 19th-century kitchen craft, doll-making, and puppetry classes are offered—all of which help children understand the life and lore of the early Virginia settlers. Among the many workshops available at the Lawrence Hall of Science are ones that help with career planning and computer use. EUREKA, the California Career Information System, offers the most up-to-date information about occupations, job profiles, salaries, future employment, outlook employment tips, and more, and combines these with information about training programs in educational institutions. A three-hour workshop led by a professional career counselor assists with a personality, ability, and needs study as they analyze and explore potential job possibilities.

Art schools, available during the week and on weekends, have developed in several museums around the country. For example, at the Colorado Springs Fine Arts Center, an art school called Bemis, works with approximately 500 students ages 3–18, during each of its three sessions. Children participate in these tuition classes in the visual arts, drama, movement, and literature. The Museum School of the Philbrook Art Center offers a variety of classes, workshops, and lecture programs that integrate the study of the museum's collections and exhibitions with studio classes in the fine arts. These three-hour classes, which take place over a 10-week period, are available to children and adults. As exhibitions change, so do the themes of the workshops and lecture series, while the basic studio courses offered to groups as diverse as pre-schoolers and senior citizens remain constant.

One other approach to the museum school format is offered at the Albright-Knox Art Gallery in Buffalo, where gifted and talented sixth-graders recommended by the school art and classroom teachers, are introduced to the process of organizing an art exhibition. Through gallery and studio activities, stemming from the museum's collection, the groups investigate topics such as perspective or physical space, and then observe the installation of major exhibitions at the museum, which leads to the development and design of their own exhibition on the course of study that they are completing. This program offers students opportunities to meet with artists and museum professionals with whom they discuss their exhibition and program activities.

Family-shared experiences generally account for the first educational contact children receive in museums. Parents can consider the museum an educational environment, which can provide a great variety of learning experiences. Most family programs in museums are designed to help parents and children work together developing skills, interests, and capabilities. The family audience is a changing one. For example, an increasing number of single parents are seeking organized activities with their children. Museums can play an important role not only in opening museum opportunities to single-parents but also in creating networks that can be supportive for single parents.

At the Staten Island Children's Museum, parent-child workshops are available every Saturday afternoon for children 5 to 14. The workshops highlight themes of the museum's current exhibitions and encourage creative problem-solving and interaction between the parents and children. For example, in a workshop entitled, "Anything Can Happen in a Dream," discussions considered dreams are examples of experiences that involved the unusual and unexpected and focused on paintings by Salvador Dali and Rene Magritte. Before creating a surrealist collage made from magazine cut-outs, the parents and children engage in round-robin storytelling. Workshops can suggest at-home follow-up activities as well.

The National Zoo in Washington, D.C., and Old Sturbridge Village in Massachusetts both have adapted some existing tours and educational programs to accommodate the social and educational processes of children and families. Each has developed family programs that actively involve children and adults in learning and working together. At Old Sturbridge Village, a series of winter family workshops for creating Christmas cards, wrapping, small gifts, and tree ornaments, and for learning how 19th-century families lived. A five-part, full-day program on the natural habitat and history of the panda included observation of the panda, an audiovisual presentation on its habitat, a film showing a newborn panda cub, and discussions. Family activities ranged from making a stuffed panda for primary students to designing their own habitat in a cardboard box for later elementary students.

Science museums are able to help family groups learn more about the world in which they live, answering questions and creating special experiences. For example, family classes range from early morning walks along the lake shore to see migrating birds at the Museum of Science and Industry in Chicago, to building small take-home planetarium projector from a kit designed by the Lawrence Hall of Science in Berkeley, California.

The family activities at the Philadelphia Museum of Art include theater festivals, self tours, treasure hunts, pre-school programs, family tours, and Halloween look-alike parties. The self-tour booklets are designed to assist parents and groups of children through the museum by helping parents feel relaxed and unintimidated, by encouraging dialogues, and by suggesting new ways of approaching art and activities to reinforce the learning. Parents-booklets include a map, questions to ask children, directions for activities, factual information about the exhibits, and the rationale behind activities for children. A children's booklet, which parallels that for parents with additional space for written activities, becomes a visual souvenir of the museum experience.

One of the most successful events undertaken by the Founders Society at Detroit Institute of Art was the "Family Art Game," a Sunday newspaper supplement, which included illustrations and commentary about paintings and sculptures in the museum's collection. Prizes were awarded to families answering questions in the supplement.

The Performing Arts
Recognizing the appeal of the performing arts for both parents and children, several museums have expanded their offerings in this area. Live professional performing arts programs during the school year at the Detroit Institute of Arts are selected to suit particular age groups with "Wiggle Club" shows, for the three to five year olds, and musicals, plays, concerts, and films for those over 5 years of age. Following each live performance, children meet the professional performers, tour backstage, and see how performances happen.

"Wiggle Club" members participate in five specially selected shows designed for pre-schoolers, receive membership pass cards, and official club button, and a "graduation" certificate when they reach five years of age and are welcomed to attend the regular performances.

Some of the finest puppeteers in the area, present productions ranging from *Punch and Judy* to *Cinderella* and other classics in Saturday programs at the Museum of the City of New York. Following the puppet presentation, children take part in a step-by-step program on puppetry, including puppet-making, costuming, and stage design. Museums can also work with other cultural organizations to develop special performing arts programs. Working with the New Hampshire Historical Society in Concord, the Small World Theater has developed a puppet play *Ocean Born Mary*. The Small World Theater carefully researched a 257-year-old incident, tracing the legend in books, periodicals, diaries, correspondence and interviews. The play emphasizes a concern for genealogy, and is based around imaginary encounters between real persons involved in the legend and a contemporary child. At the Mayo Medical Museum, a professional performer concerned with the children's health education wrote an original puppet musical on the problems of smoking, *The Tragedy of McBreath*. The play trades on youngsters imaginative empathy with puppets to carry a specific message. The puppets were created by volunteers and staff, who performed the play for children, parents, and health care professionals.

The Milwaukee Art Center offers a series of programs that correlate art tours with the young people's symphony programs. The art museum and symphony work together to combine performances of the symphony's youth concerts with tours of the museums. Objects exhibited follow themes of the concerts, and relate the art to the music or to the flavor of the times.

Two examples of the way museums accommodate community groups in the performing arts can be illustrated by the Chinese Cultural Center in San Francisco, and the Corpus Christi Museum in Texas. The Front Porch of the Corpus Christi Museum, an indoor performing area, is a fully-equipped stage available weekend afternoons to anyone who would like to put on a performance. The Front Porch has been the scene of a wide range of folk dancing by Mexican children, high school student plays, poetry readings, pagents and parades, church choir recitals, holiday choir singing, piano concerts, and opera or symphony performances. The performers are all ages and all degrees of professionalism. The museum schedules the presentations and the performances are open to the drop-in audiences from the museum's visitors. The Chinese Cultural Center in San Francisco showcases community groups, providing rehearsal, training, and performance facilities. By sponsoring professional performances in music and dance, the center exposes the community and general public to first-rank performers and enhances the general level of the performing arts appreciation in the community. The center's youth orchestra has attained a high level of skill and has become a model for similar programs throughout the area. This program gives young musicians an opportunity to perform Chinese music using original Chinese musical instruments and adapted to western instrumentation.

The Children's Museum in Indianapolis has the only theater in Indiana which offers live performances for children on a regular basis. Performances are sold out almost as soon as they are announced, and reach a regional audience. Outstanding local opera, ballet, and modern dance companies, award-winning marionette and puppet troups, a nationally acclaimed theater storyteller and former lead circus clowns, as well as famous characters from Sesame Street, are among the many performers that have been presented on this stage.

Museums find performing arts programs advantageous because they can draw large and diverse audiences. However, performing arts programs also require consideration regarding fee structures, publicity, and attention to a number of scheduling and logistical details. Among the concerns are appropriate stage facilities: for example, dancers need very different requirements than puppet or small concert presentations. Museums frequently have made the mistake of not providing adequate facilities for the performers to change costumes, have appropriate lighting, or create a sense of intimacy in the staging of the presentation, which may be essential for the appropriate understanding of its aesthetics.

Summer Programs

The summer is a special time for children to take advantage of museums. In response to the extended amount of time that children have during the summer, museums have developed workshops, internships and field trips. Frequently, museums work not only with their membership, but with the large number of summer day camps that take place in the city, and frequent museums on rainy days. Multiple visit classes, film festivals, courses for scouts, member-only and pre-school classes, and workshops similar to those for school groups and families throughout the year.

Summer day camp groups that come from church groups, neighborhood associations, and all kinds of other camps that operate throughout the summer bring to the museum a series of unique problems. Children from day camps come to a museum for reasons ranging from a need to escape from a rainy day to a need for professionally led activities, since many of the day camp summer groups are led by unskilled high school students. Traditional formats are not appropriate for working with day camp groups. The attention span of the children is often very short, as the age groups can range from 5 to 13 years, and the organizational problems and staffing problems of the summer months can be insurmountable.

The Brooklyn Museum model combines summer internships for high school students with effective theater events, participatory workshops, and an examination of the museum's galleries. Interns learn how to operate shadow puppets, create puppets and scenery, and attend art history lectures to develop a program for the summer day camp students. When the day camps come for a fee, the children can observe a shadow puppet performance produced by the interns, and then produce their own shadow puppets and act it out. The format has allowed the museum to work with a large number of children, with some audiences exceeding 115 campers.

"Summer Camps" at the Herbert F. Johnson Museum in New York provide art museum experiences for children attending summer camps throughout the city. Pre-visit collaboration is close: the museum suggests "field trip" experiences to the various community day camps, and camp leaders choose from four possible workshops. Workshops are developed around the summer exhibition, and in the past have included Buddhas, farmers, poets, queens, and trees. Activities included searching, drawing, acting, talking, and more. "Articipation," day events held at both the museum and in the community during the summer, aims to promote the museum, art, esthetics, and the environment. Activities have ranged from building a fantasy environment to creating a stage set or collage. Materials are provided free of charge to participants for this program, which encourages a broad range of experiences with the museum staff and brings its resources to new community groups.

In-depth experience in history is provided to school-age children during the summer months for ten weeks at the Littleton Historical Museum. Children "build" their own communities just as the settlers of the past did: they learn blacksmithing, weaving, farming, carpentry, and printing, and the skills of cooperation that pioneers needed to transform an area from a raw settlement into a thriving community. Town meetings are held to elect city officials and to establish a form of government.

Festivals and Special Events

Festivals and special events are an excellent way of involving large numbers of people, often those who have never come to the museum before. Some events enhance special exhibitions: the Pompeii Festival at the Art Institute of Chicago, for example, complemented the Pompeii show with a Roman play given by high school drama students; demonstrations by artists of fresco-painting, work on parchment paper, and other techniques; and a dramatic eruption of a model Mount Vesuvius. The general topic of a museum can suggest other events: The Museum of Science and Industry, Chicago, hosts an annual student science fair with exhibits, papers, and prizes, as well as an annual children's science book fair.

Cultural heritage is a common thread in festivals and special events. Bilingual drama, dance recitals, musicians, and art exhibitions bring together students, teachers, and the public in an annual celebration of their cultural heritage at the Chamizal National Memorial in El Paso, Texas, on the Mexican border. The rich cultural heritage of the Southern Appalachians is the focus of the annual music and crafts festival sponsored by the Children's Museum of Oak Ridge, Tennessee, which features foods, blue grass and country music, and crafts demonstrations. Competitions in dancing, musical instrument playing, and other skills involve both children and adults, while making the denizen more aware of their local traditions.

At the Carnegie Museum of Natural History and many museums, members have an opportunity to discover the "behind-the-scenes" of museums in annual members' evenings. Curators and staff bring specimens and artifacts from their research collections into the galleries, and demonstrations and activities are developed to help members understand the functions and purposes of the museums.

Another approach to assisting not only the members of the museum but its community is the "Cabin Fever Sundays" at the Adirondacks Museum in Blue Mountain Lake, New York. In this isolated area, the winters are long, cold, and severe, and the population is quite spread out. Social gatherings are at a premium, and the museum has sponsored a series of "Cabin Fever Sundays." At these informal afternoons friends can meet and at the same time can learn and feel comfortable in the museum. Films are shown about the early logging of the Adirondacks and nearby Shaker Village, and lectures and demonstrations on the museum's collections are given.

During the year the Jacksonville Museum of Arts and Sciences offers many different festivals and special events. The Halloween "lock-in" takes place the last Friday in October. Children from eight to 11 years remain in the museum from 7 p. m. until 9 a. m. After a brief orientation outlining the rules of the evening, the children participate in a scavenger hunt to familiarize them with the layout and contents of the museum. Activities include a planetarium show, a trip to the rooftop observatory, mask-making and other art activities, Halloween games, movies, and refreshments. "Make-it-and-take-it" days are offered in conjunction with the major holidays throughout the year. For example, on Valentine's Day, children make folding cards, create small gifts and toys, do block printing, and build heart-shaped kites.

Honoring special holidays is an important part of many museums that are associated with cultural or traditional heritages. Kwanzaa festivals are becoming more common in museums serving black communities. In honor of "El Dia de Los Muertos," (The Day of the Dead), special exhibits, workshop activities, and slide presentations on the folk art and customs related to the day are offered in Hispanic neighborhood museums. Heralding the beginning of the farmer's growing season, Bauerntag (Farm Day) is an annual event at Historic Bethelehem in Pennsylvania. This event involves the sowing of vegetables actually grown in colonial Bethelehem. In addition to sheep-shearing, horse-shoeing, and other agricultural demonstrations, Bauerntag features food, drink, and a Moravian brass choir.

Christmas is a special time of celebration for museums with unlimited opportunities. At the Blandford Nature and Science Center, more than 2,000 visitors participate in log cabin Christmas, complete with antique toys, simulated feasts, seed and cone tree decorations, taffy pulls, and candle dipping. The annual Origami Folding Day takes place for five Saturdays at the American Museum of Natural History beginning in November. A huge tree is placed in the lobby of the museum is decorated with an array of natural history figures in origami made by museum members in artist-lead workshops. A local bank and the Children's Museum of Denver help children share unselfishly during the holiday season, children bring in two or more toys or games from home. The first toy is given to a child in an institution and coupons are given for additional toys. The coupons may be exchanged for any other toy displayed in the ballroom. Families also participate in raffles; watch jugglers, magicians, mimes; and meet with Santa Claus. The Franklin Institute Science Museum has combined "celebrations of light," which honor both Hannukah and Christmas with a variety of cultural events and science programs dealing with light.

The role of the museum as a community center—a meeting place and performance space—has grown over the years, especially in museums with facilities for drama, ballet, dance, and musical performances. Some museums fear that the basic mission of the museum may ultimately be lost if performing arts programs assume too large a role. The reasons for cooperating with performing arts groups in festivals can far outweigh such consequences: the public becomes more aware of the institution itself and its value to the community. Cultural institutions within a community also have a certain responsibility to maintain high artistic standards and to increase the potentials for arts in an area. Nevertheless, museums must be aware of the costs of such programs (guards, heat, light, etc.), and either arrange for adequate compensation or recognize the program as a donation to the community.

PROGRAMS OUTSIDE THE MUSEUM

Outreach activities in museums have been growing over the past years. These range from satellite facilities and mobile vans that travel to distant communities, to the development of publications and games that can be taken home or used by health organizations. The advantage of working outside of the museum are numerous, especially when incorporated into an existing program to serve several new audiences.

Field Trips

Field trips to historical, scientific, or natural sites can complement museum workshops. For example, the Museum of History and Science in Louisville sponsors Saturday morning field activities such as strolls through valuable local resources of the county forest, work with nationally recognized experts examining the falls of Ohio, or expeditions to unique Kentucky caves in their area. These field trips are available to high school students or family groups.

The Saturday Science Safaris of the Oakland Museum in California involve morning tours of the natural science galleries and afternoon visits to a Bay area natural environments such as a tidepool. The teenagers learn about the California history and natural environment while developing specific scientific skills.

Museums in cities have a special need to develop resources, maps, walking tours, and subway tours to help familiarize children with their diverse communities. The Junior Museum at the Art Institute of Chicago has developed a series of self-guided tours that take children to surrounding areas to study various elements in architecture and sculpture of the city. At G.A.M.E., a map of upper westside Manhattan has been developed by children to help others find out more about their community and favorite shopping places. The map includes favorite places to eat, shop, gather, and rent or purchase items ranging from a hamburger to favorite celebrations such as block parties.

Encouraging teenagers to explore the city has been the major focus of *Detours,* the Children's Museum of Boston's new travel center. *Detours* provides teenagers with basic information about Boston's transportation system, food, sports, music, work, and clothing. Twelve tour guides have been developed and keyed to *Detour's* own illustrated map of Boston's major transportation systems, and travel information is available for a nominal charge to walk-in visitors in the *Detours* office. A transit workshop and *Detours'* "passport" are part of the membership package. The "passport" entitles members to discounts on travel, admissions, and special events. At the travel center, questions are fielded by "teen agents," teenagers from neighborhood youth centers and clubs who have undergone special training sessions with the *Detours'* staff.

Located in central Oregon's John Day River Valley, the Hancock Field Station serves as the outdoor learning center in the natural sciences for the Oregon Museum of Science and Industry. Its programs include geology, paleontology, botany, zoology, and archeology. Emphasis is on assembling information gathered in the field investigations into a total picture of the natural world. Children older than nine years of age go to Camp Hancock for varying periods throughout the summer, and explore the natural history of the area in morning field trips. The importance of comprehensive field notes and photography as a means of recording field observations is stressed. Afternoons are spent in interest groups such as lapidary, photography, survival skills, and lab studies with specimen identification.

Outreach Programs

Many museums offer extension programs: traveling exhibits, mobile vans, speakers and loan kits. Many museums have adopted the programs described in the chapter on outreach programs to schools for community groups. Museums have also developed cooperative efforts with local recreation departments. The Museum-Goes-To-Camp at the Siouxland Heritage Museum in Sioux Falls, South Dakota is such an example. Pioneer and Indian artifacts are taken to children in the Jaycee Camps for the Handicapped, where the campers' disabilities range from mental retardation to cerebral palsy. Each session includes handling materials and answering questions that appeal to as many age and interest levels as possible. The success of the program has been varied, with the major difficulty being the short attention spans of the campers. The staff believes this program format, which complemented museum outreach programs in the city playgrounds, is a major community service.

Outreach programs to hospitals provide effective ways of reaching an audience that not only appreciates the programs tremendously, but often needs a pleasurable and intellectually stimulating experience. In developing hospital programs, museums should contact individuals within the institution who are familiar with the needs and requirements of working with hospital patients. It is essential to spend time with the hospital staff and the patients to become familiar with the children, the hospital routines, and physical requirements of operating a program in the hospital. The children's behavior, attention span, mobility level, and type of equipment to be used will vary according to their age and cultural background, as well as their illness and medication. The National Museum of Natural History developed a kit, "Indians of Long Ago, Washington" for use at the National Children's Hospital in Washington, D.C. The hour-long program begins with a slide show on Native Americans and their way of life, which involves the children in dialogue. Following this, objects that illustrate different aspects of Native American culture, such as feathers, acorns, and grinding stones, are passed among the children, who talk about their experiences with Native Americans and ask questions about their way of life. The Children's Museum of West Hartford, Connecticut, circulates boxes with artifacts and cards to patients in hospitals. Materials are occasionally exhibited in special hospital areas when space is available.

Museums and zoos have mobile units that bring staff members and volunteers with equipment, learning resources, and live animals into community centers. "The Haul of Science" travels to schools and community groups as part of the extension programs of the Buffalo Museum of Science. Program subjects range from reptiles, birds, and mammals of Western New York to the Iroquois Indians and fossils of the area. The Staten Island Zoo is one of many zoos that has adapted school programs to also accommodate hospitals and community organizations throughout the year.

The current "Museum-on-Wheels" of the Oakland Museum houses tactile exhibits on fibers. The van visits schools, senior citizen centers, hospitals, and community centers on request. The van is totally accessible to blind and visually handicapped people, and all labels are printed in bold type for the partially sighted and are in braille as well. The exhibit, "Fiber," focuses on animal, vegetable, and man-made fibers. Children can touch raw wool, feel the card that prepares the wool, and work a loom. They can examine sisal hangings and a spidery web, and see strands of grass, soap, netting, and linen. A slide show further illustrates fibers and their origins. All programs for the "Museum-on-Wheels" are tactile, with an emphasis on content as well as sensory experiences.

The Franklin Institute Science Museum began an exciting experiment in museum outreach with the opening of "Museums-on-the-Mall," a gallery and demonstration space located in Philadelphia's Gallery, an enclosed, four-story retail complex that is considered a prototype for a new generation of urban malls, designed to revitalize old central business districts. The "Museum-on-the-Mall" is a semi-permanent, admission free attraction, which presents brief yet rich museum experiences. The Franklin Institute Science Museum's most popular and exciting science programs are presented seven days a week and include live "science sampler" demonstrations and hands-on experiments. Four hands-on science stations and a two-dimensional display are in continuous operation during regular mall hours. Science stations include a zoetrope motion picture device, a giant mathematical puzzle, shadows experiment, and a Jacob's ladder electrical device. The two-dimensional display includes a set of perceptual puzzles and illusions, many of which span the art/science boundary in an interesting fashion.

A formative evaluation study indicated that the "Museum-on-the-Mall" reaches a significantly different, more diverse audience from that of the parent museum: more adults, fewer children, more unskilled and semi-skilled workers, more individuals versus family groups, and a much higher percentage of inner-city residents. The museum is also circulating *It's All Done with Mirrors,* an interactive exhibit that includes dozens of experiments and a mirror-maze. Shown at regional shopping malls, the exhibit takes one basic scientific principle—the law of reflection—and explores some of its myriad applications in science, technology and the visual arts.

The Museum of Fine Arts of Boston and the Lawrence Hall of Science are just a few of the museums that have expanded successfully in this area. South Street Seaport is developing a large part of its complex in association with a corporation that designs urban malls and will incorporate participatory exhibits and craft demonstrations along with the shops. Marketplace museum-satellites are an effective and important way for museums to reach new audiences.

Television Programming

Museums are beginning to explore the use of television and radio as a cost-effective way to reach large audiences. Museums have traditionally felt that the public should come to museums to see collections and use resources, because the most effective experiences occur through actual observation in galleries. Nevertheless, some museums have effectively cooperated with local television on weekly shows and special broadcasts.

Some museums, such as the Corpus Christi Museum in Texas and the Arizona-Sonora Desert Museum, have been working with local television stations for more than two decades. The Arizona museum's programs focus on animals and the special natural science aspects of the desert, while the Corpus Christi show is more general in its offerings. The director of the Corpus Christi Museum has been presenting a half-hour Saturday morning program for almost 25 years, and now it is a central point of community life. Children have grown up learning how to start a fire by rubbing sticks together, understanding how to examine a sea shell, and examining with the museum director a new acquisition at the museum.

Several museums, such as the Science Museum of Virginia, have cooperated with local television stations to produce broadcasts for a state educational television network, while others have developed specials with their local stations. Others have encouraged local public and cable stations to carry special broadcasts (such as, Saturn fly-by broadcasts), for which the museum provides special programs or commentary. Radio, which has primarily been used as a promotional vehicle, also offers educational opportunities. The McDonald Observatory, for example, began a short astronomy program for public radio stations with federal funding. When funding ran out, demand for the *Star Date* series was so strong that the program was syndicated for broadcast on public and commercial radio.

In developing broadcast programming, museums must consider the unique characteristics of the medium and how to tailor programming to use the medium to its best advantage. The sophistication of the youthful audience may lead museums to cooperate with the professionals of local and national broadcasting, rather than to develop their own individual programs.

The impact of video discs, cable television, and other new media technologies will dramatically affect the way museums communicate with their public in the years ahead. Several issues must be considered when viewing the potential of cable and video discs as technologies in the future of museums. Wiring for cable will increase the number of available channels to as many as 125, and may make channels devoted to educational or cultural programming for children economically feasible. Video discs and cassettes may make it possible to

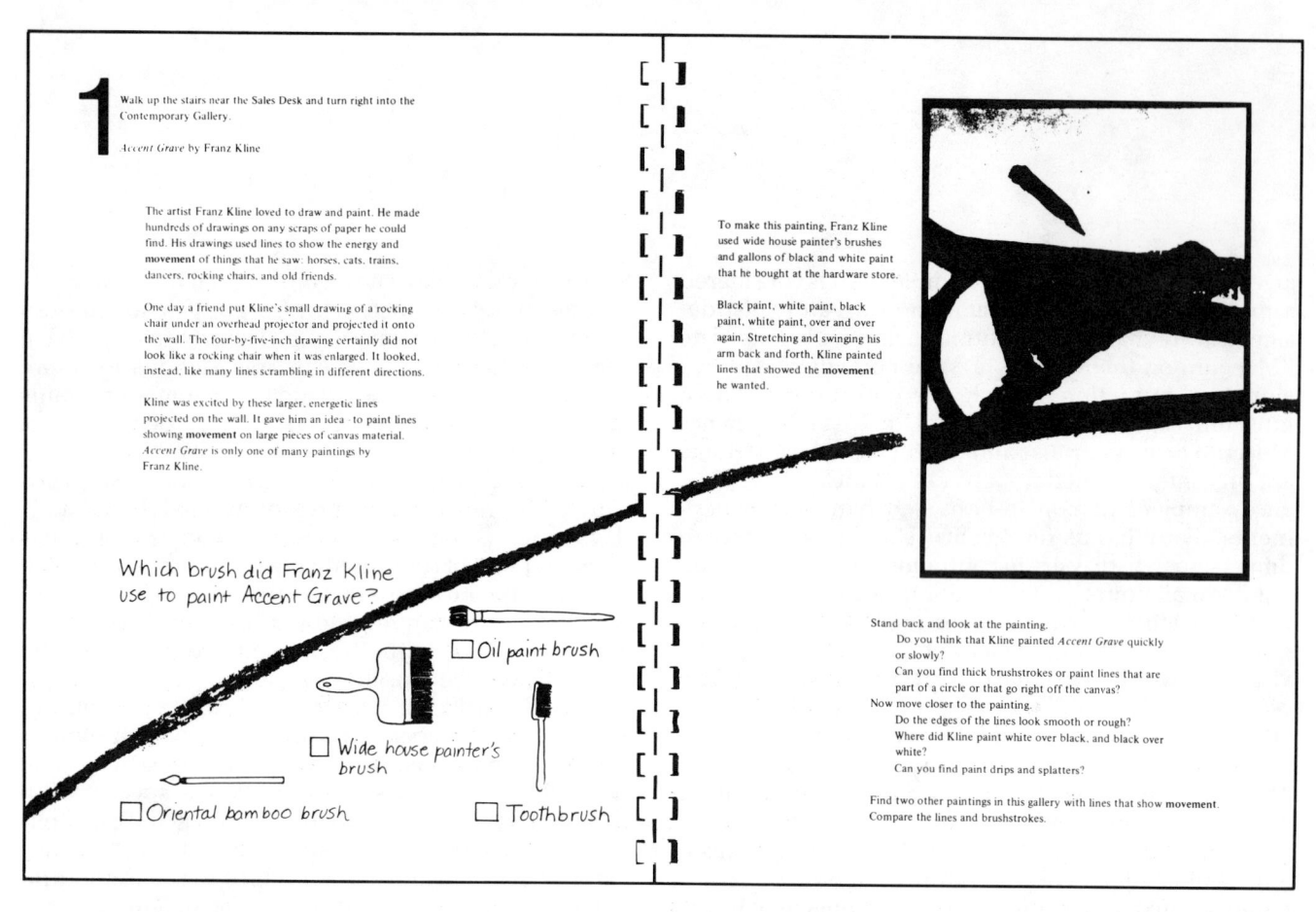

> **1** Walk up the stairs near the Sales Desk and turn right into the Contemporary Gallery.
>
> *Accent Grave* by Franz Kline
>
> The artist Franz Kline loved to draw and paint. He made hundreds of drawings on any scraps of paper he could find. His drawings used lines to show the energy and **movement** of things that he saw: horses, cats, trains, dancers, rocking chairs, and old friends.
>
> One day a friend put Kline's small drawing of a rocking chair under an overhead projector and projected it onto the wall. The four-by-five-inch drawing certainly did not look like a rocking chair when it was enlarged. It looked, instead, like many lines scrambling in different directions.
>
> Kline was excited by these larger, energetic lines projected on the wall. It gave him an idea – to paint lines showing **movement** on large pieces of canvas material. *Accent Grave* is only one of many paintings by Franz Kline.
>
> Which brush did Franz Kline use to paint Accent Grave?
> ☐ Oil paint brush
> ☐ Wide house painter's brush
> ☐ Oriental bamboo brush
> ☐ Toothbrush
>
> To make this painting, Franz Kline used wide house painter's brushes and gallons of black and white paint that he bought at the hardware store.
>
> Black paint, white paint, black paint, white paint, over and over again. Stretching and swinging his arm back and forth, Kline painted lines that showed the **movement** he wanted.
>
> Stand back and look at the painting.
> Do you think that Kline painted *Accent Grave* quickly or slowly?
> Can you find thick brushstrokes or paint lines that are part of a circle or that go right off the canvas?
> Now move closer to the painting.
> Do the edges of the lines look smooth or rough?
> Where did Kline paint white over black, and black over white?
> Can you find paint drips and splatters?
>
> Find two other paintings in this gallery with lines that show **movement**. Compare the lines and brushstrokes.

create visual libraries in the home, so that an entire home library of *3-2-1-Contact* may be possible.

Perhaps the most dramatic changes will occur in the linking of television and computers to create interactive television, which can register responses of children to the screen. Hooking computers to video discs will mean that children will be able to master elaborate data-retrieval systems, to create their own learning programs, and to store information for later use.

The opportunities of media have not been fully explored. While there is a great deal of criticism about television and the "30-second blitz of ideas and information" in some programming, technology's importance to and impact on the children of today cannot be overlooked. For example, six-year-olds entering first grade already have seen the moon, ocean floor, death and destruction throughout the ages, and some of the mysteries of the world. They have "traveled" more than the most literate man of 50 years ago. The children of tomorrow will have seen even more.

Publications and Written Resources

Museums produce different types of publications for children and adults. Written resource materials allow families and children to take part of the museum home with them. Often accompanied by slides or other resources, these formats have increased in popularity. The element of "fun" has played a major role, as museums have adopted formats that have worked with school groups to materials for parents, community leaders, and children.

As in all written materials, careful consideration must be given to clear layout and design, as well as to the kinds of activities the children will be asked to complete. The following materials have been tested and revised several times before their final publication. They illustrate the range of informational levels that can be accommodated with this format. While some are designed as games or workbooks, they all have an educational value and directly relate to the museum's permanent collections.

Museums have started to increase this particular format of reaching a diverse audience, because it can produce revenue and increase the public's awareness of the resources of the museum. In addition, developing high-quality resource materials can enhance the museum's ability to provide public services that otherwise would not be available. Although staff time is required to research, write, illustrate, and supervise publication, written materials are an excellent way for museums to communicate with large audiences that otherwise might not be tapped.

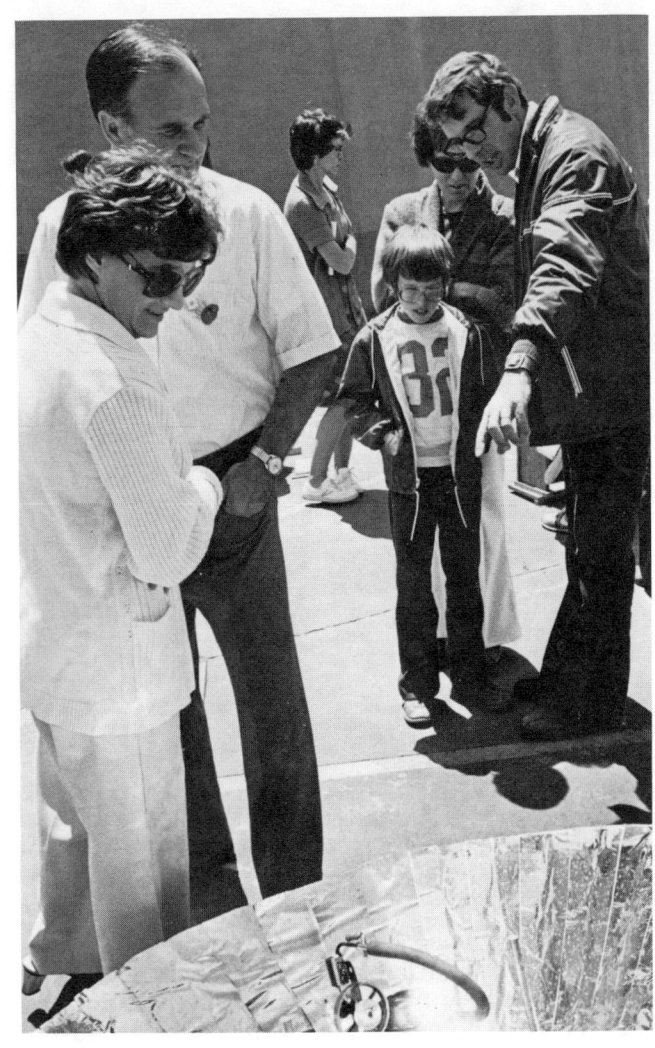

The following collection of written resource materials have been developed for parents, children, and community group leaders. They should be considered only as a sampling of the tremendous range of resources that are available in museums around the country and as illustrations of various types of documents that have proven to be effective.

Coming to a museum may be a special event for a parent and child or a community group. Creating a memory of that experience is essential, and carefully prepared self-guided materials that involve children in looking at the museum's resources can be effective ways of communicating with children while they are at the museum, and also when they are home. These pieces can become memory banks, conjuring up images of the time spent at the museum, and provoking study or investigations into new areas.

Several self-guided materials have been developed and discussed previously in the chapter on exhibitions and on school materials. Museums are developing more types of resource materials that can be used by families while they are in the museum. *Line Find*, for the galleries of the Cleveland Museum of Art, is a workbook for children to use while they explore the museum of galleries. Children investigate the way artists use and create lines as they examine a Franz Kline painting created with a housepainting brush and compare it with the outlined portrait of the Queen Nefertiti. The booklet illustrates print making with photographs of a printer at work in his studio, so children can understand the techniques used to create a Durer etching. Illustrated with drawings and stories by children, *Line Find* also includes activities that can be completed in the galleries and that provoke looking at the world outside the museum for additional characteristics of lines.

A very different approach to a self-guided tour can be seen in the Dennis the Menace comic book, in which the cartoon character visits the Alabama Space and Rocket Center. Dennis and his parents tour the entire space museum in Huntsville, Alabama, led by a guide dressed in his astronaut suit. Dennis gets into the usual amounts of trouble that are a part of his everyday life. The comic book is not only available for sale in the museum, but has been on newsstands around the country.

The Discovery Catalogue, designed by the Delaware Art Museum as a self-guided tour and follow-up to the exhibition, *The Consumer's Choice—The American Home, 1890–1940*, provokes careful looking in the museum and comparison to their own homes. The catalogue helps children trace the lifestyle changes over this 50-year period through the designs and functions of mass-produced and mass-consumed household goods. For example, children follow the development of a toaster or clock over a period of time, ending with an imaginary drawing of what they will be in the future. They examine photographs of homes and try to analyze how the rooms are different and similar to each other and to their own houses. In addition, they can create personal spaces for a family at different periods of time, and consider the invention of an electric dishwasher (first introduced in 1907) in comparison to current models. The museum found that the catalogue was effective not only with visiting school groups, but also with families, who were able to talk about their homes, the homes of their grandparents, and how things have changed today.

A Book to Color, a collection from the Worcester Art Museum, provides line drawings for children to color, based on the museum's collections. Eight drawn reproductions of sculpture, mosaics, tapestry, stained glass and paintings can be purchased at the book store. Children can use the coloring book to examine the museum's collections more carefully and to develop their own interpretations of works of art while they are at home.

The Franklin Institute's science museum game, *Expert,* orients visitors to the science museum and increases their comprehension of basic science concepts presented there. To appeal to players of various ages and educational backgrounds, the games may be played on a number of different levels. The simplest version, pre-school to aporoximately age nine, requires no reading ability or scientific knowledge. The intermediate level, aged 10 and up, parallels a visit to the museum, with the objective not simply to win a race around the board but to become an expert in one or more fields of science and technology. Playing pieces, molded on transportation objects from the museum's collections, are moved around a colorful game board representing the museum's floor plan. After landing in an exhibit hall space, players answer multiple-choice questions based on facts and concepts presented in the exhibit and in related demonstrations call for drawing chance cards and "do its." Chance cards give special directions that provide a balance of luck and skill. "Do its," simple science experiments or problems using materials commonly found around the house, involve other players and equalize opportunities to earn points. In the most advanced version, players can become experts in several fields and contract for one another's services as consultants. The game is sold in the museum shop.

The *Sky Challenger,* a star-finder kit with easy-to-do activities for families, was produced by the Lawrence Hall of Science, Berkeley. More than a map of the heavens, *Sky Challenger* is an exciting new tool for learning astronomy: What constellations did Native Americans see when they looked at the night skies? Where should you look to find planets, nebula, star clusters and other sky treasures? *Sky Challenger* works anywhere in the continental United States and includes six interchangeable star wheels, which can be used on a clear night to guide the star gazers' observations of the night skies. The introductory wheel, which shows only brighter, easy to find star patterns, acquaints beginners with the night sky. The Native American Constellations Wheel shows how to find the spider god, the raven, and the six wives who ate onions, and information about the rich lore developed by the tribes of North America about the night heavens. The Binocular Sky Treasure Hunt locates star clusters, nebulae, double stars, colored stars, and the andromeda galaxy, which can be seen with binoculars. Other wheels include activities such as finding the planets as they wander through the zodiac, and inventing your own constellations.

The Lawrence Hall of Science also has developed the "Outdoor Biology Instructional Strategies" (OBIS), a program on ecological relationships for youngsters 10-15 years of age. Activities focus on available environments—lawns, urban ponds and vacant lots—and involve children in a series of instructional activities, such as games, simulations, craft activities, experiments, and data analysis. Activities, which can be led by adults, include investigating ant behavior, searching for signs of animal and plant life on the beach, learning how aquatic animals move under water, and assuming the roles of birds and using beaks of different organisms that birds might eat.

The Children's Museum of Denver produces a variety of educational family publications (some of which include advertising) designed to help children understand more about the world in which they live. For example, *A-Maze-Ing Denver* illustrates 36 natural mazes of Denver's sites. Children follow a maze of the golden ball cactus, which is displayed year round at the Denver Botanical Gardens. Other mazes illustrate works of art from the local museums of natural history and art, and the downtown regional transportation district in Denver. It helps children learn more about their city and develop a closer sense of observation, while having a great deal of fun. The museum has produced a number of other game books such as *Denver City Games,* which is a guidebook to Denver; the *Babysitter's Guide* is a book for parents, babysitters, and children that makes child care more effective for all three groups and offers helpful hints about activities for children and the responsibilities of a babysitter; and the *In-Flight Activity Book* of games to engage children on airplanes.

The Children's Museum in Boston has cooperated with commercial publishers to publish books written by the staff. For example, a series of children's activity books *(Bubbles, Ball Point Pens, Milk Carton Blocks)* based on activities developed by one of the museum's staff members have been published. For example, *Bubbles* helps children to understand how and why bubbles float and shimmer and how to construct, blow, and form bubbles. As a result of bubble experiments, children learn more about geometric shapes and simple scientific concepts such as suspension and cell growth. *What If I Couldn't . . . ?*, based on a museum exhibit, is a book designed to teach about various physical and learning disabilities. By reviewing how children in wheelchairs play basketball and how children who are hard of hearing communicate, it helps clarify the complications and issues of being disabled. The clear language and approach of this book makes adults and children feel comfortable as they become acquainted with the needs and skills of people who are handicapped.

> *"Discover all the good things in LIFE. There is so much to discover in life . . . at museums, in libraries and the world around you. To enjoy life to its fullest, you need a strong healthy body. . . ."*

These are the lead lines on a LIFE cereal box advertisement and information panel on the Field Museum of Natural History. The museum in cooperation with Quaker Oats Company produced information panels on the back and side panels of the cereal boxes. The descriptions, intended to be read while eating the cereal, include illustrations and information on a number of dinosaurs, the size and weight ranges, and ways to distinguish between plant- and meat-eating dinosaurs. The response has been tremendous, with thousands of children writing the museum for "all the information that they have on dinosaurs." A form letter includes a list of books and encourages children to do research in their local libraries. Plans are underway for additional cereal box panels.

Obviously the union between museums and corporations in formats such as this helps increase the visibility of the institution and to educate a broad public.

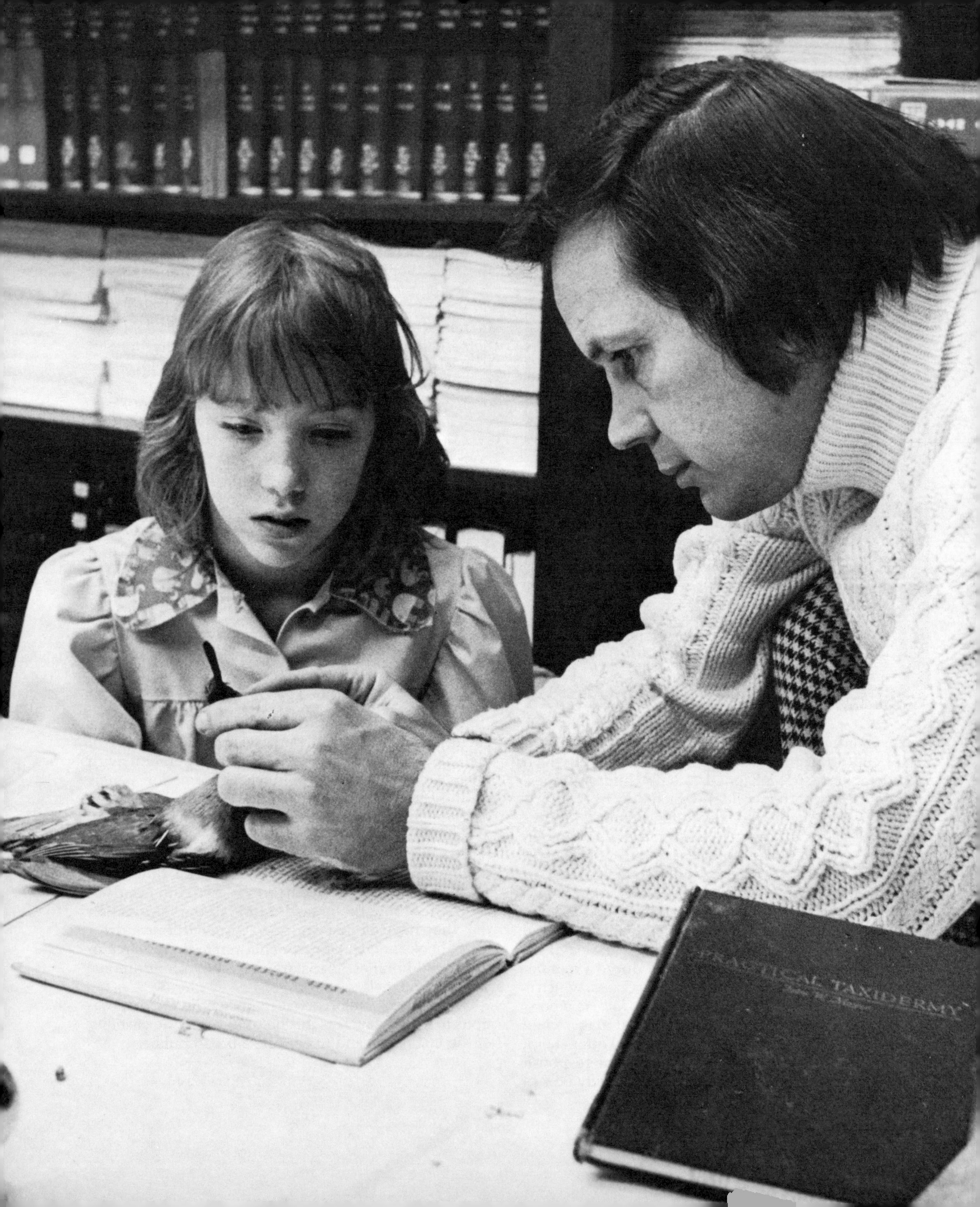
PRACTICAL TAXIDERMY

8. VOLUNTEERS IN THE MUSEUM

Volunteers help link the museum to the public. Museum guilds and volunteer committees offer people in the communities an opportunity to provide services both to the museum and to the community. They bring a wealth of resources: special skills, knowledge, time, energy, and a commitment to the museum. Volunteers provide a range of services: teaching in exhibit areas; assisting with research in the laboratories or collections; greeting school groups; providing information to the visitors; hosting special events; working in the museum's libraries; assisting the membership office; and many others.

Benjamin Ives Gilman, Secretary of the Museum of Fine Arts in Boston, is credited with employing the first docents to serve has guides and teachers to help with the exhibit interpretations in 1907. The American Museum of Natural History and The Metropolitan Museum of Art soon followed suit, developing their own volunteer programs to provide public services. During the last 70 years, the number of volunteers who work in museums has steadily expanded. In *Museums, U.S.A.*, it was reported that in 1971-72, nearly 64,200 volunteers were working in museums of all types. Nearly 60 percent of the museums in this survey used volunteers, and of those, 38 percent showed volunteers working in education departments.

There are no current estimates as to the number of volunteers involved in work with museums, but surely this number has increased over the past years. Volunteers work not only during the weekdays, but also in evenings, on weekends, and for special events. The image of a volunteer in a museum can no longer be limited to that of an upper middle-class woman who has time on her hands. Professional men and women, senior citizens, teenagers, handicapped persons—people from all walks of life—volunteer in museums in all kinds of ways. The type of work that volunteers are responsible for has expanded beyond guiding school groups. It now includes presenting puppet programs, managing museum shops, operating films, and assisting in fundraising, special events, demonstrations, and many other jobs.

Volunteers in museum programs for children are similar in most respects to volunteers in any museum program. The most important consideration for volunteers working with children is the caring for the child's learning process, rather than the communication of a specific amount of quantitative information. Volunteers should recognize the value of play as a way of learning and should place the child's needs over the information to be learned. An enjoyable museum experience can create continued interest in a topic and/a life-long respect for a museum as a place to learn and have fun.

Within the museum field, there is considerable controversy about the role of the volunteer. The Corpus Christi Museum defines members of its Guild as "volunteer staff members." The Guild's handbook explains," . . . you are now a staff member, and you have the same duties and privileges as the professional employees, not more, and not less." At Old Economy in Ambridge, Pennsylvania, the volunteers are also referred to as "basically an unpaid employee." In communities where the volunteer's role is highly valued, it is because the museum sees these volunteers as the public face of the museum, a link between the museum and its community. Museums that utilize and believe in volunteer programs probably succeed because they provide careful training, adequate supervision, proper recognition, and evaluation for those involved.

In her article, "Getting Decent Docents," Ann Bay recounts reasons that some museums have difficulties with their volunteers. "There was wide disagreement among the (24) museums visited about the merits of the volunteer docent programs. At some of the museums, volunteers had been banished from the scene, and part-time persons hired in their place; at others, the thought of using volunteers had never been seriously entertained. In both cases, volunteers were considered unreliable, difficult to train and manage, and unable to relate to children who are culturally different. Several museums had been sobered by cases in which wealthy, influential volunteers had virtually taken over museum education programs. The homogeneity of the typical docent program was frequently criticized, and a number of docent organizations are all too often social clubs that exist more for the docents than for the public."

However, most museums vigorously employ volunteers, realizing that their knowledge, skills, and enthusiasm make the museum come alive, and extend the museum's visibility far into the community. Volunteers, of course, must have certain qualifications, and must make a commitment to the museum, as do members of the professional staff. Treated as professionals and given responsibility, proper training, and encouragement, volunteers can do a professional job for a museum. Although the following ideas emphasize volunteers involved in educational activities, they are equally applicable to volunteer work in other parts of the museum.

THE NEED FOR A VOLUNTEER PROGRAM

The first stage in developing a volunteer program is the recognition of need for services. This need may be identified by curatorial, education, or membership departments, which have more work than can be accommodated with the existing staff. The museum must first of all carefully consider whether or not the service requested can be undertaken by volunteers. Volunteers must supplement the staff, not replace them. If the museum staff feels that volunteers are taking over their work, or keeping their salaries low, morale will suffer. However, if the museum staff needs assistance at the information desk, with in-school programs, to research animal behavior, or some other task that the staff agrees will complement and enrich the museum's goal, then the development of a volunteer program should proceed.

Several types of volunteers can assist the museum. Direct service volunteers are assigned regularly to such specific tasks as touring, research, inventory, preparation of school materials, or cataloging the library's acquisitions. Special service volunteers assist with special events or for a more confined period of time, such as entertainment, fundraising, and party functions. A list of some of the volunteer opportunities that are available in different museums are shown here.

Volunteer Opportunities

The following list is a sampling of the volunteer opportunities available in some museums.

Anthropology: Inventory and maintenance of collections; catalogue of artifacts, ability to read in German and Dutch; typing and preparing textiles for storage, and making of padded hangers.

Botany: Reorganize fungi collection; catalogue literature, type specimen labels; sort herbarium specimens; fold packets; file and index specimens; scientific illustration.

Building Operations: Indoor gardening; watering and repotting.

Clerical: Typing, mailing, filing, in all departments for special projects.

Demonstrators: Explain and demonstrate scientific equipment and concepts; interact with public answering questions.

Education: Docent tours, in-school programs, demonstration programs, assisting with public programs and special events, assisting with workshops and field trips.

Exhibition: Photo and design research; clay modeling; general assistance in exhibition preparation.

Geology: Wash and sort fossils; inventory of collections; upkeep of reprint library; catalogue of fossil vertebrates.

Gift Shop: Assisting at the sales desk, assisting with accounting and ordering, upkeep of records.

Information Desk: Ability to respond to requests for information about the museum's services and programs and collections.

The next important step is to secure a commitment to a volunteer program from the entire staff of the museum. Volunteers will be working throughout the museum, and should be recognized and respected, not ignored or treated like second-class citizens by all members of the professional staff. The staff must know why the volunteers are needed, understand their role, and training process, and assist in the evaluation of the program. Before proceeding to the operating phase of a volunteer program, those in charge should ask and answer some pertinent questions:

○ Who will administer the volunteer program?
○ How will the volunteers be trained?
○ Who will provide professional guidance and supervision?
○ How will volunteer needs and concerns be presented to the staff?
○ How will the program be evaluated by the staff and volunteers?
○ How will the volunteers receive recognition for their services?

One staff member should be assigned responsibility for supervising the volunteers. Some museums have hired volunteer coordinators to supervise the recruiting, placement, training, and evaluation of volunteers. In other institutions, the museum educator, director, or volunteer guilds or councils may handle the responsibility. Whoever is chosen must have certain qualifications: the ability to get along with people; the ability to inspire and motivate others; the facility for fostering staff and volunteers interaction; and an understanding of the audience encompassed by the museum's programs. Provisions should be made for office space, or at least an area that will be a central gathering place for the volunteers. Some museums have designed smocks or special badges as a way of identifying the volunteers to the museum staff and visitors. A bright, hospitable working environment, and a supportive, interested staff will do much to keep the program going.

The volunteer coordinator should be responsible for planning the programs with volunteers and staff; organizing, coordinating, and delegating work; staffing programs; assuring the accuracy of attendance records; directing and controlling the overall program; and developing leadership among volunteers. In addition, the coordinator should remain aware of legislative trends and decisions regarding volunteer benefits and insurance regulations. The importance of selecting the right person for the volunteer coordinator's job cannot be overestimated. The goals and policies of the volunteer program must be clearly understood by the coordinator, members of the staff, and prospective volunteers. Written policies should define the relationships and performance expectations of both the staff and the volunteers. Plans for volunteer recruitment, placement, training, supervision, methods of evaluation, types of benefits and termination should be agreed upon by staff and volunteers and put in writing. A uniform system of recording volunteer hours and a minimum

Hospitality: Serve at evening receptions and morning coffee hours for special events, trustees; plan and supervise food preparation, table decoration, care of tablecloths, etc.

Library: Catalogue acquisitions; book repair and conservation; shelving in general and departmental libraries; maintain card files.

Membership: Develop and record prospects; file; type; staff information and membership booths on weekends and holidays; assist with membership promotions.

Photography: Catalogue slides and prints.

Planning and Development: Individual prospect research.

Public Relations: Assist with general office activities; research facts; organize, write, and produce press releases, photocaptions, radio and tv public service announcements, research media coverage through press clippings, and electronic media reports.

Speakers Bureau: Present general talks on the museum, using slides to community groups; present lectures on special events or topics of particular interest.

Special Events: Assist with special fundraising events, such as concert benefits, lectures, films, parties, craft shows, etc.

Zoology: Assist in on-going research through observation, documentation; general maintenance of collection; prepare and catalogue cards for the reprint library; label specimens; maintain fish tanks or other special areas, inventory contents of tanks or areas of the zoo; scientific illustrations; skin mammals; flesh and clean bones; label specimen boxes; install new specimens in collection.

standard for the number of hours to be worked should be defined in advance. As has been stated before, mutual respect and understanding between volunteers and the professional staff is a critical element in the successful volunteer program. Some museums, for example, the Science Museums of Charlotte, North Carolina, and the Wadsworth Atheneum, Hartford, Connecticut, have guilds or volunteer committees with established bylaws and constitutions. These documents define the objectives of the program, the relationship between staff and volunteers, and the rules governing the volunteers. In addition, such documents define the objectives of the program, the relationship between staff and volunteers, and the rules governing the volunteers. In addition, such documents show that the staff and volunteers have decided together how they can most effectively serve each other and the public.

RECRUITMENT

Potential volunteers are attracted to a museum for a variety of reasons: the challenge of the work, increased responsibility, personal growth and development, recognition by the museum and the community, continuing educational opportunities, utilization of special skills, development of new interests, and the opportunity to make friends. Special skills—experience with the handicapped, facility with foreign language, abilities to spin or weave—can all be put to use.

Some museums have faced problems recruiting volunteers while others have two-year waiting lists of people who want to get into the programs. Plans for recruiting volunteers must be thought out carefully and implemented cautiously. An overabundance of volunteers can lead to unrest and dissatisfaction. Too many volunteers and not enough work to be accomplished can weaken the program and discourage the more qualified.

After determining the skills required for the program, the coordinator must explain the job requirements to prospective volunteers. Specific job descriptions are important tools in placing the volunteers in the right position. A clear definition of the volunteer's role and relationship to the goals of the overall museum is essential. Recruitment materials should explain who the volunteer will be helping, what audience they will be working with, and why the program is being offered. Recruitment materials must also clearly state the requirements regarding attendance at training sessions and the commitment of time considered to be a minimum for completing the tasks at hand.

There is no better recruiter than a satisfied volunteer. Word of mouth, the invitation to a friend who is not already involved, or letters to the museum's membership are frequent methods of recruitment. Media publicity to television, radio, and local newspapers, assures coverage throughout the community. Enlisting the aid of existing volunteer community organizations can often help with preliminary screening of potential applicants. Organizations—such as the National Council for Jewish Women, the Volunteer Bureau, Volunteer Action Centers, the Junior League—, educational societies, sororities, colleges, and universities are possible reservoirs of volunteer help. Service clubs, such as Rotary and Lions, are likely gatherings for men interested in volunteer work on weekends or evenings. Along these lines, volunteer programs involving entire families can fulfill certain needs. Senior citizens also offer a wealth of talent and time, and help to illustrate the positive aspects of working with these people The Capital Children's Museum in Washington, D.C., and the Carnegie Institute in Pittsburgh, both have senior citizens working in their museums in different program areas. The Retired Senior Volunteer Program (RSVP), the Foster Grandparents, the Senior Service Corps, and the American Association of Retired People are all active groups with potential museum volunteers.

Seeking to create an intergenerational program that would use the museum as a setting for children and older people to meet and work together, the Capital Children's Museum developed "Across the Generations." The volunteer program uses senior citizens, from all economic, racial, and social levels of the Washington, D.C. community, in all aspects of the museum's operations. Residents in homes of senior citizens prepare exhibit materials. Volunteers use their special skills for student enrichment programs, such as piano classes. Others are trained as guides and demonstrators. A special program brings students together with older volunteers for candid, valuable discussions of what it means to age and to be old. The museum recognizes that the older person is a dedicated, reliable worker who can bring years of personal skills and experience to assignments. Grants have made it possible for the museum to provide senior volunteers with transportation subsidies and for information for other museums interested in similar programs.

Reaching out to inner city volunteers is often difficult. If the museum is not located in their neighborhood, these people may not be aware of the museum's needs and programs. Contact with neighborhood recreation and nutrition centers as well as churches is a good beginning. Programs having the greatest appeal to such volunteers are short-term, high visibility projects involving their neighborhoods.

Involving the corporate and business community through "release time" programs can assist the museum in gaining the valuable expertise of these professionals and help the corporations fulfill community service commitments. For example, in the National Air and Space Museum in Washington, D.C., professionals from NASA and other federal agencies involved with air and space concerns, serve as "rovers" in the exhibits areas, available to answer questions to the visitors. Other professionals—engineers, public relations staff, lawyers, and accountants—can assist the museum in a variety of ways by donating their time and expertise not only during the week, but on weekends and evenings.

Young people are a wonderful source of energy and enthusiasm. The Children's Museum of Indianapolis has an extensive volunteer program for young people that allows them to "grow up in the museum." Currently, some high school volunteers are working on the weekends demonstrating different crafts in the American gallery. Museums such as the Memphis Pink Palace, have junior curator or trustee programs for young people who have become very active in the museum. The popularity of internship programs, in schools and colleges, has been increasing. Museums offer an opportunity for students to work and study with professionals. In many cases, credit for the volunteer work can be arranged with schools and universities.

SELECTION AND PLACEMENT

Once new volunteers begin to apply, the next steps are selection and placement. Application forms should include information on both the professional and personal background and the experiences of the volunteers. These applications should help to determine if the volunteer has the necessary skills to work in a particular area of the museum. It is also helpful for the application to include requests for information regarding the amount of time and periods of time when the volunteer will be available.

After studying applications, the coordinator and/or a committee of existing volunteers should conduct interviews, giving attention to the following points:
- the volunteer's goals and skills
- the volunteer's reasons for wanting to work in the museum
- the different opportunities available, for example, docent, exhibit research, museums on wheels, research, library, fund raising
- the areas of responsibility
- the qualifications needed
- the training and attendance requirements.

The interview is a critical time in the selection and placement of volunteers. In addition to determining if the volunteers have the necessary skills to do the job, such factors as their attitude and willingness to seek advice and ability to work with other people as well as their expectations about their service to the museum can be determined. If the volunteer's skills seem better suited for another area of the museum, now is the time to make such a recommendation. The interview should also include a review of the duties, commitment of time, schedule for training, and other requirements that will be asked of the volunteer. Many museums are beginning to use volunteer contracts such as the one illustrated from by the High Museum of Art in Atlanta. These contracts contain two parts: an agreement by the museum to the volunteer and from the volunteer to the museum.

At the end of the interview, a prospective volunteer must have a clear understanding of the schedule of performance to be agreed upon, the duties to be performed, the nature and schedule of the evaluations to be performed, an understanding of what will happen if they miss their assigned working period, the length of their service, and a clear understanding of the training program.

The placement of the volunteer, whether in an educational or research area of the museum, must be carefully done. Prospective volunteers should meet with the staff member who will be primarily responsible for working with them. The staff member should have the final say as to whether or not they will be able to work effectively with this particular individual. Misplacing a volunteer will often do more harm than good. The placement process requires a sensitivity to both the staff and the volunteer.

ORIENTATION PROGRAM

Staff members who will be working with volunteers should be familiar with the volunteer's job description and individual background. They should, therefore, participate in the orientation session, which may occur as part of the training program or prior to the program. It is important for the trainee to understand the total concerns of the museum, as well as the particular department for which they will be working. The responsibilities and functions of staff members in the museum (director, guards, curators, educators, maintenance personnel), should all be described. Background information on the founding of the museum, when it was built, what the building contains, what the museum offers the community, the scope of the exhibits and collections, the research and conservation responsibilities, the main educational activities, the management and structure of the museum, annual operating budget, endowment funds, hours that the museum is

---

VOLUNTEER CONTRACT
High Museum of Art, Atlanta, Georgia

The Museum's Curator of Education and her staff, assisted by the Department of Children's Education Volunteer Advisory Board, agree to:

1. Place the Volunteer in the program most suited to the Volunteer's special abilities through pre-placement interviews and if necessary, in consultation, reassign a volunteer at the discretion of the Curator of Education, the Executive Committee of the DCE Volunteer Advisory Board and/or the Director of the Museum.

2. Provide appropriate and complete training for the Volunteer to enable the Volunteer to work confidently.

3. Make available on-going training on current exhibitions and give sufficient advance notice of those lectures designated "required."

4. Grant, upon written request, a two-month extraordinary leave without substitute (maternity, special travel, etc.).

5. Maintain insurance coverage for the DCE volunteer during those hours when he/she is carrying out Museum business, whether within the Museum or at another location. (The Volunteer's personal property is not covered.)

6. Keep accurate records of the Volunteer's service. Repeated absence and/or tardiness will be reviewed by the Volunteer Program Chairman and, in extraordinary cases, referred to the Executive Committee of the Volunteer Advisory Board for final review.

7. Inform the Volunteer of any public holidays or days when individual program is not operating, and of cancellation of tours when office is notified in advance by participating school.

8. Review all suggestions of the Volunteer regarding the operation and content of her/his individual program.

9. Provide a reference based on the Volunteer's record of service at the Museum, if such a reference is requested by the Volunteer.

10. Provide personal assistance in art education and teaching techniques on a one-to-one basis by observing the Volunteer's on-the-job performance.

Staff Signature _____ Date _____   Advisory Board Signature _____ Date _____

The High Museum of Art
Department of Children's Education
VOLUNTEER SERVICE AGREEMENT

The purpose of the VOLUNTEER SERVICE AGREEMENT is to make clear the mutual responsibilities which enable each volunteer to give meaningful and competent service to the High Museum through the Department of Children's Education.

The Volunteer agrees to:

1. Carry out responsibilities in good faith and to the best of his/her abilities.

2. Fulfill the training requirements of his/her program, including attendance at on-going training lectures or training exhibitions where designated "required."

3. In case of absence during fall or on-going training, arrange to view videotape as soon as possible and prior to (next) working date.

4. Arrive on time and remain for full working and/or training sessions.

5. In case of absence, secure a substitute and provide advance notice to the Day Chairman or Program Chairman.

Program _____ Day _____ Working Hours _____

Date _____ Volunteer Signature _____

open, the costs of visiting the museum, and how to book a tour, or schedule special events, should all be reviewed because these questions will be frequently asked of all volunteers. The use and purpose of evaluation should be introduced at this time, so that the concept of review can be discussed openly.

The orientation program is a chance to answer the volunteer's questions. It should provide them with the necessary background information to answer some of the most frequently asked questions about the museum and to understand their role and function within the institution. It is also the time to get a clear understanding of the expectations that the volunteers have of their training and responsibilities in the museum.

TRAINING PROGRAM

Training programs vary in length and number of sessions, depending on the responsibilities of the volunteers. The training programs should be designed to provide information and skills necessary to carry out their work. These sessions should allow volunteers to learn about specific subject matter and effective methods of communication. Volunteers involved in scientific research are often trained one-on-one, while docents involved in teaching of children of adults, are trained in groups. Volunteers working with collections need to learn how to catalogue, record, photograph, mount, measure, and store specimens. Volunteers involved in the educational aspects of the museum need to know the collections, and how to handle equipment, such as film, slides, and tape recorders, as well as how to get groups in and out of the galleries or special educational areas. Specific information on the logistics (where to sign in, where to store coats and lunches, and what to do in case of accident or fire) should be a part of all training programs. Depending on the specific nature of their work, a variety of professionals can be involved in the training session, including educators, curators, professionals from outside the museum.

Training sessions should make good use of the volunteer's time and be offered when they will reach the maximum number of trainees. Therefore, sessions might be offered on the weekends, in the evenings, as well as during the weekdays. Training schedules are usually rigorous and requirements for entry into service quite high. Some museums charge a training fee, which ranges from $5 to $80, and covers the cost of books, outside lecturers, film rentals, and miscellaneous materials.

Others require attendance at colleges for specific courses. Necessary resource materials should be prepared or made available to volunteers, with shelves set aside in the library, and special books ordered or printed in advance.

Involving the volunteers in setting the goals of the training sessions can increase the program's applicability to their work as a volunteer. Concerned with doing a good job, the volunteers will want a variety of information, as well as opportunities to try out their skills as teachers, operators of film equipment, or mounting specimens. The goal of the volunteer should be to continually learn how to do their job better. From the outset, the training program should help to establish a feeling of trust between the volunteers and the staff, so that improvements can continually be made in the training sessions and in the volunteer's performance. Questions should be addressed on topics such as what is expected of them, what they expect to learn in the training program, what their areas of need are, and where they feel comfortable and confident, as well as what will make them feel that their gift of time to the museum is worthwhile. Trainees should evaluate the training programs, and this will make the evaluation of their performance more acceptable.

Each volunteer training program is different. Docents require special communication skills, while volunteers working with collections or exhibits need research skills. It is important to remember that the volunteers will teach in the way in which they have been taught. Therefore, the training session should include opportunities to practice what they have been told to do. Lectures, research projects, demonstrations, role-playing, observational practice, small group discussions, and understanding of the needs of the handicapped should all be included in the program. The training programs should also have time for personal growth and development of self-confidence. It is a time for volunteers to get together, to learn to know each other, and to articulate their expectations about their commitment of service to the museum.

DOCENT TRAINING

Training docents requires special attention to a number of areas, including the content of the museum's exhibits and collections, communication skills and developmental levels. In some museums, the emphasis in the training program is on the content of the collections to the exclusion of all else. Remembering that the way a volunteer is trained will influence the way they communicate, it is important to provide time in the training program for the reinterpretation of the museum's collections by the docents. A good training program, of course, must help the volunteer learn how to utilize the resources of the collections creatively. For example, docents in a zoo or natural history museum, might study adaptation, ecology, or family structure; in an art museum, such themes as color, family life, the nature and images of life and death might be the threads used to weave the diverse elements of the collections together.

Part of the training should be devoted to developing model tours so that docents learn how to organize their subject matter. Utilization of themes and varied teaching techniques should be an integral part of the program. The docent training program should also include information about how adults and children learn, learning strategies, and communication techniques. The docent must be able to help children realize that the museum is not a schoolroom. Here they can stroke the skin of a boa constrictor, watch the evening sky as it was 2,000 years ago, or feel a pre-Columbia culinary vessel. These experiences are unique and the volunteers will need to feel comfortable not only in teaching children and adults how to look at artifacts and animals, but also in awakening their sensibilities.

Flexibility is the key to success for a docent. Different groups will respond differently to a topic, according to such things as the time of day, the weather, and their curriculum under study. Children can be restless during a storm, anxious to be outside in the spring, or lethargic before lunch. Children with handicaps require special attention. Children who are bilingual may call for a more detailed explanation of certain concepts or facts. Whatever their level, students do not like to be talked down to. A docent must learn not only to be enthusiastic and cheerful, but to be comfortable and unafraid to answer a question by saying, "I do not know." The dynamics of working with groups may mean that classes arrive late, that tour groups are too large, or that disciplinary problems may arise. Volunteers should know how to cope with these situations, and feel confident in the decisions that will have to be made. Volunteers should also remember how to dress: comfortably and neatly, without ostentation.

Techniques for handling a group of children in the museum are varied, but it is always important to smile and to be friendly and flexible. Probably the most important time of the tour is the first five minutes, when docents welcome the children at the bus and bring them into the museum. During this time one docent can talk informally to the teacher and another to the children. In the process, they will acquire some important clues about the group: their reasons for coming, their familiarity with the museum, their energy level, their behavior patterns. After the group has entered the museum, it may be necessary to continue the introduction if the group has not been there before. It is important to tell the children where they will go, what they will see, and what the experience will lead to several times throughout the tour.

Some museums have the docents train and work in teams, a helpful way to bring new docents into the program, enabling them at the same time to benefit from experienced docents. Team teaching is also an effective way to remove the pressure from docents who are nervous about the first few museum lessons. Work-

Developing Gallery Tours

This outline could be helpful to docents in developing ideas for tours.
1. Age of Group

2. Theme

3. Museum Objects
   a.   d.
   b.   e.
   c.   f.

Organizing the Tour
1. How will you learn about your group?
2. What concepts will be taught?
3. Museum objects:
   a. Looking skills
   b. Information about the objects
   c. Special vocabulary
4. How will you make transitions from one object to another? Or one gallery to another? Questions or statements?
5. Conclusion: Coming together—what do they remember? What do you think they will remember and why?

ing in teams, the volunteers also begin to develop a sense of self-criticism by spending time after the tour in a review of the materials presented and the effectiveness of their teaching approach with the children. During these review sessions, volunteers can exchange experiences and comments on each other's performance. Some museums use videotapes of tours and training sessions, so that docents can see themselves in action and evaluate their own performances. The quality of the training program will do much to set the tone for this kind of interchange. The staff must also allow docents to be critical of them—as well as of each other—and to comment on their effectiveness as teachers. After participating in the training workshop, and absorbing a vast amount of information, docents often have unrealistic expectations about how much information, and how many experiences can be crammed into a school program limited to one or two hours. Care should be taken to help the docents understand and fully realize the value of the simple, well-constructed learning experience.

A museum wishing to illustrate the importance of relating the museum experience to the student's everyday life, must do the same for the docent. The training program should clearly indicate that learning is not a one-time proposition. All effective docents need to study, learn, and prepare for the tours each week. Since it is impossible for the staff to provide all the information about subject areas in a matter of hours, most training programs extend beyond opening sessions, with workshops once or twice a month throughout the year to discuss techniques, problems, and future events.

For example, the Oakland Museum has a training course offered every two years to replace volunteers who have dropped out of the program. The training program includes a general survey of the museums' galleries in which the docent chooses to work, plus two semesters at a junior college studying California ecology and other related subjects. Docents who have served for two years of regular duty can be trained to give total communication for the deaf tours. The language of total communications is not so much a method of combining sign language with voice as it is a philosophy, a way of thinking that considers the needs of the deaf and involves gestures, speech, formal signs, finger spelling, speech reading, reading, and sometimes writing or drawing. The volunteers are trained by the California School for the Deaf, as part of its community outreach program. The volunteers must learn to understand in the language used by the deaf people, which differs in syntax and concept from English.

Many would-be docents who have returned to full-time work and cannot participate in the weekday docent program. The weekend docent program of the North Carolina State Museum of Natural History is designed to train volunteers in the evenings and to have them provide services on Sunday afternoons, the museum's peak visitation period. At that time, the volunteers station themselves in the exhibits areas with objects and specimens, and talk to the visitors, and give talks at designated times. They not only provide factual information on natural history but also inform the public about museum educational programs. They also distribute postcards on which visitors can ask a question (which cannot be answered by the docent), write their address, and, thus, expect a reply from the museum staff the following week. The program has been extremely successful and is being expanded because it serves as a personal touch to the visitors.

ADVANCED TRAINING PROGRAMS

Seminars and study trips are incentives for continuing involvement in the volunteer program. After one year of work at the San Diego Zoological Garden, volunteers may take a 12-week advanced course in a specialized areas of study, such as the earth sciences and anthropology, taught by curators. At the New Orleans Museum of Art, docents who have successfully completed one full year in the program conduct docent research projects, which are designed to provide them with fresh, thematic approaches to viewing art works in the museum's collection, and to draw relationships between the various museum's galleries. Each participant researches, writes, and presents a paper to the research group. Experienced and motivated volunteers in a museum's program can help prepare special educational materials, train teachers, give public presentations, or provide counseling to new volunteers entering the programs. Advanced programs, whether they involve specific training or additional responsibilities given to exceptional volunteers, are an important way to continually recognize the value of a volunteer's service to the museum.

EVALUATION

The general aim of the evaluation is to improve the quality of the volunteer program, preserving what is good and improving the rest. An effective evaluation must include a review of the total program: the training, the service of the volunteer, and the response by the audience. The need for an evaluation should be agreed upon from the beginning, and both staff and volunteers should clearly understand the critieria for the evaluation.

An evaluation should be continuous, and should take many forms—interviews, questionnaires, observations, records of attendance, and records of accomplishments. Evaluations should include comments from the staff, volunteer coordinator, volunteers themselves, and the audiences that they are serving. Ned and Mary Flanders have developed a useful method of evaluating the performance of docents which includes the measurement of factual content, communication skills, and the group response.

Problems that occur should be discussed openly and resolved immediately. Often when a volunteer needs to improve techniques in touring, a meeting with the staff or other volunteers can be the fastest and best solution. Constructive suggestions should be the rule. Personalities will play a large role in an evaluation, but firm leadership can guide the way. If there is a high turnover rate among the volunteers, or a dwindling enrollment in the program, the staff should immediately begin a thorough review of the entire program.

One of the most difficult issues surrounding volunteer programs is that of dismissing a volunteer. There are occasions when volunteers, like paid professional staff members, do not work out. They may not fulfill their commitment to the museum, perhaps by being consistently late, not finding a substitute, or failing to complete a training program. In some cases, even with the most careful placement program, the volunteer may not meet the standards of the job. Handling the review of a volunteer's performance need not be a difficult matter, if the museum has clearly stated the objectives of the program, the commitment required of the volunteers, the evaluation process, and the criteria for review, and has maintained careful records of the volunteer's performance. With this material in hand, the museum can use evaluation committees or volunteer advisory boards, composed of all volunteers or volunteers and staff, to assess the performance of each volunteer. The longer a problem volunteer remains a part of the program, the more difficult the management of the program, the maintenance of morale between the other volunteers and the staff will be. In general, evaluations should be seen as a method of improving the training program offered by the staff, and the performance of the volunteer.

COMMUNICATION

Newsletters can be published by volunteers to maintain communication with the staff and volunteers who work at a variety of jobs in the museum. Typically such publications advise of future exhibitions and events, the needs of different programs, special requests from the staff, and personnel changes in the staff or volunteer corps. *Pawprints*, a newsletter for the junior membership of the FONZ (Friends of the National Zoo) include submissions by the volunteers such as poems, sketches, and short stories about their experiences at the zoo.

Another useful communication system used by many of the museums is an advisory board to serve as a liaison between the volunteers and the staff. Composed of volunteers and staff directly involved in the program, such boards maintain standards and formulate policy. For example, volunteers having difficulty meeting the time commitment required by the museum may ask the advisory board to review their problem. These advisory bodies allow volunteers to share actively in planning and decision-making, and thus enjoy a sense of responsibility for their service.

RECOGNITION

A program with good recruitment, an intelligent orientation, purposeful and relevant training, and well-defined assignments still needs one more ingredient: recognition of the work done by the volunteer. The desire for recognition for a job well done is a human need, and a staff too busy to acknowledge the achievement of volunteers may lose them. Recognition—whether formal or informal—is a way of saying that the museum cares. It also bolsters the volunteer's self confidence, and provides an incentive for future service.

Informal recognition is evident in the daily acceptance of the volunteer as an effective member of a team. In the working environment of a museum, such social amenities as "good morning," "we missed you," and "thank you," will carry the volunteer a long way.

Formal recognition may take many forms:
o a well-managed volunteer program
o quality training
o comfortable volunteer headquarters.

Seminars and articles for volunteer administrators on interpretation and management have been produced by the American Association for State and Local History, American Association of Museums, and professional journals.

The following are excellent sources for information about volunteer programs:
o The National Center for Voluntary Action
  Box 4179
  Boulder, Colorado 80302
o The Association of Volunteer Bureaus
  801 North Fairfax Street
  Alexandria, Virginia 22314

References Cited
Bay, Ann. "Getting Decent Docents," *Museum News*, 52 (April, 1974), pp. 25-29.
Flanders, Ned and Mary. "Evaluating Docent Performance," *Curator*, 3, No. 19 (1976), pp. 198-225.
Museums U.S.A.: Art, History, Science and Others. Washington, D.C.: National Endowment for the Arts, 1974, pp. 92.
Sutherland, Mimi. "Total Communication," *Museum News* 55 (January/February, 1977), pp. 24.26.

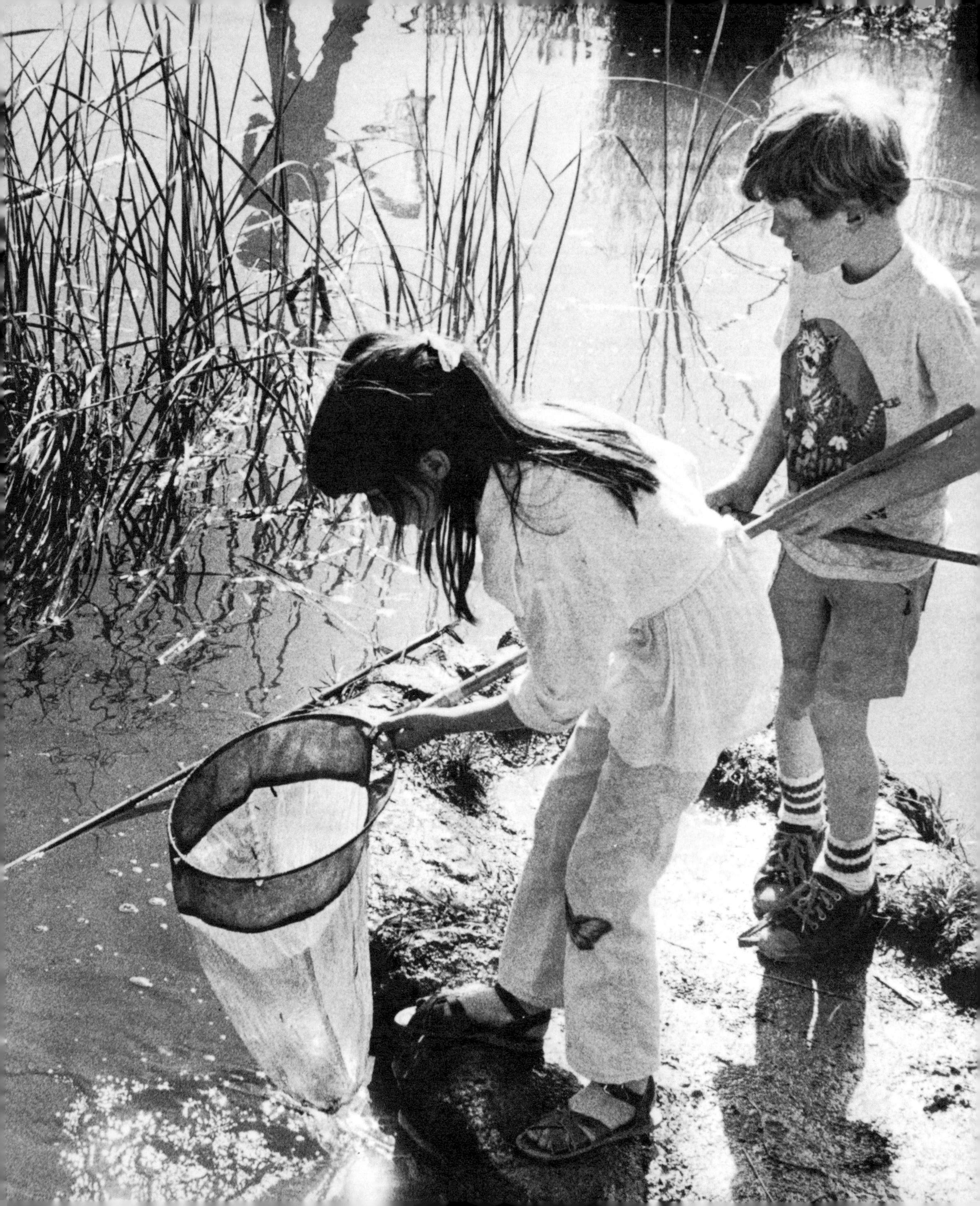

PROGRAM DESCRIPTIONS

These program descriptions represent a selection of ideas, philosophies, techniques and formats to youth education in museums. Each has been prepared in cooperation with the museum offering the program. This section is only a sampling of representative programs in art, history, natural history, children's museums, science-technology centers, zoos and aquaria. In most cases only one or two examples of the many programs available at a museum is illustrated.

Each program description illustrates a particular type of activity, format, use of materials, or teaching technique that has been found to be effective with children of a particular age group. The various categories, such as single visit programs, workshops and classes, or loan materials, should be seen as a unit, with the program descriptions illustrating the range of activities that are available. The descriptions have been grouped into eight categories. Not surprisingly, the largest three categories are single visit programs, in-depth programs, and workshops and classes. The other categories with descriptions include courses for credit, in-school programs, loan materials, junior curators, interns and clubs, festivals and special events.

Because of space limitations, only basic information about the programs has been included. In many cases a fee is charged for the museums' services; because these change frequently, they are not listed.

Although care was taken to include only current programs, some of these programs may have been discontinued or altered. Whether or not the sponsoring institutions still offer the programs, they are excellent representatives of possibilities.

One word of caution: museums are flooded with requests for information, and a questionnaire, or general request may be set aside. Often a telephone call is the most expeditious way to garner the details needed, particularly since museums are continually developing new programs and activities. The Museum Reference Center, Office of Museum Programs, Room 2235, Arts and Industries Building, Smithsonian Institution, Washington, DC 20560, is a repository for information on museum programs throughout the country and should be consulted.

Hopefully, these program descriptions will stimulate ideas for the development of new programs and encourage museum professionals to share information about their successes and failures.

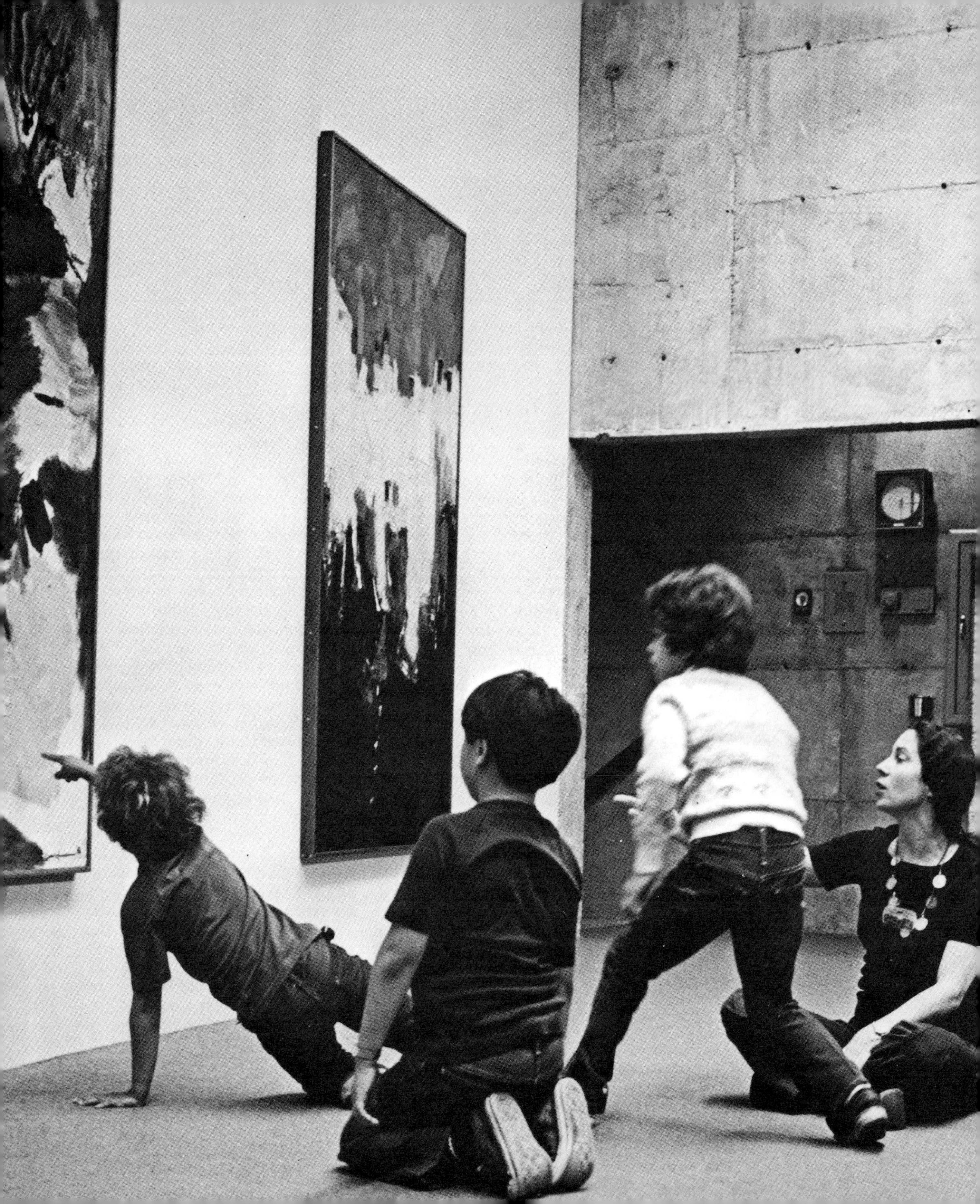

9. SINGLE VISIT PROGRAMS

Children often receive their first introduction to museums when they come for a tour with their school class. These visits generally last one to two hours and present a single concept about the collections or period in history. Pre-visit materials may be sent to classroom teachers to help the students and teachers prepare for the tour.

Pioneer Heritage Program
Blandford Nature Center
1715 Hillburn Ave. NW, Grand Rapids, MI 49504
(616) 453-6192
Users: Grade 3
Length/frequency: 90 minutes

The program consists of three parts: a visit to an 1866 log cabin homestead, a smokehouse, and a barn; a nature walk emphasizing the plants used by the pioneers; and a visit to a schoolhouse to participate in such activities as candle dipping, cider pressing, or butter churning. The program focuses on the integral relationship between man and nature comparing rural Michigan life of 100 years ago to today. For example children learn how herbs and mushrooms were dried and later stored with potatoes and other vegetables in the cellar. The cabin area includes an herb garden and family vegetable garden with such plants as safflower and indigo, which were used for dying. During the nature walk, the children learn to look more closely at plants. They learn, for example, that staghorn sumac berries not only make a good drink but that the sumac bark could be used for a tan or grey dye. A teacher resource kit provides ideas for preparation and follow-up activities, identification of plants and herbs and a guide to their use, and methods of forecasting weather changes.

Artworks—
A Learning Center
Brooks Memorial Art Gallery
Overton Park, Memphis, TN 38112
(901) 726-5266
Users: Age 4—young adults
Length/frequency: 45-90 minutes

Artworks is a multi-arts experience center where activities and programs emphasizing aspects of the collection are conducted. Students are first taken on a tour of the Gallery; sometimes the tour includes a film on one of the elements of art, such as line or color. The Artworks activities are designed to stress points raised in the film, ideas emphasized on the tour, or to stress concepts the teacher has introduced earlier in the classroom. Activities might include dressing in costumes and drawing portraits of each other after having seen a multi-screen slide and music presentation, called "About Faces", dealing with portraiture. While costumed, students might enact "living" portraits or write a verbal portrait. Students might also do drawings that express feelings through the types of lines or colors they use. Regardless of the activity planned, the purpose is to have the student become an active participant in the museum tour by providing an opportunity to interpret certain aspects of the tour through creation of art.

The Five Senses—
Hall of Health
Charlotte Nature Museum
1658 Sterling Rd., Charlotte, NC 28209
(704) 333-0506
Users: Grades K-6, and mentally and physically handicapped
Length/frequency: One-hour school group presentation plus a 90-minute workshop

This program introduces small children to sensory functions of the human body through the Eye, Ear, Taste, Smell, and Touch Centers. The Touch Center offer 10 different sensations (e.g., hot, cold, shock) and eight small compartments where children can use the sense of touch to identify such simple objects as door knobs or teddy bears. Although a baseball is easily identified by boys, most girls feel that it is only a ball. On the other hand, girls can identify a can opener by touch but the boys cannot. Puppets supplement the program. Mr. Turtle, for example, discusses the sense of hearing. Although humans have the outer ear to assist in collecting sounds, the turtle has a small hole on each side of its head, which it must turn in the direction of the sound. Miss Blue Fish discusses the sense of smell: Since fish do not have noses and their sense of smell is located in their fins, they must swim close to their food in order to "smell" it. Miss Butterfly explains the sense of taste: Because the tastebuds of butterflies are located on their feet, they must "walk" in their food in order to taste it.

Special Education
Field Trip
The Children's Museum
Museum Wharf, 300 Congress St., Boston, MA 02210
(617) 426-6500
Users: People of all ages with impairments and special education classes
Length/frequency: One hour

Visitors are paired with museum interns, staff and public school teachers, who serve as companions and guides through the participatory exhibits, encouraging exploration and interaction on whatever level is possible. In the computer section, for instance, a visitor with reading skills can play games like *Hangman* or *U Guess*. The companion also has the option of switching the terminal to "type" in order for the participants to do name-spelling or simply to watch the letters and numerals appear on the screen. In other exhibit areas, visitors can touch a snake for the first time, examine a snake skeleton, or learn factual information about reptile life. Interns and public school teachers are trained for the special education visits on a continuing basis through orientation programs and weekly support meetings. Educators from the Boston Public Schools can receive in-service credit for their work.

The Dinosaurs
The Children's Museum,
The Arts and Science Center
14 Court St., Nashua, NH 03060
(603) 883-1506
Users: Pre-school and older
Length/frequency: 40 minutes

How did the earth begin and who were the first creatures to live on it? These questions and many more are discussed in this learning program featuring dinosaurs: brontosaurus, triceratops, tyrannosaurs, stegosaurus and pteranodon. A special feltboard clock compares a child's daily activities with the earth's beginnings and the coming of the dinosaurs. Time and the many ages of the earth are explained. The group is then broken up into five smaller sections. Giant hand-crafted dinosaur puzzles are introduced and assembled by the children. The puzzles, as well as additional fact cards, teach about the dinosaurs and their habits. The museum's extensive collection of fossils, dinosaur bones and related artifacts is used in the program as further resource material.

Hear Here!
Children's Museum of Hartford
950 Trout Brook Dr.,
West Hartford, CT 06119
(203) 236-2961
Users: Grades 2-6, in groups of 150 per performance
Length/frequency: Two-hour session, including 50-minute performance

As part of an ongoing program in natural and physical sciences, students attend to live multimedia stage program on the concept of sound, which covers vibration, transmission, reception and communication. The demonstrator uses a bass fiddle and a trombone during the lecture, and supplements the performance with live animals, such as a snake, rabbit and a screech owl. Students participate in the stage demonstrations, as they attempt to put out a candle using a drum and funnel. After the performance, the audience breaks up into three groups of 50 each, for a subsequent tour through the Live Animal Center and Aquarium, to learn about audible communication with animals.

Architecture is Elementary
Corcoran Gallery of Art,
Education Department
17th St. and New York Ave. NW,
Washington, DC 20006
(202) 638-3211
Users: Grades K-6
Length/frequency: One hour

The Corcoran's building is used to introduce children to some basic architectural concepts (space, structure, decoration, and floor plan) and to make children visually, physically, and emotionally responsive to building in general. Styrofoam building blocks and the children's bodies are used as aids in teaching space, structure, and scale. For example, in learning about structure, the children compare the compression and support of post and lintel systems to support in their own bodies. With similar explorations, they may study walls, doorways, arches, and vaults. The concepts and exercises are adapted to the age and learning abilities of children. A Teacher handbook, complete with an introductory essay, vocabulary words and classroom activities to prepare and follow-up the museum experience is available when reservations for the tour are made.

Sully Plantation, Chantilly, Virginia
Fairfax County Park Authority,
Division of History
4030 Hummer Rd., Annandale,
VA 22003
(703) 437-1794
Users: Grades 3-5; suitable Grades 2-8
Length/frequency: Two hours

Students visiting Sully Plantation, the home of an 18-century planter, explore four aspects of plantation life. Before coming to the site, teachers receive a set of pre-trip materials, consisting of facsimiles of original documents and suggested classroom discussion questions. At school, each student selects one of the following activities to do during the museum visit. In the textile center the group discusses the process of making cloth by teasing, carding and weaving wool. In the kitchen, the students learn about the life of the slave cook and about open hearth cooking, as they prepare and eat batter cakes. Recreating a typical 18th-century school day in the schoolroom, children read from hornbooks, write with quill pens, take part in a spelling bee and play games. Another group discovers various 18th-century children's games, amusements and pastimes by playing "Thread the Needle" and making a pin-prick picture. After the visit the teacher receives a list of suggested classroom activities and students are encouraged to share their experiences and show the various products they made in the different learning centers, including a sachet linen freshener, a string of apples, a sample of quill penmanship and a pin-prick picture.

Exploring the Zoo
Fort Worth Zoological Park
2727 Zoological Park Dr., Fort
Worth, TX 76110
(817) 870-7055
Users: Grades 2-6
Length/frequency: Two hours, offered during fall season only

Exploring the Zoo utilizes selected animals and exhibits to teach a variety of natural history concepts while involving students in active learning experiences. Following a slide-show introduction to the various functions of a zoo, students divide into small groups for visits to specific areas. In the Primate House, each student makes a handprint beside a duplicate of a gorilla's handprint, as a lesson in comparative anatomy. This activity follows a slide lecture on the basic characteristics of primates. After a demonstration on how to set up an aquarium, another group tours behind the scenes in the zoo's aquarium. The third group is given an introduction to taxonomy and instructions on how to use senses other than vision in examining different species of animals. They then examine unusual animals such as ferrets, cockatoos, and African ball pythons, using their new evaluation techniques. Groups rotate and, by the end of the morning, each student has visited all teaching areas. The Zoo provides teacher supplements, suggesting follow-up classroom activities.

Biological Aspects of Sexuality
Fernbank Science Center
156 Heaton Park Dr., Atlanta, GA 30307
(404) 378-4311
Users: High school biology classes
Length/frequency: Half-day seminar

Designed to complement the biology curriculums in the schools and a human development exhibition, this seminar's discussion leaders are usually nurses or other trained health-care professionals. The following topics are discussed and supplemented by the exhibit materials: male and female anatomy and physiology, human sexual response, pregnancy and childbirth, fetal development, population explosion, contraception, and venereal disease. Students are encouraged to ask questions. Follow-up activities include visits to, or speakers from, the Center for Disease Control and Planned Parenthood. Future programs and exhibits are being developed in human genetics. The museum offers seminars and workshop in many subject areas in cooperation with the school system.

Tea: A Revolutionary Tradition
Fraunces Tavern Museum
54 Pearl St., New York, NY 10004
(212) 425-1778
Users: High School students
Length/frequency: Two hours

High school students visit an exhibition dealing with 18th-century tea drinking habits, and are assigned role cards with characters who lived during America's colonial period, and who might have been affected by the Stamp Act Crisis and the Boston Tea Party. Students tour the exhibition from the vantage point of one particular character who, in turn, is defined by occupation, socio-economic status, and certain very definite attitudes. They are asked to study prints and paintings in order to hypothesize how their characters might have looked and behaved, and to find the decorative arts objects their respective characters might have owned or used. Then, they participate in a tea party in the gallery, and their participation depends upon how each one of their characters feels about the burning issue of the British tax on tea. How each student behaves during the tea party and speaks—indeed whether or not each chooses to drink tea at all—depends upon information gleaned about the character while touring the exhibition *Tea: A Revolutionary Tradition*.

Eskimo Daily Life
Haffenreffer Museum of Anthropology of Brown University
Mount Hope Grant, Bristol, RI 02809
(401) 253-8388
Users: Grades 3-6
Length/frequency: Two hours

A slide show about Eskimo daily life introduces this exhibit and helps the children to learn several Eskimo dances. The class divides into small groups to visit three different areas. In an igloo reconstruction, students examine objects that Eskimo women use at home and eat smoked fish and sourdough pancakes served on an Eskimo platter. They handle children's mukluks, a sealskin sewing kit, birchbark utensils, and other household items by the light of an oil lamp. Hunting and carving implements from the museum's collection are also examined. Students try their hand at using the bow drill on a piece of soapstone and feel a hunting knife. In the main gallery, surrounded by the major part of the Eskimo collection, students play Eskimo games such as pick-up-sticks, ring toss, cats-cradle and keep-away with a caribou ball, and discuss other objects in the gallery. A mask-making workshop (using plywood) and a discussion of the uses of masks in Eskimo culture is followed by the children demonstrating how they might use masks during the hunt or in the ceremonial dances.

On-Site Programs/Vertebrate Class Orientations and Tours
Houston Zoological Gardens
P.O. Box 1562, Houston, TX 77001
(713) 522-0276
Users: Middle School through adult
Length/frequency: 90 minutes

Birds, reptiles or mammals are examined during a three-part program that includes an orientation with films or slides, a tour in the zoo, and an opportunity to handle animals in the education facility. For example, while studying the different orders of mammals such as felines, primates, or rodents, students learn how the animals have adapted for survival, their roles in the food chain and balance of nature, and man's responsibility to all living things. While in the education center, they compare and contrast skins and skeletons, handle live animals, and learn about written references that are available for further study.

Library Class On Original Source Materials: How Do We Know The Past?
Huntington Library, Art Gallery, and Botanical Gardens
1151 Oxford Rd., San Marino, CA 91108
(213) 792-6141
Users: High school and junior high school students and physically handicapped
Length/frequency: One hour

This class introduces students to research materials used by historians. Special displays feature items from the collections that document the past: letters, diaries, books, newspapers, maps, drawings, and photographs. Although the exhibits and discussion focus on the California Gold Rush, 1848-1858, they raise wider questions about verifying history and about how historians select and use their sources. A bibliography and suggestions for follow-up study are provided.

Holocaust Studies:
"A Human Response: Artwork from the Holocaust"
The Jewish Museum
1109 Fifth Ave., New York, NY 10028
(212) 860-1888
Users: Grades 9-12
Length/frequency: One hour

A small collection of original art works done by Jews in hiding and in concentration camps in Europe from 1939-45 is used to examine individual responses to prejudice and dehumanization. The program emphasizes art as a vehicle for expressing emotion and for recording history. Examination of the artwork, coupled with details of the artists' lives leads to a discussion of human rights, stereotypes, and prejudice. The goal of the program is to help the student realize that people can offer resistance to intolerable situations in many ways. The program is tailored to meet individual needs of each class. For example, literature classes reading "The Diary of Anne Frank" focus on survival and history classes may focus on events that lead up to the Holocaust.

Holt Planetarium
Lawrence Hall of Science
University of California,
Centennial Dr., Berkeley, CA 94720
(415) 642-5132
Users: School groups of all ages
Length/frequency: 45 minutes

Hands-on experiences and flexibility characterize these live presentations. In "Constellations Tonight," each member of the audience is given a star-finder's map. After a 10-minute briefing on how to use it, participants are assigned a constellation to find both on the map and then on the planetarium dome. Team heads then point out their findings to the grouping using a battery-operated light pointer. In "Stonehenge," participants select what they think might be significant points on the horizon, mark these with wooden sticks, and compare the orientations with the directions that have been found at Stonehenge.

Man and the Mississippi
Louisiana Arts and Science Center
P.O. Box 3373, Baton Rouge, LA 70821
(502) 344-9463
Users: Primarily elementary and junior high groups, and handicapped
Length/frequency: Approximately 25 minutes

"Man and the Mississippi" is a nine-part multimedia presentation on the economic, historic, and social significance of the Mississippi River to the city of Baton Rouge. Students are able to relate their study of Louisiana history, geography, United States history, or transportation to the economic, political, and geological factors that have shaped the cultural inheritance of the Mississippi River community. Further, they learn how important the river has been in shaping the characteristics of their city. For example, a class studying the economic significance of the Port of Baton Rouge walk a few feet beyond this exhibit to see a panoramic view of the commerce on the river, barges, towboats, tugboats, and ships, many from foreign ports, loading grain and general cargo as they rest at dock. The subjects covered in the presentations are specifically about the Mississippi—its geology, geography, the ancient Indian tribes living nearby, commerce, warfare, historic sites, ecology, the evolution of river transportation, and the future of the river.

Making A Living in Minnesota
Minnesota Historical Society
690 Cedar St., St. Paul MN 55101
(612) 296-2881
Users: Elementary and secondary students
Length/frequency: 90 minutes

Saint Paul in the booming period of the 1880s is the backdrop for this historical investigation of job choice and the task of making a living. In the museum's teaching gallery, students examine slides of photographs and lithographs of St. Paul in the 1880s, paying particular attention to the work lives of residents. Then students focus on four young people who lived and worked in St. Paul at that time. Drawing information from primary sources such as census records, photographs, newspaper ads, city directories, and work tools and equipment, students piece together biographies of the four people and their solutions to the problem of making a living in an urban setting. The program encourages students to look at the impact of age, sex, ethnic origin, social mobility and job skills on job choice. In addition to developing these ideas, close examination of four individual life stories gives students a vivid sense of the reality of the 1880s and continuity with young people 100 years ago.

Asian Arts Program
Minnesota Museum of Art
30 E. 10th St., St. Paul, MN 55101
(612) 227-7613
Users: Grades 4-12
Length/frequency: Two and one-half hours

Through active study of the various art forms of Asia and the philosophies pervading them, students gain insight into the technical, aesthetic and metaphysical accomplishments of Asian artists as contrasted to Western attitudes to life and aesthetics. The setting, modeled after an imperial courtyard, presents changing exhibits from the museum's Oriental collection. After close examination and discussions about the objects, students embark on projects using the materials, techniques and concepts of the Asian artists including Sumi painting, Haiku and Takna writing, I Ching divination patterns, and calligraphy. Other similar programs using the museum collections and workshop activities include "Ritual Arts," which focuses on the relationship of art and ritual in tribal societies, such as the African and Pre-Columbian sculptures and masks. "American Indian Art" examines the use of pre- and post-contact materials (hides, quills, beads, and trade cloth) in art and decorative design to illustrate the impact of European contact on the Ojigwa and Eastern Dakota tribes.

Science, Technology and You
Morris Museum of Arts and Sciences
Normandy Heights and Columbia Rds., Morristown, NJ 07960
(201) 538-0454
Users: Grades 4-8
Length/frequency: One hour

Exploring plastics, electricity, lasers, and space research, children learn how science and technology relate to their everyday lives. Representatives from local and national industries, as well as from federal agencies, present programs at the museum to acquaint the audience with a particular industry or technical field. Many lectures relate to the museum's exhibitions, such as the solar telescope or another on the chemistry of fiber and dyes. Question-and-answer sessions follow each lecture. The speakers have represented Exxon Research and Engineering, Jersey Central Power and Light, New Jersey Bell and Bell Telephone Laboratories, the National Aeronautics and Space Administration (NASA) and the Oak Ridge Associated Universities. Some of the most successful programs have been about the atom, crude oil, solar energy, sound, rocks and minerals, and dinosaurs.

Learning Tours: 19th-century American Painting
The Museums of Stony Brook
Stony Brook, Long Island, NY 11790
(516) 751-0066
Users: Grade 3 through adults
Length/frequency: Two hours

Students stretch canvas, examine a canvas showing preparation through final painting, and place a canvas in a 19th-century frame. They grind rocks into pigment, mix pigment into paint, and paint with it, creating textures and blending colors. After learning observational skills, they act out paintings (people, trees, lunch pails) to understand perspective; arrange scenes to explore composition; and draw the scenes to experience the thought processes, skills, and individuality of artists. Guides help students relate these activities to their own lives.

Genealogical Treasure Hunt
National Archives
8th & Pennsylvania Ave., NW,
Washington, DC 20408
(202) 523-3183
Users: Elementary school groups
Length/frequency: 90 minutes

Classes that use family histories as an approach to studying American history participate in this program. Each student is assigned an "ancestor," and makes their own discoveries through facsimiles of original documents from federal records. The "ancestors" may be "grandmother Livia who came to America from Yugoslavia in 1921 on the same passenger ship as President Wilson," or "great-grandfather William, listed as a deserter on the 1876 muster roll from the battle of Little Big Horn." Pre-visit materials provided to the school help prepare students for their investigations. Students also tour the public exhibitions and document preservation laboratories.

Indian Tools
New Jersey State Museum
205 W. State St., Trenton, NJ 08625
(609) 984-3896
Users: Grades 4-6
Length/frequency: One hour

Benjamin Franklin thought that an important difference between people and animals is that people have the ability to make tools, animals don't. After considering similarities and differences between people and animals, the group discusses interpretations of Franklin's idea. With this discussion in mind, a student is asked to choose one of nine early 20th-century workbench tools that he recognizes. The group names the tool, discusses its function and determines the most necessary part for performing that function. The student then examines a group of Indian artifacts to find one that might perform a similar function. After eliminating those that are obviously unsatisfactory, the student examines those that remain, eliminating others until only one is left, or a fairly certain guess can be made. As each object is eliminated, the reason or reasons are stated. As the correct items are matched, information about the Indian's use of the tools is given.

Building A Community
Old Economy Village
Ambridge, PA 15003
(412) 266-4500
Users: Grades 4-6
Length/frequency: 90 minutes.

The village setting provides a laboratory for children to investigate the community's history. The architecture, geography and function of the buildings enable them to study the town planning and influences of transportation. The program is divided into three sections, the first focusing on town planning. Using a feltboard, the children create a town. The process allows them to consider business districts and residential areas, townspeople, and other considerations. During the second section, which is a tour, each child is given a personality card containing information about a particular individual who lived in the Harmonist Communal Society. The visitors participate in role playing their personalities during the tour, while they look for evidence of where their characters might have worked or lived in the village. To conclude the program, the students cite reasons why this town developed and how it compares to their feltboard town and their hometown.

Whales And Whaling
Peabody Museum of Salem
East India Square, Salem, MA 01970
(617) 745-1876
Users: Grades 4-5
Length/Frequency: One hour

The whale, its physical characteristics, struggle for survival, and death, and the whaler, his life and the events of the hunt are the focus of this program. A slide presentation introduces the museum's collection of whaling materials and the natural history of the whale. The similarities and differences between people and whales are discussed as children are asked to breathe like whales, and then discuss other shared mammalian characteristics. The size comparison is demonstrated by having the children stand inside a life-size whale outlined on the floor and letting them handle a whale vertebra and compare it to their own backbones. Next they examine whale oil, baleen and whale teeth, both scrimshawed and natural, and view a 50-foot-long panorama of a whaling voyage that tells the story of the expedition in all of its melodrama. Children enact scenes from the panorama, imagining storms at sea, life aboard the whaling vessel, and the killing of the whale itself. After the children become familiar with the details of a whaler's life, they tour the rest of the whaling collection of prints, paintings, and scrimshaw.

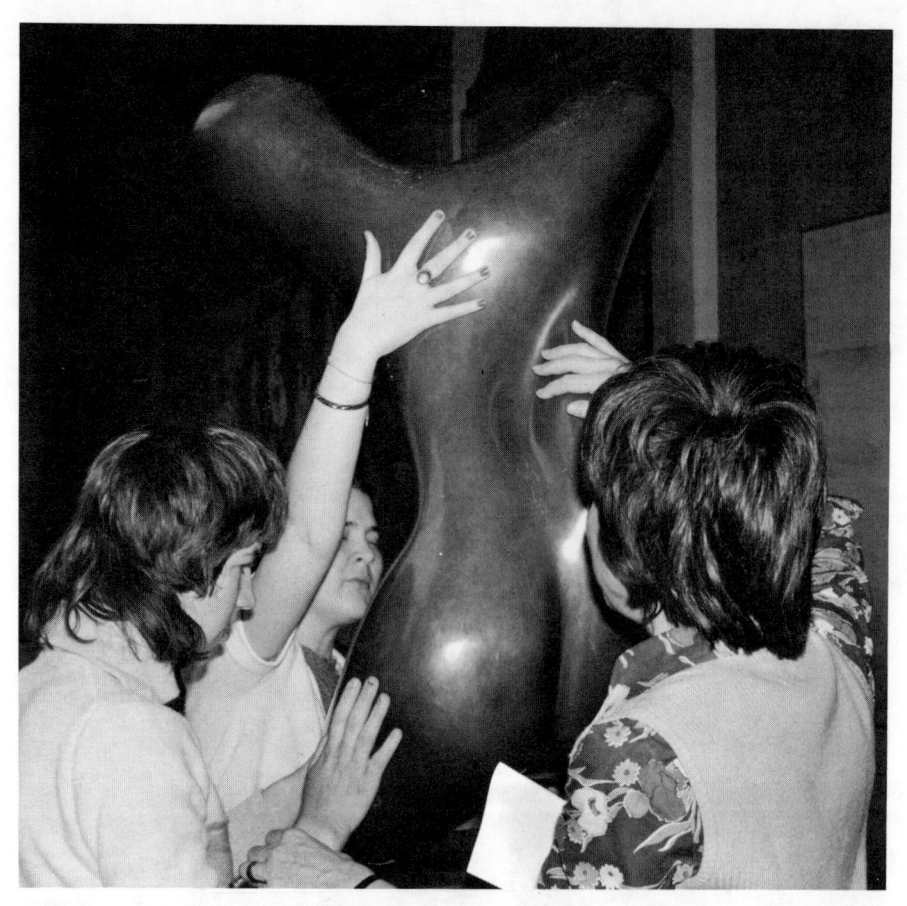

Foraging For Natural Food (Wild Salad Class)
Queens Botanical Garden
43-50 Main St., Flushing, NY 11355
(212) 886-3800
Users: Grade 3 and up, plus handicapped.
Length/frequency: 90 minutes.

Children participate in a brief discussion of the ways early Americans provided for their shelter, clothing and food. Outdoors, the children observe plans used by colonists and native Americans (e.g., white birch for canoes, pine for pitch, acorns for flour, etc.) After learning to identify plants such as chickweed, dandelion, and plantain, they pick, sort and wash the plants to make a salad. A natural dressing is prepared, and the salad tasted. This program not only involves senses of sight, touch, taste and smell, but also develops awareness of the importance of accurate plant identification.

Circus Magic
The Ringling Museum
P.O. Box 1838, Sarasota, FL 33578
(813) 355-5101
Users: Grade 3
Length/frequency: 90 minutes.

"Circus Magic," a tour supplemented by pre-and post-visit activities, examines the circus of yesteryear, focusing on the sense of community among the performers and other circus workers and relating the curriculum to community life. The pre-visit package helps the teachers to introduce the circus world and its magical lingo such as "joey" and "klinkers." The tour focuses on the community: how they lived, traveled, worked and helped one another. The "back-yard community" is examined as children consider what life would be like as a member of a circus family. The special roles of the clown, the laborers and other performers are discussed, using objects from the collection. The circus wagons, with wheels weighing 400 pounds, culminate the tour, as children learn how they were operated, their many functions and the people who maintained and used them. The program provides opportunities for pantomine and creating banners, as well as studying the collections. Teachers are provided with pre-and post-visit activities to accompany the tour.

Seasonal Programs
Roaring Brook Nature Center
70 Gracey Rd., Canton, CT 06019
(203) 693-0263
Users: Grades K-8
Length/frequency: 60-90 minutes

These outdoor programs offered throughout the school year help students understand the impact of the seasons on them as individuals as well as on their environment. Activities include hiking through the woods to determine how individuals affect the environment; studying the interactions of living and non-living components in an ecosystem to learn about habitats, adaptations, and predator-prey relationships among plants and animals; sampling soil from several areas to find its physical characteristics (temperature, texture, organic content) and how it supports vegetation; learning to identify and attract winter birds and discussing how they find food and shelter; and using a simple key to identify trees and shrubs (e.g., by their bark, buds, and twig patterns) after their leaves have fallen.

Second Grade Field Trip Program
San Diego Zoo
P.O. Box 551, San Diego, CA 92112
(714) 231-1515
Users: Grade 2
Length/frequency: Two hours

Teachers receive study guides to help prepare for the field trip, which introduces the concept of animal identification. During guided tours of the zoo's primate mesa and reptile house, students learn field observation techniques and methods for identifying the four major classes of animals at the zoo (amphibians, reptiles, birds and mammals). Students become acquainted with some live animals by touching them while they learn about the animals' habits and characteristics. An education study kit in preparation will include film strips, tapes, wall chart, game board, study prints, work sheets, duplication masters, and complete teacher's guide.

Broadsides and **Going Aloft Workshops**
South Street Seaport Museum
203 Front St., New York, NY 10038
(212) 766-9020
Users: Grades 4-6
Length/frequency: Two hours

Broune & Co., Stationers, a restored letter press print shop, houses an activity that helps students understand the history and practice of hand printing. During the workshop, the students learn that in the 19th century a broadside was a flyer printed on one side, which was posted to announce the latest opinions and shipping news. Demonstrations of printing tools and techniques are part of the press exhibit tour, and students print their own broadsides using wood type under the supervision of a printer. The "Going Aloft" workshop gives the students an opportunity to experience some aspects of life at sea in the days of the great sailing ships. This workshop includes a film (with footage of sailors in the riggings or a large sailing ship in heavy seas), singing sea chanteys, and reading short passages in American literature, such as Herman Melville and others. All relate to "going aloft" on a square-rigged ship. Materials used during the workshop include a diagram of the four-masted bark *Peking* for parts identification, word games, vocabulary lists and a bibliography. Weather permitting, a short visit to the ship *Peking*, moored at the museum, is included.

Painting and Other Arts
Sterling and Francine Clark Art Institute
Williamstown, MA 01267
(413) 458-8109
Users: Elementary school classes
Length/frequency: 50-75 minutes

Common links between the visual arts and dance, drama, music and literature are explored and developed, using the visual arts as a point of departure. Abstract paintings, selected for their contrasting moods, are compared to a variety of musical excerpts played on a cassette player. Children choose the musical piece that best reflects the feeling of each painting, and then, the piece that works least well with the painting. Next, students stand in front of a large Monet waterlily painting and try to imagine sounds that might be heard in this scene. They then combine the various sounds into the "Water Lilies Symphony of Noises." To further draw parallels between music and painting, the instructor illustrates that just as silences or pauses in music help to emphasize the stronger sections in a piece, a dark or indefinite background in a portrait might be used as a foil for a strongly lit figure, and might, therefore, focus attention on that figure.

Child Life in Colonial North Carolina
Tryon Palace Restoration Complex
New Bern, North Carolina
(919) 638-5109
Users: Grades 3-4, in school and community groups
Frequency: One hour

A child's daily life in 18th-century colonial North Carolina is the focus of this tour. In the kitchen, under supervision, children grate nutmeg, grind salt in a stone mortar and pestle, examine wooden cookie molds and other kitchen implements, and crush and use herbs. In another room, after watching a weaving demonstration, they card wool, spin on a drop spindle, wind handspun on the niddy-noddy and weave on a tape loom. While an instructor demonstrates how to dip a candle, students examine a block of tallow and a rotary candle maker. They also play with colonial toys and try on small pieces of clothing such as vests, tricorns and mob caps. This entire experience puts modern children in touch with processes and skills that were very much a part of the lives of North Carolina's colonial children.

Awareness Program
Cleveland Health Education Museum
8911 Euclid Ave., Cleveland, OH 44106
(216) 231-5011
Users: Grades K-12
Length/frequency: 45 minute program, part of the two-hour session available at the museum

Introducing children to the similarities and differences of people with special needs is part of each Awareness Program offered at the primary, intermediate and advanced level. Emphasis is placed on physical, emotional, and mental handicaps, which create differences in all people. Students acquire a greater understanding of each other and experience some of the effects of being handicapped through audio-visual, multi-sensory approaches. For example, simulated experiences reduce their levels of hearing and abilities to see, so they can more clearly understand some of the physical handicaps. Audiovisual programs and graphics emphasize similarities; for example, posters show a child in a wheelchair during a daily routine of waking up, grooming and dressing. The Awareness Program is one of the selections that teachers can choose for their classe's three-part visit. Other subjects include anatomy and physiology, dental health, drugs, genetics, nutrition, and parenting.

Space and Form: Sculpture From Around The World
Honolulu Academy of Arts
900 South Beretania, St.,
Honolulu, HI 96814
(808) 539-3693
Users: Grades 4-12
Length/frequency: One hour or more, depending on the group

Visiting the sculpture garden and galleries, students study the three-dimensional expressions of artists from Asia, Europe, the Pacific, the Americas, and Africa. Comparing and contrasting how sculptors have dealt with the problems of volume, light, and space while creating statements about their cultures and themselves is the focus of this tour. Teachers may elect to concentrate on just one country, a continent, the type of material, or different techniques (casting, carving, or modeling) that are used by the artist. For example, in studying the sculpture of India, the images of deities and spirits, encompassing diverse artistic styles from the second century A.D., are discussed in the context of several religions. Celestial beauties, winged beings, and fantastic creatures carved on the architecture are on view in a gallery that captures the feeling of a darkened, dramatically lit temple setting. Bronze and stucco images are discussed in relationship to sculptures of sandstone, schist and granite. Information sheets and slide packets have been prepared and are sent to teachers prior to their visit.

The Musement Park
Milwaukee Public Museum
800 W. Wells St., Milwaukee, WI 53233
(414) 278-2713
Users: Children ages 4-7, primarily school, day care groups, general public
Length/frequency: 45 minute visits

The Musement Park is a discovery center that allows children to touch, learn, and explore their natural world. Four learning environments are rotated in the existing space and, at times, shared at other sites. An example is "Come Crawl with Me," consisting of larger-than-life insect environments for children to crawl into, over, under and through while wearing antenna and an extra pair of legs. In addition to the gross motor activities the environments allow, the children have the opportunity to make spider webs, to build bee hives, to draw butterflies, and to closely examine a selection of mounted specimens. The exploratory opportunity is concluded with a sing-a-long, "Come Crawl," which reviews in song the insects represented by the environments. Teachers can purchase coloring books that reinforce the museum experience. One new program theme is developed each year.

Biology Programs
Museum of Science
Science Park
Boston, Massachusetts 02114
(617) 723-2500
Users: Grades 5-12
Length/frequency: 45 minutes

Three different programs introduce students to various aspects of biology including human reproduction, living organisms, and natural systems. "How Your Life Began," (K-12) uses models, slides, and films to discuss a variety of topics related to human reproduction, including puberty, reproductive anatomy, fertilization, fetal development and birth. A pre-visit telephone discussion is required in order to tailor the programs to the students' needs and interests. "Animal, Vegetable or Mineral" (Grades 5-12) looks at a variety of living organisms and inanimate forms. Students compare microscopic animals, plants, and geological specimens, discussing the similarities of forms, and systems of classifications. Microprojection equipment, electron micrographs, and close-up photography are all used to present familiar and unfamiliar organisms in detail. "River: Highway, Swimming hole, or Sewer?" (Grade 5-9) explores the effects of people on a natural system. Through chemical analysis of the Charles River, observation of the live animals and other techniques, students extend their awareness of the interrelationships in a river community to other environments.

Transporting Handicapped Children Into the Horse-Drawn Era
The Museum of Stony Brook
Stony Brook, New York 11790
(516) 751-0066
Users: Handicapped youth 3-21; instructors are high school students
Length/frequency: Two-hour sessions for disabled visitors; one day to train high school students as instructors

Students learn to understand the relationship of carriages to horses and to do the work of 19th-century Long Island blacksmiths. Children ride in a pony cart and learn about former modes of horse-drawn transportation in America. Throughout the program, history is made relevant by relating it to current analogous situations. Horse-drawn transportation is compared with bikes, motorcycles, and sports cars, historical objects are seen as serving specific needs within their own time and are compared to today's solutions to similar situations. High school students are trained to teach this program by studying primary materials: 19th-century diaries that relate stories about stagecoach trips; broadsides advertising stagecoach, steamer, canal and railroad travel; maps; blacksmiths' and wheelwrights account books describing transactions, paintings and drawings of blacksmithing, sleighing and driving; and 19th-century poems, stories and songs. The high school students are guided in their use of primary source material by meetings with a local university historian and consultants who work with people who have special needs.

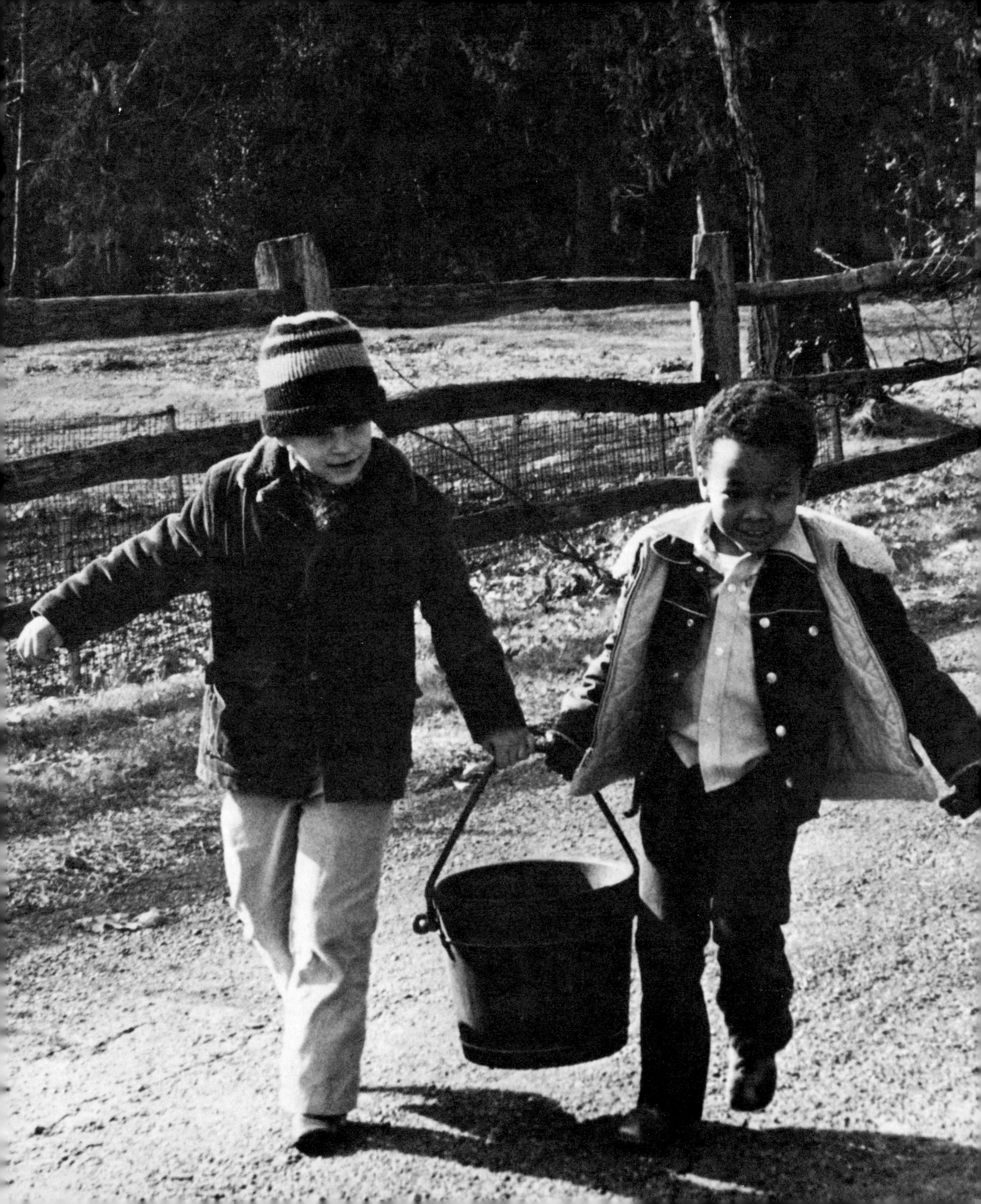

10.
IN-DEPTH AND SERIES PROGRAMS

Recognizing the importance of preparing for a museum visit, returning several times and/or following up in the classroom with additional activities has led museums to develop a variety of series and in-depth programs for schools. The sessions may last for half a day, overnight or several months with repeated visits to the museum. Many of these programs include teacher-training sessions and special resource materials that increase students' involvement with the museum experience.

Seminars In Action
Apprenticeship, Maine Maritime Museum
375 Front St., Bath, ME 04530
(207) 443-5638
Users: High school students
Length/frequency: One day

The Apprenticeship helps to develop and sustain the traditional craftsmanship of half-hull model boat building. The program emphasizes the need for patience, steady application, and freedom from interruption. Small groups of highly motivated students are supervised by two apprentices from the museum boat-building program. Each student carves a "half-model" from a block of wood during the one-day session. All tools and materials are provided.

Arts and Language Arts
Brockton Art Museum
Oak St., Brockton, MA 02401
(617) 588-6000
Users: Grades 5-8
Length/frequency: Four sessions, 90 minutes each

Developed by the museum's staff and the schools' language arts faculty, this program incorporates much of the language arts curriculum with an examination of art and the creative process. In the first session, a museum instructor visits the classroom with a slide presentation, introducing the relationship between elements of visual art and the written word, and how each functions to create imagery. For instance, slides of a written haiku poem and a Japanese brush painting, or a William Carlos Williams poem and Charles DeMuth's painting done in response to this poem, are compared and discussed. In the second classroom session, docents introduce small sculpture reproductions that students handle and discuss. Working in small groups, the student list 27 words in response to their particular sculpture, which develop into a group poem and is presented to the entire class. During the third session in the museum galleries, students write prose or poetry, a reaction to something they have seen. The final classroom session continues work on written pieces to initiate discussions about how one decides that a work of art or literature is completed. The artists' points of view are revealed in slide presentations of both finished and unfinished works, and through the writing of various artists. The museum publishes a literary magazine at the end of each school year, with a sample of each participant's writing.

A COSI School Field Day
Center of Science and Industry
280 East Broad Street, Columbus, Ohio 43215
(614) 228-6362
Users: Schools, minimum 300 students
Length/frequency: One day, plus training sessions for teachers

The School Field Day provides an elementary or junior high school total access to all COSI's exhibits, programs and workshops for a full day, providing science and history enrichment for the school curriculum. The full-day reservation of the entire museum facility for a school may be made any day from October to February. Advanced planning sessions between the school and museum staffs help develop programs that fit the needs of the teachers and students. The Field Day offers three types of experiences for all the participants: 1) Teachers select particular exhibits to focus their students' experiences and develop discussions; 2) Each class selects two or three demonstrations that relate to their theme and exhibits; and 3) "Make-it and take-it" workshops are chosen to lead the students into a science or history investigation activity and provide materials, direction and stimulus for continued activity following the COSI experience. Past workshops have included such topics as the life cycle of a butterfly, light and color, and historic apple crafts.

Art And Artifacts
Children's Museum,
Detroit Public Schools
67 E. Kirby, Detroit, MI 48202
(313) 494-1210
Users: Grades 4-7
Length/frequency: Seven sessions with workshops at the museum; follow-up materials available from the Lending Department

In this seven-visit series, students explore different areas of the museum's collection, in conjunction with classroom curriculum. For example, in one week's session, "What is Ecology?", the relationship of the American Indian to the environment is explored. In the galleries, students examine Indian crafts, artifacts, and animal specimens, such as baskets, bowls, boxes, hunting tools, birch bark, maple sugar, beaver skin, deer antlers, and porcupine quills. Based on an exploration of additional materials from the museum's collection, they discuss how Indians considered the earth and its resources as being in partnership with themselves. After seeing a short movie that shows Southwest Indians creating pottery similar to that studied in the museum, students craft a clay bowl. During the following weeks, the Eskimo collection is studied to answer the question "What is Adaptation?"; African masks help deal with the question "What is Myth?"; and musical instruments are examined to answer the question "What is Sound?" Workshop activities accompanying these programs include printmaking with modern Eskimo methods, maskmaking with a sculptural material, and xylophone construction.

The Pursuit of Happiness
The Colonial Williamsburg Foundation
P.O. Box 627, Williamsburg, VA 23815
(804) 229-1000
Users: Grades 10-12
Length/frequency: Full day generally, but varies according to needs of the teacher

What choices do young men and women have in their lives today about education, work, marriage, political and spiritual involvement, and recreation? What did it mean for young men and women of 18th-century Virginia to face their life choices: What were their chances—youth of all races and classes—for a life of liberty and happiness? The tour focuses on the crucial decisions, opportunities and obstacles facing young adults in Williamsburg by examining the economic, social and cultural life of the time. Working with an escort, students explore public buildings, tavern, shops, market places, and family homes. Students are encouraged to discover for themselves how 18th-century individuals fashioned a life within the limits imposed upon them by society and by chance.

Exploring Cranbrook's Science Museum
Cranbrook Institute of Science
P.O. Box 801,
Bloomfield Hills, MI 48013
(313) 645-3230
Users: Kindergarten classes
Length/frequency: One-hour sessions, once a week for four weeks

Children explore the world of science by handling museum artifacts and zoological specimens. In a class called "Insects and Reptiles" students learn to recognize various butterflies, beetles, and snakes, and to understand man's relationship to these animals. In a program about birds, they learn about such concepts as evolution, adaptation, and extinction, as well as nesting, migration, and camouflage. In a class about mammals, Michigan species are studied in relationship to their home, defenses, and skills. Another program about the origins and culture of the Native American uses such artifacts as masks, baskets, dolls, games, and clothing as teaching tools.

Oral History of World War II
Florida State Museum
126 Florida State Museum,
University of Florida, Gainesville,
FL 32611
(904) 392-1721
Users: High school history classes and public
Length/frequency: Project and four-day exhibit

Students prepare an oral history of World War II by conducting taped interviews with local people who lived on the home front during that time: the market owner who sold rationed meat, the woman who ran the recreation center, and the draft board official who inducted young men in the area. After obtaining exhibit space at the museum in conjunction with the anniversary of Pearl Harbor, the students advertise with silk-screen posters they themselves make using museum facilities. During the exhibit, visitors can listen to the unedited tapes on equipment furnished by the telephone company and installed by students. Artifacts from that era, such as ration books, are also displayed.

Fort Point Environmental Living
Fort Point National Historic Site,
National Park Service
P.O. Box 29333, Presidio of San Francisco, CA 94129
(415) 556-1693 or 556-2857
Users: Grades 4-6
Length/frequency: Overnight visit, preceded by teacher workshops and classroom presentation

The Environmental Living Project gets children into another time, another culture, and another environment. Historical parks are living examples of man's interrelationship with his environment. The heart of the project is involvement. Thus, the emphasis is on processes and activities that bring out the most enthusiasm, feeling, and confidence in the child. After careful classroom preparation, they arrive at the fort in the afternoon and tour the area along with other visitors. When the park closes officially, the class takes over as the garrison of Fort Point for the night. A Civil War-period meal is prepared, and tin cups and metal utensils are used to help simulate an 1860 Army mess hall. After the meal, the mess hall and kitchen are cleaned up. The youngsters sleep in a simulated barrack, taking turns on guard duty throughout the night. Candles provide the only available light. All troops participate in flag raising and calisthenics the next morning, followed by breakfast, cleanup, and inspection of quarters.

One-Room Schools
Greenfield Village and Henry Ford Museum
Dearborn, MI 48121
(313) 271-1620, ext. 535
Users: Grades 1-8
Length/frequency: Single full day

Three one-room school programs are available to groups visiting Greenfield Village. The McGuffey school is representative of a frontier school of the early 1800's. Furnished with hornbooks, slates, wall-fastened writing shelves, and narrow wooden benches, it provides an authentic setting for young people to re-create an entire classroom day of that era. Miller School is a replica of a school attended by Henry Ford in the 1870's. Scoth Settlement School is the actual building in which he began his education. In both of these schools children sit at handmade wooden desks, practice penmanship on slates and read from McGuffey's Eclectic Readers. Teacher's guide materials, including a filmstrip, help in planning the day's activities, which can be tailored to any one of the first eight grades.

Museum Utilization for Student Education (M.U.S.E.)
Hebrew Union College Skirball Museum
3077 University Ave., Los Angeles, CA 90007
(213) 749-3424
Users: Grades 3-9
Length/frequency: One to 10 90-minute classroom sessions; three-hour museum visits

The M.U.S.E. project loans out self-contained kits of classroom materials to public and religious school teachers. The kits, which emphasize the multicultural parallels in Jewish historical events and cultural phenomena, are available in four subject areas: "Immigration and Family History" (grades 7-9), "Celebrations" (grades 3-5), "The Torah" (grades 4-6), and "Archeology" (grades 4-7). Each kit contains artifacts, workbooks, games, charts, and audiovisual materials. Three kits are complemented by morning-long visits to the museum, which include a tour, class, and hands-on experiences. In "Celebrations," for example, the pre-visit lesson describes five celebrations in five different cultures. In the museum visit, students learn about two Jewish celebrations, Shabbat and Hanukah, through food, songs, a ceremony, examination of ceremonial objects, and a hands-on crafts project. Back in the classroom, student create their own museum of ceremonial objects from their own homes. The "Immigration and Family History" kit includes a multicultural family history workbook; documents and artifacts about a German-Jewish immigrant family; a slide/tape presentation; and role-playing exercises about a Polish-German immigrant family.

Museum In The Schools
Herbert F. Johnson Museum of Art
Cornell University, Ithaca, NY 14853
(607) 256-6464
Users: All grades, including group homes, delinquent education centers and developmentally disabled schools
Length/frequency: Two-part program: one hour in the classroom and one hour in the museum; program can vary

Museum In The Schools is a collaborative effort between school and museum educators. The format uses original works of art and participatory activity workshops utilizing museum resources. For example, 18th-century French landscapes may be used to teach creative writing, or Margaret Bourke White photographs may be used to teach the concept of discrimination. Sculptures from the permanent collection may be used to introduce the concept of self image and the museum's architecture may be used to explore geometry.

Workshops are designed individually to meet the teacher's needs, with one workshop taking place in the classroom and one in the museum galleries. Workshops involve participatory activities, such as writing, drawing, talking, or dramatics, to explore original works of art. The activity provides the structure in which to approach the work of art. Programs developed with the teachers have included a high school ceramics class studying form versus function using the museum's Asian and contemporary American ceramics, or a second-grade class' introduction to the museum with an emphasis on color. Each workshop is documented with written materials and includes an evaluation from the teacher.

Highsites
The High Museum of Art
1280 Peachtree St, NW, Atlanta, GA 30309
(404) 892-3600
Users: Elementary age children and teachers
Length/frequency: Three sessions

Playscapes, the children's play environment at Piedmont Park, is the basis for "Highsites," a three-part program that begins with an introductory session for children and teachers in the classroom. Later, student visit *Playscapes* and explore the variety of forms, textures, and space in the play sculptures. At the end of the free-play session, children are grouped together according to their colored arm bands to explore such themes as line (at the triple slide) or pattern (at the cubes). Several weeks later, the children return to the museum for games and dialogue. At this time they begin applying their newly acquired concepts in looking at art and the environment.

Arts in Education
Huntsville Museum of Art
700 Monroe St., SW, Huntsville, AL 35801
(205) 534-4566
Users: Grades 5-6
Length/frequency: Twelve lessons in the classroom over a two-year period, plus two museum visits per year

This program corresponds to the public school's social studies curricula by demonstrating the relationships between art and culture. Classroom presentations examine art from a design standpoint and in regard to its social content. For example, students pretend they are detectives as they view a slide of the Henry Laurens portrait by John Singleton Copley. Using clues found in the painting—facial expression, pose, clothing, props and background detail—they determine the subject's personality, the time period in which he lived, his social status, and his occupation. The docent lecturer then relates information about Laurens' place in history and discusses the artist's technique. Fifth graders study American culture through early American portraits and folk art. In sixth grade, cultures such as those of China and Egypt provide the subject matter for an exploration of art and culture. Students continue their investigation of art objects in a cultural context by visiting the museum's changing exhibitions twice each year.

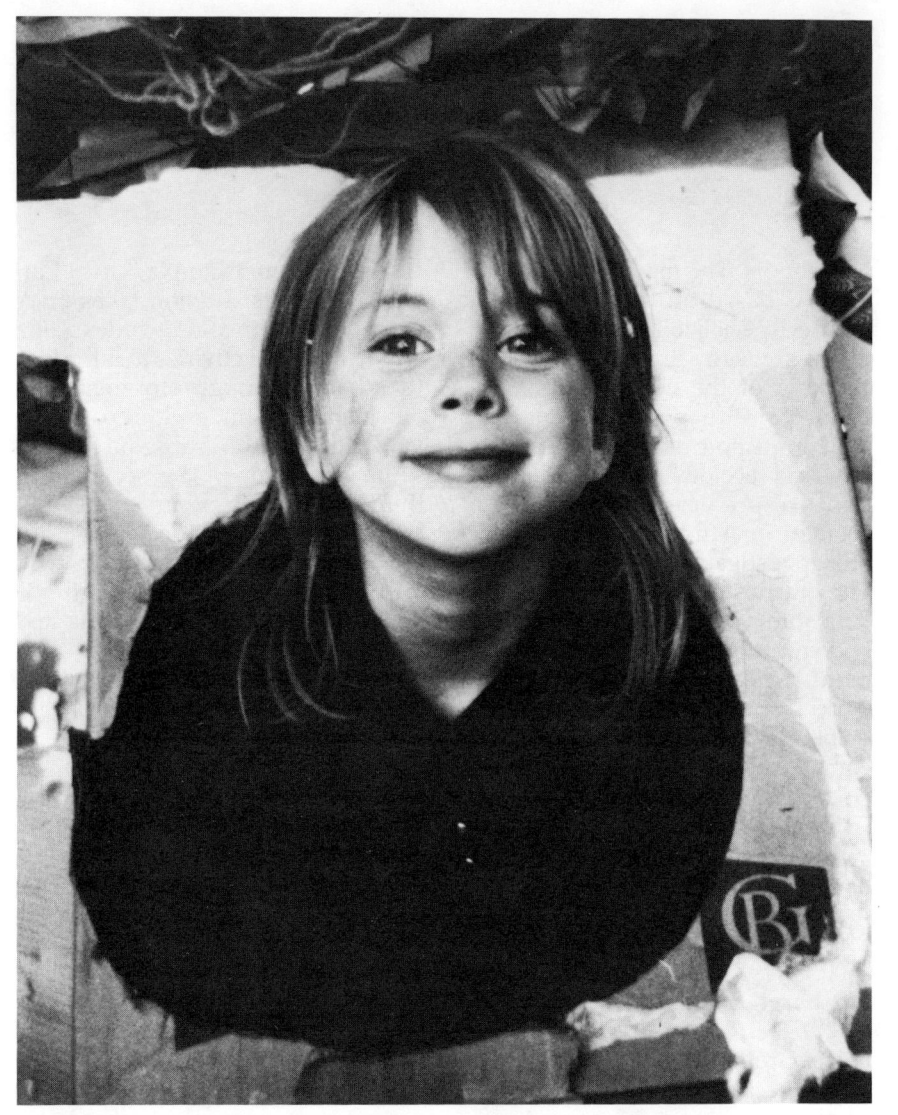

Survivors in the Woods
Jacksonville Museum of Arts and Sciences
1025 Gulf Life Dr.,
Jacksonville, FL 32207
(904) 396-7062
Users: Grade 6
Length/frequency: 90 minutes once a week

Using artifacts, live animals, and environmental exhibits, the life styles of Florida's Indians and pioneers from 1870-1900 are compared and contrasted. In four different exhibits illustrating adaptations and survival in semitropical environments, students learn about daily life in an Indian chickee, log cabin, and country store. They role-play the people of that period, handling kettles, light sources, clothing, and other materials. In addition, they learn about the environment of that period, in comparison to the current environment, and what the differences mean to life styles. When birds were more plentiful, for example, there were fewer mosquitoes, and egrets were plentiful before their plumes became fashionable in hats.

Animal Discovery Units
John Ball Zoological Gardens
301 Market St. SW, Grand Rapids, MI 49503
(616) 456-3811
Users: All elementary students in Western Michigan
Length/frequency: Three 90-minute sessions over three weeks.

The "Predator-Prey Discovery Unit" typifies the zoo's three-part interrelated programs that include two classroom visits and a zoo tour, accompanied by extensive preparatory and follow-up materials. Part 1, "The Coyote Program," presented at the school by trained volunteers, deals with basic predator-prey concepts and relationships, focusing specifically on the coyote. Concepts are presented using inquiry techniques, incorporating a variety of methods, such as study skills, slides, pelts, cassettes of howling coyotes, and a hunting-simulation game. The program was developed by Michigan United Conservation Clubs. In Part 2, "Live Animals," two trained volunteers visit the classroom with live animals such as boa constrictors, ferrets, rabbits, alligators, turtles, etc. The presentation focuses on the specific physical and behavioral adaptations of predators and/or prey animals. The final section, a "Guided Tour of the Zoo," stresses the balance of predator-prey relationships, the concept of stewardship, and identifiable characteristics and adaptations of predators and prey. Other Animal Discovery Units deal with vertebrate classification (grades 1-3) and predator-prey relationships.

Student Science Seminars
Maryland Academy of Sciences
601 Light St., Baltimore, MD 21230
(301) 685-2370
Users: Gifted students in Grades 11-12
Length/frequency: Eight two and one-half hour sessions

The academy works closely with science supervisors in public, parochial, and private school systems in planning the program. Because seminar leaders encourage independent study, many students begin major research projects under the direction of local scientists. One course in neurology called, "An Overview of the Brain," uses lecture-discussion and laboratory sessions to examine major features of the nervous system and to illustrate research methods used in the neurological sciences. In a course entitled, "Electronic Circuit Design and Application," students build and operate transistor amplifiers and computer logic circuits. In "The Stars in the Milky Way," students combine photoelectric data, photographs, and radio observations to find the ages of stars and the shape of our galaxy.

Plant Ecology Program
Missouri Botanical Garden
2248 Tower Grove Ave., St. Louis, MO 63110
(314) 772-7600
Users: Grades 4-8
Length/frequency: Two to three times per month, per student

The educational staff of the Missouri Botanical Garden is directly involved in the St. Louis Public Schools' effort to reduce racial isolation through the establishment of magnet schools. The magnet school program is based on the premise that highly specialized curricular programs serve to attract students from all parts of the city and thus voluntarily reduce racial isolation. Drawing upon its expertise in botany and ecology, the Garden designed a specialized program in plant ecology for students attending the Stix Investigative Learning Center. The purpose of the program is to help students develop an awareness and appreciation of their environment. Activities include mapping a park; planting and caring for a vegetable garden; and studying various climate zones in the Garden's Desert House, Mediterranean House, and Tropical Climatron.

Artexpress School Museum Projects
Museum of Art, Carnegie Institute
4400 Forbes Ave.,
Pittsburgh, PA 15213
(412) 622-3144
Users: Grades 3-5, 25 classrooms
Length/frequency: Three 90-minute sessions

Classroom, art, and museum teachers have collaborated on the curriculum design and implementation of a program that connects the visual arts and academic subjects in imaginative and informative ways. Six different themes are outlined in a series of sample lesson plans that can be adapted to the ages and needs of each participating group. The themes include: "Portraits—People from the Past"; "The Peaceful Hopi—Symbols and Ceremonies"; "Treasures of the Earth"; "Earth, Sky and Water"; "Many Faces, Many Friends"; and "Dragons and Dinosaurs." Each project consists of three sessions. For example, in "Portraits," the first session takes place in the classroom and includes a film and related art activities to introduce the theme through storytelling of Huckleberry Finn, and prepares the students for the subsequent museum workshops. The second and third workshops occur in the museum, combining storytelling, gallery games, museum workbooks, and art projects. The children might examine portraits by Frans Hals and John Singer, discussing their similarities and differences, improvising conversations and creating collages and puppets.

Costume Design
Museum of Art, Rhode Island School of Design
224 Benefit St., Providence, RI 02903
(401) 331-3512
Users: Eight students at a time; ages 12-15
Length/frequency: Eleven weeks, 90-minute sessions

The education department creates special programs to take advantage of temporary exhibits. Design workshops using the museum galleries as classrooms were offered in conjunction with two exhibitions: "Costumes in Context" and "Designed for Another Age: Decorative Arts from Newport Mansions." Participants saw slide presentations and visited the Rhode Island Historical Society to study its collection of imported dolls in period costumes in order to understand more fully how these fashions were created. The students learned design, draping and construction of 19th-century costumes as they studied the Museum's collection, and, simultaneously, they produced their own period costumes. These were worn at the opening for the children's art classes exhibition where all participants in the after-school program displayed their work.

Neighborhood History

Museum of Transportation
The Wharf, Boston, MA 02130
(617) 426-6633
Users: Grades 3-5
Length/frequency: Ten weeks, one hour per week

The museum demonstrates how new ways of moving people, things, and ideas have caused dramatic changes in the shape of the city and the lives of its citizens. Children explore how their own or their school's neighborhoods used to be and are now. They study neighborhood history, map the area, explore it, interview people who live and work in it, and take pictures of it. In these ways, they learn about what makes up a community. Subsequently, the students display maps and pictures of their neighborhood in school exhibits.

Overnight Aboard the Joseph Conrad

Mystic Seaport Museum, Inc.
Mystic, CT 06355
(203) 536-2631
Users: All grade levels
Length/frequency: Two days with one overnight; Three days with two overnights

A sailmaker's palm, a drawknife, tarred hemp, scrimshaw, harpoons—these are just a few of the objects used so that school groups can gain a greater understanding of life in a 19th-century seaport town. This program delves into the study of whaling, fishing, shipbuilding and 19th-century home life. Students visit a sailmaker's loft and a cooper's shop, climb the rigging of a ship, row a fishing boat, and sail a dinghy. In the evening, students are berthed aboard the former Danish training ship *Joseph Conrad*. After dinner, they sing sea chanties, and see a movie appropriate to their visit, such as "Moby Dick," or "Captains Courageous."

C. A. THAYER—Overnight Program

National Park Service, Golden Gate National Recreation Area, National Maritime Museum
2905 Hyde St., San Francisco, CA 94109
(415) 556-6435
Users: Grades 4-6
Length/frequency: 24-hour overnight sessions, 35 per year

The *Thayer*, a three-masted, schooner-rigged 1890 sailing ship, is the focal point for the park's Environmental Living Program. Here children can experience something of the life of a sailor through role-playing, exploration, and problem-solving. The program is handled in five stages: a 24-hour training session for teachers, a preliminary visit by the children to the *Thayer* and other historic ships at the park; preparation and planning in the classroom for the trip; the overnight outing itself; the classroom follow-up. The National Park Service's Environmental Living Program Packet describes other programs throughout the United States.

Monkeys, Apes, and Humans: The Story of Primates

National Museum of Natural History and the National Zoo
Smithsonian Institution,
Washington, DC 20560
(202) 381-5304
Users: Secondary Students
Length/frequency: Three two and one-half hour sessions

This jointly sponsored program combines the resources and viewpoints of both zoology and anthropology. Students learn to observe and collect data on primate behavior, formulate hypotheses based on observation of living and skeletal forms, and compare and contrast the physical and social development of monkeys, great apes and humans. Students are introduced to the appropriate scientific techniques on the first day of the program at the Zoo. Then they observe primate behavior, concentrating on interaction, locomotion or communication. On the second day at the Museum of Natural History, students participate in exercises where they classify primates and make a detailed comparison of the major primates. On the third day, at the museum, students use exhibits and actual skeletal material to focus on the development of humans through time. A final discussion reviews the highlights of primate physical and social development and the unique nature of our cultural heritage. At each session, students work in small study groups, making clearly defined observations and attempting to find answers to a variety of problems.

I, Too, am America
National Portrait Gallery
Eighth and F St., NW,
Washington, DC 20560
(202) 357-2920
Users: Grades 7-12
Length/frequency: One classroom visit followed by a museum tour

Black history comes alive during this program, which exposes students to the Harlem Renaissance Period of the 1920's. A museum instructor visits the classroom to introduce the divergent philosophies of three men who shaped this era: Booker T. Washington, W. E. B. DuBois, and Marcus Garvey. Students receive role cards of individuals who lived in New York City in the 1920s. According to the roles they have assumed, the students must decide which man's philosophy each would have followed. Issues involved would be the ability to join a union, the right to sit anywhere on a bus, insurance of the right to vote, and, in general, the issues that served as the basis of the Civil Rights struggle. A follow-up tour of the museum's portraits of educators, musicians, politicians, writers and others related to the Harlem Renaissance and the subsequent Civil Rights movement, furnishes students an opportunity to explore the emergence of the black community as a powerful and vital force in America. The trial of John Brown is the subject of another program based on this model.

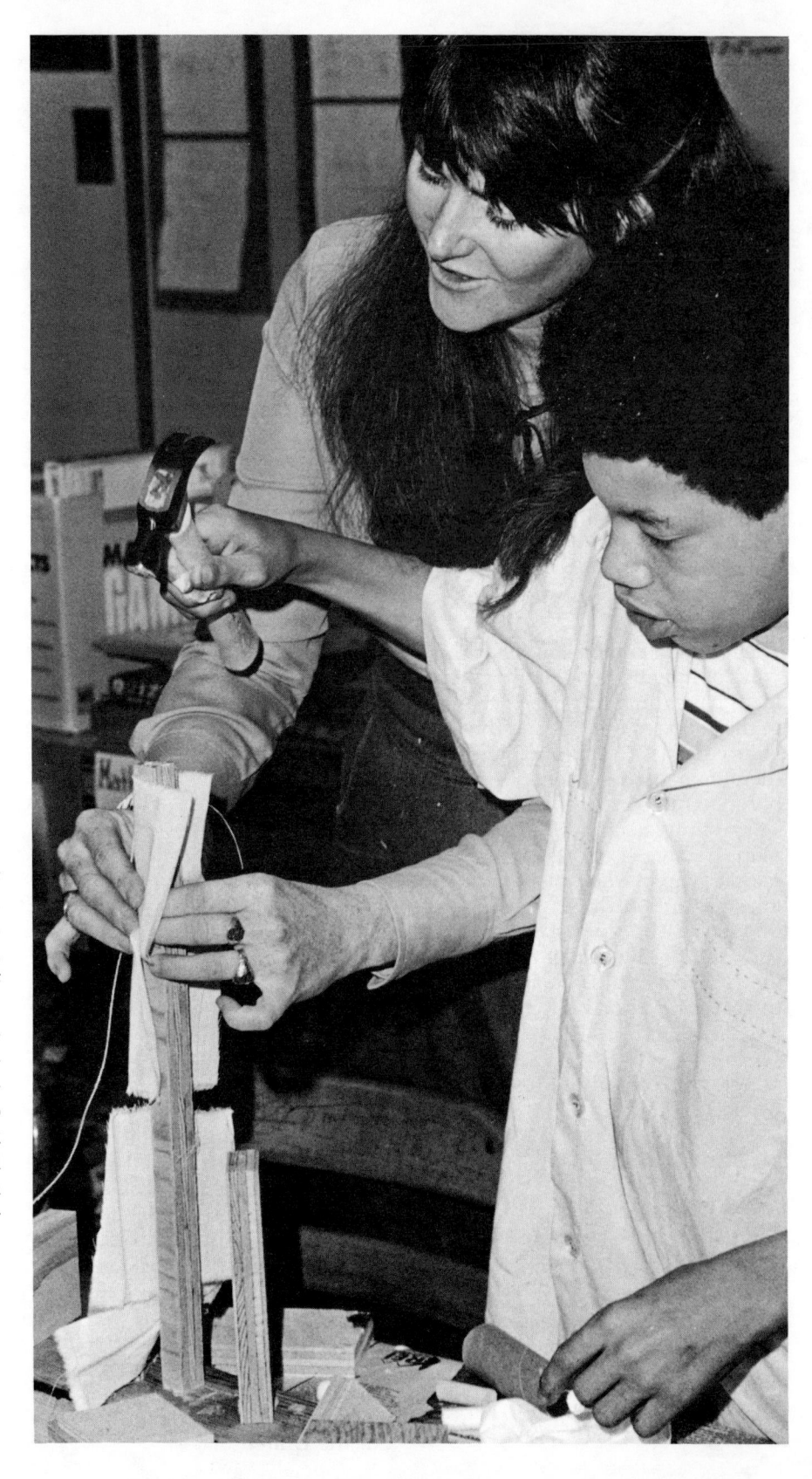

Zoo Animals—A Closer Look
National Zoological Park,
Smithsonian Institution
Washington, DC 20008
(202) 673-4724
Users: Grade 4
Length/frequency: Seven sessions: one in classroom, six at zoo; teacher workshops preceeding program

This program reinforces the skills of observing, classifying and recording data. Teachers attend a preliminary series of workshops at the zoo where they learn how to participate as instructors and become familiar with the follow-up materials the zoo provides. Zoo staff and volunteers first visit the classroom to show a film on general zoo operations and to answer questions. During the next five lessons, children work at the zoo in small groups looking closely at animals to see what they are like, how they behave, and how they are suited for different habitats. For example, in a lesson on animals of the African plains, the students closely observe a live meerkat in a zoo workroom. They learn how to describe its appearance and behavior, and determine how it is adapted to its savannah habitat. In the park, the students observe other inhabitants of the African savannah while looking at and describing these animals in a "Mammal Book." They discuss how each animal's adaptive features (feet, limbs, body shapes, eye placement and color) help it compete and survive on the savannah. Follow-up classroom activities include researching a variety of mammals and watching films. A month later, the class returns to the zoo, to observe and share information about their favorite animals with the rest of the group. Other lessons are on reptiles, amphibians, birds, primates, and aquatic animals.

Museum History Seminar
Natural History Museum of Los Angeles
900 Exposition Blvd., Los Angeles, CA 90007
(213) 744-3342
Users: 60 selected high school and college freshmen
Length/frequency: Two semesters on Saturdays

This yearly seminar supplements the curriculum of high school and college students with a critical examination of a topic in American history. The students selected for the seminar (six from each school) study with the history staff of the museum, professors from local colleges and universities, and their peers. One topic, "American History: Backwards and Forwards," offers students an opportunity to study their family in relation to the past and examine everyday implements on display at the museum. Sample topics include the "Ubiquitous Artifact," "The Original Americans," "After the Gold Rush," and "Abolutionism: the Anti-Slavery Impulse."

School Service Program
Ontario Science Centre
770 Don Mills Road, Don Mills, Ont M3C IT3
(416) 429-4100
Users: Grades K-13
Length/frequency: Two-to-three-day workshops; 30 to 60-minute presentations, demonstrations, and exhibit inquiries

The program adapts the Centre's biology programs on evolution, genetics, physiology, hormones, reproduction, and nutrition to the needs of visiting classes through presentations that make extensive use of slides, movies, models, and biological specimens. Students also learn how the human body is organized, participate in a submaximal oxygen uptake test to understand how fitness is measured, and observe the locomotion of pond life on a television monitor. In addition to these programs, students handle equipment and artifacts in laboratory workshops. For example, in the three-day "Electron Microscopy Workshop," students explore the optical principles of light and electron microscopes, the function of components in a transmission electron microscope, and the preparation of specimens and electron micrographs. Exhibit inquiries involve students in an exploration of specific exhibit areas such as hormones, the Canadian North, and food webs.

California Rancho
Petaluma Adobe State Historic Park
Sonoma Area, P.O. Box 167, Sonoma, CA 95476
(707) 996-1744
Users: Grade 4
Length/frequency: Overnight session, available once a week

Students experience the life of a cook, woodworker, or artisan on a working Mexican ranch by spending 24 hours at the park. Depending on their role assignment, the students bake bread in beehive ovens, make candles, tend the fires, or take turns at the night watch. Activities are flexible and adaptable for use by each teacher, who participates in a training session and a pre-visit with the class before the live-in experience. Students also make bricks, card and spin wool, and weave on old oak floor looms.

Museum Journey
Philadelphia Museum of Art
P.O. Box 7646, Philadelphia, PA 19101
(215) 763-8100
User: Grades 4-6
Length/frequency: Four 90-minute sessions

"Museum Journey" is a multivisit introduction to appreciating art and using art museums. Each of the four sessions is devoted to a specific approach to art, building from one set of skills to the next. The first visit deals with visual perception in art: Students learn to improve observation skills and become aware of themselves as perceivers. Visual memory tests, optical illusions, and experiments with distance and point of view are used to emphasize that seeing is an active skill. Visit two focuses on emotion and reaction to art. Students discover and analyze their affective responses to a variety of objects, discovering that works of art affect people in different ways and that artists can only partially control the effect an object will have on a viewer. Art as an historical document is studied in the third visit as students gather information about objects produced in a particular time and place (Medieval France, or Colonial America, for example). They then attempt to "read through" the objects to the people and culture that produced them, drawing some conclusions about the lifestyle and attitudes of people in other times and places. The goal in the final session is for students to make personal value judgments and to better understand the nature of their own value systems and those of others. Students participate in a word game in which they privately match value-laden words to a variety of paintings and then cast public votes for the objects they value most. For the final activity, small groups discuss their words, their preferences, and their ways of judging and valuing art objects.

The Coyote And The Raven
San Diego Museum of Man
1350 El Prado, Balboa Park,
San Diego, CA 92101
(714) 239-2001
Users: Grades 3-6 Gifted
Length/frequency: Two, two-and-one-half-hour lessons, one at school, one in the museum

The diverse cultures of the California Indians from the southern desert to the northern forest are compared to the cultures of the American Plains Indians in this two-part program. Emphasis is placed on the myths, art and language of these people as represented in various artifacts. The classroom slide presentation illustrates how the environment helps to shape different cultural patterns. The museum tour compares California and Plains Indians artifacts such as baskets, pottery, clothing and games. These are carefully studied for distinguishing characteristics in the design, materials, and use.

Participatory Tours
The San Francisco Museum of Modern Art
Van Ness and McAllister,
San Francisco, CA 94102
(415) 863-8800
Users: Primarily elementary school groups
Length/frequency: Three weekly 90-minute sessions

The philosophy of see, think, do, and learn is reflected in these participatory tours. Students visit the Hands-On Gallery, where props, large-scale graphic designs, colored slides, and participatory exhibits are used to illustrate art concepts, elements, and materials. In other exhibitions, gallery games are used to develop "creative looking" and to teach students to conceptualize and fantasize about art. The children are given an art project to do that relates to the works seen. With any given exhibition, children examine the various conceptions of traditional and modern painting or sculpture, determine how the work they are examining is or is not consistent with those conventions, and then take on the task of creating their own painting or sculpture out of simple materials (e.g., wood dowels, twine) in the same galleries where the artist's work is shown.

Fun Physics
Science Museum of Virginia
2500 W. Broad St.,
Richmond, VA 23220
(804) 257-1013
Users: Elementary school age groups
Length/frequency: One three-hour session followed by a full day session

"Fun Physics" is designed to actively involve students in the physical sciences of motion. This is first accomplished by demonstrating principles of motion and then by providing a firsthand opportunity to experience these principles. The first three-hour session is conducted at the museum by the staff and probes physical principles dealing with motion. Demonstrations include a twirling cup of water, a model rocket, and the familiar tablecloth-under-the-china trick. Students are encouraged to try many of the demonstrations themselves. The second session is a day-long trip to a major amusement park where the students experience some of the principles of motion and the forces associated with them (centripetal force and weightlessness) by riding the amusements. A continuous conversation between students and facilitator encourage both understanding and an excitement for science.

South Dakota—A Four Part Series
Siouxland Heritage Museums
200 W. 6th, Sioux Falls, SD 57102
(605) 335-4210
Users: Grade 6 (primarily)
Length/frequency: Four consecutive, one-hour programs

This program developed from an analysis of the South Dakota history text used in most schools of Minnehaha County and Sioux Falls. The first session acquaints students with the geology and prehistory of South Dakota, stressing that an understanding of the land and the forces that shaped it is essential to begin the study of the people. Prehistory takes the first people in the Americas from their arrival until just before the area's cultures were changed

167

by European arrivals. The second session deals with the changes brought about by the introduction of goods and culture from about 1600 to 1820. The third session covers the topics of frontier army, gold mining, the start of ranching in western South Dakota, and their interrelationships. The final session deals with the relatively short period of 1858-1890 and the concepts of homesteading and town building, culminating in a slide presentation on the development of Sioux Falls and area towns. Each presentation makes extensive use of the inquiry method coupled with some role playing and storytelling.

American Arts, Discovery Tours
Reynolda House, American Art
P.O. Box 11765, Winston-Salem, NC 27106
(919) 725-5325
Users: Grades 1-12
Length/frequency: Two hours to two days depending on the needs of the class

"Discovery Tours" on a range of topics are designed to relate to the individual curricula of each grade level and tours are developed in partnership with the teachers. A range of topics are available for the teachers to choose from depending on their needs. "American History through Art", available to grades 4-12, begins with a 1775 portrait of Mrs. Thomas Lynch, mother of one of the signers of the Declaration of Independence, and examines other portraits of 18th- and 19th-century Americans. Landscape and everyday life scenes complete an in-depth look at the changing American scene as students study works by Andrew Wyeth, T. Hart Benton, A. Bierstadt and other artists whose works are represented in school textbooks. In "Correlation of Art, Literature and Music," available to all grades, specific works of art, literature and music which express similar points of view are examined, for example T. H. Benton's painting "The Bootleggers," F. Scott Fitzgerald's "The Great Gatsby," and Scott Joplin's "The Entertainer." Grades 4 to 12, can participate in "American Printmaking," examining works by J. Sloan, Jim Dine and Jasper Johns followed by experiences in printmaking. Other topics are available and using the same format of studying objects in the collection followed by an activity session which helps the students understand the creative process more clearly.

Eye-Openers Programs
Wadsworth Atheneum
600 Main St., Hartford, CT 06103
(203) 278-2670
Users: Grades 4-6
Length/frequency: 45 minutes in school and 45 minutes in the museum

These two-part programs introduce students to the vocabulary of art, facilitate an understanding of artistic processes, and develop skills in analyzing works of art. Through the use of slides, art reproductions and artists' materials, each in-school component introduces the basic concepts to be developed on the museum tour. Approximately 10 objects from the permanent collections are used in the museum tour to illustrate the tour theme and expose students to the diversity of artistic expression and meaning. "Things Made of Wood" illustrates the grain, color, relative ease of carving, and the wide range of possible surface textures and treatments that have made wood an appealing material for the craftsman and sculptor. Students learn about the techniques and tools of wood carving, and differences in style and purpose as they compare objects ranging from a 13-century madonna to a 20th-century abstract work. During the tour in the "Shape" program, students compare such objects as a suit of armor and an abstract Picasso painting as they learn the vocabulary of shapes and how to look at shapes in the man-made and natural world. Additional Eye-Opener themes have been developed.

SEE (Special Extended Enriched) Programs
Western Reserve Historical Society
10825 East Blvd., Cleveland, OH 44106
(216) 721-5722
Users: Grades 5-9
Length/frequency: Four hours (one full day or two consecutive days)

"The People Who Built Cleveland" focuses on the experiences of the immigrants and their participation in the city's growth. Using excerpts from diaries, letters, and other first person accounts, children role play and simulate leaving the old country and travelling by steerage to Ellis Island. Maps of Cleveland settlement patterns in 1930 and 1970 guide their study of origins and changes in ethnic neighborhoods. The day ends with a craft project using ethnic designs. Teachers receive study sheets for making family trees, conducting oral interviews with immigrants, and exploring ethnic neighborhoods as post-visit activities. "Museum Careers are Fundamental," for students in grades 6-9, was developed in cooperation with school career education coordinators. The variety of museum jobs are used as examples of the academic and interpersonal skills needed in the adult working world. After touring the museum and interviewing staff members from the curatorial, exhibit, education, and restoration departments, the students are given data sheets that explain the job roles they will assume as they practice museum activities. Among the pre- and post-visit activities, interviewing techniques are discussed before the visits, and the various jobs are compared and analyzed afterwards.

Art Enrichment for the Gifted and Talented
Hirschhorn Museum and
Sculpture Garden
Smithsonian Institution,
Washington, DC 20560
(202) 381-6713
Users: Grade 6, talented and gifted
Length/frequency: Eight one-hour weekly sessions: five in the classroom and three museum visits

The changing world of 20th-century art and the reasons for these changes are presented in the classroom, lectures, and museum tours. The program develops the students' aesthetic awareness and understanding of the tools and vocabulary used by artists as it offers an historical perspective of the changes that brought about the creative work of the 20th century. The classroom sessions develop the students' sensory and perceptual levels for looking at works of art. The students learn how artists translate the three-dimensional world onto a two-dimensional surface by examining the relationships between size, space, and positioning in works by Eakins, Sargent, and Magritte. New materials, communications, exploration of space, psychological analysis, the computer and other elements of the 20th-century world are discussed as they influenced the artist. In addition, they learn about basic compositional elements and their application to painting and sculpture throughout the history of art. The tours of the museum's collection include: the material of the artist, which emphasizes the media and methods of 20th-century painting and sculpture; modern painting, which emphasizes the development of the modern idiom in American painting; and modern sculpture, which surveys the complete development of the sculptural medium in the United States and Europe from the 19th century to the present.

Nineteenth-Century Day
The Hagley Museum
Greenville, Wilmington, DE 19807
(302) 658-2400, Ext. 259
Users: Ages 9-12; available to school and community groups
Length/frequency: Five hours

Children spend a day in three different structures that help illustrate the life and work of young people in an 1880s industrial community. The structures are: an 1850s house for a workman and his family, the Brandywine Manufacturer's Sunday School attended by children who lived and worked in the area, and the powderyard, where black powder was manufactured in the late 19th-century. The program stresses the relationship of the 19th-century family to the community and the changes in technology over the years. The children do sums with slates and chalk, practice penmanship with quill pens, scrub clothes on a washboard, bake biscuits on a wood-burning stove, and iron with a flat iron heated on the stove. The powderyard foreman helps them with outdoor chores and takes them through the yard, where he operates a turbine-powered roll wheel in one of the mills. He also demonstrates stone cutting techniques in a quarry and sets up outdoor drying tables so that the young powder workers can rake and dry the black powder. During the tour of the home, children do household chores, sing 19th-century songs while playing an autoharp, and try on replicas of period clothing. Kitchen activities allow them to focus on how a household operated without electricity and to make comparisons with their own homes. A suitcase-like kit, available for pre-visit work, includes lesson plans, learning station activities, artifacts, slides, books, and pamphlets.

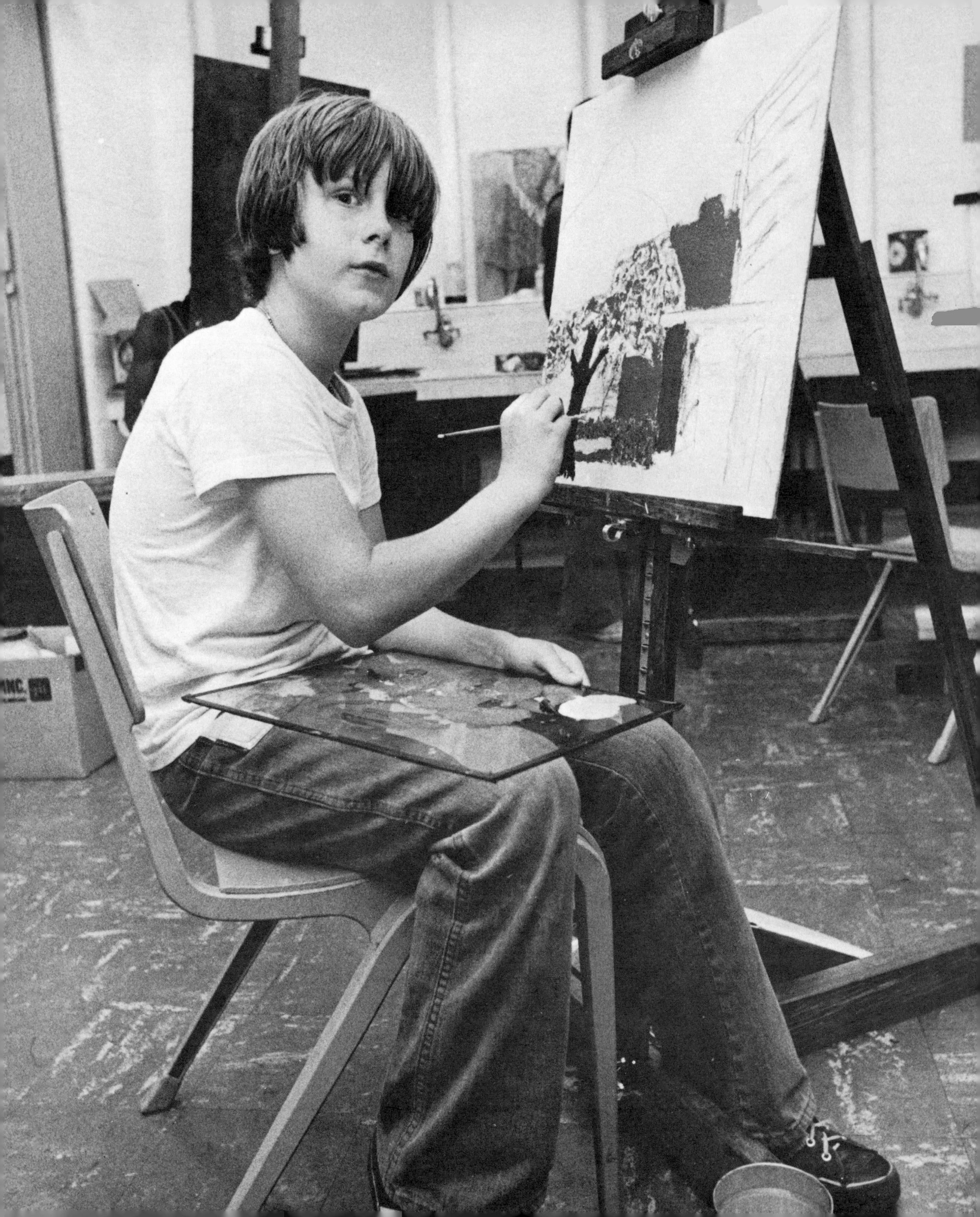

11.
COURSES FOR CREDIT

Museums have developed courses for academic credit in cooperation with their local school districts. Using the collections, staff and resources of the museum, students come to study the history of art, the built environment, wild life, and the history of their community. These courses are offered for a specified number of weeks or during the entire year.

Scientific Tools And Techniques
Fernbank Science Center
156 Heaton Park NE, Atlanta, GA 30307
(404) 378-4311
Users: Grades 9-10, 60 per quarter
Length/frequency: Entire quarter: 12 weeks, 9 a.m.—2 p.m. daily

Methodologies and techniques of scientific studies are emphasized in this program, as is the knowledge needed to understand them. Selected aspects of the physical and biological sciences are covered by using the equipment, skills and expertise of the staff. More specifically, the students learn: scientific methodology, including planning, observational, and experimental techniques; the performance of field investigations, including how to draw reasonable conclusions and inference from readings and observations; the writing of quantitative and qualitative field and laboratory notes; the interrelationships among sciences and within a given science; and how to utilize and research topics in the scientific library. Each student receives six weeks of training in both areas. Offerings in the physical sciences include physics, chemistry, observational astronomy, computer science, regional field geology, and meteorology. In the biological sciences, the topics include ornithology, animal behavior, scanning electron microscopy, terrestrial ecology, invertebrate zoology, entomology, horticulture, and physiology. Students, selected on the basis of academic achievement, enthusiasm for science, and maturity, receive two elective credits. The "concentrated science quarter" enables students to make better decisions regarding their future academic and professional careers.

Beaumont U.S.A.: Our Built Environment
Beaumont Art Museum
1111 Ninth St., Beaumont, TX 77702
(713) 832-3432
Users: Grade 8
Length/frequency: Eight months

American and local history are taught through architecture and environmental awareness in a program that is an addition to the curriculum. The program revolves around a student text and workbook, "Beaumont USA," written by the art museum and heritage society staffs. The book combines factual material about architecture, Beaumont history, and historical preservation, with a variety of activities to be carried out individually or in class. These activities include: downtown discovery hikes, house hunts, design problems, map skill sheets, vocabulary review, role playing, restoration and adaptation planning, drawing exercises and National Register application forms. In the course of the school year, volunteers visit the classroom twice a month, and the teachers attend six in-service workshops. The program introduces the concept of architecture and the built environment as a fine art embodying the elements of briefly introduces Asia, Africa and the Americas. This study is conducted using the museum's collection as a primary source, and augmented with slide-lectures, guest speakers, visits to other cultural institutions. An Advanced Placement (AP) exam qualifies the student to participate in the museology course offered in the spring. In the museology course, the students explore the role of a museum and its operations by researching and presenting an exhibition of museum works of art. Students receive college credit in English and in art upon successful completion of the AP exam and/or the museology course.

Adopt A Building
The New Jersey Historical Society
230 Broadway, Newark, NJ 07104
(201) 483-3939
Users: Elementary and secondary students
Length/frequency: Part of school curriculum

A special statewide outreach program for the 1981-82 school year, "Adopt A Building" is sponsored by the historical society to involve youth in grassroot preservation. Young people will academically "adopt" a structure that interests them in their community. Through oral history, three-dimensional models, audio-visual presentations and other activities, the youth research and share the building's role in the community with other young people and with the public. At the end of the school year all participants will be recognized. Outstanding projects will receive awards and will be published in a special edition of *New Jersey History*.

The Oakland Museum Classroom
Oakland Museum
1000 Oak St., Oakland, CA 94607
(415) 273-3401
Users: Grade 5, bilingual and handicapped
Length/frequency: Week long

This program provides interdisciplinary learning experiences in natural science, history, and art as these subjects pertain to California. The *Natural Science Gallery* provides opportunities for map making and animal identification and studies of animal population, water resources, land management, geography, and bird migrations. In the *History Gallery*, impromptu drama and identification of family artifacts supplement problem-solving questions on worksheets to develop a child's sense of his own place in history. Often, as the court calendar permits, the class visits a session of the county's superior court to compare today's legal procedures with yesterday's vigilante era. Art is taught as a record of the historical, as well as aesthetic, development of early California and Oakland. Sculpture in the garden provides a geometry lesson, an introduction to physics (optics), and a stimulus for haiku poetry.

Curriculum Projects
Pacific Science Center
200 Second Ave. N., Seattle, WA 98109
(206) 625-9333
Users: Grades 5-8
Length/frequency: Curriculum developed for 12-week program in the public school

The curriculum, "Project Archeology: Saving Traditions," helps students in grades 6-8 explore the prehistory of the Puget Sound region and the evolving life styles of Northwest Coast people. They gain respect for earlier cultures and an appreciation of the need to protect archeological sites. Students inventory, survey, make their own tools, excavate a simulated site to discover artifacts, analyze data, and formulate and defend conclusions. School districts may apply for funding to adopt the program, which was developed under a state-administered grant. Students play an active role in "You Are Here", an environmental science curriculum developed for gifted fifth to seventh graders. Activities are designed to help them learn from their own discussions, problem-solving sessions, laboratories, and field observations. The curriculum is divided into three units: "Common Ground," which looks at local plants and animals; "Adaptation," which focuses on living things and adaptations that have occurred; and "City-scape," which looks at Seattle's past and how the natural environment influences the present.

Interdisciplinary Science Program
Roger Williams Park Zoo
Providence, RI 02905
(401) 467-9230
Users: Grades 5 and 6
Length/frequency: One-year project, two semesters

Students explore wetland ecosystems and animal ecology, behavior, and adaptations. These topics are developed through course materials and activities performed in the classroom and at the zoo. After teacher orientation, a specially trained docent makes a slide presentation in the classroom focusing on animal adaptations and components of wetlands ecosystems. In addition, such objects as antlers, snake skins, eggs, and shells are examined and handled. During the next four to eight weeks, teachers and students study developed texts and explore activities suggested in the teacher's guide. At the end of each semester, students visit the zoo for an activity-oriented wetlands exploration day or zoo discovery day. The last segment involves a follow-up activity period in the classroom, supplemented by a Zoomobile visit.

Agriculture Education: Animal Care
Toledo Zoological Society
2700 Broadway, Toledo, OH 43609
(419) 385-5721
Users: Grades 11 and 12 (accredited high school program)
Length/frequency: Thirty-six weeks (regular school year), 4 hours each day on the zoo grounds; two-year program

This vocational program includes technical instruction, laboratory activities, and occupational experience as preparation for employment in the animal care field. Students are in class for two weeks and then rotate to work on the zoo grounds for two weeks. This processs continues for the length of the school year. For example, they may have the responsibility of running Wonder Valley, the children's zoo, after preparation in the classroom for tasks they are to perform: handling animals, caring for them, feeding them, and keeping a watch on their public contact.

The Arts Infusion Project
The George Walter Vincent Smith Art Museum
222 State St., Springfield, MA 01103
(413) 733-4214
Users: Elementary and junior high school students
Length/frequency: One to twelve sessions using packets

The "Arts Infusion Project" teaches basic curriculum through the arts, and encourages the arts as an integral part of education. The program is organized around nine different learning packets, such as storytelling, geometry, the Renaissance, and classification. Learning packets are designed to provide the classroom teacher with materials and experiences necessary to infuse art, music, and drama into the basic curriculum. Created by teachers and representatives of the Springfield Symphony, two art museums, and theater, each packet consists of between 15 and 25 activities, which teach a particular subject area in the curriculum and make connections between what the children learn in the school and what they find at the arts institutions. A typical situation might be a second grade class, which visits the museum as part of their unit on geometric shapes. Having studied shapes in the classroom, each child receives a geometric shape cut from wall paper when they arrive at the museum. The children are asked to look around the gallery and select works that have their shapes. They select, focus and react to the art works. Their discoveries lead to discussions about their choices, what the objects are, and how they were used. In the Oriental rug collection, for example, the children take a selection of geometric shapes, carefully examine the designs in the carpets, and then design their own rugs. Careful study reveals the variations in the design and sizes of the shapes in the museum's rug collection.

Humanities Class
Rocky Mountain Historical Association
Rt. 2 Box 70, Piney Flats, TN 37659
(615) 538-7396
Users: Grade 8, gifted
Length/frequency: Ten hours per week for 27 weeks

The museum and classroom teachers have developed a humanities curriculum for the study of state history, required of all eighth graders. Students participate in the program for 10 hours each week, both in school and at the museum. For example, in one week's humanities unit on the local Cherokee tribe, students tour the museum's Indian galleries and collections, and study Indian migrations, contact with Europeans, and Indian history, myths and legends. Activities include listening to native music, making flint arrowheads, and crafting pottery with traditional designs. Another unit on the Spanish settlements in eastern Tennessee involves a study of Spanish explorers, a slide show prepared by the museum on the painting of El Greco and Moorish architecture, and other related programs. This format continues until the class completes the entire study of the state's history. Approximately 130 students from four junior high schools participate in this course.

Career Preparation in Natural Resource Management
Cincinnati Zoo
3400 Vine St., Cincinnati, OH 45220
(513) 281-4701
Users: Students entering 11th grade
Length/frequency: Two-year program: five hours a day, five days a week; 36 weeks

Through a cooperative program between the Cincinnati Public Schools and the Cincinnati Zoo, students prepare for entry-level jobs in animal care, wildlife management, landscape gardening, park and recreation maintenance, and soil, water and air testing and control. Training includes working experience within such areas as the zoo's animal hospital, children's zoo, bird house, aquarium and commissary. The students have additional field experiences in city park and recreation areas, the Cincinnati Nature Center, and the Hamilton County Parks. Students devote three hours a day to laboratory and/or field experiences, and two hours a day to related areas in science, math, English and communication skills. An accredited high school diploma and a vocational certificate are awarded upon graduation.

Independent Study For High School Seniors
The Cleveland Museum of Art
11150 East Blvd., Cleveland, OH 44106
(216) 421-7340
Users: High school seniors
Length/frequency: 30 hours a week, for varying numbers of weeks

Since 1974, the museum has offered independent art-related projects to high school seniors whose schools give them release time as well as academic credit in some cases. For some students, the project revives a once-traditional form of instruction: copying masterpieces in the gallery. Others assist in studio classes and write research papers using the museum's library and slide collection. In addition to the journal kept and submitted by the student, the museum staff coordinator provides an evaluation of the student's work to the school.

School In The Exploratorium
The Exploratorium
3601 Lyon St.,
San Francisco, CA 94123
(415) 563-7337
Users: Grades 3-7
Length/frequency: Full-day classes, three to five consecutive weeks

The School in the Exploratorium has been experimenting since its inception eight years ago with projects directed toward improving science instruction in the public schools and in discovering ways in which teachers, students, and curriculum developers can rely on the museum as an adjunctive learning and teaching resource. Through the School in the Exploratorium program (SITE) a school class can pursue a curriculum based on Exploratorium exhibits under the guidance of a SITE instructor. Public school classes spend one full school day each week for three to five weeks in the museum. The curricula, developed by SITE staff, is based on the study of light, sound and perception and includes such topics as reflection, refraction, color, eye physiology, visual perception, strobe and motionmakers, the physics of sound and music makers. Before the first session, the class visits the Exploratorium on a field trip and participating teachers attend a teachers' workshop. Each session combines discussion, experimentation, and small group exploration of exhibits. Students and teachers make projects associated with the session's ideas to take back to school. A typical session includes the study of eye physiology and its relationship to seeing. Students look at their own eyes in a mirror and draw what they see, paying particular attention to the pupil as the classroom lights are turned on and off. In studying the unseen parts of the eye, the students experiment with small convex lenses to get a sense of the relationship between the lens and retina. They take an "image walk" through the museum to see what images of the museum and exhibits they can make with a convex lens and a 3-by-5 inch card. The rest of the morning is spent exploring the exhibits in the eye section. Here the students can see the blood vessels in their retinas, measure their peripheral vision and locate their blind spots. Finally, they dissect a cow's eye to see the clear flexible lens and "empty" pupil. At the end of each museum session the class is given lending library kits which contain small exhibit-type props, books, equipment, such as light sources, tuning forks, color filters, and suggested activities for experimenting.

Mentally Gifted Program
Franklin Institute Science Museum and Planetarium
20th St. and the Parkway,
Philadelphia, PA 19103
(215) 448-1111
Users: Elementary and junior high school students
Length/frequency: Total contact time 12-20 hours

Students identified by their own school systems as academically talented participate in single-topic mini-courses provided by the museum education staff. These courses emphasize hands-on experimentation and discovery in small-group workshops. Science demonstrations, relevant exhibits, the observatory, the weather center, and the planetarium are integral to the program. Topics include matter and motion, light and color, electricity, astronomy, meterology, chemistry, printing processes, forces and motion, waste and pollution, nutrition, and energy.

A School In The Zoo
John Ball Zoological Gardens
301 Market SW, Grand Rapids, MI 49503
(616) 456-3800
Users: Grade 6
Length/frequency: Full academic year

The John Ball Zoo School is a full-time sixth grade program for highly motivated children, which fulfills all of the students' academic needs and places primary emphasis on basic independent learning skills. Zoology is the central focus of the science curriculum, and the zoo and its facilities are used extensively. Students become involved in a wide variety of projects, from leading groups of younger children around the zoo to creating video tapes and slide shows about such diverse topics as animal adaptations and whales. Courses in conservation, alternative energy, current events and self sufficiency are taught to open students' eyes to the real world and to the potential problems of the 21st century. Regular classes in zoology are conducted in the zoo's classroom, taught by the zoo's director of education. These classes cover basic information such as classification, predator-prey relationships, endangered animals, animal adaptations, animal behavior and conservation, with an emphasis on stewardship. Students also become involved in major projects. For instance, zoo school students have built a greenhouse on the side of the school building, designed and built a working water wheel, constructed a windmill that generates electricity, made solar collectors, and planned a garden that is located in the zoo. They also staff one of the zoo's information windows. These projects like most of the curriculum at the zoo school, were designed to teach students to research, plan, solve problems and present their work to the public. It is a unique school that provides an education not to be found anywhere else in the country.

Urban Arts' Art History
Minneapolis Institute of Arts
2400 Third Ave. S., Minneapolis, MN 55404
(612) 870-3194
Users: High school students
Length/frequency: Two hours daily for 12 weeks

Two high school courses provide advanced study in art history and museology, with fall and winter terms devoted to exploring the history of art from prehistory through modern times. The survey concentrates on Western civilization but also space, human scale, structure, decoration and design. Architectural styles throughout the world are examined and examples are sought in the Beaumont area. Extensive walking tours of the downtown area emphasize building and street usage, architectural styles and future improvement. Students also learn about historical preservation and its impact on their community. An architect works with the students in the classroom helping them to begin a variety of projects that will make a permanent contribution to their community. Activities include planning and building models of the downtown area incorporating present plans and ideas for the future, work on actual restoration sites, and designing a riverside park.

Wildlife Education
Boston Zoological Society
Franklin Park Zoo, Boston, MA 02121
(617) 442-2005
Users: Grades 1-8
Length/frequency: Five-ten week course

"Wildlife Education" focuses on survival needs of animals and interrelationships between all animals (including humans) and their environment. The program includes live animal demonstrations, audiovisual demonstrations, and site visits to the zoo and other animal-related facilities. Students work together in small groups. The program also includes a teacher-training component in which classroom teachers gain familiarity and experience working with zoo and animal resources, curriculum and teaching techniques.

Learning To Read Through The Arts
Solomon R. Guggenheim Museum
1071 Fifth Ave., New York, NY 10028
(212) 860-1361
Users: Elementary and secondary students, groups of 15
Length/frequency: Ninety minutes twice a week for 22 weeks

In a curriculum that combines art activities with writing and reading, children participate in small groups in painting, sculpture, drawing, ceramics, book making, print making, mixed media, photography, film, video, puppetry, dance mime, music, and writing. By developing interesting themes that can be approached through art and writing, children are encouraged to explore ideas in greater depths and to express themselves in both print and visual media. Each child keeps a two-section journal of his writing activities. One section recalls the art procedures, art vocabulary, subject area vocabulary, and notes of the artist-teacher pertaining to the art activity. Section two expresses the student's personal responses to the art activity and is a creative writing activity based on the subject theme of the art project. This individualized section provides the art-related reading materials that are shared with all students in the workshop. The art activities and writing projects foster creativity on topics such as the children's memories, descriptions of imaginary people and lands, observations about life—ideas which encourage both fantasy and serious thinking. Writing includes poetry, short stories, letters and plays. Teachers work with children to increase their vocabulary and writing skills. Cognitive skills such as identification, discrimination, sequencing, and memory are intrinsic in all lesson planning. An example is an art project on the concept of creation and metamorphosis that introduced the elements of earth, air, fire, and water, and how these forces can cause great and sudden changes in the environment. The class listed images that could be associated with each element: wind was associated with kites flying, hats blowing off; fire was linked with volcanoes, gas stoves, and so forth. Following these discussions, the students created a painting. The writing project focused on reading and discussion of the e. e. cummings' poem "What If a Much of a Which of a Wind." Students wrote about the element portrayed in their painting, and together wrote a class poem about a tree in the forest, and how it would react to fire. The methodology has been applied and modified to work with different groups of children: those behind in reading skills by one-two years, the academically gifted, and the perceptionally impaired. Teacher training sessions are available.

Gifted and Talented Programs
Children's Museum
3037 SW Second Ave., Portland, OR 97201
(503) 248-4587
Users: Grades 4-9, 25 gifted and talented students
Length/frequency: One to five days

Specialized workshops available during the school year to gifted and talented students include simulated archeological digs and reconstruction of the culture that is unearthed; learning how to read and make maps and to use the tools and techniques

WHICH IS THE COLDEST BLOCK?
The principle of Conduction

• Place your hand on each of these blocks and make a guess as to their relative temperatures.

Now check your answer by reading the thermometer in each of the three blocks.

• The copper feels "cold" only because it takes heat away from your hand. Your warm hand cannot take "cold" from the copper. The three blocks are all at room temperature, but they vary considerably in their ability to conduct heat. Wood is a good insulator because it is a poor conductor. Copper is one of the best conductors known, while granite falls between these two in conductive powers.

Heat is a form of energy and can, therefore, be transmitted. "Cold" is merely the absence of heat.

Exhibit prepared at the Museum by Ward Cruickshank, Clyde Allison, and Albert Metzger

of engineering, surveying and cartography; and understanding and demonstrating the machines made by man. Schools and school districts contract with the museum to work with 25 selected students in programs that combine experience and an understanding of the collections. For example in the "Communications" program students work in the museum and with the business community for four and one-half days. They are presented with a communication problem from the Portland business community, such as the introduction of a new service or product. They participate in a series of workshops in the areas of problem solving, interpersonal and nonverbal communication, mass communication, budgets, and a special session using videotaping equipment. The team members assume the roles of professionals in specific communication areas and are responsible for identifying target audiences; selecting an appropriate media; researching effective use of media; writing, drafting, drawing, taping, or performing the communication vehicle; and practicing effective group process skills. On the last day of the program, students visit appropriate businesses presenting the finished product for critique and analysis.

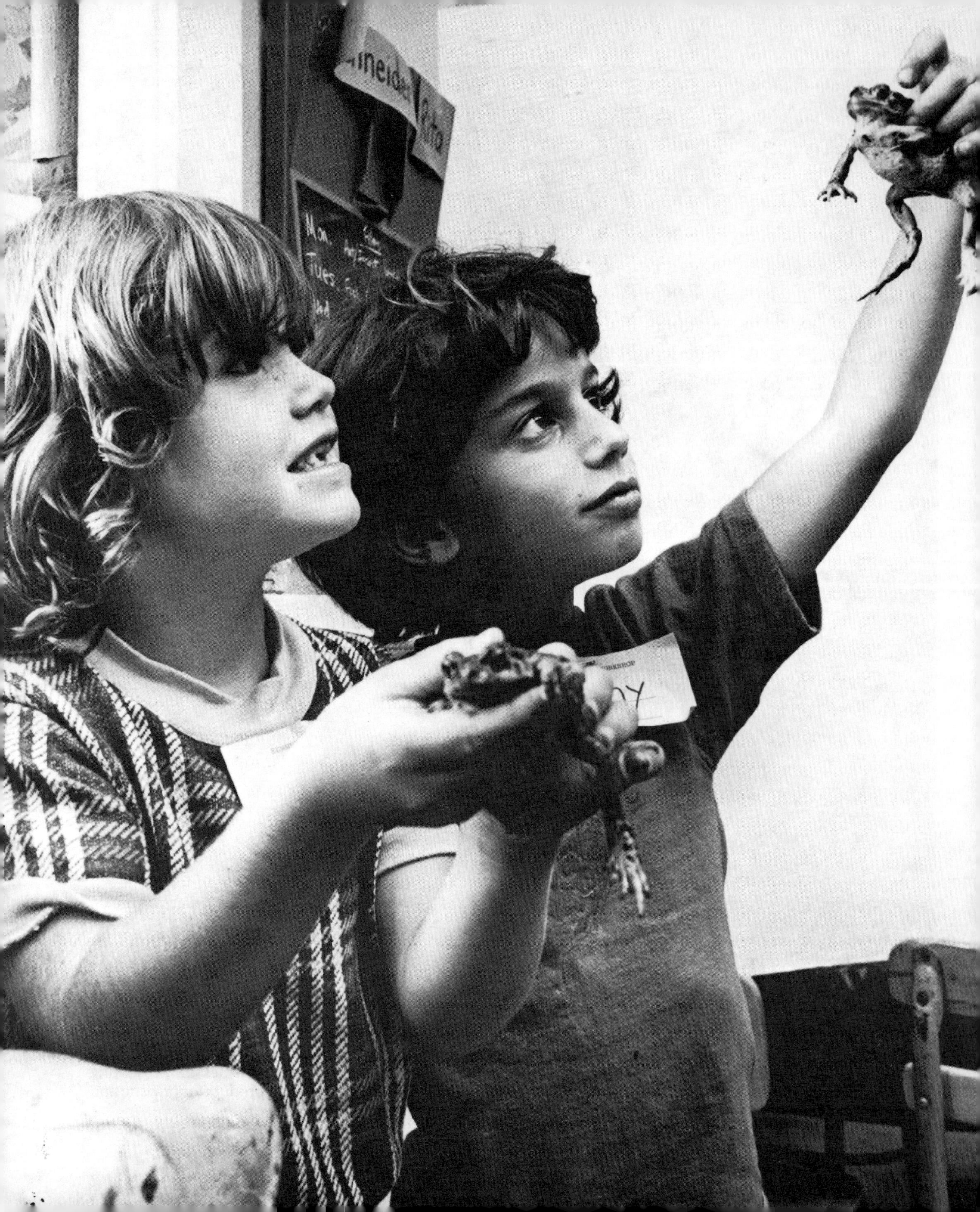
Mon.
Tues

12. IN-SCHOOL PROGRAMS

Museum staff and volunteers visit classrooms taking with them collections, live animals and slide presentations. The following in-school programs illustrate some of the many ways museums have developed outreach programs for people who cannot come to the museum or who will do so at a later time.

Art-to-the-Schools
Albright-Knox Art Gallery
1285 Elmwood Ave., Buffalo, NY 14222
(716) 882-8700
Users: Grades 3-6
Length/frequency: Class sessions, 30-45 minutes, two to four times per semester following by a gallery tour.

Original works of contemporary art and reproductions of works from earlier historical periods serve as the stimuli for classroom discussion and activities prior to gallery tours. Trained volunteers and staff carry out lessons related to the social studies, language arts, math, science, and visual arts curricula of the third, fourth, and sixth grades. For example, in the third grade program students explore aspects of the environment as depicted by artists of the past and present. During one of four classroom visits, students study a selection of landscape paintings, looking for similarities and differences between the environments. Vocabulary such as environment, landscape, mood, and perspective are introduced during this visit. During the gallery tour one activity is to compare three artists' interpretations of the same environment, New York City. Comparisons, contrast, deductive reasoning, and interpretive language are some of the skills students develop during the classroom discussions and tour. Teachers receive outlines of each grade level program and are encouraged to extend the discussion and activities between the gallery staff's visits.

Travelling Instructor
Brooklyn Botanical Garden
1000 Washington Ave., Brooklyn, NY 11225
(212) 622-4433
Users: Schools, senior citizen centers, hospitals and rehabilitation centers
Length/frequency: Ninety-minute presentation

The Travelling Instructor Program was developed to serve those physically and financially unable to come to the garden. Workshops in basic botany, economic botany, ecology, and horticulture focus on a particular botanic or ecological principal. For instance, the ecology terrarium lesson entails a discussion of tropical, desert and woodland environments, followed by the planting of individual terrariums in plastic cups. These sessions show how to maintain plants in different environments as well as to understand how plants adapt and how humans depend on them for our survival. The economic botany classes focus on man's use of plants and plant products as the students prepare bread and natural cosmetics as part of the session.

Museum To The Schools Program
Children's Museum, Detroit Public Schools
67 E. Kirby, Detroit, MI 48202
(313) 494-1210
Users: Grades 1-6
Length/frequency: One visit per participating school

Using objects from the museum's collections, museum teachers present lessons on American Indians, Eskimo and African images, and dinosaurs in school classes. "Indian Ways" introduces the first Americans to children in the primary grades, stressing the ways the Indians used natural resources such as wood, fibers, clay, bone, skin and ivory to satisfy basic needs for food, clothing and shelter. Children examine hard-and soft-soled moccasins, a birch bark canoe model, a tipi model, bow and arrows, and different baskets, pottery and costumes to learn about the different American Indian cultures. "African Images", a lesson offered to students in grades 4 to 7 explores and explodes myths and misconceptions about Africa, past and present. Textiles, baskets leather work, beadwork, and metalwork are used by the museum teacher to show how utilitarian and ceremonial artifacts relate to the different lifestyles of the American people. The focus of this program is on the diversity of economic, social and cutural backgrounds and their importance in today's world.

The Traveling Science Show
The Franklin Institute Science Museum
20th St. and the Benjamin Franklin Parkway, Philadelphia, PA 19103
(213) 448-1426
Users: Grades K-12
Length/frequency: forty-five minutes at school assemblies, science fairs, etc.

The Traveling Science Show uses a rich variety of scientific demonstrations and apparatus to dramatize and illuminate scientific concepts. Available for groups of up to 300 students, museum instructors adapt each presentation to specific school audiences. Some of the topics are "Energy Transformation," which includes demonstrations of solar-operated motors, steam engines, pulleys, and small explosions to illustrate different forms of energy, and "Chemistry," which begins with the ancient black art of alchemy and ends up with modern synthetic chemistry. In addition to the show itself, the program includes a question-and-answer session, program resource sheets for teachers, and individual discount coupons to encourage students to follow up on the program by a visit to the museum.

In-School Programs/ "Texas Wildlife"
Houston Zoological Gardens
P.O. Box 1562, Houston, TX 77001
(713) 522-0276
Users: Grades 4-6
Length/frequency: 30-45 minutes in the classroom

How prairie dogs, alligators, racoons and kingsnakes live in Texas is explored in classroom sessions. A slide presentation presents five biomes including the desert, grasslands, and marshes. Posters provide additional illustrations of the state and its varied environments. Live animals and "ecology jars" for each biome are also brought to the classroom for careful examination. Other in-school programs include an introduction to mammals and ecological concepts for the primary grades and school assemblies on endangered species for middle-school children.

Classroom Visit Program: History of Textile Techniques
Merrimack Valley Textile Museum
800 Massachusetts Ave., North Andover, MA 01845
(617) 686-0191
Users: Grades 4-6
Length/frequency: Three-hour session in the classroom

Through actual practice with hand tools, children learn the cloth-making techniques of pre-industrial America and gain greater insight into the transition from hand to mechanized cloth production during the Industrial Revolution. A museum teacher brings to the classroom a slide presentation illustrating the history and process of making woolen cloth in the 18th-century home, from shearing the sheep to finishing the cloth. Following a demonstration of carding, spinning, and weaving, children then carry out the principal elements of turning fleece into fabric, using hand cards, drop spindles, and small waist loom. The classroom visit is designed to serve as preparation for a trip to the museum galleries, where children see colonial hand looms and spinning wheels, as well as a power-driven carding engine, a spinning jack, and an automatic loom from the industrial era in operation.

Connecticut Animal Presentation
New Britain Youth Museum
30 High Street, New Britain, CT 06051
(203) 225-3020
Users: Preschool through Grade 6, including the disabled.
Length/frequency: One hour.

Live skunks, rabbits, gartersnakes, chickens, and pigeons are used in this program in which children make comparisons between their own needs and those of the animals for food, shelter, protection, and survival. For example, in comparing homes and habitats, the children discuss seasonal variations, migrations, hibernation, and location of the home or habitat. A discussion of enemies includes the use of camouflage and methods of escaping or fighting. The animal is passed to the children so that they may have the experience of touching and smelling it. Classroom materials for follow-up activities relate to the various curriculum areas. For example, math studies might include measurements as the average weight, size, and length of an animal.

School Yard Environment
Peninsula Nature and Science Center
524 J. Clyde Morris Blvd,
Newport News, VA 23601
(804) 595-1900
Users: Grade 5
Length/frequency: Two hours

Groups of four students spread out over the school yard. Each group outlines a quadrant one meter square and studies the plant and animal life and some physical factors of the environment. The students are asked to fill out a data sheet that includes numbers of plants and animals, number of species, permeability of the soil, soil acidity, and temperature. Afterwards students compare the various quadrants, analyze the data, and make diagrams of food chains. Kits for teachers also provide ideas for creative art projects, poems and short stories, and other curriculum-related projects.

Secrets from Stone
San Diego Museum of Man
1350 El Prado, Balboa Park, San Diego, CA 92101
(714) 239-2001
Users: Grades 7-9
Length/frequency: two hours

The theory and methodology of archeology, along with the museum's role in the discipline area, is studied through this classroom program. Students learn the sequence of San Diego's prehistory and play a game that helps them to reconstruct the three cultures under study. Using artifacts in the museum's collection, they compare knives and scrapers and spears from the big game culture to the simple flake tools used by the coastal people with a shellfish subsistence base. The students attempt to learn what the tools were used for, what they are made of, and how they were manufactured. A film prepared by the museum describes an actual archaeological investigation in the desert east of San Diego. The program concludes with instructions about what action to take should the students encounter an archeological site on their own and how to protect native resources.

Art Museums
Seattle Art Museum
Volunteer Park, Seattle, WA 98112
(206) 447-4790
Users: Primarily elementary school classes
Length/frequency: One hour

The museum, in a cooperative venture with the Cultural Enrichment Program of Washington State, has prepared a presentation for schools, consisting of slides, visual materials, activities, and written materials that help students become aware of the behind-the-scenes operation of an art museum, staff roles, and art museum resources inside and outside the galleries. In addition to the slide show, the presenter engages students in activities that that simulate what they see in the slides. Slides may show, for example, the installation of an exhibit: the design crew outlines the floor plan and designates the location of each artwork, with consideration for the lighting, public viewing space, and movement through the galleries, and additional materials such as text panels, photographs, labels. The class activity might include drawing a bird's eye view of your classroom, considering the reasons for its arrangement, and comparing the classroom arrangement to another room in the school used for a different purpose, such as the library, determining reasons for lighting and movement patterns.

On The Road for Health: Mobile Health Education Program
University of Nebraska State Museum, Lincoln, NB 68588
(402) 472-6365
Users: Grades 4-8
Length/frequency: Two days

Self-discovery and activities are the key terms for the Mobile Health Education Program. Students make discoveries about themselves through the Health Activities Project (HAP), units, a health/science curriculum developed at the Lawrence Hall of Science in Berkeley, California. The Mobile Health Education Specialist works with the teacher prior to the visit and facilitates the students' health experiences during the two-day school visit. The specialist is assisted by volunteers from local medical auxiliaries. There are explorations, conducted in the areas of heart fitness and action, breathing fitness, sight and sound, and action/reaction, through the use of hands-on devices, such as stethoscopes, lung volume bags, vision disks, and reaction timers. The HAP materials supplement and enrich existing school programs in health, physical education, and science.

Travelling Zoo
Staten Island Zoo
614 Broadway, Staten Island, NY 10310
(212) 442-3174
Users: Grades 1-6, special education classes, nursing homes and other audiences
Length/frequency: forty-five minutes

Exploring how snakes, turtles, lizards, rabbits, ferrets and humans use eyes, noses, mouths, feet, and tails in special ways is the focus of one of the Travelling Zoo visits, "Animal Senses as Tools." The Travelling Zoo brings live animals to schools, special education centers and people in other places who are unable to come to the zoo, so that they can learn how to handle animals and develop an appreciation for the individual uniqueness of other living creatures. Discovery activities and discussions involve the children in developing their understanding of how animals are a vital part of our world. Activity packets on animal senses and adaptation help teachers to prepare their children for the visit of the travelling instructor.

The Creepy Crawler Zoomobile Program
Washington Park Zoo
4001 SW Canyon Rd., Portland, OR 97221
(503) 226-1561
Users: Grades 4-6
Length/frequency: forty-five minutes

"The Creepy Crawler" program is designed to increase the students awareness of the insect group, arthropods, one of the most ubiquitous of animals. Students learn to recognize members of the arthropod insect group, identify subgroups on the basis of observable characteristics, and learn the general life cycles of these insects. Teachers receive written materials that include information and questions that help students to master a basic concepts prior to the visit from the Zoomobile. For example, after a general introduction the students are asked to invent and draw an example of an arthropod based on the information about basic characteristics. The Zoomobile visit includes a slide presentation, and first-hand examination of live arthropods including crabs, tarantulas, scorpions, and insect colonies. The life cycles of two different arthropods are illustrated by the milkweed bugs and meal worms. The conclusion of the program includes suggestions for subsequent activities such as how to arrange an insect safari walk on the school grounds.

The Age of the Dinosaur
Carnegie Museum of Natural History
4400 Forbes Ave., Pittsburgh, PA 15213
(412) 622-3283
Users: Grades 2-6
Length/frequency: One hour

The "Age of the Dinosaur" is unfolded by exploring the environment of the Mesozioc era and the interactions between various organisms at this time. The evolution of dinosaurs, the time periods in which they lived, and some of their adaptations are explained. Trained volunteers present the program, in which students handle a selection of fossils and rocks that record some of the interesting events of this period. Visual aids are used to demonstrate and animate the past and to help students in their understanding of what life on earth was like millions of years ago. The presentation is designed to help students learn that dinosaurs were reptiles and shared characteristics of all reptiles: that they varied in structure, behavior, and time period in which they lived; that the Mesozoic era was especially conducive to the growth and development of reptiles; and at the end of that era, for many reasons, the dinosaur became extinct. The dinosaur skeletons on exhibit and in storage at the museum are emphasized, and students are encouraged to come to the museum. Another in-school program, "The Story Fossils Tell," introduces the Paleozoic Era, which discusses the environment and survival techniques of various forms of life during this time. Special attention is given to prehistoric vertebrates which have living relatives which are found today.

Road Shows
Department of Museums, City of El Paso, El Paso Museum of Art, Cavalry Museum, and Wilderness Park Museum
Education Office, 1211 Montana, El Paso, TX 79902
(915) 543-3800
Users: Elementary, intermediate, and secondary school pupils
Length/frequency: Fifty minutes

A variety of slide programs are designed to increase art awareness, appreciation, and historical knowledge, as well as to inform the public of changes in the three museums. These "Road Shows," shown at schools and civic groups upon request, include a 20-minute slide/tape presentations. An interpretation of the program includes vocabulary clarification, demonstrations, and informal discussion. Current selections, include programs on art, science, and history, covering a wide range of programs from prehistoric Indians to the most modern painters in the Rio Grande area.

Horticultural Therapy
Fernbank Science Center
156 Heaton Park Dr., NE, Atlanta, GA 30307
(404) 378-4311
Users: Handicapped and non-handicapped persons, groups of 15
Length/frequency: One to three hours, depending on the group

The therapeutic aspects of horticulture come from caring for something living. Although success cannot always be realized, failure can be turned into something positive by emphasizing the plant's living quality. Science center horticultural specialists travel to schools and hospitals, reaching groups unable to attend programs at the greenhouse facility and botanical gardens. Horticultural therapy provides people with recreation and an opportunity to work with plants, gaining skills necessary for possible future employment, as well as being a type of preventive medicine for everyday stress. The program is activity-oriented, and each participant can pot a plant, build a terrarium, propagate various plants, examine seed parts, or trigger a venus fly trap, among other activities. Colorful visuals, a variety of plant material, and necessary supplies are packaged for travel, and found or recycled items, such as plastic dishpans, milk containers, and styrofoam cups, serve as pots and watering cans for these projects. When possible, the classes take place outdoors, and at some sites, small gardens have been developed. Teaching techniques are geared to the special needs of the group: hearing impaired, emotionally disturbed, and mentally retarded. When possible, teachers and program directors are encouraged to participate in in-service training so that they can make full use of the garden, including site selection, planting techniques, watering, weeding and harvesting.

Trip-Out-Trucks and Trip-Out-Trunks
The Fine Arts Museum of San Francisco
Golden Gate Park, San Francisco, CA 94118
(415) 558-3109
Users: Schools, neighborhood groups, community centers, senior centers, libraries and parks; also disabled
Length/frequency: Three classroom visits, followed by a museum visit; two to six community visits (no museum visits)

Trucks are fully equipped with supplies and trained professional artists. When working in the community, the artists engage participants in such projects as kite making, face painting, sculpture, mural painting, pinhole photography, super-8 mm filmmaking, improvisational drama, puppet plays, and movement activities. The trucks visit classrooms three or four times in order to develop a continuing program that relates both to the museum's collection and to the classroom curriculum. The artists work with the classroom teacher to plan a curriculum prior to the truck visit. The museum also has trunks containing artifacts, folk art, photographs, and explanatory materials. Designed as teaching aids, the objects are used to create an environment in the classroom. The themes are cross-cultural and include textiles, masks, puppets, basketry, ceramics, printmaking, and body adornment.

Visits to the School
Siouxland Heritage Museums
200 W. Sixth Ave., Sioux Falls,
SD 57102
(605) 335-4210
Users: Grades 4-6
Length/frequency: One hour, four sessions

Scales for weighing gold, army food utensils, Chinese coins, high button shoes, and various rock samples are among the objects taken to the classroom in a program that helps children to learn the history of South Dakota. This four-part program, presented by the staff, complements the social studies curriculum and illustrates (with objects that can be handled) the changes that have taken place over the years in the land, the environment, and the people. Fossils, rock specimens, and artifacts of the early Plains Indians are used in the geology and prehistory session to relate the earliest life in the region. The rapid changes water made on the culture of the Sioux Indians in the mid-1800s after they were in contact with white trappers and traders is the focus of the second session, as children examine bead work and hides. The conflicts between the gold miners, ranchers and frontier army as well as the breaking of the treaties with the Sioux are explored in the third session. The final program includes a slide show on the development of Sioux Falls and illustrates the life of the early pioneers in the region. Examining household objects, eye glasses and high button shoes, students begin to see the changes in farming and business life during this period. After completing all four sessions in the classroom, classes come to the museum to tour the history exhibits.

Tree Senses
Museums at Sunrise
746 Myrtle Rd., Charleston, WV 25314
(304) 344-8035
Users: Grade 2
Length/frequency: One hour

This multidisciplinary program is designed to illustrate the interdependence of all living things, including relationships in nature and the community. Library books on related subjects, which are delivered to the school by the museum, remain for two weeks after the classroom presentation. Volunteers visit the school and explore with the children the natural environment (grass, soil, insects, rocks, and birds) and their role in the ecological system. Food and growth cycles of plants and insects also are discussed, and the students are given the opportunity to be adopted by a tree on the school grounds. The teacher finds out what kind of tree it is and receives adoption papers from the museum, as well as a wooden plaque to identify it during class nature walks. In the classroom, a "community web"—a peg board with strings—illustrates relationships in the food chain and what happens if one of the components is missing. This concept of interdependence is transferred to the children's social community—the fire department, the school, parents. Puppets, live animals, and music are part of the program. The teacher is provided with a package of resources including games, follow-up activities and information on the Forestry Department, which will send a representative to the school to help the students plant a tree seedling or a vegetable garden.

Instant Theatre Traveling Trunk Show
Los Angeles Children's Museum
310 N. Main St., Los Angeles, CA 90012
(213) 687-8801
Users: Schools and other learning centers
Length/frequency: One full day in the schools including three workshop sessions with children and a teacher in-service.

The Instant Theatre Traveling Trunk Show, an outreach program for the school children of Southern California, is designed to bring the museum's philosophy of experiential learning into classrooms. The two trunks that make up the equipment are old but refurbished and colorfully decorated theater trunks containing costumes, make-up and props. The goal of the trunk "show" is to enhance oral and written narrative skills for the children and to bring new and innovative curriculum techniques to the teachers. The Instant Theatre Traveling Trunk Show is an involving, creative experience for children and teachers with a built-in learning factor far beyond the simple performance in which it culminates. The trunk show develops a better understanding of the basic narrative structure with improved oral and written skills. Staff works with two classes at a time in 90-minute sessions, and leaves a curriculum guide in the school.

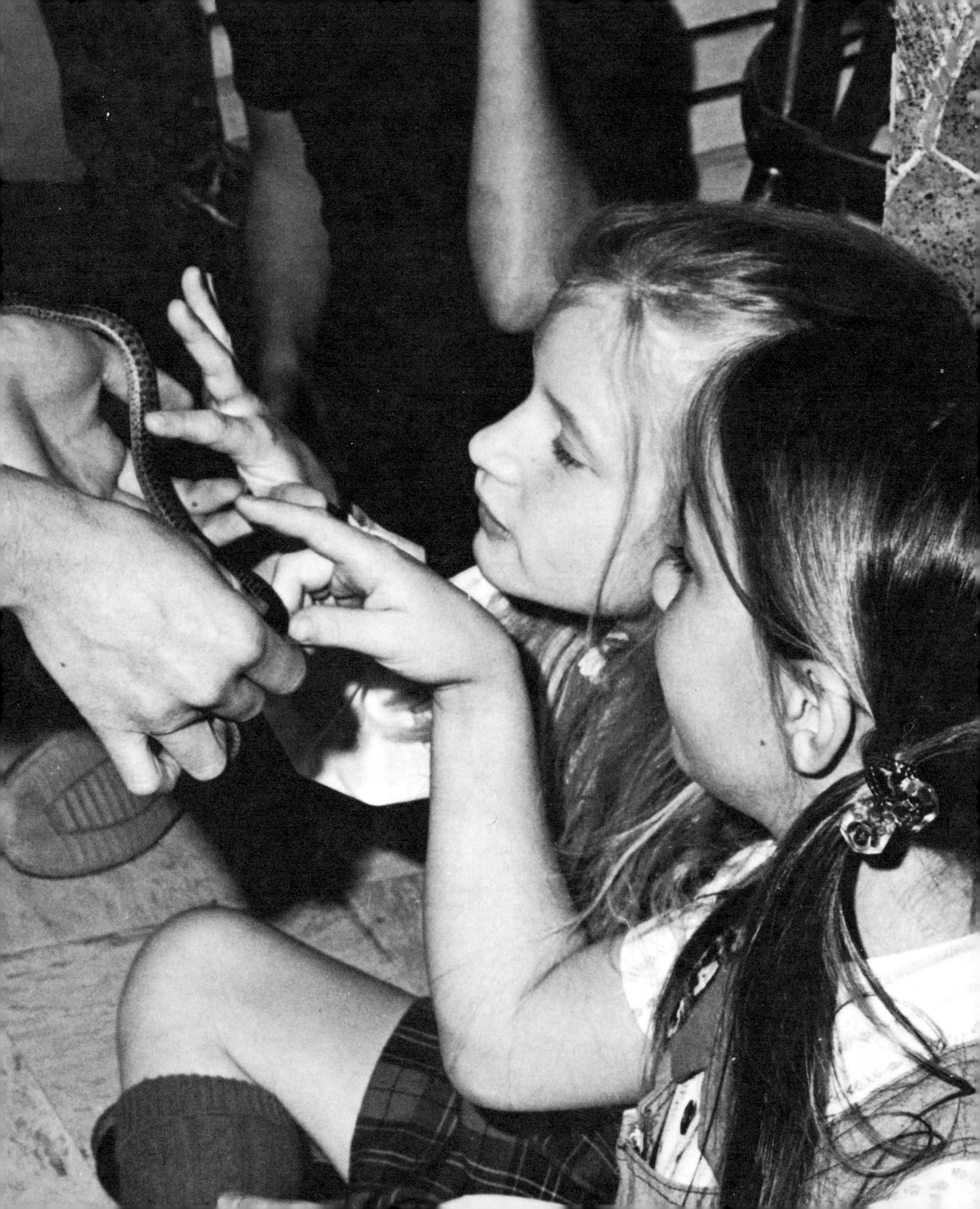

13. KITS AND LOAN MATERIALS

Objects from the collections, specimens, slides, video tapes, films, books, photographs, documents, maps and reproductions are packaged in hundreds of different ways for loan to schools or community groups. Available in trunks, boxes, or envelopes, these resource materials can supplement the curriculum of a class or bring the museum into the classroom. Usually a fee is charged for the loan or purchase of these materials, but in some cases they are available free of charge. Managing a loan program includes careful attention to the distribution and maintenance of the kits. A more extensive listing of resource materials produced by museums is listed in Chapter 16.

Alaska Multimedia Education Program
Alaska State Museum
Pouch FM, Juneau, AK 99811
(907) 586-1224
Users: Grades 1-2 statewide

More than 35 learning kits on Alaskan history, cultural heritage, art, and natural history are available for distribution to rural schools throughout the state. These learning kits combine authentic artifacts and other resource materials from the museum with films, videotapes, games, puzzles and other instructional materials. A teacher resource manual offers suggestions for presenting the concepts in each kit. Eskimo Archaeology, a typical learning kit for upper primary and junior high students, includes authentic artifacts, films, videotapes, booklets, educational games, and other resources required for a class to conduct a simulated dig at two precontact Eskimo sites. Other kits provide students with the opportunity to learn about the Tlingit, Haida, and Aleut cultures; Alaskan myths and legends; the peregrine falcon; and Alaskan gold rushes. The museum also produces and distributes television programs statewide and provides assistance to schools in the development of Alaskan studies curriculum.

Grandmothers' Trunks and Case Histories
Colorado Historical Society, The Heritage Center
1300 Broadway, Denver, CO 80203
(303) 839-3682
Users: Intermediate grades
Length/frequency: Three-day periods

The Colorado Historical Society distributes two types of educational loan kits known as "grandmother's trunks" and "case histories," designed to provide schools throughout the state with hands-on educational experiences. The kits contain a variety of artifacts and are supplemented with background information for the teacher.

The "grandmothers' trunks" contain objects and artifacts reflecting the culture and traditions of four of Colorado's ethnic minority groups: Plains Indian, black, Japanese and Chicano. For example, one trunk contains objects that might have been treasured by a Colorado woman of Spanish Colonial descent who is still alive and has a grandchild in the fifth grade: many religious items, native craft products (weaving and wood carvings), personal accessories, and a family portrait album. As a follow-up activity, children may trace their own family histories or experiment with cooking an ethnic recipe included in the trunk.

The "case histories" trunks contain objects and artifacts related to the Anasazi (prehistoric) Indians, Plains Indians, fur trappers and traders, and miners. The cases contain material such as beadwork and weapons, beaver pelts and traps, and gold pans and mining equipment. The "Cliff Dweller," a simulated archaeological "dig" housed in a picnic cooler, is complete with artifacts buried in "earth" and the tools and instructions necessary for excavation.

Articulation: The Gallery Game
Columbus Museum of Art
480 E. Broad St., Columbus, OH 43215
(614) 221-6801
Users: All ages

Twenty-five full color reproductions of paintings in the permanent collection are the focus of a game that helps the player learn to make appropriate donations for an exhibition. The gallery space is the game board. Three to five players choose a deck of requirement cards that establish an arena of ideas for discussion. According to the roll of a die, the player moves a token the appropriate number of board spaces and decides whether to donate one of the art cards he holds or to challenge a present installation with a new gift. The player must defend the donation with reasons for the choice. Heated, inventive, and surprisingly witty debate is assured since the judgment of a challenged donation is by consensus of the players. The game is over when all the gallery spaces are filled by a group consensus. A unique feature of "Articulation" is its inclusion of three decks of requirement cards, permitting the players to choose one of three different approaches to the game. Art cards deal with the visual qualities of the images themselves; humanities cards attend to cultural and social qualities suggested by the reproductions; aesthetic cards permit players to explore criteria for personal response.

Experience Boxes and Discovery Units
Field Museum of Natural History
Roosevelt Rd. at Lake Shore Dr., Chicago, IL 60605
(312) 922-9410
Users: Classroom groups, intermediate through college
Length/frequency: Two weeks

The *Experience Boxes* contain a variety of resources that help students to learn more about their environment of different cultures. For example the "Chicago: Past and Present," for studying changes in the shoreline and natural environment of Chicago, contains a map illustrating Chicago's vegetation and shoreline in 1821 and a clear acetate overlay that permits students to outline the city's present form and to design its future development. Included as well are slides showing past and present city sites, activity suggestions, an information chart about the growth of the city. Also available are plant boxes containing samples from the woodlands, prairie, and a vacant lot, and boxes on such topics as animal tracks, African life, Mexico and prehistoric life. The museum's *Discovery Units* is a series of teacher manuals about the permanent collections. Most are included in the *Experience Boxes*, and are retained by the teachers when borrowed box is returned. Each *Discovery Unit* is a self-contained resource that includes the geographic characteristics setting, characteristics of the human or natural population, pre- and post-activities, activities in the museum matched to the collections, and a bibliography. Available titles in addition to those in the *Experience Boxes* are "Imperial China," "Woodland Indians," "Prairie," and "Hidden Environment."

Lost Kingdoms, Lost Worlds
Indianapolis Museum of Art
1200 W. 38th St., Indianapolis, IN 46208
(317) 923-1331, Ext. 31
Users: Community groups such as boys clubs, girls clubs, YM and YWCA, multi-service organizations

"Lost Kingdoms, Lost Worlds," is an experience in looking at the lost worlds of the African kingdoms of Egypt, Ife and Benin; Mediterranean kingdoms of Crete, Greece and Rome; and the ancient Indian civilizations in the Americas. As archeologists, the students use the kit's collection of objects, costumes, games, decorated panels, books, and suggested activities to investigate these past cultures and to find traces of them in today's architecture, art, language and music. Buildings in Indianapolis are compared to those from Greece and Rome. Seals and stamps like those from Egypt and Crete are used to decorate paper and clothes. Ceremonies are reenacted with costumes, music, games and food, as children begin to understand that in some ways the people of the past were like those of today. The kits may only be used after the group leaders have been trained. A notebook, available to the leaders, explains the panels and artifacts, contains games, rituals, recipes, art activities, myths and historical information, and encourages active use of the museum.

The Immigrant Experience Resource Unit
Minnesota Historical Society
690 Cedar St., St. Paul, MN 55101
(612) 296-2881
Users: Intermediate and secondary school students and teachers

"The Immigrant Experience" is one in a series of *Minnesota History Resource Units* designed to make the results of historical research available for classroom study. The unit considers immigration history as the history of individuals—people who made personal choices, people with hopes and fears, people whose expectations were often at odds with the realities of life in Minnesota. Teachers may use the unit in its entirety, as a full-scale, self-contained curriculum, or they may select particular components for study. The unit includes 35 students booklets (either the intermediate booklet, "Three Immigrant Stories," or the secondary booklet, "The Immigrant in the American Experience"), eight filmstrips, and records. The material outlines the history of migration and immigration to Minnesota and explores key issues, such as assimilation. Also included are biography banners (each tells the story of a particular family), reproduced documents related to the journey to Minnesota, reproduced posters encouraging immigration to Minnesota, and other materials. Fees are charged.

The Mathematics of Islamic Art, A Resource Packet
Metropolitan Museum of Art
82nd St. and Fifth Ave., New York, NY 10028
(212) 879-5500
Users: Grades 1-12

The resource packet was designed for use in the classroom, by mathematics, social studies, art and elementary classroom teachers. It includes 20 color slides of objects in the museum's Islamic collection, overhead transparencies, ditto masters, activity sheets and notes on the slides. The students learn that all Islamic designs are constructed with a compass and straight edge. They examine the circle, learn its important role as the organizing element of the designs, and explore other basic characteristics of Islamic geometric design. In the junior high school or middle school, the geometry teacher may include a two- or three-week unit on the geometry of Islamic art in the curriculum, working with teachers of social studies and art to provide a truly interdisciplinary learning experience. Elementary school teachers may use the materials to design an interdisciplinary introduction to Islam in the fifth or sixth grades. High school teachers of remedial mathematics have found the materials stimulating to students having difficulty with the subject. Classes have done related studio projects with geometric patterns on paper, clay, and in textiles.

The Arts and Human Values
The Minneapolis Institute of Arts
2400 Third Ave. S., Minneapolis, MN 55404
(612) 870-3046
Users: Grades 1-12

This humanities curriculum, consisting of teacher guides and accompanying slides of major works in the museum's collections, has been developed to illustrate the eternal values of our civilization. The program is divided into the five concepts of truth, beauty, love, justice and faith. The teacher's guide contains background information on the historical era in which the objects were made, artists' biographies, descriptions of the works, comparisons with other objects in the unit, study questions, suggested classroom activities, selected bibliographies, and lists of available community resources. By studying a wide range of objects from different periods and cultures (paintings, sculptures, prints, drawings and furniture), students will learn to perceive an idealized "beauty" in a carving of an ancient Greek warrior, see a realistic version of "truth" in a portrait of an aging Roman matron, or see the embodiment of "justice" in Henry Moore's "Warrior with a Shield." The program's underlying theme is that, although values change from century to century and culture to culture, they remain an integral part of human thought and understanding.

Preview: Pre-Visit Orientation Materials
The Museum of Modern Art
11 W. 53rd St., New York, NY 10019
(212) 956-6100
Users: Grades 6-12

Developed as an alternative to the single visit guided tour, this kit consists of two sections: an envelope with procedures and information about the museum, the mechanics of planning a tour; and an envelope with "preview resource materials," focusing on 17 art works selected from the painting, sculpture, design and photography collections. Included in preview are postcard reproductions of each art work, photographs of the artists in their studios, quotations by artists, a glossary, a banner, pre-visit activities, a question/itinerary foldout, and current exhibition materials. The pre-visit activities are designed to illuminate artists' issues and ideas and to point out ways to compare and contrast the selected works of art. There are conceptual activities such as studying hue intensity as value changes occur and activities such as making a collage and painting it. Students can take an active role in making visual and compositional choices by assembling elements such as the postcards, pictures and quotations on a nylon banner for classroom display. The questions/itinerary foldout provides a structure for leading discussions while touring the museum. The questions, written with the curators, encourage students to focus on the works of art, to discover relevant issues and to explore the artist's intention. The kit's current exhibition materials component parallels the materials on the permanent collections, and is updated for every major exhibition and designed in collaboration with the exhibition's curator.

Traveling Exhibits and Kits
Museum of Natural History
University of Kansas,
Lawrence, KS 66045
(913) 864-4173
Users: Grades K-12
Length/frequency: One week by reservation

Each traveling kit contains specimens which can be handled either directly or in protective mounts), cards identifying and introducing the specimens, and various combinations of posters, pictures, books, and slides to complement the theme. The kits currently available are "Mammals of Kansas," "Birds of Kansas," "Insect Classification and Morphology," "Insect Ecology and Behavior," and "The Bones Tell a Story" (mammal skulls). Traveling exhibits are designed for display in classrooms and other locations and contain materials that may not be handled. In addition to the completed "What is a Fossil?", untitled works in process include exhibits on bird beaks and feet, the taxidermic process used for mounting bird specimens, and adaptations for flight in birds. Kits and exhibits are available to schools throughout the state.

Family Learning Kits
Museum of New Mexico
P.O. Box 2087, Santa Fe, NM 87501
(505) 827-2030
Users: Intermediate grades, also visually impaired and mentally retarded
Length/frequency: Minimum one month

Learning kits designed for classroom use deal with the predominant cultural-historical groups in the Southwest—the Navajo, Pueblo, Apache, Spanish frontier, and Anglo pioneer. The kits introduce the concepts of shelter, food gathering, and food preparation and instill a sense of the past and a sensitivity towards the the cultures that produced the items. Each kit deals with the everyday lives of the depicted group and includes toys, cooking utensils, clothing and tools, all of which can be handled or worn. Objects from the museum's collections illustrate unique cultural and historical aspects of each of the four separate groups. Extensive supplemental reading and audio materials, activity cards, and a teacher's manual are included.

Supplemental Teaching Units
National Archives and Records Service
8th and Pennsylvania Ave. NW, Washington, DC 20408
(202) 523-3347
Users: Secondary social studies

As a supplement to classroom texts, the units provide reinforcing information and critical guidance to all students with varying levels of experience and achievement. Primary sources fascinate students because they are real and personal. Using original materials in four teaching units, students touch the lives of people about whom history is written: "World War I, The Home Front;" "World War II, The Home Front;" "The Great Depression and New Deal;" and "The Civil War—Soldiers and Civilians." These materials deal with certain key issues of a period including governmental and political responses and public attitudes. Each unit contains 30 to 50 facsimiles of documents from the National Archives and a teacher's guide. The documents include written materials (memos, letters, newspapers) as well as posters, charts, maps, photographs, and cassette tapes. In each teacher's guide, suggested activities emphasize such skills as identifying bias and fact, weighing evidence, drawing logical conclusions, and developing generalizations. Students come to recognize different points of view towards an event and learn to form their own thoughtful conclusions. Materials available nationwide.

Tide Pool Kit
New England Aquarium
Central Wharf, Boston, MA 02110
(617) 742-8830
Users: Elementary and junior high school

Crabs, mussels, periwinkles, barnacles, and seaweed are among the animal and plant specimens that live in tidepools. Designed to complement the tidepool exhibit, this resource unit includes dry specimens, curriculum materials, illustrations, books, slides with a script, and field trip information. Slides help to illustrate a tidepool environment and place the specimens in their natural setting. Curriculum related activities are suggested for the teacher in a variety of subject areas including the sciences, language arts, and crafts. For example, while working with the kit, a class might plan a collecting trip to a tidepool. The gathered specimens can be studied and documented for science projects; later they can be used to create a mobile or to write stories about the lives of the animals. Large illustrations can be reproduced for the students to identify species, to color, or to cut up for cards or puzzles.

The World of Work
Old Sturbridge Village
Sturbridge, MA 01566
(617) 347-3362
Users: Grades 4-12

The *World of Work Resource Kits* and curriculum include historical documents, study prints and slides of period graphics, artifact reproductions, and suggestions for classroom teaching. Two kits which teachers may purchase are "Farming was Family Work," and "From Farm to Factory." Project materials and learning activities assist students in acquiring a set of concepts for analyzing work in modern society as well as understanding its meaning in history. Students can develop an understanding of key concepts like work environment, work schedule, and work process by keeping work journals, charting their days and weeks into periods of work and leisure, mapping their own work spaces and those of their parents, and interviewing parents on their work routines. They can also examine their families as workers: are their fathers and mothers self-employed, employers, or employees? Do they carry on family businesses (a farm, retail store or restaurant)? Do their families directly produce anything? These concepts and questions are used as a basis for investigating work in the past. Early 19th-century documents, such as a farmer's diary, a craftsman's manual, a store's account book, a factory's ledger, and a mill worker's letters reveal much about the impact of work upon the daily experiences of New Englanders. These sources, along with paintings, woodcuts of work scenes, and reproductions of workers' tools, clothing and production, permit students to explore what it was like to work during the 19th century, and to apply that knowledge to understanding work experiences today.

The Art-Ful Boxes
Spencer Museum of Art,
The University of Kansas,
Lawrence, KS 66045
(913) 864-4710
Users: Grades 1-12

In addition to exercises written in game format, each kit contains 60 slides of art objects in the museum's collections. Students participate in sensory and aesthetic awareness activities by responding to open-ended questions designed to stimulate the imagination, to strengthen problem-solving skills, and to develop an awareness of aesthetic choices. Intended for use by the regular classroom teacher, the activities can be coordinated with literature, music, science, and other disciplines. For example, "Rough Waters/Calm Waters" compares the styles of four different artworks depicting water. The students might be asked to imagine the purpose of the boat trip, the feelings one would experience physically and emotionally while at sea, and the sounds one would hear.

Traveling Trunks: Arizona's History
Arizona Historical Society
949 E. Second St., Tucson, AZ 85719
(602) 882-5774
Users: Elementary grades

The legacy of the vaqueros, cowboys, mountain men, miners and Spanish settlers is told through the resources found in four different steamer trunks. Each of the traveling trunks contains 40 artifacts (originals and reproductions), slide shows, photographs, drawings, and teacher manuals that include activities and introduce the theme. "The Life of a Miner" examines the work and daily life of an underground miner in Arizona around 1900. Activities include panning for gold, mining copper, faro (a gambling game), and other role-playing activities that explore the hardships, safety conditions, and sources of entertainment enjoyed by the miners. The life of the "Arizona Mountain Men" is told through the resources and activities on trapping, bartering for beaver pelts, clothes that include the various essentials for survival, and the dangers encountered. The "Vaqueros and Cowboys" trunk presents the life of cattle ranching from the Spanish period to the 19th century. It includes a saddle, chaps, hat, spurs, clothing, directions for rope tricks and tying, and branding irons and information on how outlaws changed them. "The Spanish Settlement of Arizona" trunk examines the different lives of priests, soldiers, ranches and miners who lived together. The information presented in the trunks can be enhanced through museum-supplied slide shows, 16mm films, film strips, videotapes, and speakers.

Loan Kits: "What If You Couldn't . . ."
The Children's Museum
Museum Wharf, 300 Congress St., Boston, MA 02216
(617) 426-6500
Users: Children with families and teachers
Length/frequency: One month in the classroom

The museum has a variety of loan materials available to schools, community groups and homes. The *Activity Kits* deal with a single activity and include resources and instructions for crafts and games; while *Exhibit Kits* use objects from the museum's teaching collections and are accompanied by teaching guides with suggested activities. *Curriculum Units* include teaching collections, audiovisual resources and teacher guides including structured lesson plans. For example, "What If You Couldn't? . . ." helps the mainstreaming of handicapped children by encouraging children to see handicapped persons as people first and handicapped second. The kit is useful in changing attitudes about the handicapped in teachers and other adults, too. Activities include simulations of handicapping conditions, experiences with remedial devices (leg braces, etc.), and role-playing exercises. "What If You Couldn't? . . ." contains an introductory unit on each of six disabilities: visual impairments, hearing impairments, mental retardation, learning disabilities, emotional problems, and orthopedic handicaps.

SCIENTOYFIC: A Traveling Exhibit
The Children's Museum
931 Bannock St., Denver, CO 80204
(303) 571-5198
Users: Schools
Length/frequency: One to three days

Portable, participatory exhibits can be rented or leased to bring the excitement, discovery, and learning associated with the museum into the classroom. More than six exhibits, which require a well-lit 500-square-foot room, are used by schools to supplement their curriculum, and by shopping centers and banks for promotion. Each exhibit involves participatory activities and is accompanied by written resource materials and a staff person. "Scientoyfic" capitalizes on a child's natural enjoyment of toys to teach basic scientific principles. Controlled scientific experiments help children learn the fundamental laws of the universe and practice scientific behaviors of experimenting, observing, and drawing conclusions. Children study balance using their own bodies, spinning tops, and cars with rubber band motors; action/reaction and motion are illustrated through items that travel in a straight line; and simple machines investigate fulcrums, balances, gears, and pulleys. Other exhibits include "Movies-To-Go," an introduction to animation using zoetropes, flip cards and more; "Colors-To-Go," which explores the aesthetic and scientific principles of color in three participatory areas—rainbows, color tricks, and color mixing; "Figure-It-Out," which provides concrete activities, games, and puzzles to give children a chance to practice computation and mathematical thinking; and "Like-Me-Like-You-To-Go," which teach children about being handicapped.

Loan Programs From The Resource Center
The Children's Museum
3000 N. Meridian St., Indianapolis, IN 46208
(313) 924-5431
Users: Grades 1-12

Classroom discussions of the ancient world, pioneer life, American Indians, Chinese crafts and many other topics come to life with artifacts and supplemental information found in the museum's loan exhibits. The materials are available in several formats: portables, charts, specials and kits. Portables are self-contained glass-fronted exhibits with artifacts, labels, and pictures demonstrating such topics as flax spinning, a Seminole family or African children. Charts are mounted photographs or illustrations, on such topics as the polar region, prehistoric reptiles or U.S. cities of the 1800s. Specials are artifacts with labels for locked showcase display only, and include topics such as pioneer schools and 19th-century toys. Kits contain artifacts for students to handle along with a teacher's information booklet; some include filmstrips and cassette tapes. One kit, which creates an awareness of the use of masks in the Iroquois society, contains newly, but traditionally, carved false face masks and a filmstrip. "The Natural Materials and Clothing" kit includes old and new hides including buffalo, moose, elk and deer, and a child's leggings under plexi.

Loan Kits Program
Denver Museum of Natural
History
City Park, Denver, CO 80205
(303) 575-3618
Users: Grades 3-7

In "Who Went There?" children examine a dinosaur track and hooves from sable antelope, water buffalo and mule deer to learn about animals from what it leaves behind. This is typical of the multimedia educational loan kits designed to help children learn about the role of animals in the environment. Each kit includes specimens to be handled, a teacher's manual with classroom activities, charts, slides, and tapes. The "Feathered Friends" kit explores the avian world by comparing various feathers, bird skulls, nests, and eggs as well as human sight with that of a hawk. The museum also has *Insect Visual Aides*, which are framed exhibits of specimens and charts on topics such as the development and metamorphosis of butterflies; how insects protect themselves with color and shape; or how fast fruit flies multiply and how much an ant can carry for its size.

West Virginia Heritage Trunks
Museums at Sunrise
746 Myrtle Rd., Charleston, WV 25314
(304) 344-8035
Users: Grade 8
Length/frequency: Two weeks

An antique camelback trunk houses a traveling exhibit of reproductions, original artifacts, and curriculum materials on West Virginia history. Among the artifacts are clothing, quilts, toys, documents, and musical instruments. Thirty-six characters grouped into six families have been researched so that roles may be assumed by the entire classroom. The role playing includes a preacher-teacher and his wife, a lawyer merchant, a doctor, a miner, a riverboat captain, and a farmer. Each trunk contains two full costumes—one for a man, the other for a woman—as well as fashion prints, photographs, films on West Virginia crafts, two puppets, cornhusk dolls, and letters that tell of the hardships of frontier life. Spelling bees, quilting parties, box suppers at a barn raising, a sing-along, a meeting at the country store, and making apple butter are among the suggested activities in the teacher's guide. The trunks are currently circulated by the Cultural Center, Charleston, West Virginia 25314.

**Buckaroos In Paradise—
A Teacher Resource Kit**
National Museum of American History
Smithsonian Institution,
14th and Constitution Ave.,
Washington, DC 20560
(202) 357-3030
Users: School groups

A traditional way of life in the American West—the cowboy trade as practiced since the 1860s by the buckaroos who live in Nevada—is presented in this kit, which accompanies a museum exhibit. The kit contains 40 slides, printed and cassette scripts, suggested activities, bibliography, a poster for classroom use, 35 copies of topic-related crossword puzzles, and general information about the museum. Three perspectives of the life of these modern cowboys are presented: first, the geographical setting; second, the tools and materials used in their work, crafts and part-time activities; and third, the bunkhouses where they live. The daily life of the cowboy is explained in detail, and the script describes where and how the cowboy tradition is being altered by modern technology. As one suggested classroom discussion topics, students watch a typical television western and compare similarities and differences between the television program and the cowboys depicted in the Buckaroo slide presentation. The resource kit contains the cowboy's cryptic alphabet, or brands which buckaroos use to identify cattle. As an art project, students design their own brands, using initials or signs special to them. The crossword puzzle is based on vocabulary related to cowboys and used in the slide presentation.

Extension Programs
National Gallery of Art
Constitution Ave., NW.,
Washington, DC 20565
(202) 737-4215
Users: Schools, community groups, all over the United States
Length/frequency: Color slide programs may be kept for five days, films for three

Videotapes, 16mm color/sound motion pictures, and color slide programs circulate throughout the United States, as the National Gallery of Art attempts to make its collections accessible to everyone. Color slide programs include mounted slides, a printed text, an audio recording, and, very often, color study prints of selected works as additional resource material for classroom display. The 85 available programs deal with a wide range of subjects drawn from the Gallery's permanent collections and special exhibitions. Among the 50 color slide programs offered are surveys such as "700 Years of Art" and "Introduction to Understanding Art;" a series of programs on American folk arts and crafts such as woodcarving, textiles, costume, and Pennsylvanian/German folk art; "The Far North," based on an exhibition of Eskimo and Indian art of Alaska; as well as programs dealing with such elements as color and light in painting. Many of the slide programs are augmented by music of the period or culture, poetry, folklore, and excerpts from lectures by experts in the field. Films available free of charge include such titles as *The American Vision, Adventures in Art, The Eye of Thomas Jefferson,* and *Treasures of Tutankhamun. Rembrandt, Renoir,* and *Cezanne* are a few in the film series based on the works of major artists in the gallery's collections. Selected films are also available in videocassette form.

Marine Education Activity Packets And Teaching Kits
Pacific Science Center
200 Second Ave. N., Seattle, WA 98109
(206) 627-9333
Users: Elementary and secondary students and teachers

The marine education project provides students and teachers of the Puget Sound area with resources to develop an awareness of the Pacific Northwest marine environment. The activity packets, which supplement existing school courses, are interdis-

195

ciplinary with subjects ranging from math, literature, and sciences to social studies. Designed to involve the students actively in conducting experiments, analyzing, testing and participating in simulations, the activity packets include American poetry from the sea, marine biology field trip activities, and a field trip guide to Puget Sound. Packets and teaching kits have been created to supplement the activity packets for the elementary-aged and visually impaired students. These kits cover a range of topics including whales,' tides, the migration game, and beach life. Resources such as a whale model, teeth, baleen, and other materials are included in the kits. Developed for use by teachers and students, a resource center of marine education materials includes 300 curriculum and reference volumes, a vertical file of more than 1,500 additional items, and a file of 500 names of resource people and marine educators in the Northwest and the nation.

Teaching Materials for the Visually Challenged
John G. Shedd Aquarium
1200 S. Lake Shore Dr., Chicago, IL 60605
(312) 939-2426
Users: Visually handicapped children and adults

Twelve coral reef fish and how their body shapes and fins indicate various aspects of adaptation are the subject for these teaching materials. The sting ray, nurse shark, moray eel, trigger fish, and angel fish are among those illustrated through raised shapes and large line drawings that allow students to feel the shapes of the fish. The worksheets are available in both braille and large print. Examining the shapes of the fish through comparison and contrasts, students learn to tell something about the lifestyle of that fish. For example, a flat body has adapted for laying on the bottom as illustrated by the sting ray, while the streamlined body adapted for fast swimming is seen in the tarpon and jack fish. The type of mouth a fish has sometimes indicates the type of food it eats. Students examine fish with lots of teeth, such as the nurse shark and moray eel, or the upturned mouth of the tarpon to understand the different foods they eat. Each kit also contains floor maps of the aquarium, in large print and braille.

Loan Materials
Anacostia Neighborhood
Museum, Smithsonian Institution
2405 Martin Luther King, Jr. Ave.
SE, Washington, DC 20020
(202) 381-2558
Users:

The museum has a variety of loan materials that help teachers learn about their community, the history of black people and the Kwanza celebration. "How and Why Black People Came To North America" is a felt board and activity book for teachers designed to communicate this story to preschool and elementary students in a simple, graphic and participatory way. The story deals with the location of the different people in the world, the relocation of the Africans to the Americas, their struggles during slavery and fight for freedom. Throughout the story telling the students place felt pieces on the board, develop their motor skills, reading-readiness, listening, speaking, spelling, problem solving and other skills. Follow-up activities include visits to the museums and further study of Africa and its people.

The "Kwanza Kit" accompanies a workshop for the teachers and community group leaders on the Kwanza symbols and use of the kit. A slides show tells how a black family celebrates Kwanza during seven days in December. Following the introduction students prepare to celebrate their own Kwanza by learning African songs and music, preparing food, and designing and making clothes. The parents are included as often as possible as the students learn about Africa and its peoples, visit embassies, compile scrap books on the geography and cultures, and learn where other festivals are taking place in the community. All of the resource materials designed by the museum can be used in association with a group or individual trip to the museum.

Health Activities Project: HAP
Lawrence Hall of Science
University of California, Berkeley, Centennial Dr., Berkeley, CA 94720
(415) 645-5132
Users: Grades 4-8

Students become involved as they count and record respiration rates, take strength tests, perform exercises, measure lung volume, monitor pulse rates, and make choices through a whole range of health-, safety-, and nutrition-related activities. HAP is a modular curriculum of 64 student-centered activities grouped into 13 modules that can complement existing health, science and physical education programs or stand alone. The resources for teachers include a guide with instructions for implementing HAP, activity folios with specific information on the health unit and activities, and activity work sheets for recording and charting the information collected. Specially designed apparatus such as grips testers, limber gauges, balance boards, temperature gauge strips, reaction timers, lung volume and gas exchange bags are included in most of the modules, as well as reusable charts and crayons. The simple and functional apparatus helps familiarize the students with health fitness and medical devices while eliminating much of their mystery.

The HAP modules include such topics as: "Breathing Fitness," "Sight and Sound," "Action/Reaction," "Balance in Movement," "Heart Fitness," and "Personal Health."

Lawrence Hall has produced a number of other curriculum programs with resource materials such as OBIS (Outdoor Biology Instructional Strategies), SCIS (Science Curriculum Improvement Study), SAVI (Science Activities for the Visually Impaired) and CHEM study.

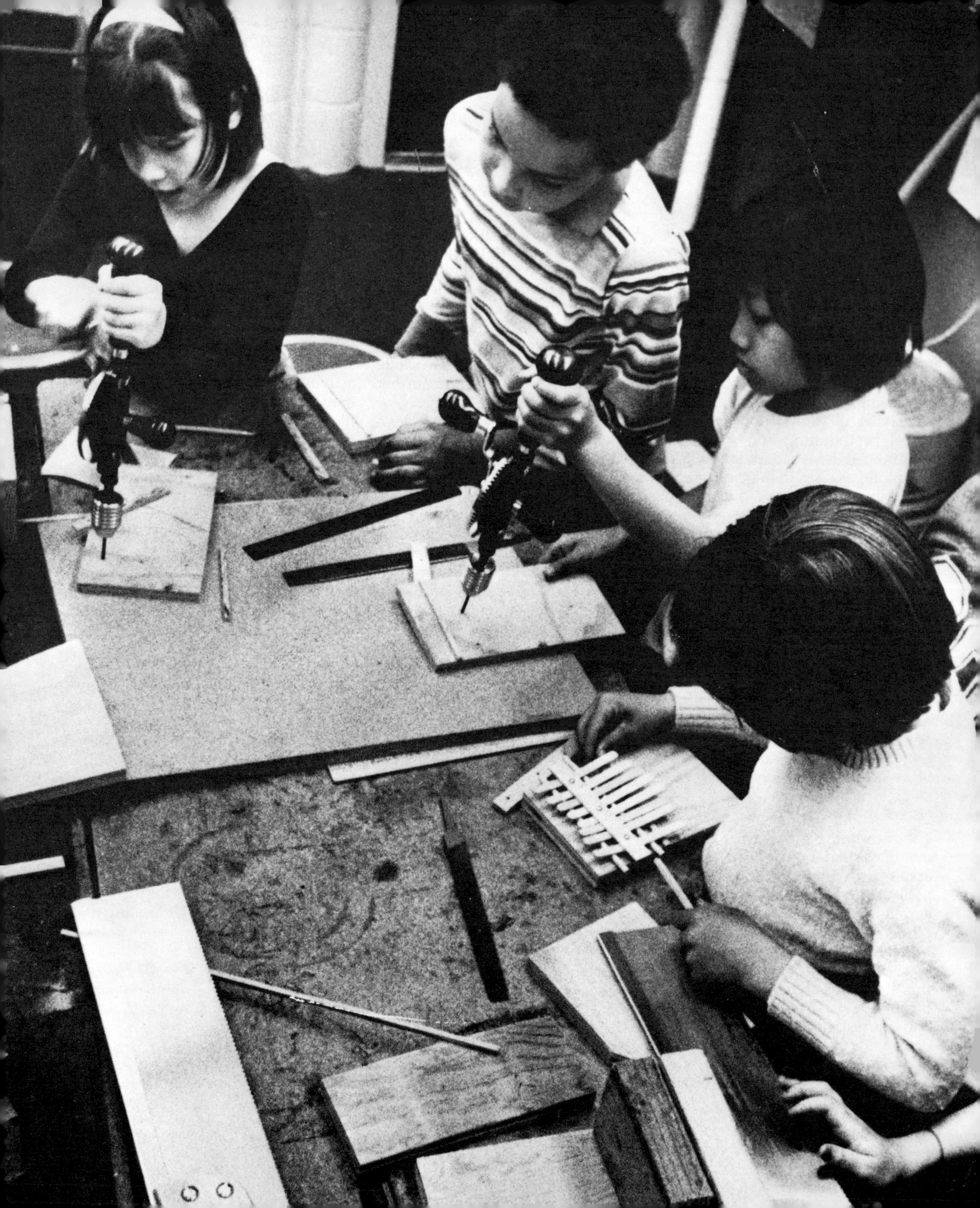

14. WORKSHOPS AND CLASSES

Children come to museums after school, in the evenings, on weekends and during the summer to attend classes and workshops. In many cases this may be their first introduction to the museum. They may study the collections, learn how to do research, conduct experiments, learn how artists have worked with the different materials and participate on field trips.

Museum School
Amarillo Art Center
2200 Van Buren St., P.O. Box 447,
Amarillo, TX 79178
(806) 372-8356
Users: Pre-schoolers, ages 6-8; ages 9-12
Length/frequency: 90 minute session, once a week for 8 weeks all term

The Museum School develops children's understanding of and ability to use a number of art media. Pre-schoolers learn the media through more familiar experiences, such as story-telling, music, nature or drama. For example, after telling a story about an animal adventure, the teacher then asks the children to think about what the animal looks like, where it lives, what it eats, and what kind of noise it makes. Given clay, the children create their version of that animal. In the next session they might draw an environment for their animals. The Discovery Classes, for children ages 6 to 8 and 9 to 12, focuses on a variety of art processes such as papermaking, printmaking, weaving, and painting. Children 10 years and older can learn specific skills in a single medium, such as oil painting or pottery. Instructors are urged to take students of all ages into the galleries in order to see the museum exhibits. Once a year the museum exhibits work done by students in the art school.

Children's Classes
The Baltimore Museum of Art
Art Museum Dr.,
Baltimore, MD 21218
(301) 396-6321
Users: Elementary classes
Length/frequency: Four to six weeks

Students examine artworks in a museum setting, while learning about different media and developing art skills. Working with artists from the community, children explore the permanent collections and special exhibitions and then create their own costumes, masks and musical instruments. For example, Miro's *Portrait No. 1* is used to encourage the students' fantasies first in poetry, and then in two- or three-dimensional collage, while the exuberant colors and patterns of the Matisses in The Cone Collection inspire a personal interpretation of the traditional techniques of block printing, wax-resist and tie-dye.

Camp-In
The Center of Science and Industry
280 E. Broad St.,
Columbus, OH 43215
(614) 228-6361
Users: Youth agencies
Length/frequency: One overnight visit

A one-night special program, the COSI Camp-In, is set aside for youth agencies in the states of Ohio and West Virginia. The overnight program gives participants a chance to see all of the exhibits, demonstrations and shows at the Center of Science and Industry. This includes a visit to the Battelle Planetarium, an exploration of the *Jeffery Coal Mine,* a chance to explore the history of Ohio in the time train, and an opportunity to hold and examine the Center's pet boa constrictor. Several hundred youths, from agencies such as the Boy Scouts, 4-H, or CampFire Girls, arrive at the museum in time for a late afternoon snack. Divided into smaller groups, the youths attend demonstrations on special topics; do participatory experiments, activities, and demonstrations; and view the museum's exhibits. Nutritious but "camp-like" dinner and breakfast are served. When the workshop program was initiated several years ago, the youths slept in the museum; currently, they "camp out" in nearby gymnasium. Adult and senior members of the youth agencies work with the staff on the program.

Children's Garden Program
Brooklyn Botanic Garden
1000 Washington Ave., Brooklyn, NY 11225
(212) 622-4433
Users: Ages 9-17
Length/frequency: Projects run from the spring through the fall

Designed to introduce city children to the world of plants, the program allows students to plant and maintain individual vegetable and flower plots. In the spring, after instruction in the classroom and greenhouse, the children prepare the seedlings for the garden. During the school year, they come on the weekends, but during the summer they tend their gardens two mornings a week. They weed, hoe, fertilize, and harvest their own crop and maintain a record of the annual crop. During the summer the gardeners attend a series of workshops in nature studies. At the end of the summer, the beds are spaded and planted with a cover crop. In addition to learning about botany, the students learn to respect the rights and property of others and to assume responsibility for their own garden.

Shadow Puppet Theater and Workshop
The Brooklyn Museum
Eastern Brooklyn, NY 11238
(212) 638-5000
Users: Ages 6-12, day camps and other summer groups
Length/frequency: Twenty-minute theater production and thirty-minute workshop

"Catching Shadows Across the Nile," illustrating the legend of Ibis and the Egyptian collections, and "Children of the Sun" dealing with Quetzalcoatl and the pre-Columbian collections are among the themes used for this summer program. Each year the staff writes a new script for a shadow puppet theater based on a real or imaginary myth that can be illustrated through objects in the collection. Summer interns learn how to present the play, build the puppets, stage and run the workshops, in which the children make their own puppets. For example, the workshop that accompanied the production of "Catching Shadows Across the Nile," included an exploration of objects in the Egyptian collection such as statues of Ibis and the barque of the dead, followed by the making of their own puppets and musical instruments that incorporated the images and symbols that were seen in the play and in the collection. Some groups also make brief presentations with their puppets on stage.

Telescope Making and Astronomy
Buhl Planetarium and Institute of Popular Science
Allegheny Square, Pittsburgh, PA 15212
(412) 321-4300
Users: Elementary and intermediate school age children
Length/frequency: Two hours a week for eight weeks

Students learn the fundamentals of optics by making their own reflector telescope. Activities range from the use of simple kits by the younger children to the grinding of mirrors and assembling more sophisticated instruments by the older ones. In addition, students learn how to use a telescope to observe the moon, planets, and stars. Older students often proceed to active membership in the local amateur astronomers' association.

Science Workshops
California Museum of Science and Industry
700 State Dr.,
Los Angeles, CA 90037
(213) 744-7441
Users: All ages
Length/frequency: One- to two-week classes, two hours per session

Workshop topics examine insects, lasers, optics and light, marine ecology, computer power, photography, electronics and animal behavior among other subjects. Staffed by local outstanding science educators, the programs emphasize a laboratory and field work approach to learning. Problem solving, puzzles, games, demonstrations, participation, and creation all become a part of the learning experience. For example, preschool children learn to formulate new concepts and thinking skills in a program that combines body movement, art, cooking, block play and more. Children in grade school experiment with lasers, optics, light, a pinhole camera, telescope, solar cooker and simple microscope. In addition, college credit courses are offered for teachers, and informal classes are available for parents.

Out of Doors Days
Carnegie Museum of Natural History
4400 Forbes Ave.,
Pittsburgh, PA 15213
(412) 622-3283
Users: Family groups and adults
Length/frequency: A two-hour workshop and an eight-hour field trip per topic

Examining the changes of the seasons, rafting a river to investigate a unique environment in the state park, or learning about the habitats of animals and birds along the Allegheny are all part of the field trips cosponsored by the museum and the Western Pennsylvania Conservancy. The museum organizes eight to twelve different programs during the year, each combines an evening workshop at the museum with a field trip. During the orientation workshop, objects from the collection are used to illustrate such topics as western Pennsylvania geology, stream life, and animals at night. The field trips visit a number of different areas throughout the state. As part of the stream life program, the group canoes on a creek and takes water samples, as part of the geology program students investigate an area where glacial activity changed the landscape 10,000 years ago.

Learning Enrichment Programs
The Children's Museum
3000 N. Meridian St., Indianapolis, IN 46208
(317) 924-5431
Users: Ages 8 and up
Length/frequency: Varies according to the program

Learning Enrichment experiences are offered as daily after-school activities, half-day and summer events, theater performances, field trips, special events, and the museum choir. Attention is given to attracting youth to the museum for an enjoyable yet meaningful adventure, and importantly to developing a skill that may be called upon during an entire life time. In addition, they assist youth in understanding the environment in which they live, and to help them function more successfully in it. An example of a *Learning Enrichment Program* series was entitled "What Makes the World Tick." Taught by members of the National Society of Black Engineers, students viewed a demonstration of a particular theory and went on to complete individual projects during each class session. These projects included making steam engines, windmills, rockets, electromagnets, motors, radios and cameras. The *Learning Enrichment Programs*, part of the *Neighbors Programs*, are available to children living in the museum's neighborhood.

Communiversity
The Cincinnati Zoo (and The University of Cincinnati)
3400 Vine St.,
Cincinnati, OH 45220
(513) 475-6836
Users: Participants 15 years old and older
Length/frequency: from 3 to 5 weeks; 2 hour sessions

Curators, teach this series of courses that combine classroom study with work in the zoo among the animals. In "Photographing Wildlife," students learn how to capture animals on film and how to simulate natural backgrounds. In "Zooming In," students investigate aspects of zoo management such as how the zoo obtains its animals and propagate endangered species. In "The Fascinating World of Animals," eight different members of the zoo's professional staff tour their areas and present their views with slides, movies, and live animals.

Evening Programs
The Colonial Williamsburg Foundation
P.O. Box 627,
Williamsburg, VA 23815
(804) 229-1000
Users: All ages
Length/frequency: One to two hours

An orientation to Tidewater Virginia, and introduction to plantation life, learning the games, stories, songs, music and lifestyles of the people in the 18th century are possible through the many different evening programs. Activities range from visiting candlelit craftshops with costumed interpreters to comparing and contrasting the games, songs and stories of children today with those who lived 200 years ago. Theatrical dramatizations draw students into personal contact with several characters from different levels of colonial Virginia society and make vividly real their conflicting views of the revolutionary cause in Virginia in another program. Actors and actresses assume typical characters of the community, (a Tory female shop owner, a male militia recruiter, a black minister, and Patrick Henry) presenting their view points and soliciting the audience's reactions and perspectives. A range of musical activities are available every evening including programs of popular songs, and demonstrations of military music, including signals, calls, ceremonies evening and dance music and fifes and drums with a brief explanation of uniforms, instruments and accoutrements. Using period rooms and music, costumed dancers join with students to demonstrate colonial dances.

Holiday Workshops
The Dayton Art Institute
Forest and Riverview Ave., P.O. Box 941, Dayton, OH 45401
(513) 223-5277
Users: Ages 7-18
Length/frequency: First two workshops 2 ½ hours each, third workshop 4 hours. Children may participate in single workshops, or in all three.

These special workshops are offered in December to help celebrate the holiday season. In the first, students tour the museum's collection to learn about different symbols and patterns throughout history. The class cuts patterns and silkscreens sheets of giftwrapping paper. In the second workshop, students create a permanent holiday wreath, done in the spirit of a Della Robbia sculpture. The third workshop is designed to help students make Victorian Christmas tree ornaments, before attending a local theater for a performance of the Dickens' classic *A Christmas Carol*.

High School Gallery Course
The Detroit Institute of Arts
5200 Woodward Ave.,
Detroit, MI 48202
(313) 833-7900
Users: Graduating senior high school students
Length/frequency: Five two-hour sessions

The summer gallery course for high school students, originally part of a program to interest minority students in the museum profession, is now open to all students with high academic standing. Teachers recommend students for the course, which is structured as an introduction to college-level art history through the study of a selected works in the collections. Classes are actually taught in the galleries to provide direct exploration of the objects discussed. The museum's comprehensive collection allows a broad sampling of art objects of different types, periods, and cultures. Reading assignments supplement the gallery discussions for a thorough study of the objects. Classes are conducted as discussions rather than lectures.

Family Activities
John G. Shedd Aquarium
1200 S. Lake Shore Dr.,
Chicago, IL 60605
(312) 939-2426
Users: Parents and children together
Length/frequency: Three hours

Depending on the subject, these events and activities take place on weekends at the aquarium or nearby sites. The age of the children varies with the activity. Learning what fish are and how to snorkel illustrate the range of subjects that are covered during this weekend special. Topics have included "Canoeing and River Ecology," (ages 10 and up) in which families have paddled a local area, stopping to sample the water for plankton, clams and fish, climbed on sandstone cliffs and been guided through the vegetation. "What is a Fish," ages 5 and up, combines lecture and discussion followed by a dissection to introduce fish, their shapes and structures and how they live in water. "Introduction to Snorkeling and Scuba" (ages 10 and up) involves families in learning how to use the equipment under the supervision of trained instructors. Activities are available throughout the year and children must attend with an adult family member.

The Renewable Resource Economy of Northeast Vermont: Past, Present & Future
Fairbank Museum and Planetarium
83 Main St., St. Johnsbury,
VT 05819
(802) 743-3413
Users: High school and college students

A matched pair of Belgian draft horses, a treadle-driven spinning wheel, the enduring utility of fine carpentry tools, and a solar-heated dairy barn all illustrate the historical developments of technology. This after-school program seeks to perpetuate local traditional rural values such as independence, personal ingenuity, and respect for the land. Under museum staff guidance, area youth use oral history interviews and photography as study tools to learn about state inhabitants, and to produce audiovisual programs, newspaper articles, radio features, and an interpretive exhibition at the museum. Areas of study have been how fiddles are handcrafted, how to heat water for a barn with solar energy, and how simple windmills can be designed to meet energy needs. The students helped to produce an exhibition on traditional crafts, which included the various stages in the handcrafting of a fiddle and examples of the weaver's art. They used photographs and puppets for interpretive purposes and wrote a comprehensive exhibition catalogue.

Classes For Children and Families
Florida State Museum
University of Florida, Museum Road, Gainesville, FL 32611
(904) 392-1721
Users: All ages
Length/frequency: Six 75-minute; six three-hour; 10 one-hour sessions

Participatory programs in the natural and social sciences are offered on many levels. Most classes are scheduled for Saturday mornings and afternoons. Preschoolers participate in story telling, simple science experiments, visits to the object gallery, nature walks, ecology study programs, and natural history and cultural arts and crafts projects. Students in grades one and two enroll in classes on specific subjects. In a "Toys and Puzzles" class, for example, they examine 19th-century toys from the collections and use files, coping saws, drills, and sandpaper to make their own facsimiles. Third through fifth graders enroll in various classes in nature study, earth sciences, physical sciences, and social studies. Florida's unique ecosystems are stressed in many of these. Children set up terrariums and aquariums, work in laboratories, and go on field trips. Middle and high school students and their parents may work together in classes on plant life, freshwater biology, and the like. Some evening and afterschool classes are offered that provide instruction in basic observational skills.

Zoo Summer School Classes
Fort Worth Zoological Park
2727 Zoological Park Dr.,
Forth Worth, TX 76110
(317) 870-7055
Users: Ages 6-16
Length/frequency: six two-hour class sessions

Zoo summer school classes introduce children to the five groups of vertebrate animals and their basic similarities and differences. Animal adaptations, behavior, ecology, taxonomy and zoo animal care and management are some of the concepts encountered. Divided into three levels by age (6-7 beginning zoology; 8-12 intermediate zoology; 12-16 advanced zoology), these concepts are approached at levels appropriate to the age group. For example, the two younger classes may assist in food preparation and actually feed such animals as wallabies, guinea pigs, tortoises, and seals. They are encouraged to become careful observers of animals and to use all of their senses in discovering animals. During discussion of the taxonomy and comparative anatomy of the five groups of vertebrate animals, students in advanced zoology participate in dissections of fish, toads, snakes, chicks and mice. In all cases, students are encouraged to actively participate in whatever topic the classes are studying so that the entire zoo becomes a classroom.

Indian Lore Merit Badge
The Heard Museum
22 E. Monte Vista Rd.,
Phoenix, AZ
(602) 252-8848
Users: Girl and Boy Scouts
Length/frequency: Four two-hour sessions on Saturday morning

Scouts who wish to work towards their merit badges in Indian lore, participate in this program, focused on the Native American cultures of the Southwest. Instructors stress how each culture adapts to its own environment and utilizes the materials found in the area it inhabits. To illustrate this concept, the children look at models of different Native American dwellings and discuss why Navajos live in hogans while Pueblo Indians live in compact, apartment-like houses. Within the program's framework, children meet specific requirements for obtaining their merit badge, such as learning an Indian song or dance, or constructing a clay model of an Indian home. Children gain a better understanding of cultural differences, but they also become aware of the many of the cultural similarities shared with Indian children such as games.

Math and Computer Education Project
Lawrence Hall of Science
University of California,
Centennial Dr., Berkeley,
CA 94720
(415) 642-3167
Users: All ages and the handicapped
Length/frequency: Eight-week courses, weekly throughout the year

Computer exhibits, workshops, and in-depth coursework are offered for school groups and the general public at all age levels. Terminals in the exhibit area informally introduce the public to computer games and simulations. Single-visit workshops demystify the computer and allow participants to use it as a tool for learning, exploring, and creating. On weekends, the labs offer public access to the computer for $3 per hour. Special classes designed for school groups often combine computer experience with other sciences. In "Programming in BASIC," beginning and advanced students learn to create math games, solve problems, make pictures, and construct simple scientific simulations on the computer. A wide variety of other computer courses are offered throughout the year. In addition, more than 40 schools reach the Lawrence Hall computer over telephone lines using computer terminals in the classroom for every sort of educational purpose.

Experiences in History
Littleton Historical Museum
6028 S. Gallup, Littleton, CO 80120
(303) 795-3850
Users: Grades 2-6, and handicapped
Length/frequency: Ten week-long sessions

Children assume the roles of pioneers traveling to a new frontier in this summer program. After reviewing maps, they determine a starting point and destination for their journey. On arrival they set up their own 19th-century community. For five days, the community members act out daily activities in the blacksmith shop, the print shop, the carpenter's shed, the farmhouse, and the barn and garden. Children experience daily living and working routines in the museum complex using artifacts and reproductions. As community members the children are in turn the interpreters for other 20th-century visitors to the museum and the historical farm.

Summer Camp Program
Living History Farms
R. Rte 1, Des Moines, IA 50322
(515) 278-5286
Users: Grades 3-6
Length/frequency: Nine weekly sessions

Children learn about mid- and late-19th-century farmlife in Iowa, by spending a week in this summer program and by actually living the lives of their 19th-century counterparts. One day of the week is spent on each of the following themes: the first Iowa farmer, Indian heritage, Pioneer family life, craftsman of the 1870s, family life on a 1900 farm, exploring family histories. For example, during the "pioneer family life" segment of camp, children do the farm chores: hoeing the fields, gathering wood, starting the fire, cleaning the farmhouse, and eating a meal they have all helped to prepare. After dinner, they sing and play games, amusing themselves the way early Iowa farmers might have done at the end of an active day. During the day devoted to crafts of the 1870s, campers see demonstrations performed by blacksmiths, potters, cabinet makers, quiltmakers, weavers and broom makers, and try some of these crafts themselves.

Summer Field Schools
Memphis Pink Palace Museum
3050 Central Ave.,
Memphis, TN 38111
(901) 454-5600
Users: High school students
Length/frequency: Three-week summer courses

The museum offers a series of summer field schools in archaeology, geology, astronomy, and vertebrate paleontology. The students learn archaeological techniques and assist for two weeks in field studies coordinated by Memphis State University. In addition, they learn laboratory techniques, as well as methods of identifying stone, bone, and clay implements. In "The Caves of Tennessee," students spend a week at different cave sites identifying and studying geological formations. The vertebrate paleontology field school, which is coordinated with the University of Oklahoma, provides students with an opportunity to study and excavate various forms of vertebrate fossil, including lung fish and fossil reptiles.

Vision Quest
Milwaukee Public Museum
800 W. Wells St., Milwaukee, WI 53233
(414) 278-2714
Users: High school students
Length/frequency: Three-week session

"Vision Quest" brings high school students into the museum during the summer and gives them a view of career opportunities in various fields of interest. Topics over the years have included archeology, botany, history and taxidermy. In the taxidermy program teenagers master the skills necessary in mounting a fish skin, and a bird skin. In addition to procedures and experience, heavy emphasis is placed upon taxidermy as a means of preserving endangered species for future study. Concurrently, students learn about laws concerning collecting and possession of mounts.

Catskill Mountain Hiking Tour
Munson-Williams-Proctor Institute
310 Genessee St., Utica, NY 13502
(315) 797-0000
Users: Member family groups and individuals
Length/frequency: Day trip

The Hudson River School of painting is introduced through a program that combines a study of the museum's collection and a tour of the sites painted by these artists. A briefing is conducted on the bus using books and illustrations of paintings of the areas to be visited. Guides who live in Catskill and are teachers take the group to Kaaterskill Falls; the site of the former Mountain House (America's first famous vacation resort); Haines Falls; Artist's Ledge; and "Olana," Frederic Church's home. The history and literature, by such famous writers as Washington Irving and James Fenimore Cooper, connected with the areas is also discussed and related to the works of art by America's first school of painters.

Pre-School Program
Museum of Fine Arts
Boston, MA 02115
(617) 267-9300
Users: Ages 3-5, accompanied by a parent
Length/frequency: Four to six weekly sessions; of 75 minutes

Preschool children and their parents learn about aspects of the museum's collection, including the Egyptian, classical, Medieval and contemporary collections. Storytelling, creative movement, music and pantomine are an integral part of each session. Individual sessions have included activities such as exploring outdoor works by Anthony Caro and David Smith, followed by a studio project in which participants collaborate on a large sculpture. In a segment called "S is for Sculpture," children are both sculptures and sculptors as they dance to the lines of the sculptures and create their own sculpture using a variety of materials. In "P is for Portrait," children add to their own self-portraits each week: facial details and hair are added after they study the curves and curls in classical portraits; background settings and inclusion of the sitter's favorite object complemented a visit to the American portrait gallery.

Sometimes parents and children work together on art projects and other times each works on a complementary part of the same project. For example, if a child is making a puppet based on a character from the collection, the parent will work on the puppet stage. In creating additive sculpture, parents and children work together.

Discovery Club
Museum of Northern Arizona
Rte. 4, Box 720, Flagstaff, AZ 86001
(602) 774-5211
Users: Grades 4-12
Length/frequency: All-day Saturday

The Discovery Club is a series of outings offered each fall and spring for children throughout the community. Each outing visits sites of special interest in Northern Arizona, with an emphasis on anthropology, geology or biology. A specialist in one of those areas leads the outing. All outings take place on Saturdays and include hiking, discussions, observations, or identification, depending on the outing emphasis. Outings have included trips to unexcavated archeological sites with identification and discussion of pot-hunting activities; a hike into the Grand Canyon observing wildlife, identifying flowers and discussing concepts in geology and environmental issues; and insect-collecting trips that included identification techniques, trapping and preservation techniques. The goal is to increase the participants' awareness of their surroundings and to improve and teach skills that will benefit them in school and later life.

Family Classes
Museum of Science and Industry
57th Street and Lake Shore Drive, Chicago, Illinois 60637
(312) 684-1414
Users: Elementary school children and their parents
Length/frequency: One, two, or three two-hour classes

Family classes provide children and parents with opportunities to share the joy of learning together. These classes include experiments, tours of museum exhibits that complement the class theme, and plans for further investigations that can be done at home. "Make-it, take-it" activities are featured. Topics for family classes include the themes of the *3-2-1 Contact* science series from Children's Television Network, tesselation, weather, fossils, nature study, hot air balloons, pond and insect life, construction of a home planetarium, aviation, and rocketry. The emphasis is on presenting the family group with insights and materials for continued investigations. Small classes assure individual attention and families may register for one or several classes. In the *3-2-1 Program*, children and their parents practice hands-on activities, prepare materials to take home for continued experimentation, and receive guidelines for follow-up gallery tours. The gallery tour guides are keyed to the weekly *3-2-1 Contact* themes, pointing out exhibit units related to the themes.

Summer Workshops For Young People
Museums of Natural History
University of Kansas, Lawrence, KS 66045
(913) 864-4173
Users: Ages 5-13
Length/frequency: Week-long sessions meeting two or three hours per day

Twenty-five different courses in natural history, anthropology, and astronomy are available throughout the summer offerred by all of the university's natural history museums. In these workshops, which promote an understanding of the natural world, children learn how to identify animals and plants, locate them, and understand their importance to each other and to humans. Trained naturalists lead students on field trips to nearby ponds, streams, woodlands, prairies and rock outcrops. The children might study a prairie dog colony or other habitats harboring a variety of wildlife, or collect samples of water, soil and plant life for analysis in the field and laboratories. Classes make use of the collections, exhibits and other facilities of the museums throughout the program.

Place-Name Research
National Museum of Natural History
Smithsonian Insititution, Washington, DC 20560
(202) 381-6212
Users: High school juniors and seniors
Length/frequency: Two-hour sessions for 12 weeks, plus one Saturday field trip

This after-school program is designed to familiarize young people with local geology, history and architecture, and to teach them a specific set of research skills. Each student receives the name of a neighborhood located close to his own home, which have not been formally presented to a U.S. Commission that validates place names. The student researches the origin of the neighborhood name and comes up with information such as "Chevy Chase derives from the English word Cheviot meaning "hunting area." The student also ascertains the boundaries of the neighborhood in terms of longitude and latitude. Research involves researching at local archives (city hall, church registries and town planning boards); interviewing area residents such as religious leaders, politicians and longtime residents who have seen the neighborhood change; and studying old maps and other regional source materials. At the end of the 12 sessions, each student makes a presentation to the States Place/Name Board, with substantiating evidence, so that the place name will become official. Students give a corresponding report to the neighborhood association.

Natural Science Workshop
Los Angeles Natural History Museum
900 Exposition Blvd., Los Angeles, CA 90007
(213) 744-3343
Users: Superior high school students
Length/frequency: Ten sessions, three-hour weekly

This workshop, held in the museum laboratory, is designed to acquaint superior students with methods of collecting, identifying, preparing, and studying biological specimens. Under the direction of the curators, students learn proper techniques for handling study collections and participating in field work. Those who return for a second, third, or fourth year may take additional classes or embark on research projects of their own choice providing their grades remain high. Some of the subjects usually offered are anthropology, comparative anatomy, entomology, herpetology, ichthyology, invertebrate marine zoology, mammalogy, mineralogy, and ornithology.

Art in Nature
William Rockhill Nelson Gallery of Art
Atkins Museum of Fine Arts
4525 Oak, Kansas City, MO 64111
(816) 561-4000
Users: Ages 5-11
Length/frequency: seven two-hour Saturday sessions

Art projects such as rubbings, paintings, drawings, printmaking and ceramics are combined to study design patterns found in nature. Students visit different section of the gallery's collection and grounds to observe the various aspects of nature as they relate to the creative art projects. For example, children go on safaris to hunt for specific wild animals or insects with wings as depicted in famous artworks. They closely observe the beautifully painted flower studies to compare the various techniques employed by Redon, LaTour, Van Huysen and Monet. Films, film loops and visuals covering nature-related phenomena (seeds sprouting, flowers blooming, birds nesting and hatching, and bees pollinating) supplement science study projects. Children prepare a garden to take home and learn the procedures of planting different seeds and starting plants from cuttings. Each week, they gather wild flower specimens and press them between blotters in a wooden flower press. Botanical keys are consulted to determine the genus and species as well as common names. Field trips to nearby gardens and farms are sponsored by one of the local garden clubs, allowing students the opportunity to sketch and collect a variety of specimens.

Natural Sciences Bicycle Tour
Oakland Museum
1000 Oak St., Oakland, CA 94607
(415) 273-3818
Users: Families
Length/frequency: All day

Families join a museum naturalist for a three-mile bicycle trip around Lake Merritt in the heart of Oakland. They stop at the Rotary Science Center to learn about migrating waterfowl on the lake in a lecture by City of Oakland Naturalists. Participants compare the current city environment and the former "natural" environment of the Bay Area. After playing nature games, they pedal back to the museum for refreshments and an opportunity to visit the natural sciences gallery.

OMSI Summer Research Teams
Oregon Museum of Science and Industry
4015 SW Canyon Rd., Portland, OR 97221
(503) 248-5944
Users: High school age
Length/frequency: One eight-week session for each team

The summer research program offers high school students opportunities to work with professionals in field research experiences in the areas of archeology, ecology, and paleoecology. All three teams conduct their studies in central and eastern Oregon, with the archeology and paleoecology groups based at OMSI's Hancock Field Station, and the ecology team based at Crooked River National Grasslands. Individual research is encouraged. Requirements for participation are an interest in the area of study, an ability to work well on a team, and an enjoyment of field-oriented experiences. Selection to the team is based upon completion of an application form and a combination of personal and/or written interviews and recommendations.

ZooCamp
Philadelphia Zoological Garden
34th and Girard,
Philadelphia, PA 19104
(215) 387-6400
Users: Neighborhood children
Length/frequency: All day, one week

ZooCamp's objective is to develop awareness, appreciation, and respect for all living things among neighborhood children. In addition to meeting, handling, and caring for a full range of zoo animals, the children study nutrition and concern themselves with the diet of humans and other animals. For example, the campers mix a batch of the omnivore diet used at the zoo with ingredients such as oats, oystershell flour, and cottonseed oil supplied by the zoo staff. The children also sprout seeds hydroponically for use in a natural food lunch, and take seed kits home to share with their families. A behind-the-scenes visit to the exhibits department teaches campers how an animal exhibit is designed, how artificial rocks and trees are created, and how an artificial nesting tree is fabricated. On daily tours to different areas of the zoo, the children use worksheets to gather information for discussions and word games, math puzzles, and craft activities that are also part of the program.

Museum School
Philbrook Art Center
2727 S. Rockford Rd.,
Tulsa, OK 74114
(918) 749-7941
Users: Pre-school through Adults
Length/frequency: Three-hour classes for 10 weeks.

This museum school integrates the study of the museum's collections and exhibitions with studio classes in the fine arts through classes, workshops and lectures. For example, in conjunction with the museum's *Gloria Dell'Arte* exhibition on the Italian Renaissance, the museum school offered the lectures on Renaissance cooking, Renaissance calligraphy, goldsmithing, and the transition from egg tempera into oils during the period. Workshops and demonstrations were given on the art of bas relief, goldsmithing, and other Renaissance metal casting techniques. Ten-week participatory classes on Renaissance dancing and enameling were also available. As exhibitions change, so do themes of the workshops and lecture series, while basic studio courses offered to groups as diverse as preschoolers and senior citizens remain constant.

The Inside Story
Science Museum of Virginia
2500 W. Broad St.,
Richmond, VA 23220
(804) 257-1013
Users: Grades 5-7
Length/frequency: Four to six two-hour sessions

To stimulate in-depth scientific inquiry in physiology, a series of Saturday morning courses, taught by a university biology professor, examine physiological systems in detail. An informal discussion format encourages easy interchanges between students and teacher. Anatomical hand-outs, hands-on experience with models, and dissection materials provide stimulation through sight, sound and touch experiences. Students develop their own interests, delving deeply into different areas: dissecting a cow's heart, listening to their heart sounds, taking their blood pressures, or microscopically observing capillary blood flow in a frog's foot. The university and museum award a certificate of completion to the students.

Parent-Child Workshops
Staten Island Children's Museum
15 Beach St.,
Staten Island, NY 10304
(212) 273-2060
Users: Ages 5-14 and parents
Length/frequency: Ninety-minute sessions, Saturday afternoons

Workshops are designed to encourage creative problem-solving and interaction between parent and child through exploration of a variety of art media, theatre and movement. As an example, the exhibition *HOCUS-FOCUS* concerned itself with visual perception and art. In the workshop "Anything Can Happen in a Dream," dreams were discussed as examples of experiences that involve the unusual and the unexpected. Examining surrealistic paintings by Salvador Dali and Rene Magritte in the exhibit the group participated in a round robin storytelling activity and cooperated in creating a surrealistic collage made from magazine cut-outs. Another workshop called "String, Straw, Sponge, Spatter," explores methods of painting other than traditional brush on paper form. Studying paintings by Jackson Pollack and Paul Jenkins, students use a variety of atypical painting implements, such as string dipped in paint and sponges, to create abstract paintings on large pieces of paper.

Whale Watch Trips
San Diego Natural History Museum
P.O. Box 1390,
San Diego, CA 92112
(714) 232-3821
Users: All ages
Length/frequency: Thirty two-hour trips each season (December-January)

Visitors are taken by boat two miles off the Pacific Coast to view the California gray whales on their annual southward migration to winter courting and calving grounds in the lagoons of Baja, California. Observers see these animals as they spout through blowholes and dive with an impressive show of tail flukes on their graceful journey through the water. The trip also affords opportunities to observe sea lions, pilot whales, porpoises, pelicans, gulls, terns, and other marine animals.

Chop Suey
Toledo Museum of Art
Monroe at Scottwood,
Toledo, OH 43697
(419) 255-8000
Users: Ages 4-6
Length/frequency: One hour each week for ten weeks

Young children are introduced to the thoughts and ways of the Oriental culture through weekly lessons focus on customs, dress, music, dance, language, ancient traditions, daily life and geography. Children examine art works in the Oriental galleries and participate in creative movement activities that reenact painting and sculpture in these halls. In an Oriental classroom environment, children work with brush and ink, printing materials and other traditional tools. Each week new vocabulary is introduced and parents receive a newsletter identifying the various concepts and vocabulary being taught. During the final week, children and their parents participate in a matsuri, or Oriental festival, with costumes, feasting and music.

Junior Science Academy Winter and Summer Programs
Utah Museum of Natural History
University of Utah, Salt Lake City, UT 84112
(801) 581-6927
Users: Grade 4 (winter programs), grades 4-10 (summer programs)
Length/frequency: Two hours per week for three weeks (winter); four weeks with field trips (summer)

Emphasizing participation, these programs are designed to stimulate a lasting interest in the natural sciences. The children, divided into three groups, rotate among the areas of biology, geology, and anthropology during each session. In geology they work with fossils and igneous and sedimentary rocks, observe a stream table, and cast fossils. Biology includes simple experiments illustrating the single cell, genetics, the sense of taste, and chromatography. In anthropology, students are involved in simulated archaeological excavations. Actual artifacts are used in student activities (grinding corn on a metate with a mano). The summer program includes multidisciplinary field work. For example a two-day field trip would include experience in an archeological excavation, field biology, fossil collecting, and nature trail hikes. Programs for gifted children and younger grades are designed using the same interdisciplinary format.

Herbs For Medicines, Food and Fragrance
Van Cortlandt Manor, Sleepy Hollow Restorations
150 White Plains Rd., Tarrytown, NY 10591
(914) 631-8200
Users: 10 years or older
Length/frequency: Four-hour sessions for three Saturdays

These workshops explore the use of herbs, plants and flowers as medicines, foods and fragrances. In "18th-century Medicine and Treatment of Disease," participants focus on the preparations of early medicinal treatments and learn about distillates, decoctions, infusions and alchemical approaches to medical treatment using different herbs. Attention is given to medical history, herbs, and plant lore, in the preparation of early mixtures and compounds. In another workshop, "Culinary and Other Uses of Herbs," students learn about the versatility of herbs in cooking, and "Fragrance," allows participants to combine roots, barks and oils with herbs to produce sweet scents for their homes.

Three Days in March
The Virginia Museum
Boulevard and Grove,
Richmond, VA 23221
(804) 257-0885
Users: Junior and senior high school students, educators
Length/frequency: Three days and two nights, annually

Each of the museum's 32 chapters and affiliates cooperate with high school principals and teachers in selecting two students—one boy and one girl—from its area high school. These students, chosen for academic excellence, and an educator from each of the chapter/affiliate communities attend this three-day residency program. The program includes lectures, demonstrations, tours, and creative arts activities centered around the theme "The Presence of the Past." On the first day various art experts demonstrate the reasons why an artist turns to the past for inspiration. On the second day, students divide into small groups to look carefully at objects taken from the museum's collection to determine the ways in which an artist can use the past. On the final day, the groups make presentations to fellow students, educators and museum staff, based on their three days at the Virginia Museum.

Discovery Unlimited
Worcester Science Center
222 Harrington Way, Worcester
MA 01604
(617) 791-9211
Users: Ages 4-13
Length/frequency: Six weeks during the summer; sporadically during the rest of the year

This environmental educational facility is located on more than 100 acres with varying habitats. During the summer it functions as a day camp, offering classes in astronomy, bird study, geology, trailcraft, biology, trees, flowers, weather, and animal life. A "hands-on" approach is used to involve children in activities that stimulate their curiosity about nature. By the end of the program, the children have collected and identified rocks, insects, and trees; pressed flowers; and made tea from wild edible plants.

Grandparents and Grandkids
The Los Angeles Children's Museum
310 N. Main St.,
Los Angeles, CA 90012
(213) 687-8801
Users: Grandparents and grandchildren (over 5 years old)
Length/frequency: 2-hour session

"Grandparents and Grandkids" is a workshop for children and their grandparents designed to help different generations share a positive creative art experience. In the workshop, participants focus on color, space, light, texture and sound through various art activities and explore ways of bringing these art activities into the home. The workshop emphasizes the use of recycled materials found at home in art activities. Slides, photographs, art books, nature, and the environment are used as resource materials for the workshop activities. The grandparents and grandchildren are encouraged to express and share their own ideas and feelings through a variety of collaborative art projects.

Discovery and Science Explorers
Museum of Science
Science Park, Boston, MA 02114
(617) 723-2500
Users: Discovery: Grades K-3;
Explorers: Grades 4-8
Length/frequency: Twelve 45-minute Saturday programs

In *Discovery* young children learn about science by watching demonstrations, manipulating materials, and making objects to take home. Among the subjects taught are weather, insects, light, metrics, vertebrate and invertebrate animals, static electricity, and plastics. Live animal demonstrations and simple experiments dramatize the subjects and programs often related to the museum's exhibitions. *Science Explorers* is a similar program in the natural and physical sciences for older children presented primarily as lecture/demonstrations.

The High School Visual Arts Seminar
The St. Louis Art Museum
Forest Park, St. Louis, MO 63110
(314) 721-0067
Users: High school students recommended by their teachers
Length/frequency: Fourteen 90-minute Saturday sessions

Students study the visual arts of painting, sculpture, and architecture in the museum galleries, with lectures, discussions, and individual projects. Meeting with key staff members (the director, registrar, librarian, conservator, and education department personnel) allows students to learn the basics of museum operations. Field trips to art galleries, artist studios, and important architectural sites supplement the students' knowledge of the St. Louis arts community. A subsequent intern program provides graduates of the seminar with opportunities to work in the museum, as both paid and volunteer assistants. Students who satisfactorily complete the seminar with regular attendance, receive a certificate of achievement from the museum.

Young Associate Workshops
Smithsonian Resident Associate Program
Smithsonian Institution,
Washington, DC 20560
(202) 357-3030
Users: Ages 3-15
Length/frequency: One- to three-hour sessions on weekends

Celebrating several traditional activities associated with the Chinese New Year; examining the many shades of red in a Valentine; comparing oak, elm, and dogwood trees to learn about the cycle of the seasons. These are only a few of the events offered to the Associates. Children come to one of the Smithsonian museums to participate in such workshops, which often use the exhibits and include creative projects. For example, in honor of the Year of the Rooster, children listen to ancient Oriental folktales about the naming of the years, create rooster shadow puppets, learn the calligraphic symbol for this animal, try ribbon dancing, and decorate and stage an impromptu dragon dance. The "Winging It" workshop examines lift, drag, thrust, and gravity: four forces that affect the flight of all airplanes. After learning about the basic principles of flight, the children test several airplane designs by creating and flying different paper airplanes. The "Clockwork Universe," an exhibit at the National Museum of American History, provided the focus for a workshop on the history of timekeeping devices and their mechanics. Children became clock makers, expressing on paper their ideas for clocks with elaborate automata. As exhibits and seasons change, so do the offerings of this program, which is complemented by the Resident Associates Family Programs and series of classes for young associates.

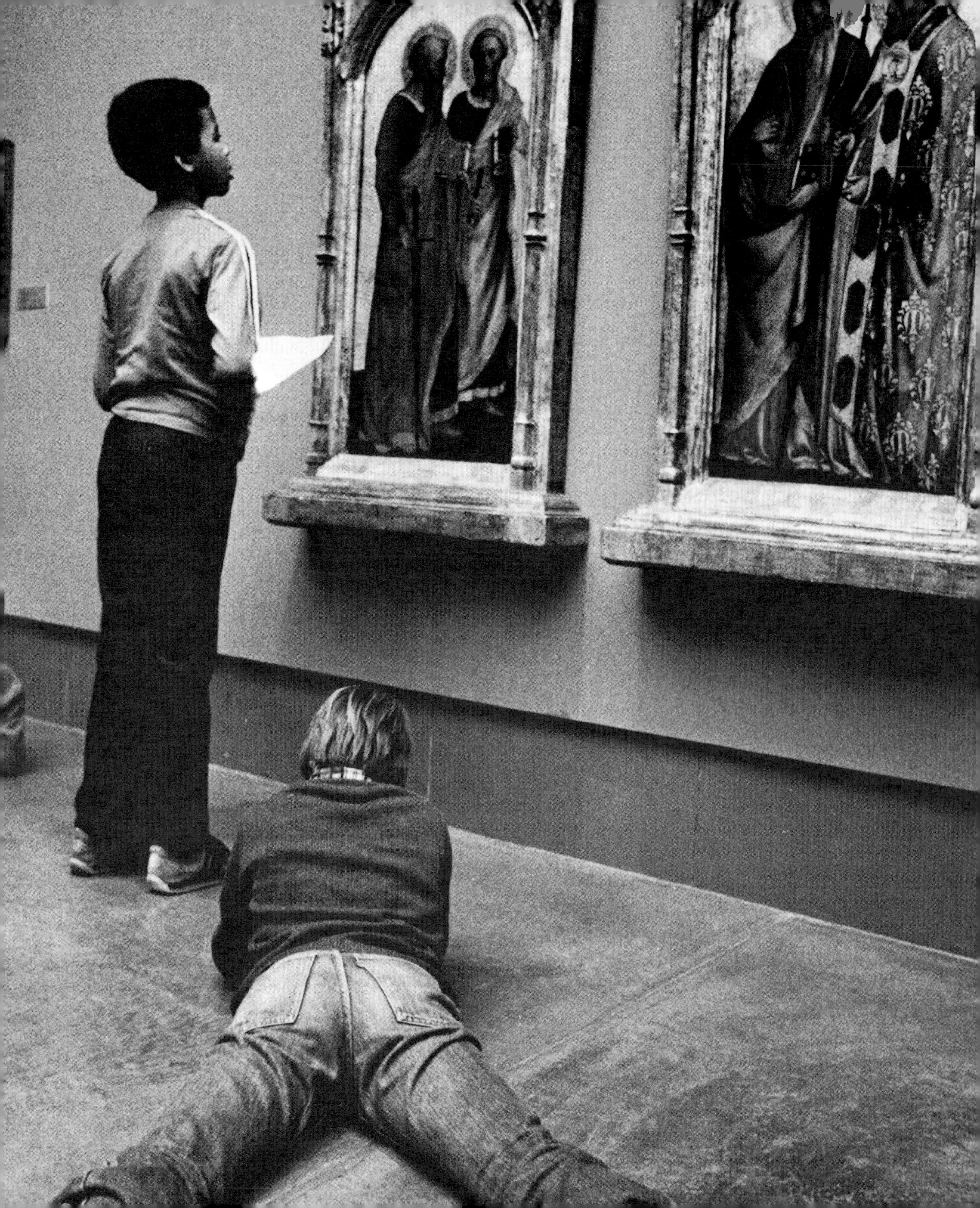

15. JUNIOR CURATORS, INTERNS AND CLUBS

Through these programs children become involved in a museum in significant ways, assuming responsibilities for managing projects, learning about collections and assisting staff. Often well-suited for teenagers, the range of activities varies from clubs studying local history or working as an interpreter for exhibits to helping with construction.

Prospector Club
Idaho State Historical Society
610 North Julia Dan's Dr.,
Boise, ID 84702
(208) 334-2120
Users: Grade 4
Length/frequency: weekly

More than one-half of the state's fourth graders belong to the 287 chapters of the Prospector Club. This junior historian program is coordinated with the social studies curriculum yet most of the activities take place after school and on the weekends. Students pay 50 cents and receive membership cards, newsletters, organize a club and participate in activities. A series of 22 topics are explored and researched by the club members including the Lewis and Clark expedition, the naming of the state, and the past and present occupations of its people. Each month the museum publishes a newsletter using essays prepared by the students, which examine different issues relating to the state's history. The clubs also participate in a number of different activities such as writing skits, plays, painting murals, and doing research on goldmining, trapping, historic sites and people to learn about their community. Awards are made annually for the best project. Teachers serve as facilitators for the club's activities and receive information and assistance from the museum.

Junior Docents
Cavalry Museum
12901 Gateway W.,
El Paso, TX 79936
(915) 543-3828
Users: Girl Scouts
Length/frequency: One-hour sessions weekly for two months

Girl Scouts are trained for two months to become junior docents for the museum. Each week the girls receive information about another section of the museum, with the five main topics being: Conquistadors, Indians, Mexicans, frontiermen, and the military. The junior docents study objects from the museum's collection that are relevant to these various cultural groups that formed the southwest. After the initial training period, the girls serve as guides and give tours after school and on Saturdays for young visitors.

Junior Intern Program
The Capitol Children's Museum
800 Third St. NE,
Washington, DC 20002
(202) 544-2244
Users: Junior and senior high school students
Length/frequency: Depends on the individual

After an initial training period, the junior interns work as interpreters of the museum's exhibits assisting younger children with their explorations. The exhibits and programs provide learning opportunities on two levels. First, the interns themselves must learn the information behind the exhibits, such as Mexico and simple machines. They then must learn how to communicate this to others. Thus, the interns who explain the pulley system in the simple machine exhibit both reinforce their own understanding of mechanical principles and know how to describe them to others. The interns rotate to all of the exhibits and gain a sense of accomplishment as they teach young visitors how to make chocolate in the Mexico exhibit or how to measure their height in centimeters. The program helps the interns develop their personal and communication skills. The staff assists them to prepare for job interviews and to write a resume when they are ready to leave.

Future Scientists
Cleveland Museum of Natural History
Wade Oval, University Circle,
Cleveland, OH 44106
(216) 231-4600
Users: High school students
Length/frequency: Seven hours on Saturdays during school term; two days per week during summer

Museum biologists, assisted by university faculty and scientists from industry have developed this combined laboratory/field program. During the course of study, students learn field techniques, actively participate in field experiences, and learn methods of processing, preserving, and curating materials brought to the museum from the field. In a series of laboratory sessions, archeological, biological and geological specimens are examined using investigation techniques, including microscopic analysis. One recent project involved an archeological salvage excavation of a Whittlesey culture village site. Students studied archeological field methods and received background information on the Whittlesey culture before actually working at the site with museum scientists. Back in the laboratory, they analyzed materials and artifacts excavated during their field work. Other projects involved fossil collecting and compiling nesting bird records for the Cornell Laboratory of Ornithology. Museum instructors emphasize the importance of teamwork and outdoor survival techniques, important skills that must be mastered in the making of future scientists.

Summer Intern Program
The Cloisters
Fort Tryon Park,
New York, NY 10040
(212) 923-3700
Users: Twelve senior high and college students
Length/frequency: Three-week training session; full-time summer

Five cloisters from the Romanesque to the Gothic period form the backdrop as summer interns study the collection, medieval history, medieval art, and crafts and gallery teaching techniques in preparation for leading summer day camp groups on treasure hunts. During the three-week training program, interns practice crafts such as weaving and metalwork, and lead one another on hunts for specific treasures such as gold, unicorns and jesters. Later, the interns lead 120 campers per day, in groups of four and five. Treasure hunts through the museum's collection of architectural structures, tapestries, ivories, illuminated manuscripts, stained glass, paintings and metal works help children to discover, and then compare and contrast, specific motifs (kings, queens, jesters, unicorns) as well as precious materials.

Junior Curators Program
The Corning Museum of Glass
Centerway, Corning, NY 14830
(607) 937-5371
Users: Grade 6, 20 students
Length/frequency: Sixteen 90-minute after-school sessions

This cooperative junior curator program uses the resources of three museums that have distinctly different collections. Approximately eight weeks are spent at the Museum of Glass, two weeks at the Rockwell-Corning Museum (western art), and six weeks in the Benjamin Patterson Inn, a restored 1790s inn and tavern. Each week, the students consider a subject relative to the collections in one of the museums. A curator or community person leads a discussion and the students participate in a workshop. For instance, at the Museum of Glass, one program focuses on reflections, or the mirror image: Students see a film on the pouring of the Hale telescope mirror, study the original casting in the museum, and discuss its uses and construction, considering the idea behind reflections, or the mirror-image. At the end of the session, the students make their own paperboard periscopes. Sessions at the Inn include the study of 19th-century building tools and their use in the construction of the Inn, followed by a lecture on architectural preservation and the reuse of old buildings. Each session provides the interns with an opportunity to study a museum collection and a chance to learn from curators and other staff members.

Junior Rangers
Environmental Education Center
Tilden Nature Area, Berkeley, CA 94708
(415) 525-2233
Users: Ages 8-12
Length/frequency: Full year program

The main purpose of this program is to develop an appreciation of the environment and an understanding of the need to conserve resources. To further these goals, the program provides instruction in the care and use of tools, in camping techniques for minimizing human impact on land, in first aid, and in methods of identifying plants, animals, and minerals. Rangers participate in a number of group environmental and conservation projects.

The Explainer Program
The Exploratorium
3601 Lyon St., San Francisco, CA 94123
(415) 563-7337
Users: High school students
Length/frequency: 20 students hired every four months

The Exploratorium hires high school students as floor staff for the science center. Instructed by the staff during their entire tenure, these Explainers learn through teaching and help maintain exhibits. Personal contact with the visitor is a major function of the program, as the students work with adults and children demonstrating, dissecting, explaining, and helping visitors themselves use and understand the participatory exhibits. They are paid for their services through grant funds received by the Exploratorium. A number of Explainers have ultimately become permanent staff members and others were influenced towards science careers.

ArtScene
The Hunter Museum of Art
10 Bluff View, Chattanooga, TN 37403
(615) 267-0968
Users: 46 High school students grades 10-12
Length/frequency: Regularly scheduled monthly meetings throughout the school year

ArtScene involves high school students in the inner workings of an art museum, introducing them to museum volunteerism, as well as of-

215

fering them a variety of stimulating art enrichment programs. Annual projects give the youths training in specialized areas of museum work include: "Spectrum", the museum's annual fundraising event/art auction; and "ArtScene Exhibition," a local high school juried exhibition during which students work with museum staff and volunteer coordinators to receive, photograph and hang the exhibit, publish a catalogue of the show and present the opening reception. Members assist with children's art Workshops, attend "learn-how-to" sessions with guest instructors, visit local artists' studios, and find out more about their field of interest during an "art career night." *ArtScene* members who regularly attend monthly meetings receive a complimentary student museum membership.

Junior Curators
Memphis Pink Palace Museum
3050 Central Ave., Memphis, TN 38111
(901) 454-5600
Users: Grades 9-12
Length/frequency: Four monthly meetings, two monthly field trips

Junior curators are instructed in all aspects of museum operation—collecting, identifying, processing materials, and developing exhibit concepts. In addition, each participant is encouraged to pursue some aspect of geology, anthropology, or biology under the supervision of the professional staff and outside consultants. During the summer months, the junior curators are encouraged to participate in museum activities on a volunteer basis, although if funds are available they are paid for their efforts.

Teenage Volunteer Program
Museum of the Hudson Highlands
Cornwall-on-the-Hudson, NY 12520
(914) 534-2320
Users: Junior and senior high school students
Length/frequency: Full year

Teenage volunteers are the backbone of this small, regional natural history museum. Through the senior workshop program, volunteers assist with curatorial duties in the animal hall where live regional animals are exhibited. Teenage volunteers also participate in the construction stages of cultural and scientific exhibits. They serve as field assistants and work closely with the staff collecting baseline scientific data on the natural resources of the county. Students involved in the program also participate in several camping trips each year.

Jerseymen State Association of History Clubs
The New Jersey Historical Society
230 Broadway, Newark, NJ 07104
(201) 483-3939
Users: Elementary and secondary students
Length/frequency: Once a week, after school

This junior historian program encourages students to take an active approach to state and local history, by developing club projects, participating in an annual calendar of events and creating projects that reflect New Jersey's history. Annual events include "Sight and Sound Festivals," "November Election Debates," "Leadership Workshops," and history fairs. Students also attend a Tri-State Junior Historians Convention with young people from New York and Pennsylvania.

The Yorker Program
New York State Historical Association
Cooperstown, NY 13326
(607) 547-2533
Users: School clubs, Grades 5-12
Length/frequency: Full year program

Encouraged by the Historical Association as their parent sponsor, Yorker Clubs throughout the state conduct architectural surveys, research topics for publication in *The Yorker* magazine, document and restore cemeteries and schoolhouses, and prepare exhibits for the annual state convention. A Yorker club at Sherman, New York, began collecting old objects from students' homes some 30 years ago. In the process of finding a home for the collections, members (now including second-generation Yorkers) have raised funds to move six historic buildings onto the village common to form a museum that is equipped, staffed, and maintained by Yorkers.

FANS (Fine Art Novices)
San Diego Museum of Art
Balboa Park, P.O. Box 2107, San Diego, CA 92117
(714) 232-7931
Users: Ages 12 to 20
Length/frequency: One morning each month during school year

FANS is a group of teenagers interested in all aspects of art and the museum, who are members or children of members. The museum provides a behind-the-scenes view of the art world including visits to artists' studios and homes of collectors, as well as tours to other museums. *FAN* members study art history, participate in studio art classes and learn about potential of careers in art-related fields. In addition they assist in a variety of museum projects such as sorting and filing catalogues in the museum's library, and helping to host the Junior Art Festival, which brings together children and local artists in an exciting studio experience.

Saturday Science Clubhouse
The Science Museum of Minnesota
30 E. 10th St., St. Paul, MN 55101
(612) 221-9488
Users: Ages 8-14 and families
Length/frequency: Weekly one-hour programs

Science topics ranging from biology to physics and everything in between are examined in the clubhouse. The phenomena of earth formation, undersea life, and the laws of gravity have been presented on the auditorium stage where professional actors serving as clubhouse leaders pose questions and work with invited guests who are experts in their fields. Members participate on stage, receive clubhouse t-shirts and newsletters, and join with the mascot, Iggie the Iguana, in fun while learning. Two or three sessions explore different aspects of the same topic and members are encouraged to write letters, question the guests, and vote on clubhouse business.

Thomas Bailey Aldrich House Interpretation
Strawberry Banke, Inc.
P.O. Box 300, Portsmouth, NH 03801
(603) 431-4046
Users: Ages 12-16
Length/frequency: Ten weeks during the summer

The program is an interpretation of 19th-century youth experiences, based on a restored house and a literary work, given by local youth for the benefit of their peers. One of the houses at Strawberry Banke is the boyhood home of Thomas Bailey Aldrich, a 19th-century novelist who wrote about his childhood in *The Story of a Bad Boy*. Each summer, the Junior Guides, local youth aged 12-16, work as costumed interpreters in the house. They also perform a dramatic version of the story, and organize typical 19th-century childhood activities for youths visiting the museum.

Junior Curator Program
Children's Museum of Oak Ridge
P.O. Box 3066,
Oak Ridge, TN 37830
(615) 482-1074
Users: Grades 5 and 6
Length/frequency: 36 hours over six months

Teachers select fifth- and sixth-grade volunteers for this program, which focuses on museum management and maintenance. In addition to weekly meetings with the museum's program coordinator, the students commit to working 36 hours during a six-month period in six areas: assisting as tour guides and receptionists; cleaning and maintaining the museum and exhibits; assisting in classes; working as aides for special events; preparing exhibits; and conducting a research project that results in either an exhibit for the museum or an essay for the museum library. Students are solicited through contact with local elementary school teachers and newspaper articles. Special recognition is given to student volunteers after six months and one year of service. Each year, 10 to 20 students remain committed to the museum, serving as volunteers through high school. Plans are underway for a Senior Curator Program for high school students.

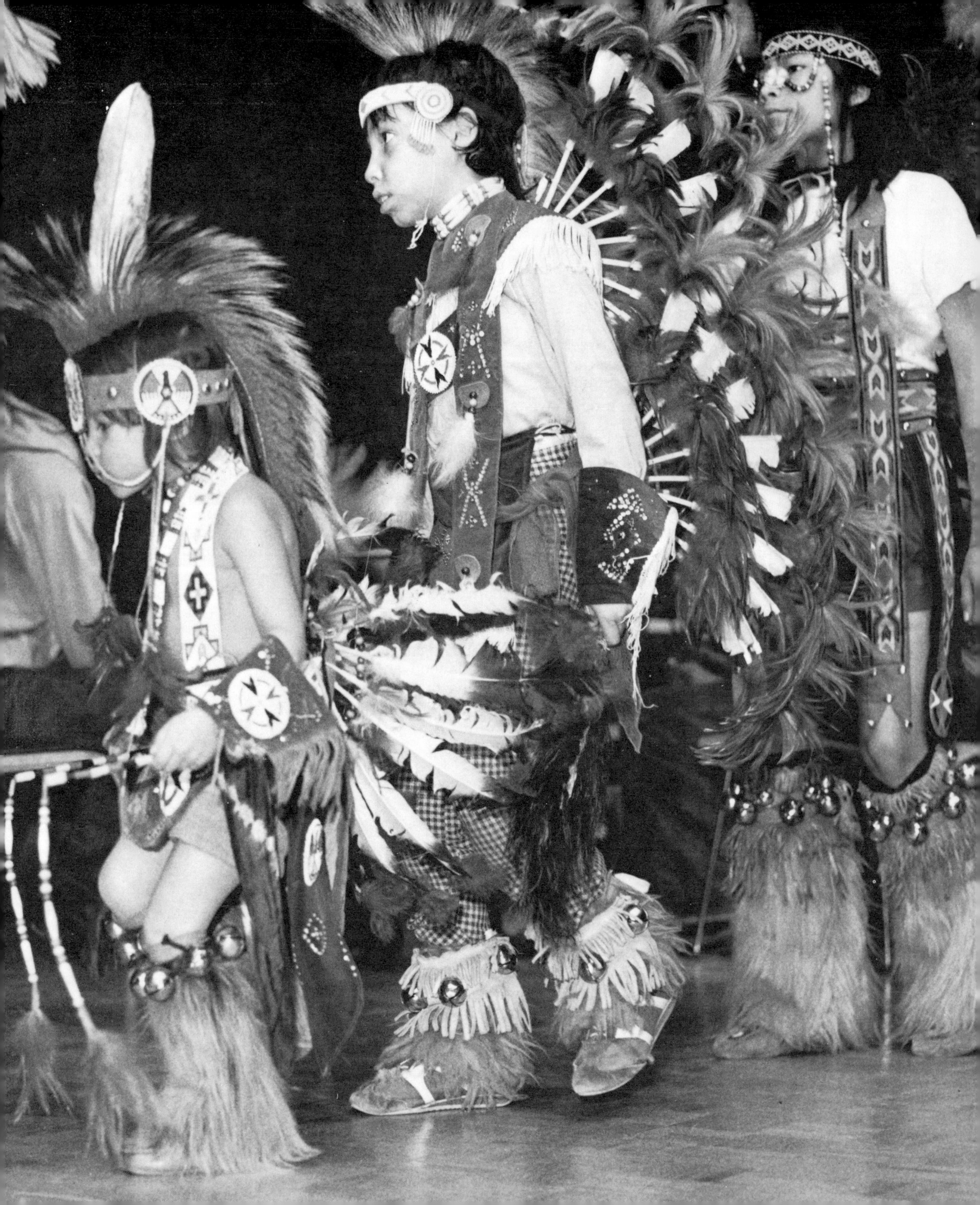

16. FESTIVALS AND SPECIAL EVENTS

Preparing to celebrate the holidays, National Historic Preservation week, special exhibitions, or the Harvest Moon are important ways to examine collections. These programs help to bring new audiences to the museum while offering opportunities for families to join together in learning about and celebrating different cultures, events and periods in history.

The People Center
American Museum of Natural History
Central Park West at 79th St., New York, NY 10024
(212) 873-1300
Users: All ages
Length/frequency: Weekends/afternoons

Designed to extend understanding of the anthropological exhibitions at the museum, the People Center provides an intimate environment for communicating feelings, values, and concepts through performance and demonstration. The People Center consists of three areas: an 80-seat theater and two smaller carpeted and terraced amphitheatres or teaching pits. Visitors may sometimes participate in the center's programs. A typical weekend program will juxtapose dance or music demonstrations from different regions and present slides, short films or mini-talks on cultures of the world. Sometimes the weekend will focus on a single cultural tradition or region such as India or Japan.

Foreign Language Festival
Buhl Planetarium and Institute of Popular Science
Allegheny Square, Pittsburgh, PA 15212
(412) 321-4300
Users: Grade 7
Length/frequency: Eleven days

General interest in the relationships between the heavenly bodies, foreign cultures and languages provides the impetus for this festival at the planetarium. Students of French, German, Russian and Spanish prepare and present dramatic performances in foreign languages, participate in dancing, singing, and instrumental presentations. Students also take part in a special sky show presented in the language they are studying. This yearly festival receives support from the Foreign Language Council and the planetarium.

Dinosaur Birthday Party
Carnegie Museum of Natural History
4400 Forbes Ave.,
Pittsburgh, PA 15213
(412) 622-3235
Users: Children ages 6-10
Length/frequency: One to two hours, Saturday and Sunday

A Dinosaur Birthday Party, complete with a dinosaur birthday cake, is offered to children ages 6-10. A docent leads the children through the Dinosaur Hall and shows them a slide presentation about how paleontologists recovered dinosaur bones, brought them to the museum, and prepared them for exhibit. Then, it's the children's turn to be paleontologists. Each child receives a box containing a plaster cast of a fossil enclosed in matrix. Carefully, the children remove their fossils, and use clues and questions written on the box to help them learn about and identify their fossils. The fee for the party includes special invitations, the fossil hunt kit, and a birthday cake with a dinosaur motif.

Surrounding Resident Programs
The Children's Museum
3000 N. Meridian St., Indianapolis, IN 46208
(317) 924-5431
Users: Families
Length/frequency: Continuous series and special events year-around

From 20 to 30 different programs are offered yearly as part of the museum's Neighbors Programs. Available to those persons living in the museum's neighborhood, they utilize top talent locally, nationally, and internationally and consist of concerts, performances, exhibit openings, classes, festivals, lecture-demonstrations, receptions and special seminars. Many programs are offered in series, such as the six-day celebration of Kwanza, while others may expand from one to 60 days as in the opening and showing of *The Great Beautiful Black Women Exhibition*. With the opening of *Africa—A Look at Life Exhibit,* four United Nations ambassadors from Africa attended, the Museum of African Art Musical Ensemble performed, food representing a number of African countries was served to 275 museum visitors, and six different workshops were offered including one conducted by a famed Nigerian sculptor.

Special Events
Florida State Museum
University of Florida, Museum Rd., Gainesville, FL 32611
(904) 392-1721
Users: All ages
Length/frequency: Ninety-minutes to all day

Music, dance, theater, demonstrations, workshops, and lectures are all part of the museum's events programs for families. Visitors enjoy children's classics such as *The Little Prince, Punch and Judy,* and *Jack and the Beanstalk,* presented as drama or puppet shows. The courtyard may be filled with the toe-tapping fiddle music of the Bucksnort Barndance Band or the fife music of the Historic Florida Militia; dancers clogging or performing intricate international folk dances; craftspersons spinning, wood carving, weaving, or chair carving; museum scientists describing their work with local fossils or early peoples; or programs on edible plants, endangered species, principles of taxidermy, or how to begin a family geneology. The events offer families opportunities to see, discover, and learn about man's heritage and the world around them.

Junior Craftsmen Along The Monarchy
Historic Bethlehem, Inc.
516 Main St., Bethlehem, PA 18018
(215) 868-6311
Users: Ages 6-16
Length/frequency: Annual event in May

In this program, children teach and learn from each other. Eighth grade students work for several months researching various colonial crafts and trades. They plan how to interpret their chosen craft to an audience of fourth graders, make their own costumes, create posters and displays, and locate the necessary artifacts and objects for their craft interpretation areas. On two consecutive days during National Historic Preservation Week, the 100 costumed interpreters demonstrate crafts such as rope-making, candle dipping, masonry, trapping and carpentry in Historic Bethlehem's 18th-century industrial area. The general public is also invited to attend this living history program.

West Virginia Heritage Festival
Huntington Galleries
Park Hills, Huntington, WV 25701
(304) 529-2701
Users: Grade 8
Length/frequency: Two weeks annually (spring)

The festival helps to increase the students' appreciation of the cultural background of Appalachia and to help them to make use of this cultural heritage in their lives. Students construct quilt squares, gather traditional recipes, and learn folk dances and songs in their school classrooms. At festival time, they come to the museum in groups of 300 to participate in a full day of heritage-related activities: folk dancing and singing, marble shooting, storytelling, candlemaking, spinning, and blacksmithing. Although primarily for students, the general public attends the weekend exhibitions, lectures, and concerts related to the heritage theme.

Regional History Fairs
Illinois State Historical Society
Old State Capitol, Springfield, IL 62706
(217) 782-4836
Users: Students in grades 7-12
Length/frequency: All-day Saturday meeting, held annually in four regions of state in spring

The competition in the regional history fairs, either with papers or projects, places a strong emphasis on preparing carefully researched and documented products on Illinois history. Awards are based on how much the student has learned about Illinois rather than on how well he/she has learned to draw or sew. Research papers may be considered for publication in *Illinois History*, covering a range of topics that relate to their region of the state. Project categories include art, dioramas, models, handicraft and audiovisual or videotape presentations. For examples, submissions have included quilts with historic symbols completed in the appropriate stitching patterns of the period, models of a working windmill in South Chicago, and audiovisual presentations illustrating different aspects of neighborhood history. Students compete in a local, regional and statewide competition, with the superior award-winning projects moving onto the next level of competition. Certificates, ribbons, books, and cash prizes are awarded by the governor each May at an annual award day in Springfield. State winners may participate in the National History Day competition.

Student Science Fair/and Children's Science Book Fair
Museum of Science and Industry
57th Street and Lake Shore Drive, Chicago, IL 60637
(312) 684-1414
Users: School children
Length/frequency: Annually

The Student Science Fair is one of the oldest and most successful in the nation. Started in 1950, it is held each spring for four days by the Chicago Public Schools in cooperation with an industrial sponsor and the museum. Exhibits and research papers on science and mathematics projects are presented by some 300 finalists chosen from a series of school and district competitions. The program awards mini-grants to students to conduct research projects and approximately 500 prizes, including a dozen college scholarships. The Children's Science Book Fair is held annually for two weeks to introduce children to the joys of reading and introduce children to the joys of reading and learning about science, and to acquaint adults with the variety and quality of children's science books available today. Hundreds of recently published children's science books are shown and arranged by grade level in the following categories: animals, astronomy, aviation/space, biography/careers, earth sciences, life sciences, marine life and many others.

An annotated bibliography of the books on display is available for $3 at the Children's Science Book Fair or throughout the year from the Museum's Store. Classes are invited to attend the museum during the Book Fair to see the book exhibits and take part in the activities that may include home science experiments, live animals, story hours, demonstrations, and lectures. A special seminar for adults on children's literature is also featured. The Children's Science Book Fair is presented by the museum in cooperation with the Children's Book Council, the National Science Teachers Association, and the Association of Science and Technology Centers (which circulates a limited version of the Book Fair).

Adventures in Wool
Old Economy Village
Ambridge, PA 15003
(412) 266-4500
Users: Grade 3
Length/frequency: Every March

Guides begin by explaining how wool is an integral part of the children's clothing and how wool begins with sheep. Children are introduced to two live sheep and encouraged to examine their winter growth of wool. Each child receives a piece of wool they keep throughout the visit and later—during a demonstration of teasing and carding wool—learn how to fluff. As the children feel the animals, they are told how the lanolin serves as a conditioner to prevent excessive drying of the wool, and how lanolin is extracted and used in human skin and hair preparations. Students then visit a room equipped with a fleece (in grease and wool state), scoured wool (already washed and ready to be teased), and instruments—such as shears—used in the various stages of the preparation process. During the spinning and weaving demonstration, students assist the textile demonstrator as the steps necessary in the production of woolen cloth are explained. This process of contact and observation helps the children understand lifestyles.

Harvest Moon Festival
Science Museum of Virginia
2500 W. Broad St., Richmond, VA 23220
(804) 257-1013
Users: General audience
Length/frequency: Two hours beginning as the full moon rises each fall

The Harvest Moon Festival, an outdoor event, celebrates the first full moon following the autumnal equinox. Corn shocks, bales of hay, which serve as seats, and a bonfire create a colorful setting for the program which integrates the science of astronomy with the folklore and legends passed down about this particular full moon. The full moon itself becomes the astronomy lesson (weather permitting) and museum staff explain how to anticipate when and where the moon will rise nightly. Indians tell of their culture and what the harvest moon meant to them and children join in a snake dance. A storyteller creates with word pictures the ancient folklore of the moon, plays a guitar for a sing-along, and does juggling and other tricks. The program ends with cider and doughnut refreshments, and a look at the moon through telescopes provided by the museum and the Richmond Astronomical Society. This is an annual affair, attracting more people each year.

Story Telling
State Museum
University of Nebraska, Lincoln, NB 68588
(402) 472-2637
Users: All ages (primary ages predominant)
Length/frequency: Half-hour sessions once a week

Story telling is used as a primary tool to make exhibits come alive for visitors. Rich in historical detail, the stories are the result of extensive research. Everyday details, such as conversation and emotion, are added only when appropriate, and human characteristics are never attributed to animals. One story tells of an injured sand hill crane, found and cared for by a family and then released. Others illustrate the symbolic importance of the elephant to an African tribe. No audiovisuals or specimens are used; instead exhibits that contain appropriate animals are used as backgrounds for the storytelling events. One concern is the need to recruit experienced story tellers to fill this truly artistic role. A distinct talent is required to successfully accomplish this type of story telling, which relies on the story teller becoming the focus of attention as he/she completely absorbs the audience utilizing theatrical and mood-setting abilities.

Land Between the Lakes
Tennessee Valley Authority
Golden Pond, KY 42231
(502) 924-5602
Users: Families
Length/frequency: One hour to two days, depending on the programs

Numerous special events and programs, field trips and workshops at the TVA interpretive facilities cover topics, such as woodworking skills of the mid-19th century and wild-game gourmet cooking, that celebrate the history and traditional craft activities of the western Cumberland. Weekend events are offered periodically. Examples are: a celebration of the natural wonders of Western Kentucky; field trips dedicated to the conservation and understanding of eagles and other birds of prey; or an introduction to archeology through presentations by archeologists and anthropologists and visits to sites in Kentucky and Tennessee. An annual arts and crafts festival promotes an awareness and participation in the arts and crafts of the region. Included in the festival are examples of quilting, woodworking, candle-dipping and weaving. The Devil's Elbow Fiddlers' Championships are held in conjunction with this festival.

Family Bookmaking
William Rockhill Nelson Gallery of Art, Atkins Museum of Fine Arts
4525 Oak St., Kansas City, MO 64111
(812) 561-4000
Users: Families
Length/frequency: Three hours

In conjunction with an exhibition about books, the museum offered a one afternoon workshop for families to work together on a family book. The first hour was spent looking at books in the gallery collections and a traveling exhibition. Participants made hanging scrolls inspired by the gallery's Chinese collection, hornbooks after those in the Shakespeare traveling exhibit, and illustrated books, which included contributions by each family member.

Science Circus
Pacific Science Center Foundation
200 Second Ave. N., Seattle, WA 98109
(206) 625-9333
Users: All ages
Length/frequency: Six days annually

Each year between Christmas and New Year's Day, people of all ages experience the thrill of scientific discovery amidst the sights and sounds of a circus at the center. Filling every available hall, room, and corner of the Pacific Science Center, this event features "hands-on" exhibits, science demonstrations, Indian Longhouse activities and legends, a special preschoolers' area, and—of course—balloons. With the help of the city aquarium, local businesses, community groups, and dozens of student volunteers, Science Circus has become a popular family holiday event.

Popcorn Concerts
Staten Island Children's Museum
15 Beach St., Staten Island, NY 10304
(212) 273-2060
Users: Children ages 5-14 and parents
Frequency: Three to five concerts yearly, Sunday afternoons

The museum, in conjunction with The Concert Artists Guild, brings together family audiences and emerging musicians, vocalists and ensembles in this Sunday afternoon concert series. Each year, the concert series attempts to enhance the theme of the museum's current exhibition. As an example, for an exhibition on visual perception and art the first concert was a piano recital of Mussorgsky's *Pictures at an Exhibition,* 10 short pieces of music based on sketches and drawings by Victor Hartmann. During the series, the museum highlighted music in art throughout the ages in a display of prints illustrating the musicians and the audience. As part of a concert program, musicians discuss the history of the music they are playing,

223

and any unusual or interesting information about their instruments. For example artists may present their unusual instruments and music styles throughout the ages. Popcorn is served at the conclusion of each concert.

Special Saturday Events
GAME—Growth Through Art and Museum Experience, Inc.
314 W. 54th St., New York, NY 10019
(212) 765-5904
Users: All ages, children, parents, and grandparents
Length/frequency: Special events vary in length, offered throughout the year

Saturdays in June, July, and August may bring Solar Power Day, Operation Balloon-Track, and Aerodynamics Day, among others, to the youngsters in the city and their parents. Balloons are tagged and sent into the west Manhattan sky, one by one. The most enterprising sailed on the summer winds to Manchester, New Hampshire, where it was captured and returned. Solar Power Day featured lunch cooked on solar-powered ovens, solar-designed doll houses built by New York City public school children, and music created by solar organs. Paper plane designing and flying contest offered prizes to the innovative and longest thrust (60 feet) on Aerodynamics Day. The winter months include not only celebration of the normal holidays, but also activities such as inventing animals, telling stories through textures and photography, flying kites with experts to learn aerodynamics, and being part of a participatory performance of classics with children and parents working behind the scenes with props and costumes.

Kwanzaa Festival and Workshop
Museum of African Art
Smithsonian Institution,
Washington, DC 20002
(202) 287-3490
Users: Families
Length/frequency: Annually in December

Kwanzaa (Swahili for "first"), an African-American celebration, is observed during the seven-day period from December 26th to January 1st. Kwanzaa brings together family and community to celebrate the "fruits" of the year's labor, to evaluate achievements and contributions to the family and community, and to lay plans and goals for the year ahead. Each day of Kwanzaa is devoted to a different principle of social, spiritual or moral commitment: unity, self-determination, collective work and responsibility, cooperative economics, purpose, creativity, and faith. On the seventh day a feast is held, with music and dance as part of the final celebration. On each day of Kwanzaa, families and friends gather to light a candle for that day, and to honor ancestors and cooperation. Finally, on the last day of the celebration, handmade gifts, or "zawadi," are exchanged representing the fruits of the parents' labor and reward for good acts or achievements of the children. A full range of festive activities are planned at the museum, including storytelling, African craft workshops, demonstrations of African naming ceremonies, films, and guided tours of current exhibitions. No festival is complete without music and dance to capture the spirit and excitement of the holidays. The museum offers free workshops for families and community leaders to help discover the purpose, meaning, and origins of the celebration of Kwanzaa.

Medieval Fair
The Ringling Museums
P.O. Box 1838, Sarasota, FL 33578
(813) 355-5101
Users: Families
Length/frequency: Annually for four days in March

The tumultuous atmosphere of a Medieval city, set against the Italian renaissance museum buildings, is recreated as executioners, minstrels, madrigal singers, rope and stilt walkers, fire eaters, instrumentalists, and fortune-tellers banish the many centuries between the Medieval times and the present. A grand court processional takes place each noon. The ceremony involves a dignified showcasing of some 600 participants robed in the authentic accoutrement and fittings of a Medieval society, along with elephants, horses and other animals. Fifteen separate staging areas present theater, dance, music, mime, and sporting events—all authentic to Medieval and Baroque Periods. Special events include demonstrations of jousting Renaissance knights; human chess matches on a checkered lawn board with armed combat deciding who wins the exchanges; and Medieval stonecutters, spinning contests and traditional Maypole festivals. Continuous entertainment includes stiltwalkers, jugglers, magicians, fire-eaters and madrigal performances. Craft demonstrations take place throughout the fair and include leather and glass working, bobbin lace-making, and net weaving. The fair involves many people of the community as presenters, costumed participants, and visitors help to create an authentic representation.

Performance Events
Brooklyn Museum
Eastern Pkwy, Brooklyn, NY 11238
(212) 638-5000
Users: Families
Length/frequency: Three hours to two days on the occasion of special exhibitions

For many years, the museum has offered a wide range of events including demonstrations, concerts, films, lectures and festivals to enhance the interpretation of its special exhibitions. These performance events create an atmosphere that helps visitors better understand the works of art and their historical or cultural context. For example, for the exhibit *The American Renaissance, 1876-1917*, a festival of fairs was held to examine some of the ideas and styles of that period. In the late 19th-century, the spirit of collaboration between architects, painters, sculptors, decorators and landscape architects was brought to the American public through world fairs, starting with the 1893 Columbian Exposition in Chicago. The museum's weekend event re-created the atmosphere and events that took place during that fair. A slide show and films documented three different world fairs and the events that surrounded them. Demonstrations of stained glass making and mural painting illustrated particular techniques that were seen in the works of art. Music accompanied the realistic representations of paintings as tableaux vivants, also creating a festive atmosphere through waltzes, ragtime, jazz and more. Eight tableaux vivants were created, faithfully representing every detail of the painting or sculpture. The midway of the fair was brought to life with an entertainment theater that included belly dancers and a Viennese cafe.

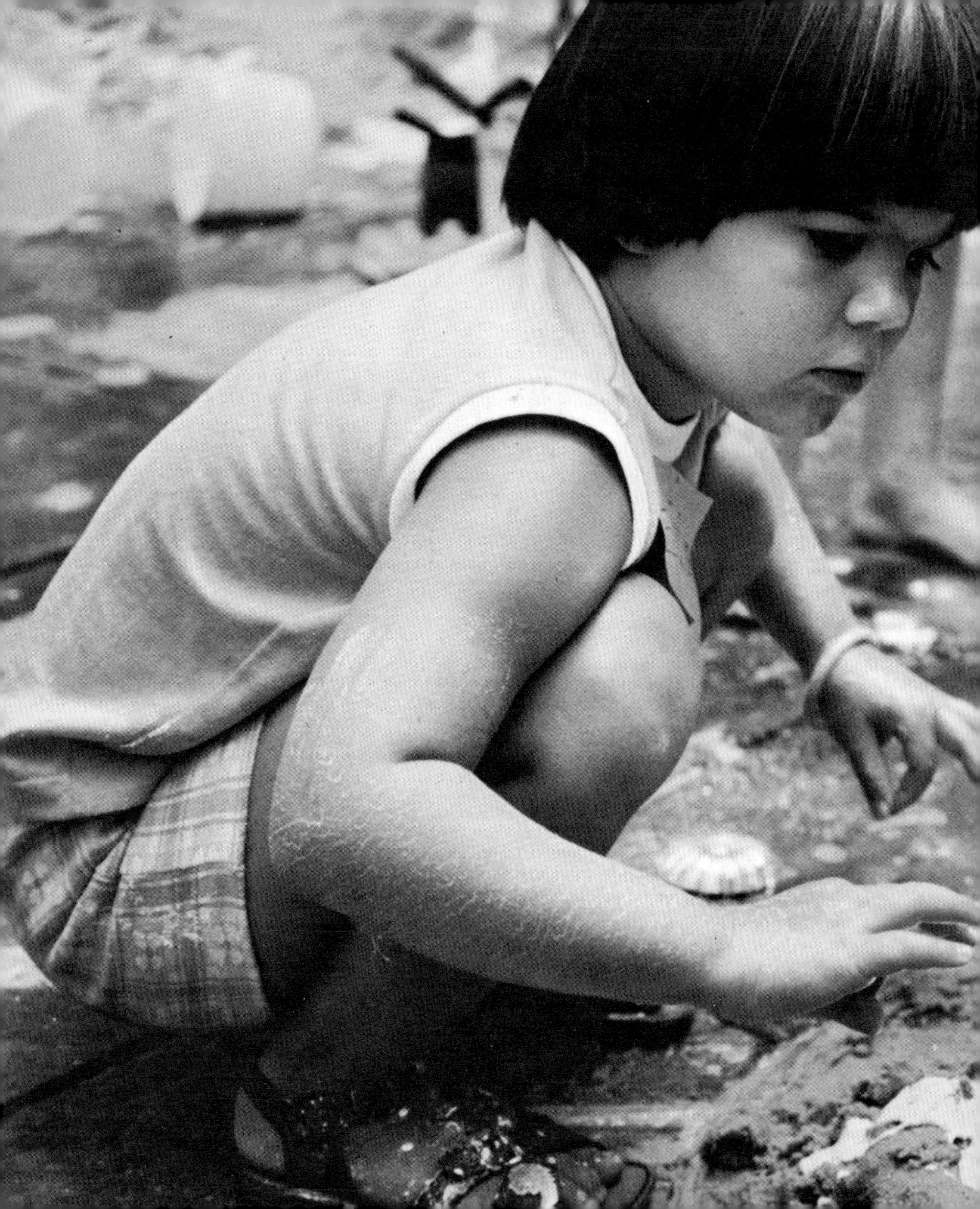

REFERENCE MATERIALS

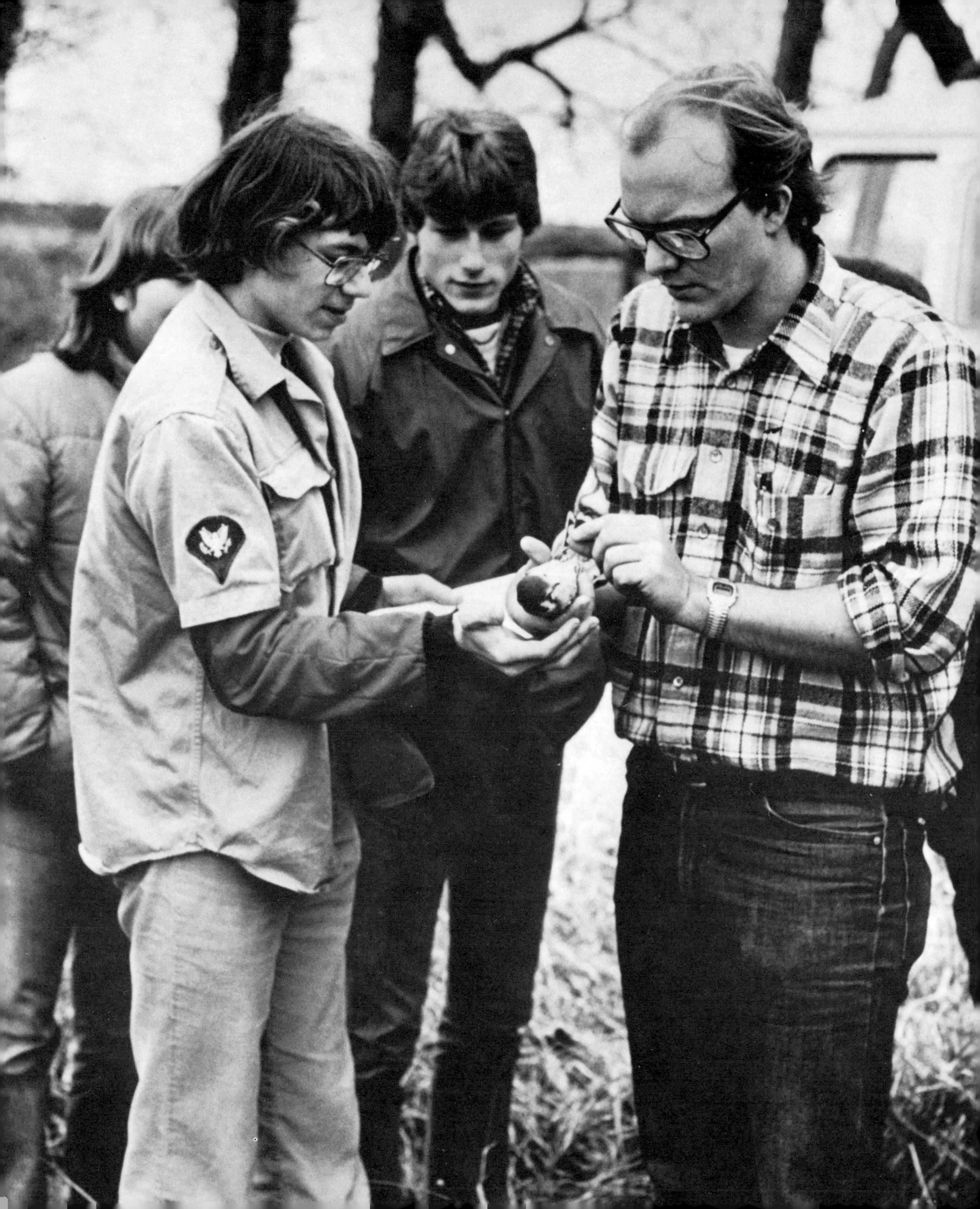

17. RESOURCES FROM MUSEUMS

This list of catalogues has been compiled from information provided by museums responding to questionnaires distributed during the research phase of this book. Many of the museums mentioned in this book, as well as those not included, also have resource materials, exhibits, kits, slide programs, films and video cassettes for loan. Therefore, this list should be seen as a beginning or illustration of the scope of materials that are available.

Alaska State Museum Alaska MultiMedia Education Program
Pouch FM
Juneau, AK 99811
Multimedia loan materials including slides, video tapes and manuals that relate the history, culture, people and environment.

Albright-Knox Art Gallery
1285 Elmwood Ave.
Buffalo, NY 14222
"Video Vasari" catalogue lists videotape interviews with leading contemporary artists and critics whose works are in the collection. Other materials, such as slides, tapes and teacher guides are listed with the Educational Resource Center.

American Association for State and Local History
1400 Eight Avenue South
Nashville, TN 37203
Publications, technical leaflets, slide and tape presentations on all areas of museum management, interpretation and collections.

American Association of Museums
1225 Eye St., NW, #200 t.,
Washington, DC 20005
Publications.

Anacostia Neighborhood Museum
Smithsonian Institution
2405 Martin Luther King Blvd., S.E.
Washington, DC 20020
Workbooks and kits: topics range from Kawanzaa festival to creating a museum in the classroom.

Appalachian Museum
Berea College
CPO Box 2298
Berea, KY 40404
Slide/tape programs of the dying Appalachian folk processes such as building a log cabin, making a rocking chair, and many others.

Apprenticeshop
375 Front St.
Bath, ME 04530
History of the Apprenticeship program on slides.

Association of Science-Technology Centers
1413 K St., NW, Tenth Fl.
Washington, DC 20005
Publications, exhibitions, and educational resources.

Arizona Historical Society
949 East 2nd St.
Tucson, AZ 85719
Slide and video resources, artifact trunks on the settlement of Arizona, mining and cowboy life and other topics.

Baltimore Museum of Art
Art Museum Drive
Baltimore, MD 21218
Slides and teacher guides on landscapes, portraiture and other topics used in the previsit programs.

Brockton Art Museum
Oak St.
Brockton, MA 02401
Publications and slide resources available on museum education and their programs.

Brooklyn Museum
188 Eastern Parkway
Brooklyn, NY 11238
Films such as "Statues Hardly Ever Smile," on the Egyptian collections and other loan materials.

Buffalo and Erie County Historical Society
25 Nottingham Court
Buffalo, NY 14216
Kits and classroom aids on topics of Western New York history.

Buffalo Museum of Science
Humboldt Parkway
Buffalo, NY 14211
Loan services including films, filmstrips, slide sets, and loan kits on different cultures and all areas of natural science.

Carnegie Museum of Art
4400 Forbes Ave.
Pittsburgh, PA 15213
Publications and curriculum guides on the ARTEXPRESS programs.

Carnegie Museum of Natural History
4400 Forbes Ave.
Pittsburgh, PA 15213
Catalogue of the collection of 2,000 items of natural history, taxidermy mounts and museum specimens.

CEMREL Aesthetic Education Program
3120 59th St.
St. Louis, MO 63139
Teacher and student workbooks, resources, exhibits and curriculum materials in aesthetic education and the humanities.

Children's Museum
300 Congress St.
Museum Wharf
Boston, MA 02210
Rentals lists of educational kits, activity units and curriculum units.

The Children's Museum
931 Bannock St.
Denver, CO 80204
Traveling exhibitions and products that deal with topics such as the handicapped, movies, and others.

Children's Museum
67 E. Kirby
Detroit, MI 48202
Picture portfolios and teacher guides on African cultures, Native American architecture, arts and costumes.

Children's Museum The Resource Center Catalogue
3000 N. Meridian St.
Indianapolis, IN 46208
Resource Center offerings in more than 60 subject areas including portable exhibits, charts, kits.

Sterling and Francine Clark Art Institute
Williamstown, MA 02167
Slide/tape programs such as "Winslow Homer at the Clark," written and narrated by Lloyd Goodrich, and videotapes on children's programs.

Cleveland Health Education Museum
8911 Euclid Ave.
Cleveland, OH 44106
Educational programs and resources on health education activities.

Cleveland Museum of Art
11150 East Blvd.
Cleveland, OH 44106
Slide programs on the collection, developed for teachers.

Cleveland Museum of Natural History
Wade Oval, University Circle
Cleveland, OH 44106
Publisher of *The Explorer* magazine, a membership benefit for 23 natural history museums; other teaching resources and other related programs.

Colonial Williamsburg Foundation
Williamsburg, VA 23185
Slide/tapes, films for docent-training in crafts and on the collections.

Cultural Education Collaborative
164 Newbury St.
Boston, MA 02116
Publications available describing the Collaborative, its partnership with schools and museums and its programs.

Delaware Art Museum
2301 Kentmere Parkway
Wilmington, DE 19806
Resources produced for children such as "Artists in Wilmington, a Discovery Sketchbook."

Denver Museum of Natural History
City Park
Denver, CO 80205
Loan materials and kits that focus on the role of animals in the environment.

Detroit Institute of Arts
5200 Woodward Ave.
Detroit, MI 48202
State-wide loan programs including traveling exhibitions, portfolios of reproductions and slides.

El Paso Department of Museums
1211 Montana
El Paso, TX 79902
Audio-visual resources for the "On the Road" program, slide presentations complementing the collections of the city's museums: El Paso Museum of Art, Museum of History and Wilderness Park.

The Exploratorium
3601 Lyon St.
San Francisco, CA 94123
Publications, teaching materials and the "recipe" book for the Exploratorium's exhibits.

Fernbank Science Center
156 Heaton Park Dr., N.E.
Atlanta, GA 30307
Catalogue of classes and publications on natural and physical sciences.

Field Museum of Natural History
Roosevelt Road and Lake Shore Dr.
Chicago, IL 60605
Loan materials relating to the collection, including discovery units and loan kits.

The Fine Arts Museum of San Francisco The deYoung Museum Art School
Golden Gate Park
San Francisco, CA 94118
Films, slides, videotapes on processes of lithography, paper conservation, pottery, careers in museum education.

The Franklin Institute Science Museum
20th St. and Benjamin Franklin Parkway
Philadelphia, PA 19103
Science enrichment activities such as perception, papermaking, that illustrate science experiments to do at home or in class.

G.A.M.E. (Growth through Art and Museum Experiences)
Manhattan Laboratory Museum
314 West 54th St.
New York, NY 10019
Publications that utilize museum collections in the classrooms.

Grand Rapids Public Museum
54 Jefferson, S.E.
Grand Rapids, MI 49503
Educational loan services, materials including slides, mounted specimens, dioramas, etc.

Greenfield Village and Henry Ford Museum
Educational Resources
  Division
Dearborn, MI 48121
Film strips and study guides on 19th-century life as it relates to the museum's collections including automobiles, schoolhouses and more.

Greenville Country Museum of Art
420 College St.
Greenville, SC 29601
Video and slide resources; special collection on Wyeth.

Solomon R. Guggenheim Museum
Learning to Read Through
  the Arts Programs, Inc.
1071 Fifth Ave.
New York, NY 10028
Publications include reports, evaluation studies and curriculum materials that document the Learning to Read Through the Arts Program.

The Hagley Museum
Box 3630
Greenville, DE 19807
Loan kits and teacher resources and pamphlets on water power and the energy it produces.

Herbert F. Johnson Museum of Art
Cornell University
Ithaca, NY 14853
"Museum in the Schools," a video documentary of the program that connects the resources of the museum to the school curriculum.

High Museum of Art
1280 Peachtree St. N.W.
Atlanta, GA 30309
Educational resources such as kits on spaces and illusion, and docent publications.

The Houston Zoological Gardens
P.O. Box 1562
Houston, TX 77001
Slide units on the animal collections and comparisons between the species.

Honolulu Academy of Arts
900 South Beretania St.
Honolulu, HI 96814
Lending collections, slide sets and extension services for the state.

The Hunter Museum of Art
10 Bluff View
Chattanooga, TN 37403
Illustrated children's book, "Bluff and the Magic Mansion."

Idaho Historical Society
610 N. Julia Davis Dr.
Boise, ID 93706
Educational resources for teachers and students on the history, events, people and geography of the state; *Prospector* and other magazines coordinated with the Junior Historian Program.

Indianapolis Museum of Art
1330 W. 38th St.
Indianapolis, IN 46208
Films produced by the museum including "Art Now On," loan kits, and slides.

Jefferson National Expansion Memorial
11 N. Fourth St.
St. Louis, MO 63102
Learning packages of slides and resource materials on American history and the westward movements.

The Jewish Museum
1109 Fifth Ave.
New York, NY 10028
Resource units with slides, photographs, loan kits and canvas bags with resources on immigration, and archeology.

Lawrence Hall of Science
University of California
Centennial Blvd.
Berkeley, CA 94720
Curriculum units, games, puzzles and other resources that can be used to teach science concepts, including OBIS, HAP, SAVI and others.

Living History Farms
R.R. 1
Des Moines, IA 50322
Teacher guides and other printed materials on family living, community living, and food production.

Louisville Zoological Garden
110 Trevilian Way
Louisville, KY 40213
Self guides, teacher and student guides and games for K-12, including observation, classification, and ecological and endangered species topics.

Metropolitan Museum of Art
Education Department
82nd and Fifth Ave.
New York, NY 10028
Slide kits, curriculum materials, picture sets and videotapes available on such topics as armor, unicorn tapestries, Monet, Islamic art.

The Milwaukee Art Center
750 N. Lincoln Memorial Dr.
Milwaukee, WI 53202
Traveling exhibitions, loan kits, slides films, and videotapes on architecture, American Indian art, fibers, modern art.

Milwaukee Public Museum
800 W. Wells St.
Milwaukee, WI 53233
Films, slides, loan kits and other educational resources.

Minneapolis Art Institute
2400 Third Ave. S.
Minneapolis, MN 55404
Loan exhibits, portfolios, slide sets on portraiture, the family of man, the collection, and a humanities curriculum, "Art and Human Values."

Minnesota Historical Society
240 Summit Ave.
St. Paul, MN 55102
Educational services including resource units, slides, traveling exhibitions.

Museum of African Art
Smithsonian Institution
Washington, DC 20560
Catalogue of the Eliot Elisofon Archives of the museum includes color slides, black-and-white photographs and films on all aspects of African art, culture and environment, both traditional and modern.

Museum of the City of New York
Fifth Ave. at 103rd St.
New York, NY 10029
Publications such as *Short History of East Harlem*, special exhibits, and audio-visual programs such as *The Big Apple*.

231

Museum of Fine Arts
Huntington Ave.
Boston, MA 02116
Videotapes from the "Eye to Eye" series, and printed resources on the collection for the handicapped.

The Museum of Modern Art
11 West 53rd St.
New York, NY 10019
Circulating films, slide sets and reproductions of paintings available to city schools.

Museum of New Mexico
P.O. Box 2087
Santa Fe, NM 87503
Loan exhibits and bilingual audio-visual packages illustrating the various lifestyles, arts and history of New Mexico cultures.

Museum of Northern Arizona
Route 4, Box 720
Flagstaff, AZ 86001
"Thieves of Time," (3/4" color videotape program) exposes the problems of pot-hunting to the general public; "Museum Backroom" (3/4" color videotape) introduces children to the basic concepts of the natural sciences and to the people who work behind the scenes in museums.

Museum of Science and Industry
57th St. at Lake Shore Dr.
Chicago, IL 60637
Teacher guides, self-guided materials for "3-2-1 CONTACT," programs, and events coordinated with the museum's exhibits in all areas of science and technology.

National Archives and Records Service
Washington, DC 20408
Supplemental teaching units on World War I, Great Depression, New Deal, and World War II, available from the Social Issues Resources Series, Inc., P.O. Box 2507, Boca Raton, FL 33432.

National Audio-Visual Center
General Services Administration
Washington, DC 20409
"Museums: Where Fun is Learning," a 16mm film showing children participating actively in museum lessons: stalking dinosaurs, sculpting noses and rubbing snake skins.

National Gallery of Art
Extension Service
Washington, DC 20565
Slide, film and video programs available on the collections, seasonal topics, special exhibitions, and technical aspects of art.

National Museum of American History
Smithsonian Institution
14th and Constitution, N.W.
Washington, DC 20560
Slides, cassettes, and teacher guides on the Afro-American traditions in decorative arts, Buckaroos and more.

New England Aquarium
Central Wharf
Boston, MA 02110
Slide presentations on the aquarium and multimedia kits on tidepool animals.

New Jersey Historical Society
230 Broadway
Newark, NJ 07104
Outreach programs and resources.

New Orleans Museum of Art
P.O. Box 19123
New Orleans, LA 70179
Publications and programs available for training docents, including *Watermelon*, a resource handbook for training volunteers, docent guides and other educational materials and catalogues.

The Oakland Museum Department of Special Exhibits and Education
1000 Oak St.
Oakland, CA 94607
Suitcase exhibits and loan materials in art, history, and natural history.

Office of Elementary and Secondary Education
Smithsonian Institution
Arts & Industries Bldg.
Washington, DC 20560
Publishes "Art to Zoo," and a film "Museums: Where Learning is Fun" illustrating a variety of participatory learning activities in a museum.

Office of Museum Programs Arts and Industries Bldg.
Smithsonian Institution
Washington, DC 20560
Videotapes such as "The Docent Doesn't," a dramatization of an "awful" school tour, for use in training docents, and other audio-visual materials.

Office of Museum Programs Division of Curriculum Services
Educational Services Bldg.
640 North Emporia
Wichita, KS 67214
Exhibits and resource materials available to schools covering topics in art, history and science.

Old Economy Village
14th and Church Sts.
Ambridge, PA 15003
Slide lectures on the pioneer kitchen, the cooper's craft and the history of lighting devices.

Old Sturbridge Village
Museum Education Dept.
Sturbridge, MA 01566
A catalogue, "Family, Work, Community-Museum Education Catalogue of Teaching Materials," ($2), includes background papers, key resource packets with documents, and supplementary media resources.

Ontario Science Center
770 Don Mills Road
Toronto, Ontario, Canada
Loan kits dealing with evolution, science and natural sciences.

Pacific Science Center
200 2nd Ave. N.
Seattle, WA 98109
Slides, tapes, and other resources for various curriculum projects, including ORCA, archeology, and others.

Peabody Museum of Salem
East India Square
Salem, MA 01970
Educational services and programs for schools including gifted and handicapped, and covering topics from whales to volcanoes.

Peninsula Nature and Science Center
524 N. Clyde Morris Blvd.
Newport News, VA 23601
Printed teacher resource kits for the educational programs.

Philadelphia Museum of Art
P.O. Box 7646
Philadelphia, PA 19101
Slides, teaching resources, activity booklets, loan kits and reproductions on artists in the collection, mythology, French art, Baroque tapestries.

John and Mable Ringling Museum of Art
Education Division
P.O. Box 1838
Sarasota, FL 33578
School programs with goals, program outlines and teaching strategies, K-6.

Roger Williams Park Zoo
Providence, RI 02905
Publications for students and teachers: *Zoo Animals and You*, and *Rhode Island's Waterworld*.

Santa Barbara Museum of Art
1130 State St.
Santa Barbara, CA 93101
Reproduction portfolios for school and handbooks on the permanent collection.

San Diego Zoo
Education Division
P.O. Box 551
San Diego, CA 92112
Resource materials available to teachers, including study kits, film strips, audio tapes and teacher guides.

Science Museum of Virginia
2500 W. Broad St.
Richmond, VA 23220
Loan materials including one on Mt. St. Helen's with experiments, slides, and volcanic rock and ash.

SITES
Smithsonian Institution
A & I Bldg., Room 2175
Washington, DC 20560
Exhibitions, kits, games, children's books, catalogues and posters.

The George Walter Vincent Smith Art Museum
222 State St.
Springfield, MA 01103
Publications on the Arts Infusion Project and self guides used in the permanent collections.

Skirball Museum
3077 University Ave.
Los Angeles, CA 90007
Multimedia kits on immigration, celebration, the Torah and archeology, including artifacts, films, written guides and resources.

Smithsonian Institution Office of Printing and Photographic Services
Washington, DC 20560
Slide kits including cassette tape on the collections, such as pandas, first ladies' gowns, "A Nation of Nations," George Catlin and more.

Spencer Museum of Art
The University of Kansas
Lawrence, KS 66045
Portfolios and slides with teacher guides, artful boxes, on the museum's collections, "Space: Inside Out," and architecture.

John G. Shedd Aquarium
1200 S. Lake Shore Dr.
Chicago, IL 60605
A catalogue, "The Marine Resources List," of aquatic science materials including self guides, puzzle kits, audio-visual unit and bibliographies on fish, animals and the lake shore environment.

The St. Louis Art Museum
Forest Park
St. Louis, MO 63110
Slide kits available to teachers on topics such as American art, Chinese art, and myths and mythology.

State Historical Society of Wisconsin
816 State St.
Madison, WI 53706
Educational services and loan programs for students and teachers covering a range of topics on state history; publication of *Badger History*, a quarterly for children in elementary schools.

Superintendent of Documents
Government Printing Office
Washington, DC 20402
Publications produced by federal agencies and museums such as the National Portrait Gallery, NEA, NEH, etc.

Turkey Run Farm
George Washington
  Memorial Parkway
McLean, VA 22101
Resource packets and loan materials focusing on the senses and relating to the farm such as sewing, farm products, and clothing.

Vermont Historical Society
Pavilion Bldg.
109 State St.
Montpelier, VT 05602
Educational materials including publications, kits, films and slides on Vermont history for use by teachers.

Wadsworth Atheneum
600 Main St.
Hartford, CT 06106
Catalogues published for The Lion's Gallery of the Senses, listing of slide programs, including *Insights: The Visual Arts in American History*, and 200 slides analyzing art and artifacts in American history.

Worcester Art Museum
Education Department
55 Salisbury St.
Worcester, MA 01608
Teacher training programs.

Zoological Society of Cincinnati
3400 Vine St.
Cincinnati, OH 45220
Self guides, teacher and student materials, and programs available at the zoo including endangered species, observation and identification game.

18. RESOURCE ORGANIZATIONS

There are numerous professional organizations, information bureaus and federal agencies that support museums and their educational activities. The following is a very *selected listing* of the major organizations and agencies that might be of assistance to you. Important reference books have been cited to aid the reader interested in more information and to locate additional contacts.

Museum Associations

African American Museums Association
P.O. Box 50061
Washington, DC 20004

American Association for State and Local History
1400 8th Ave. S.
Nashville, TN 37203

American Association of Botanical Gardens and Arboreta
Horticulture Department
Box 3530, New Mexico State University
Las Cruces, NM 88003

American Association of Museums
1225 Eye St., NW, #200
Washington, DC 20005

American Association of Youth Museums
70 P St.
Salt Lake City, UT 84103

American Association of Zoological Parks and Aquariums
Oglebay Park
Wheeling, WV 26003

Association of Science-Technology Centers
1413 K St., NW, Tenth Fl.
Washington, DC 20005

International Council of Museums
Maison de L'Unesco
1 Rue Miollis, F - 75015
Paris, France

International Council of Museums (ICOM)
Committee of the AAM
1225 Eye St., NW, #200
Washington, DC 20005

National Park Service/Division of Museum Services
Harpers Ferry Center
Harpers Ferry, WV 25425

Natural Science for Youth Foundation
763 Silvermine Road
New Canaan, CT 06840

WAAM-The Art Museum Association
270 Sutter Street
San Francisco, CA 94108

Major Museum Education Committees and Organizations

American Association of Museums
Standing Professional Committee on Education
1225 Eye St., NW, #200
Washington, DC 20005

Contact regional representatives of the committee for lists of state and local education committees and roundtables where they exist.

Cultural Education Collaborative
59 Temple Pl., #552
Boston, MA 02111

International Society of Planetarium Educators, Inc.
Strasenburgh Planetarium of the Rochester Museum and Science Center
663 East Ave.
Rochester, NY 14603

Museums Collaborative, Inc.
15 Gramercy Park, S.
New York, NY 10003

Museum Education Round Table
P.O. Box 8561
Rockville, MD 20856

Museum Reference Center (resource information only)
Office of Museum Programs
A & I Building, Room 2235
Smithsonian Institution
Washington, DC 20560

Note: For a more detailed listing, consult the American Association of Museums, which has published a *Guide to Museum-Related Resource Organizations,* 1978, which includes information on the state cultural bureaus and arts commissions, major federal agencies awarding grants to museums, and nonprofit organizations of direct interest to the profession including national, regional, and state museum organizations.

Major Educational Associations

The Association for Educational Communications and Technology
1126 16th St., N.W.
Washington, DC 20036

National Art Education Association
1916 Association Drive
Reston, VA 22091

National Association of Educational Broadcasters
1346 Connecticut Ave., N.W.
Washington, DC 20036

National Council for the Social Studies
3501 Newark St. NW
Washington, DC 20016

National Education Association
1201 16th St., N.W.
Washington, DC 20036

National Science Teachers Association
1742 Connecticut Ave., N.W.
Washington, DC 20009

Note: Consult the National Education Assocation for a list of additional educational associations in the various fields and disciplines.

Major Federal Agencies Funding Museums

Institute of Museum Services
1100 Pennsylvania Ave.
Washington, DC 20506

National Endowment for the Arts
1100 Pennsylvania Ave.
Washington, DC 20506

National Endowment for the Humanities
1100 Pennsylvania Ave.
Washington, DC 20506

National Museum Act
Office of Museum Programs
Smithsonian Institution
Washington, DC 20560

National Science Foundation
1800 G St. N.W.
Washington, DC 20550

National Trust for Historic Preservation
1785 Massachusetts Ave., NW
Washington, DC 20202

Department of Education
400 Maryland Ave., S.W.
Washington, DC 20202

Note: Consult the *Cultural Directory II: Federal Funds and Services for the Arts and Humanities,* for more information on other agencies and for detailed information on the programs in these agencies.

Major Sources of Information on Corporate and Foundation Support

American Council for the Arts
570 Seventh Ave.
New York, NY 10018

Business Committee for the Arts, Inc.
1700 Broadway, Fifth Floor
New York, NY 10019

Foundation Center
888 Seventh Ave.
New York, NY 10019
Regional offices located in major cities.

Grantsmanship Center
1015 W. Olympic Blvd.
Los Angeles, CA 90015

19.
FILM PRODUCERS AND DISTRIBUTORS

The following list has been compiled from the recommendations of museum professionals. Listings marked with a (*) were highly recommended by a number of professionals.

Acorn Films
33 Union Square West
New York, NY 10003

American Crafts Council
Research and Education
   Department
29 W. 53rd St.
New York, NY 10019

American Handicrafts Company
83 W. Van Buren St.
Chicago, IL 60605

Arco Embassy Picture Corporation
1301 Avenue of the Americas
New York, NY 10019

Audio Visual Center
Indiana University
Bloomington, IN 47401

* B.F.A. Educational Media
(Columbia Broadcasting System)
2211 Michigan Ave.
Santa Monica, CA 90404

Boston University Film Library
765 Commonwealth Ave.
Boston, MA 02215

British Information Services
30 Rockefeller Plaza
New York, NY 10020

Canadian Center for Films on Art
P.O. Box / CP 457
Ottawa, Ont., Canada

Center for Mass Communication of Columbia University Press
562 W. 113th St.
New York, NY 10025

Center for Southern Folklore
1216 Peabody Ave.
P.O. Box 4081
Memphis, TN 38104

Cinema 5, 16 MM
595 Madison Ave.
New York, NY 10022

Classic Film Museum
4 Union Square
Dover-Foxcroft, ME 04426

Contemporary Films, Inc.
330 W. 42nd St.
New York, NY 10036

Contemporary Films/McGraw-Hill
Princeton Road
Highstown, NJ 08520

Creative Film Society
7237 Canby Ave.
Reseda, CA 91350

* Ealing Corporation
2225 Massachusetts Ave.
Cambridge, MA 02140

* Educational Film Library Association
43 W. 61st St.
New York, NY 10023

* Encyclopaedia Britannica Educational Corporation
425 N. Michigan
Chicago, IL 60611

Entertainment Films
℅ The Film Scene
1 Beekman Place
New York, NY 10038

F.A.C.S.E.A.
(French-American Cultural Services)
927 Fifth Ave.
New York, NY 10022

The Film Center
915 12th St., N.W.
Washington, DC 20005

* Film Images
17 W. 60th St.
New York, NY 10023

The Haboush Company
6611 Santa Monica Blvd.
Hollywood, CA 90038

HAF—Alternatives on Film
P.O. Box 22141
San Francisco, CA 94122

* Ideal Picture
3910 Harlem Road
Buffalo, NY 14226

Impact Films
144 Bleecker St.
New York, NY 10012

* International Film Bureau, Inc.
332 S. Michigan Ave.
Chicago, IL 60604

* Janus Films
745 Fifth Ave.
New York, NY 10022

Killiam Collection
Rental Division
6 East 39th St.
New York, NY 10016

* Library of Congress
  Motion Picture Section
  Attn: David Parker
  Washington, DC 20540

* McGraw-Hill Films
  1121 Avenue of the
    Americas
  New York, NY 10036

* MacMillan Films
  34 MacQuesten Parkway S.
  Mount Vernon, NY 10550

* Media Center for Children,
    Inc.
  3 W. 29th St.
  New York, NY 10001
  (will assist with development of film programs for museums)

  Monument Film Corporation
  43 W. 16th St.
  New York, NY 10011

* Museum at Large, Ltd.
    Films
  157 W. 54th St.
  New York, NY 10019

* Museum of Modern Art
  Department of Film
  11 W. 53rd St.
  New York, NY 10019

  Museum Without Walls
  Universal City Studios, Inc.
  221 Park Ave. S.
  New York, NY 10003

* National Audio Visual
    Center
  General Services Administration
  Washington, DC 20409

  National Cinema Service
  333 W. 57th St.
  New York, NY 10019

* National Film Board of Canada
  1251 Avenue of the Americas
  New York, NY 10020

  National Film Service
  14 Glenwood Ave.
  Raleigh, NC 27602

* National Geographic Educational Services
  17 and M Streets, N.W.
  Washington, DC 20036

* NBC Educational Enterprises
  30 Rockefeller Plaza
  New York, NY 10020

  New Day Films
  P.O. Box 315
  Franklin Lakes, NJ 07417

  Odeon Films
  1619 Broadway
  New York, NY 10019

  Pennebaker, Inc.
  56 W. 45th St.
  New York, NY 10036

  Perspective Films
  369 W. Erie St.
  Chicago, IL 60610

* Pyramid Films
  Box 1048
  Santa Monica, CA 90406

  Roger Larson's Young Filmmaker's Foundation
  4 Rivington St.
  New York, NY 10002

  Roninfilms
  43 W. 61st St.
  New York, NY 10023

* Serious Business Co.
  1145 Mandana Blvd.
  Oakland, CA 94610

  Sterling Educational Films
  241 E. 34th St.
  New York, NY 10016

* Time-Life Films
  43 W. 16th St.
  New York, NY 10011

  Tricontinental Film Center
  P.O. Box 4430
  Berkeley, CA 94704

  University of Illinois
  Visual Aids Service
  704 S. 6th St.
  Champaign, IL 61820

  Westcoast Films
  25 Lusk St.
  San Francisco, CA 94107

  Walter Reade 16
  241 E. 34th St.
  New York, NY 10016

* Xerox Films
  245 Long Hill Road
  Middleton, CT 06457

* Yellow Ball Workshop
  62 Tarbell Ave.
  Lexington, MA 02173

20. SELECTED PERIODICALS

The following list of periodicals have been useful to museum professionals and includes educational, foundation, media and museum journals.

AAZPA Newsletter. Oglebay Park, Wheeling, WV 26003.

American Arts. American Council for the Arts, 570 Seventh Ave. New York, NY 10018

American Education. U.S. Government Printing Office, Washington, DC 20402

Art and Man. Scholastica Magazine, 902 Sylvian Ave. Englewood Cliffs, NJ, 07632. (published cooperatively with the National Gallery of Art).

Art Teacher. National Art Education Association, 1916 Association Drive, Reston, VA 22091.

ASTC Newsletter. Association of Science-Technology Centers, 1413 K St., NW, Tenth Floor, Washington, DC 20005.

Audiovisual Instruction and *Educational Communication and Technology: A Journal of Theory, Research and Development.* The Association for Educational Communications and Technology, 1126 16th St., N.W., Washington, DC 20036.

Aviso. American Association of Museum, 1225 Eye St., NW, #200, Washington, DC 20005.

Bank Street College of Education. 610 W. 112th St., New York, NY 10025.

BCA News. Business Committee on the Arts, Inc. 1700 Broadway, New York, NY 10019

Childhood Education. Association for Childhood Education International, 3615 Wisconsin Ave., N.W. Washington, DC 20016

Cultural Post. The National Endowment for the Arts, U.S. Government Printing Office, Washington, DC 20402.

Curator. The American Museum of Natural History, Central Park West at 79th St., New York, NY 10024.

Current Index to Journals in Education. New York: MacMillan Information.

Educational Change Magazine. Educational Change, Inc., N B W Tower, New Rochelle, NY 10801.

The Educational Forum. 121 Ramseyer Hall, 19 W. Woodruff Ave., Columbus, OH 43210.

Educational Leadership. National Education Association, 1201 16th St., N.W., Washington, DC 20036.

Eric Search. University of Minnesota Education Library, Minneapolis, MN 55455. (Index search service to educational resources.)

Foundation News. 888 Seventh Ave., New York, NY 10019.

Government and the Arts. Fraser Barron, 1054 Potomac St., N.W. Washington, DC 20007.

Grantsmanship Center News. Grantsmanship Center, 1031 S. Grand View Los Angeles, CA 90015.

Harvard Business Review. Harvard University, Cambridge, MA 02138.

Harvard Educational Review. Longfellow Hall, 13 Appian Way, Cambridge, MA 02138.

Historic Preservation. National Trust for Historic Preservation. 1785 Massachusetts Ave., NW, Washington, DC 20006.

History News. American Association for State and Local History, 1400 Eighth Ave., Nashville, TN 37203.

The History Teacher. Society for History Education, California State University, Long Beach, CA 90840.

Humanities. The National Endowment for the Humanities, U.S. Government Printing Office, Washington, DC 20402.

ICOM. (International Council of Museums Quarterly), 1225 Eye St., NW, #200, Washington, DC 20005.

Intermedia. 2431 Echo Park Ave., Los Angeles, CA 90026. (A quarterly interdisciplinary journal of arts, resources and communications.)

Learning. (The Magazine for Creative Teaching). Education Today Center, 530 University Ave., Palo Alto, CA 94301.

Mosaic. The National Science Foundation, 1800 G St., N.W., Washington, DC 20550.

Museum News. American Association of Museums, 1225 Eye St., NW, #200, Washington, DC 20005.

Museums. International Council on Museums, UNESCO House, Paris, France. (Available With ICOM membership from ICOM/AAM.)

The National Information Center of Educational Media. A User's Primer. University of Southern California, University Park, Los Angeles, CA 90007. (Index to nonbook educational resources.)

Preservation News. National Trust for Historic Preservation, 1785 Massachusetts Ave., NW, Washington, DC 20006.

Public Telecommunications Review. National Association of Educational Broadcasters, 1346 Connecticut Ave. N.W., Washington, DC 20036.

R.F. Illustrated. The Rockefeller Foundation, 1133 Avenue of the Americas, New York, NY 10036.

Roundtable Reports. Museum Education Roundtable and the AAM Standing Professional Committee on Education.

School and Society. (Journal of Educational Affairs). 1860 Broadway, New York, NY 10023.

Science and Children and *The Science Teacher.* National Science Teachers Association, 1742 Connecticut Ave. N.W., Washington, DC 20009.

Social Education. National Council of Social Studies, 3615 Wisconsin Ave. N.W., Washington, DC 20016.

The Social Studies. Heldref Publications, 4000 Albermarle St. N.W., Washington, DC 20016. (Bimonthly periodical containing articles of interest for elementary and secondary social studies teachers and administrators.)

Today's Education. National Education Association, 1201 16th St. N.W., Washington DC 20036.

Trends. Division of Federal, State and Private Liaison, National Park Service, Washington DC 20240.

Washington International Arts Letter. P.O. Box 9005, Washington DC 20003.

21. BIBLIOGRAPHIES

ADMINISTRATION: INCLUDING MANAGEMENT, LAW, TRUSTEES

Ahmanson, Caroline. "Trustees and Directors," *Museum News,* 50 (September 1971), pp. 35-36.

Alexander, Edward P. *The Museum: A Living Book of History.* Detroit: Wayne State University Press, 1959.

———. *Museums in Motion.* Nashville: American Association for State and Local History, 1979.

Alinsky, Saul. "Citizen Participation and Community Organization in Planning and Urban Renewal." In *Strategies of Community Organization: A Book of Readings.* Itasca, Illinois: F. E. Peacock, 1970.

American Anthropological Association. *Professional Ethics: Statements and Procedures of the AAA.* Washington: American Anthropological Association, 1973.

American Association of Museums. *Accreditation: Professional Standards.* H. J. Swinney, ed. Washington: American Association of Museums, 1978.

———. *America's Museums: The Belmont Report.* Washington: American Association of Museums, 1969.

———. *Museum Accounting Handbook.* Washington: American Association of Museums, 1978.

———. *Museum Accreditation: A Report to the Profession.* Washington: American Association of Museums, 1970.

———. *Museum Ethics.* Washington: American Association of Museums, 1978.

———. *The Official Museum Directory, 1980-81.* Skokie: Illinois, National Register Publishing Company, 1980.

American Council for the Arts. *Community Arts Agencies: A Handbook and Guide.* New York: American Council for the Arts, 1978.

American Law Institute/American Bar Association. *Course of Study Transcripts: Legal Proglems of Museum Administration, 1973-1975.* Philadelphia: ALI-ABA, 1976.

Anderson, Linda, and Marcia R. Collins. *Libraries for Small Museums.* Columbia, Missouri: Museum of Anthropology, University of Missouri, 1976. No. 4 of Miscellaneous Publications in Anthropology.

Arts Programming and Promotion Seminar References. Oakland: Western Association of Art Museums, 1976.

Associated Councils of the Arts. *Americans and the Arts.* New York: Associated Councils of the Arts, 1976.

Borst, Diane. *Managing Nonprofit Organizations.* New York: AMACOM, a division of American Management Associations, 1977.

Burcaw, G. Ellis. *Introduction to Museum Work.* Nashville: American Association for State and Local History, 1976.

Burt, Nathaniel. *Palaces for the People.* Boston: Little-Brown, 1977.

Creigh, Dorothy Weyer. *A Primer for Local Historical Societies.* Nashville: American Association for State and Local History, 1976.

Cultural Directory: Guide to Federal Funds and Services and Cultural Activities. New York: American Councils of the Arts, 1975.

Danilov, Victor J. *Museum Accounting Guidelines.* Washington, D.C.: Association of Science-Technology Centers, 1976.

———. *Starting A Science Center.* Washington, D.C.: Association of Science-Technology Centers, 1977.

Drucker, Peter. *Management: Tasks, Responsibilities, Practices.* New York: Harper & Row Publishers, 1974.

Educational Facilities Laboratories. *Technical Assistance for Arts Facilities: A Source Book.* New York: Educational Facilities Laboratories, 1976.

Endter, Ellen A. "Technical Assistance: How to Get It When You Need It," *Museum News,* 53 (March 1975), p. 33.

Feldman, Franklin, and Stephen E. Weil. *Art Works: Law, Policy, Practice.* New York: Practicing Law Institute, 1974.

Finlay, Ian. *Priceless Heritage: The Future of Museums.* London, Faber and Faber, 1977.

Fitzgerald, Marilyn Hicks. *Museum Accreditation: Professional Standards.* Washington, D.C.: American Association of Museums, 1973.

Gorr, Louis F. "A Museum Management Bibliography: Part I" *Museum News,* 58 (May/June 1980) pp. 71-84.

_____. "A Museum Management Bibliography: Part II" *Museum News,* 58 (July/August 1980), pp. 67-78.

Guthe, Carl E. *The Management of Small History Museums.* Nashville: Association for State and Local History, 1964.

_____. *So You Want a Good Museum.* Washington, D.C.: American Association of Museums, 1973.

Harris, Louis. *American and the Arts.* New York: American Council for the Arts, 1980.

Hudson, Kenneth and Ann Nicholls, eds. *The Directory of World Museums.* New York: Columbia University Press, 1975.

Hudson, Kenneth. *A Social History of Museums: What the Visitors Thought.* Atlantic Highlands, New Jersey: Humanities Press, 1975.

Kimche, Lee. "The AAM Trustee Committee," *Museum News,* 49 (February 1971), pp. 26-30.

Kittleman, James M. "Museum Mismanagement," *Museum News,* 54 (March/April 1976), pp. 44-46.

Lee, Sherman, ed. *On Understanding Art Museums.* Englewood Cliffs: Prentice-Hall, 1975.

Levy, Howard and Lynn Ross-Molloy. *Beginning a Community Museum.* New York: N.Y. Foundation for the Arts, 1975.

Lewis, Richard. *Field Manual for Museums.* Washington: National Park Service, 1976.

Long, Charles J. *Museum Workers' Notebook.* San Antonio: Witte Memorial Museum, 1970.

MacBeath, George, and S. James Gooding, eds. *Basic Museum Management.* Ottawa: Canadian Museums Association, 1969.

Mandl, Cynthia K., and Robert Kerr. "Museum Sponsorship of the Performing Arts," *Museum News,* 53 (June 1975), pp. 24-27.

McGrath, Kyran. "Are Your Trustees Protected?" *Museum News,* 52 (March 1974), p. 36.

_____. "A Landmark Court Decision," *Museum News,* 53 (December 1974), pp. 40-41.

_____. *1973 Museum Salary and Financial Survey.* Washington, D.C.: American Association of Museums, 1973.

McHugh, Alice, "Strategic Planning for Museums," *Museum News,* 58 (July/August, 1980) pp. 23-30.

Museum News, V. 51 (May 1973). Entire issue deals with accessioning procedures and management of collections.

_____. V. 55 (November/December 1976). Entire issue on museum accreditation.

_____. V. 58 (May/June 1980). Entire issue on the future of museums.

_____. V. 58 (July/August 1980). Several articles on federal fund raising.

_____. V. 58 (September/October 1979). Several articles on law.

_____. V. 59 (September/October 1980). Entire issue on adaptive use.

National Endowment for the Arts. *Museums USA: Art, History, Science and Others.* Washington, D.C.: Government Printing Office, 1973.

Naumer, Helmuth J. "Employment Agreement." Unpublished paper, delivered at 1972 meeting of the American Association of Museums.

_____. *Of Mutual Respect and Other Things: An Essay on Trusteeship.* Washington, D.C.: American Association of Museums, 1977.

Neal, Arminta, and Elizabeth, Webb. "Evolving a Policy Manual," *Museum News* 56, (January/February 1978) pp. 26-30.

Newgren, Donald Andrew. *A Standardized Museum Survey: A Methodology for Museums to Gather Decision-Oriented Information.* Ann Arbor: University Microfilms, 1973.

O'Doherty, Brian. *Museums in Crisis.* New York, Braziller, 1972.

ART RESOURCES

Arnheim, Rudolph. *Art and Visual Perception.* Berkeley: University of California Press, 1966.

_____. *Toward a Psychology of Art.* Berkeley: University of California Press, 1972.

_____. *Visual Thinking.* Berkeley: University of California Press, 1969.

Arts Impact: Curriculum for Change. A Summary. Washington, D.C.: Office of Education, 1973.

Arts and the Schools: Patterns for Better Education. Albany: The New York State Commission on Cultural Resources, 1972.

Babcock, Gregory, ed. *New Ideas In Art Education*. New York: E. P. Dutton, 1973.

Bassett, Richard. *The Open Eye in Learning: The Role of Art in General Education*. Cambridge, Massachusetts, MIT Press, 1969.

Berger, John. *Ways of Seeing*. London, England: The British Broadcasting Corporation, and Penguin Books, 1972.

Brodatz, Phillip. *Textures*. New York: Dover, 1974.

Brooking, Dolo. *Art is Me*. Lawrence: University of Kansas Museum of Art, 1974.

CEMREL. *Examining Point of View: Aesthetic Education Program*. New York: Viking, 1973.

Coming to our Senses: The Significance of the Arts for American Education. New York: McGraw-Hill, 1976.

Dewey, John. *Art as Experience*. New York: G.P. Putman's Sons, 1958.

D'Amico, Victor. *Assemblage*. New York: Museum of Modern Art, 1960.

Duchamp, Marcel. "The Creative Act," In *The New Art*, ed. Gregory Babcock. New York: E.P. Dutton, 1966.

Eddy, Junius. *The Upsidedown Curriculum*. New York: Ford Foundation, 1970.

Eisner, E. W. *Educating Artistic Vision*. New York: MacMillan, 1972.

Feldman, Edmund Burke. *Art as Image and Idea*. New York: Prentice-Hall, 1973.

_____. *Becoming Human Through Art*. New York: Prentice-Hall, 1970.

Gardner, Howard and Ellen Winner. "How Children Learn . . . Three Stages of Understanding Art," *Psychology Today*, March 1976.

Hurwitz, Al, and Stanley Madeja. *The Joyous Vision*. Englewood Cliffs: Prentice-Hall, 1977.

Kennet, Frances, and Terry, Measham. *Looking at Paintings*. New York: Van Nostrand and Reinhold Co., 1978.

Laliberte, Norman, and Richey Kehel. *100 Ways to Have Fun With an Alligator*. Blauvelt, New York: Art Education, Inc., 1969.

Lanier, Vincent. "Art and the Disadvantaged," In *New Ideas in Art Education*, ed. Gregory Babcock. New York: E.P. Dutton, 1973, pp. 181-202.

McKim, Robert H. *Experiences in Visual Thinking*. Monterey, California: Brooks/Cole, 1972.

Madeja, Stanley, and Sheila Onuska. *Through the Arts to the Aesthetics*. St. Louis: CEMREL, 1976.

Marcouse, Renee. *Using the Objects: Visual Learning and Visual Awareness in the Museum and Classroom*. New York: Van Nostrand and Reinhold Co., 1974.

Read, Herbert. *Education Through Art*. New York: Pantheon Books, 1956.

Samuels, Mike, and Nancy Samuels. *Seeing with the Mind's Eye*. New York: Random House, 1975.

Shuker, Nancy. *Arts in Education Partners*. New York: Associated Council of the Arts, 1977.

Taylor, Joshua C. *To See is to Think: Looking at American Art*. Washington, D.C.: Smithsonian Press, 1975.

Walker, Percy. *The Message in the Bottle*. New York City: Farrar, Straus and Giroux, Inc., 1975.

Winick, Mariann Pezella. "Value the Child's Eye View," *Art Education*, 27 (March 1974), pp. 8-11.

Parr, Albert E. "Function of Museums: Research Centers or Show Places?" *Curator*, 16, (1963), pp. 20-31.

_____. *Mostly About Museums*. New York, American Museum of Natural History, 1959.

_____. "Museums: Enriching the Urban Milieu," *Museum News*, 56 (March/April 1978), pp. 46-51.

_____. "On Museums and Directors," *Curator*, 16, (December 1973), pp. 281-285.

Prieve, E. Arthur, and Ira W. Allen. *Administration in the Arts: An Annotated Bibliography of Selected References*. Madison: University of Wisconsin-Madison, 1973.

Rath, Frederick L., Jr., and Merrilyn Rogers O'Connell, eds. *A Bibliography on Historical Organization Practices*. Nashville: American Association for State and Local History, (3 vols., 1975, 1977, 1978).

Reiss, Alvin H. *The Arts Management Handbook*. New York: Law-Arts, 1974.

Robbins, Michael W., and Kyran M. McGrath. *America's Museums: The Belmont Report*. Washington, D.C.: The American Association of Museums, 1969.

Royal Ontario Museum. *Communicating with the Museum Visitor: Guidelines for Planning*. Toronto: Royal Ontario Museum, 1976.

Schwabe, Douglas. "Are You an Amateur Administrator?" *Museum News*, 53 (April 1975), pp. 26-29.

Schwartz, Alvin. *Museum: The Story of America's Treasure Houses*. New York: Dutton, 1967.

Silvestro, Clement M. *Organizing a Local Historical Society*. Nashville: American Association for State and Local History, 1975.

Sorenson, Roy. *The Art of Board Membership.* New York: Associated Press, 1950.

Stitt, Susan. "The Search for Equality," *Museum News*, 54 (September/October 1975), pp. 17-23.

"Tax Reform Act of 1969," *Museum News*, 48, (February 1970), pp. 29-30.

Traverso, Daniel, and Cindy Sherrell. *Thoughts on Museum Planning.* Austin: Texas Historical Commission, 1976.

Washburn, Wilcomb. *Defining the Museum's Purpose.* Cooperstown: The New York State Historical Association, 1975.

Weil, Stephen E. "Vincible Ignorance: Museums and the Law," *Museum News*, 58, (September/October 1979), pp. 43-46.

Wittlin, Alma S. *Museums: In Search of a Usable Future* Cambridge, MIT Press, 1970.

COLLECTIONS: INCLUDING CONSERVATION, REGISTRATION, SHIPPING AND SECURITY

Allen, Carl G., and Huntington T. Block, "Should Museums Form a Buyer's Pool for Insurance?" *Museum News*, 52 (March 1974), pp. 32-35.

American Association for State and Local History Technical Leaflets. Nashville: AASLH, 1963.

Association of Art Museum Directors. *Professional Practices in Art Museums.* New York: AAMD, 1971.

Botwinick, Michael, Huntington Block, and John Buchanan. *Shipping, Packing and Insurance.* Washington, D.C.: American Association of Museums, 1978.

Burnham, Bonnie. *The Protection of Cultural Property: A Handbook of National Legislations.* Paris: International Council of Museums, 1974.

Chenhall, Robert G. *Museum Cataloging in the Computer Age.* Nashville: American Association for State and Local History, 1975.

———. *Nomenclature for Museum Cataloging: A System for Classifying Manmade Objects.* Nashville: AASLH, 1978.

Conservation of Collections: Recent Concepts. Moncton, New Brunswick: Canadian Conservation Institute, 1974.

Conservation of the Decorative Arts. Washington: American Association of Museums reprint, 1976.

DuBose, Beverly J. *Insuring Against Loss.* Nashville: American Association for State and Local History, 1969. Technical Leaflet No. 5.

Duckett, Kenneth W. *Modern Manuscripts: A Practical Manual for Their Management, Care and Use.* Nashville: American Association for State and Local History, 1975.

Dudley, Dorothy H. et al. *Museum Registration Methods.* Washington, D.C.: American Association of Museums, September 1979.

Dunn, Walter S. *Storing Your Collections: Problems and Solutions.* Nashville: American Association for State and Local History, 1970. Technical Leaflet No. 5.

Guldbeck, Per E. *The Care of Historical Collections: A Conservation Handbook for the Nonspecialist.* Nashville: American Association for State and Local History, 1972.

Guthe, Carl E. *The Management of Small History Museums.* Nashville: American Association for State and Local History, 1964.

Hill, John I. "A Consumer Guide to Security Systems," *Museum News*, 55 (July/August 1977), pp. 34-37.

Hours, Madelaine. *Conservation and Scientific Analysis of Painting.* Toronto: Van Nostrand, 1976.

Irwin, Howard S. et al. *America's Systematics Collections: A National Plan.* Lawrence, Kansas: Association of Systematics Collections, 1973.

Kansas State Historical Society. *A Suggested Collection Record System for Museums.* Topeka: KSHS, 1974.

Keck, Caroline K. "Conservation's Cloudy Future," *Museum News* 58 (May/June 1980), pp. 35-39.

———. *A Handbook on the Care of Painting.* New York: American Association for State and Local History, 1965.

———. "Instructions for Emergency Treatment of Water Damages." *Newsletter*, O.M.A., v. 3, No. 2 (April 1974), pp. 27-29.

———. "On Conservation," *Museum News* reprint available from American Association of Museums, 1972.

———et al. *A Primer on Museum Security.* Cooperstown, New York: New York State Historical Association, 1966.

Langwell, W. H. *The Conservation of Books and Documents.* London: Sir Isaac Pitman & Sons, 1958.

Leene, J.E., ed. *Textile Conservation.* Washington, D.C.: Smithsonian Institution, 1972.

Lewis, Ralph H. *Manual for Museums.* Washington: National Park Service, 1976.

Museum Forms Book. Austin: Texas Association of Museums, 1980.

Museum News, V. 56 (November/December 1977). Several articles on conservation and costumes.

_____. V. 56 (July/August 1978). Issue has many articles on conservation and registration.

Nicholson, Thomas D. "The Publication of a Statement of Guidelines for the Management of Collections," *Curator*, 17 (June 1974), pp. 81-82.

Pfeffer, Irving, and Daniel Herrick. *Risk Management Manual*. New York: Association of Art Museum Directors, 1974.

Plenderleith, H.J. *The Conservation of Antiques and Works of Art*. London: Oxford University Press, 1966.

Protection of Museum Collections. Boston: National Fire Protection Association, 1974.

Reibel, Daniel B. *Registration Methods for the Small Museum*. Nashville: American Association for State and Local History, 1978.

Rush, Carole E. *Information System for History Museums*. Rochester, New York: Museum Data Bank Committee, 1977.

DIRECTORIES OF MUSEUMS

American Association for State and Local History. *Directory of Historical Societies and Agencies*, 12th edition. Nashville: AASLH, 1978.

American Association of Museums. *The Official Museum Directory*. Washington, D.C., and Skokie, Illinois: The American Association of Museums and National Register Publishing Co., Inc., 1980.

Association of Science-Technology Centers. *Directory of Exhibits at Science and Technology Centers*, comp. Shabtay Levy. Washington, D.C.: Association of Science-Technology Centers, 1977.

_____. *Survey of Educational Programs at Science-Technology Centers*. Washington, D. C.: Association of Science-Technology Centers, 1976.

Exploring Science: A Guide to Contemporary Science and Technology Centers. Washington, D.C.: Association of Science-Technology Centers, 1980.

Berman, Avis. *A Handbook of Museum Related Resource Organizations*. Washington, D.C.: American Association of Museums, 1975.

Catalogue of Federal Education Assistance Programs: An Indexed Guide to the Federal Government's Programs Offering Educational Benefits to American People. Washington, D.C.: U.S. Office of Education, 1974.

Hudson, Kenneth and Ann Nicholls, eds. *The Directory of World Museums*. New York: Columbia University Press, 1975 *Museums of the World, 3rd Revised Edition*. Munich: K.G. Saur Verlag, 1981

Natural Science for Youth Foundation. *Directory of Natural Science Centers*. New Canaan: Natural Science for Youth Foundation, 1979.

Schlebecker, John, and Gale Peterson. *Living Historical Farms Handbook*. Washington, D.C.: Smithsonian Institution Press, 1972.

U.S. Department of Health, Education and Welfare. Office of Education. *Directory of Educational Information Centers*. Washington, D.C.: Government Printing Office, 1969.

Zook, Nicholas. *Museum Villages U.S.A.* Barre, Massachusetts: Barre Publishers, 1971.

Schroder, A. G., *Museum Security: An Inventory of the Problems of Security in Museums and Ways of Achieving Security*. Amsterdam: ICOM, International Committee for Museum Security, 1975.

A Suggested Collection System for Museums. Topeka: Kansas State Historical Society Museum, 1974.

Texas Historical Commission. *Thoughts on Museum Conservation*. Austin: T.H.C. Museum Services Department, 1976.

Tillotson, Robert G. *Museum Security/La Securite dans les Musees*. Washington, D. C.: American Association of Museums, 1977.

Vance, David. *Computers in the Museum*. White Plains, New York: I.B.M., 1973.

_____. *Manual for Museum Computer Network Data Preparation*. Stony Brook, New York: SPECTRA, 1975.

_____. *Manual for Museum Computer Network GRIPHOS Application*. Stony Brook, New York: SPECTRA, 1976.

_____. "Museum Computer Network: Progress Report," *The Museologist*, No. 135 (December 1975), pp. 3-10.

Additional Sources of Information

Conservation Analytical Laboratory, Smithsonian Institution, Museum of History and Technology, Washington, D.C.

Conservation Information Program, Office of Museum Programs, Smithsonian Institution, Arts & Industries Building, Washington, D.C.

American Society for Conservation Archaeology Newsletter, c/o Dept. of Anthropology, University of South Carolina, Columbia, S.C. 29208

Journal of the American Institute for Conservation, American Institute for the Conservation of Historic and Artistic Works, 1522 K Street, N.W., Washington, D.C. 20005

Journal of the Canadian Conservation Institute (CCI), Ottawa, National Museums of Canada, KIA OM8

Studies in Conservation, International Institute for the Conservation of Historic and Artistic Works, London, England WC2 N 5HN

Technology and Conservation, Technology Organization, Emerson Place, Boston, Massachusetts

EDUCATION: PHILOSOPHIES AND METHODOLOGIES

Allen, Rodney F., John V. Fleckenstein, and Peter M. Lyon, eds. *Inquiry in the Social Studies*. Washington, D.C.: National Council for the Social Studies, 1968.

Baker, Katherine. *Ideas That Work with Young Children*. Washington, D.C.: National Association for the Education of Young People, 1973.

Berne, Eric. *Games People Play, The Psychology of Human Relationships*. New York: Grove Press, 1964.

Beyer, Barry K. *Inquiry in the Social Studies Classroom: A Strategy for Teaching*. Columbus: Charles E. Merrill, 1971.

Bloom, Benjamin A., Thomas Hastings, and George Madaus. *Handbook on Formative and Summative Evaluation of Student Learning*. New York: McGraw-Hill, 1971.

_____, _____, and _____, eds. *Taxonomy of Educational Objectives, Handbook I: The Cognitive Domain*. New York: David McKay, 1956.

Boocock, Sarane S., and E.O. Schild, eds. *Simulation Games and Learning*. Beverly Hills: Sage Publications, 1968.

Boorman, Joyce. *Creative Dance in the First Three Grades*. New York: David McKay, 1969.

Bowman, Garda W., and Ray Pecheone. *The Brace System of Interaction Anaylsis as a Tool for Program Analysis*. New York: Bank Street School of Education, 1976.

Boyd, Neva L. *Handbook of Recreational Games*. New York: Dover, 1975.

Brandwein, Paul. *Permanent Agenda of Man: The Humanities, A Tactic and Strategy for Teaching the Humanities in the Elementary Schools*. New York: Harcourt, Brace, Jovanovich, 1971.

Self-Expression and Conduct: The Humanities. New York: Harcourt, Brace, Jovanovich, 1974.

Bruner, Jerome S. *On Knowing: Essays for the Left Hand*. Cambridge: Harvard, University Press 1962.

_____. *The Process of Education*. Cambridge: Harvard, 1966.

_____et. al., *A Study of Thinking*. New York: John Wiley and Sons, Inc., 1961.

_____., *Toward a Theory of Instruction*. Cambridge: The Belknap Press of Harvard University Press, 1966.

Cohen, Dorothy H. *The Learning Child*. New York: Vintage Books, 1973.

Commission Reports on Instructional Technology. *To Improve Learning: An Evaluation of Instructional Technology. Vols. I and II*. Washington, D.C.: Superintendent of Documents, 1971.

Dewey, John. *Experience and Education*. New York: Collier Books, 1938.

Erikson, Erik. *Childhood and Society*. New York: W. W. Norton, 1960.

Featherstone, Joseph. *Schools Where Children Learn*. New York: Liveright Press, 1971.

Fenton, Edwin. *The New Social Studies*. New York: Holt, Rinehart and Winston, 1967.

Flanders, Ned A. *Analyzing Teaching Behavior*. Reading, Massachusetts: Addison-Wesley, 1970.

Fraiberg, Selma. *The Magic Years*. New York: Charles Scribners & Sons, 1959.

Fraenkel, Jack R. *Helping Students to Think and Value: Strategies for Teaching the Social Studies*. Englewood Cliffs: Prentice-Hall, 1973.

Friedenber, Edgar. *The Vanishing Adolescent*. Boston: Beacon Press, 1959.

Fuller, R. Buckminster. *Ideas and Integrities*. New York: Collier, 1969.

Gagne, Robert M. *The Conditions of Learning*. New York: Holt, Rinehart & Winston, 1967.

Getzells, Jacob W., and Philip W. Jackson. *Creative Intelligence*. New York: John Wiley and Sons, 1962.

Ginott, Haim. *Teacher and Child*. New York: Macmillian, 1972.

Goldmark, Bernice. *Social Studies, A Method of Inquiry*. Belmont, California: Wadsworth, 1968.

Goodlad, John I., and M. Frances Klein. *Behind the Classroom Door*. Belmont, California: Wadsworth, 1970.

Gordon, Thomas. *Parent Effectiveness Training*. New York: Peter H. Wyden, Inc., 1970.

Gordon, W.J.J. *The Metaphorical Way of Learning and Knowing*. Cambridge; Porpoise Books, 1973.

Gregory, Richard Langton. *Eye and Brain: The Psychology of Seeing*. New York: McGraw-Hill, 1966.

Hall, Edward T. *The Hidden Dimension*. New York: Anchor Books, Doubleday, 1969.

———. *The Silent Language.* Garden City: Doubleday, 1959.

Herndon, James. *The Way It Spozed to Be.* New York: Simon & Schuster, 1968.

Holt, John. *Freedom and Beyond.* New York: E.P. Dutton, 1972.

———. *How Children Learn.* New York: Pitman, 1967.

Howe, Leland, and Mary Martha Howe. *Personalizing Education: Values Clarification and Beyond.* New York: Hart, 1975.

Hyman, Ronald T. *Ways of Teaching.* New York: J. B. Lippincott, 1974.

Isaacs, Susan. *The Children We Teach, Seven to Eleven Years.* New York: Schocken Books, 1971.

Kepes, Gyorgy. *The Education of Vision.* New York: Braziller, 1965.

———. *The Nature and Art of Motion.* New York: Braziller, 1965.

Kibler, R. J., et al. *Objectives for Instruction and Evaluation.* Boston: Allyn and Bacon, 1974.

Koch, Kenneth. *Rose, Where did you get That Red? Teaching Great Poetry to Children.* New York: Vintage Books, 1974.

———. *Wishes, Lies and Dreams.* New York: Chelsea House, 1970.

Kohl, Herbert. *36 Children.* New York: Signet Books, 1968.

———. *On Teaching.* New York: Schocken Books, 1976.

Laban, Rudolf. *Modern Educational Dance.* New York: Macdonald & Evans, [n.d.]

Lesser, Gerald S. *Children and Television: Lessons from Sesame Street.* New York: Randon House, 1974.

Levinson, Melvin. "Multi-Media Literacy and Learning: A Concept for Teacher Education." In *Concepts in Teacher Education.* Toronto, Ontario: Ontario Teacher's Federation, 1971.

Lippitt, Gordon, Leslie This, and Robert Bidwell. *Optimizing Human Resources.* Reading, Massachusetts: Addison-Wesley, 1971.

Mager, Robert F. *Measuring Instructional Intent.* Belmont, CA: Fearon Publishers, Inc., 1974.

———. *Preparing Educational Objectives.* Palo Alto, CA: Fearon Publishers, Inc., 1975.

———. *Preparing Instructional Objectives.* Palo Alto, CA: Fearon Publishers, Inc., 1962.

Marzollo, Jean, and Janice Lloyd. *Learn Through Play.* New York: Harper and Row, 1972.

Matthai, Robert A., and Neil E. Deaver. "Child-Centered Learning," *Museum News,* 54 (March/April 1976), pp. 15-19.

McLuhan, Herbert Marshall. *Understanding Media: The Extensions of Man.* New York: McGraw-Hill, 1965.

Metcalf, Lawrence E., ed. *Values Education: Rationale, Strategies, and Procedures.* Washington, D.C.: National Council for the Social Studies, 1971. 41st yearbook.

Minuchin, Patricia P. *The Middle Years of Childhood.* Monterey, Calif.: Brooks/Cole, 1977.

Mussen, Conger & Kagan. *Child Development and Personality.* New York: Harper & Row, 1978.

Neill, Alexander Sutherland. *Summerhill: A Radical Approach to Child Rearing.* New York: Hart, 1960.

Opie, Iona & Peter. *Children's Games in Street and Playground.* London: Clarendon Press, 1969.

———. *The Lore and Language of School Children.* Oxford: Oxford University Press, 1959.

Piaget, Jean. *A Child's Conception of the World.* New York: Harcourt, Brace & Co., 1929.

———. *The Essential Piaget.* Edited by H. E. Guber, New York: Basic Books, 1977.

———. *The Origins of Intelligence in Children.* New York: International Universities Press, 1952.

———, and B. Inhelder. *The Psychology of the Child.* New York: Basic Books, 1971.

Postman, Neil. *Teaching as a Conserving Activity.* New York: Delacorte Press, 1979.

———, and Charles Weingartner. *Teaching as a Subversive Activity.* New York: Delacorte, 1969.

Redfern, Betty. *Introducing Laban Art of Movement.* New York: Dance Notation Bureau, Inc., 1965.

Rogers, Carl. *Freedom to Learn, a View of What Education Might Become.* Columbus: Charles E. Merrill, 1969.

Samuels, Mike, and Nancy Samuels. *Seeing with the Mind's Eye: The History, Techniques, and Uses of Visualization.* New York: Random House, 1975.

Sapir, Selma G. & Ann C. Nitzburg. *Children with Learning Problems.* New York: Brunner/Mazel, 1973.

Saxe, Richard W., ed. *Opening the Schools: Alternative Ways of Learning.* Berkeley: McCutchan, 1972.

Shulman, Lee S., and Evan R. Keislar. *Learning by Discovery.* Chicago: Rand McNally, 1966.

Silberman, Charles E. *Crisis in the Classroom, The Remaking of American Education.* New York: Random House, 1970.

———, ed. *The Open Classroom Reader*. New York: Random House, 1973.

Simon, Sidney B., Leland W. Howe, and Howard Kirschenbaum. *Values Clarification: A Handbook of Practical Strategies for Teachers and Students*. New York: Hart, 1972.

Spolin, Viola. *Improvisation for the Theater*. Evanston: Northwestern University Press, 1963.

———. *Theater Game File*. St. Louis: CEMREL, Inc., 1976.

Stake, Robert. *Evaluating the Arts in Education*. New York: Bobbs-Merrill, 1974.

———. ed. *Evaluating the Arts in Education: A Responsive Approach*. Columbus, Ohio: Merrill, 1975.

Stone, L. J. & J. Church. *Childhood and Adolescence*. 4th Ed. New York: Random House, 1979.

Sullivan, Harry S. *The Interpersonal Theory of Psychiatry*. New York: Norton, 1953, pp. 217-227.

Taba, Hilda, Mary Durkin, Jack Frankel, and Anthony McNaughton. *A Teacher's Handbook to Elementary Social Studies: An Inductive Approach*. Reading, Massachusetts: Addison-Wesley, 1971.

Toffler, Alvin, ed. *Learning for Tomorrow: The Role of the Future in Education*. New York: Random House, 1974.

Way, Brian. *Development Through Drama*. London: Longman, 1976.

Webb, Eugene, Donald Cambell, et al. *Unobtrusive Measures: Nonreactive Research in Social Sciences*. Chicago: Rand McNally, 1966.

Wedge, Eleanor. *Nefertiti Graffiti*. New York: Brooklyn Museum, 1976.

Weinstein, Gerald, and Mario D. Fantini. *Toward Humanistic Education—a Curriculum of Affect*. New York: Praeger, 1973.

Whitehead, Alfred North. *The Aims of Education and Other Essays*. New York: McMillan, 1967.

Wilson, John et al. *Psychological Foundations of Learning and Teaching*. New York: McGraw-Hill, 1969.

Wittich, Walter, and Charles Schuller. *Instructional Technology: Nature and Use*. New York: Harper & Row, 1973.

Yarbus, A. L. *Eye Movements and Vision*. New York: Plenum Books, 1967.

EVALUATION: STRATEGIES AND METHODS

Allen, T. Harrell. *New Methods in Social Science Research*. New York: Praeger, 1978.

Anderson, Scarvia B. "Noseprints on the Glass or: How Do We Evaluate Museum Programs?" In *Museums and Education*, ed. E. Larrabee. Washington, D.C.: Smithsonian Press, 1968.

Bayless, John, "Conflicts and Confusion Over Evaluation", *Journal of Education and Recreation*, 49(7): 54-55, September, 1978.

Benjamin, Alfred, *The Helping Interview*, Boston: Houghton Mifflin, Co., 1969.

Benson, Jeri and Linda Crocker, "The Effects of Item Format and Reading Ability on Objective Test Performance: A Question of Validity", *Educational and Psychological Measurement*, 39(2): 381-87, Summer, 1979.

Bloom, B.S., Hastings, J.T., and Madaus, G.F. *Handbook on Formative and Summative Evaluation of Student Learning*. New York: McGraw-Hill Books, Co., 1971.

Bloomberg, Marguerite, "An Experiment in Museum Instruction", Publications of the *American Association of Museums, New Series*, Washington, D.C.: American Association of Museums, 1929.

Borun, Minda, "Exhibit Evaluation: An Introduction", *The Visitor and the Museum*, Washington, D.C.: Museum Educators of the American Association of Museums, 47-73, 1977.

———. *Measuring the Immeasurable: A Pilot Study of Museum Effectiveness*. Washington, D.C.: Association of Science-Technology Centers, 1977.

———. *Museum Effectiveness Study: A Bibliographic Review*. Philadelphia: The Franklin Institute, 1975.

Boulding, Kenneth. *The Image*. Ann Arbor: Ann Arbor Paperbacks, University of Michigan Press, 1961.

Bower, Robert T., Stanley K. Bigman, and S. J. Niefield, *Audience Reaction to Two ICS Cultural Exhibits: Report on the Pre-Test of a Questionnaire*, Washington D.C.: American University, Bureau of Social Science Research, 1954.

Bronfenbrenner, Urie, "The Experimental Ecology of Education", *Educational Researcher*, 5(9): 5-15, October, 1976.

Campbell, Donald T. and Julian C. Stanley, *Experimental and Quasi-Experimental Designs for Research*, Chicago: Rand McNally and Co., 1963.

Campbell, Jeff H. "CLEP Changes Teachers, Too: A Professor Works on Test Development", *The College Board Review*, 108: 20-24, Summer, 1978.

Cross, Lawrence and Robert Frary, "Empirical Choice Weighting Under 'Guess' and 'Do Not Guess' Directions", *Educational and Psychological Measurement,* 38: 613-620, 1978.

Draughon, Margaret, "Ego-building Through Art in a Museum", *Psychological Reports,* April, 1977.

Eason, Laurie, and Alan Friedman. *Star Games: The Pains and Pleasures of Formative Evaluation.* Berkeley: Lawrence Hall of Science, 1976. Unpublished manuscript.

_____, and Marcia Linn. *Effectiveness of Participatory Exhibits: Evaluation of Two Formats for Interactive Optics Exhibits.* Berkeley: Lawrence Hall of Science, 1973. Unpublished manuscript.

_____, and _____. "Evaluation of the Effectiveness of Participatory Exhibits," *Curator,* 19 (March 1976), pp. 45-62.

Ebel, Robert L., "The Role of Testing in Basic Education", *NASSP Bulletin,* 63(429): 89-93, October, 1979.

Elliot, Pamela and Ross J. Loomis, *Studies of Museum Behavior In Museums and Exhibitions: An Annotated Bibliography of Sources Primarily in the English Language,* Washington, D.C.: Smithsonian Institution, 1975.

Foster, M. S., and S. F. Kitch. "Game-Catalogue: An Educational Approach to Exhibition Viewing," *Art Education,* 27 (October 1974), pp. 6-10.

Guba, Egon G. *Toward a Methodology of Naturalistic Inquiry in Educational Evaluation.* Center for the Study of Evaluation Monograph Series in Education, Vol 8. Los Angeles: Center for the Study of Evaluation, 1978.

Linn, Marcia C. "Exhibit Evaluation—Informed Decision Making," *Curator,* 19 (December 1976), pp. 291-302.

Loomis, Ross. "Museums and Psychology: The Principle of Allometry and Museum Visitor Research." Unpublished paper synopsis, of a talk given at the Northeast Museum Conference, November 1973.

_____. "Please! Not Another Visitor Survey," *Museum News,* 52 (October 1973), pp. 21-26.

_____. *Working Papers in Visitor Studies, No. 1.* Denver: Denver Museum of Natural History, 1975.

Ott, Judy. "Learning about 'Neat Stuff' " One Approach to Evaluation," *Museum News,* 58 (November/December 1979), pp. 38-45.

Pelto, Pertti. J. *Anthropological Research: The Structure of Inquiry.* New York: Harper and Row, 1970.

Rich, John. *Interviewing Children and Adolescents.* London: Macmillan, 1968.

Schatzman, Leonard and Anselm Strauss. *Field Research: Strategies for a Natural Sociology.* Englewood Cliffs, New Jersey: Prentice-Hall, Inc., 1973.

Screven, Chandler G. "A Bibliography on Visitor Education Research," *Museum News* 57 (March/April 1979), pp. 56-59.

_____. "The Effectiveness of Guidance Devices on Visitor Learning," *Curator,* 18 (September 1975), pp. 219-243.

_____. "Exhibit Evaluation—A Goal-Referenced Approach," *Curator,* 19 (December 1976), pp. 271-290.

_____. "Learning and Exhibits: Instructional Design," *Museum News,* 52 (January/February 1974), pp. 67-75.

_____. *The Measurement and Facilitation: An Experimental Analysis of Learning in the Museum Environment.* Washington, D.C.: Smithsonian Institution Press, 1974.

_____. "The Museum as a Responsive Learning Environment," *Museum News,* 47 (June 1969), pp. 7-10.

Stake, Robert. *Evaluating the Arts in Education: A Responsive Approach.* . Columbus: Charles E. Merrill, 1974.

Webb, Eugene J., et al. *Unobtrusive Measures: Nonreactive Research in the Social Sciences.* Chicago: Rand McNally, 1966.

Willis, George, ed. *Qualitative Evaluation.* Berkeley: McCutchan, 1978.

Wolf, Robert L. "A Naturalistic View of Evaluation," *Museum News,* 58 (July/August 1980), pp. 39-45.

_____., and Barbara L. Tymitz, *A Preliminary Guide for Conducting Naturalistic Evaluation in Studying Museum Environments.* Washington, D.C.: Office of Museum Programs, Smithsonian Institution, 1977.

_____, *Whatever Happened To The Giant Wombat: An Investigation of The Impact of the Ice Age Mammals and Emergence of Man Exhibit, National Museum of Natural History, Smithsonian Institution.* Washington, D.C.: Smithsonian Institution, May, 1978.

_____, *Do Giraffes Ever Sit?, A Study of Visitor Perceptions At the National Zoological Park, Smithsonian Institution.* Washington, D.C.: Smithsonian Institution, March, 1979.

_____. "East Side, West Side Straight Down the Middle": *A Study of Visitor Perceptions of "Our Changing Land", The Bicentennial Exhibit, National Museum of Natural History, Smithsonian Institution.* Washington, D.C.: Smithsonian Institution, April, 1979.

EXHIBITIONS: PLANNING, DESIGN AND EVALUATION

Anderson, D. C. "Creative Teaching, Temporary Exhibits, and Vitality for the Small Museum," *Curator*, v. 12, No. 3 (September 1969), pp. 180-184.

Arth, Malcolm. "The People Center—Anthropology for the Layman," *Curator*, 18 (December 1975), pp. 315-325.

Borhegyi, Stephan F. de, and Irene Hanson. "Chronological Bibliography of Museum Visitor Surveys," *Museum News*, 42 (February 1964), pp. 39-41.

_____ and _____, eds. *The Museum Visitors: Selected Essays and Surveys of Visitor Reaction to Exhibits in the Milwaukee Public Museum.* Milwaukee: Public Museum, 1968. No. 3 in publications in Museology.

Borun, Minda. *What's In A Name: A Study of the Effectiveness of Explanatory Labels in a Science Museum.* Washington, D.C.: Association of Science-Technology Centers, 1980.

Bowditch, George. "Preparing Your Exhibits: Methods, Materials and Bibliography," *American Association for State and Local History Technical Leaflet No. 4.* Nashville, AASLH, 1969.

Brawne, Michael. *The New Museum: Architecture and Display.* New York: Praeger, 1965.

Cameron, Duncan F. "A Viewpoint: The Museum as a Communications System and Implications for Museum Education," *Curator*, 11, (March 1968), pp. 33-40.

Canadian Museums Association. "Ten Commandments for Museum Exhibitors," *Alberta Museums Review*, 2, (March 1975), p. 27.

Carmel, James H. *Exhibition Techniques: Traveling and Temporary.* New York: Reinhold, 1962.

Casterline, Gail Farr. "Exhibiting Archival Material: Many Faceted Manuscript," *Museum News*, 58, (September/October, 1979), pp. 50-54.

Communicating with the Museum Visitor: Guidelines for Planning. Toronto: Royal Ontario Museum, 1976.

Danilov, Victor. "American's Contemporary Science Museums," *Museums Journal*, 75 (March 1976), pp. 145-148.

Draper, Linda, ed. *The Visitor and the Museum.* Berkeley: Lowie Museum of Anthropology, 1977.

"Educational Role of Science Museums Sparks Debate at ASTC Conference," *Association of Science-Technology Centers Newsletter*, 4, no. 1 (1977), p. 9.

Elliott, Pamela, and Ross J. Loomis. *Studies of Visitor Behavior in Museums and Exhibitions: An Annotated Bibliography of Sources Primarily in the English Language.* Washington, D.C.: Office of Museums Programs, Smithsonian Institution, 1975.

The Exploratorium Cookbook. San Francisco: The Exploratorium, 1977. A manual on how to design and build exhibits like those in the Exploratorium.

Feller, Robert L. "Control of Deteriorating Effects of Light upon Museum Objects," *Museum*, 17 (1964), pp. 57-98.

Gabianelli, Vincent J., and Edward Munyer. "A Place to Learn," *Museum News*, 53 (December 1974), pp. 28-33.

Gleadowe, Teresa. *Organizing Exhibitions: A Manual Outlining the Methods Used to Organize Temporary Exhibitions of Works of Art.* London: Arts Council of Great Britain, 1975.

Grinell, Sheila. *Exploratorium: Light, Sight, Sound and Hearing.* San Francisco: The Exploratorium, 1974.

Herman, Judy, and Barbara Fertig. "Learning, Plan and Fantasy," *Roundtable Reports* (Summer 1976), pp. 9-11.

Lusk, Carroll B. "Museum Lighting," *Museum News*, 49 (November 1971), pp. 20-23; v. 49 (December 1971), pp. 25-29; v. 49 (February 1971), pp. 18-22.

_____. "The Invisible Danger of Visible Light," *Museum News*, 53 (April 1975), pp. 22-23.

Museum News, 50 (February 1972), pp. 15-35. Five articles relating to current exhibit practices.

Neal, Arminta. *Exhibits for the Small Museum.* Nashville: American Association for State and Local History, 1976.

_____. *Help! for the Small Museum: A Handbook of Exhibit Ideas and Methods.* Boulder: Pruett, 1969.

Nicol, Elizabeth. *The Development of Validated Museum Exhibits.* Boston: The Children's Museum, 1969.

Noble, Joseph V. "The Museum of Ideas," *Museum News*, 59 (September/October, 1980)

O'Hare, Michael. "The Audience of the Museum of Fine Arts," *Curator*, 17 (June 1974), pp. 126-128.

_____. "The Public's Use of Art—Visitor Behavior in an Art Museum," *Curator*, 17 (December 1974), pp. 309-320.

_____. "Why do People go to Museums: The Effect of Prices and Hours on Museum Utilization," *Museum*, 27, no. 3 (1975), pp. 134-146.

One Hundred and One Ideas from History News. Nashville: American Association for State and Local History, 1975.

Parr, Albert E. "Marketing the Message," *Curator*, 12 (June 1969), pp. 77-82.

_____, "Museums: Enriching the Urban Milieu," *Museum News* 56 (March/April 1978), pp. 46-51.

_____. "Some Basic Problems of Visual Education by Means of Exhibits," *Curator*, 5, no. 4 (1962), pp. 369-370.

_____. "Theater or Playground," *Curator*, 16 (June 1973), pp. 103-106.

Peithman, Russell. "Live Animals in Museums," *Curator*, 18 (June 1975), pp. 11-14.

Rhees, David. "Exhibits About Computers." Washington, D.C.: Association of Science-Technology Centers, 1981. Occasional Report Series.

Schroeder, Fred. *Designing Your Exhibits: Seven Ways to Look at an Artifact.* Nashville: American Association for State and Local History, 1976. Technical Leaflet 91.

Screven, Chandler. "A Bibliography on Visitor Education Research," *Museum News* 57 (March/April 1979), pp. 56-59.

Shettel, Harris H. "Exhibits: Art Form or Educational Medium?" *Museum News*, 52 (September 1973), pp. 32-34.

_____. *An Evaluation of Visitor Response to "Man in his Environment."* Washington, D.C.: American Institutes for Research, 1976.

Swauger, James L. "Anthropological Exhibits Should be More Than Curio Cabinets," *Curator*, 18 (June 1975), pp. 115-119.

Vigtel, Gudmund. "Child's Work," *Museum News*, 55 (September/October 1976), pp. 32-35.

Wilson, Don W., and Dennis Medina. *Exhibit Labels: A Consideration of Content.* Nashville: American Association for State and Local History, 1972. Technical Leaflet 60.

Wolf, Robert L. "A Naturalistic View of Evaluation," *Museum News*, 58 (July/August 1980), pp. 39-45.

FUNDRAISING: GRANTSMANSHIP AND MARKETING

Alderson, William T. "Grantsmanship: A Primer," *Museum News*, 51 (February 1973), pp. 40-43.

_____. "Securing Grant Support: Effective Planning and Preparation," American Association for State and Local History Technical Leaflet #62. Nashville, AASLH, 1972.

Annual Register of Grant Support. Chicago: Marquis Publications, 1978.

Barron, Jean McC. *Marketing Strategies for Non-Profit Institutions; A Blueprint for Survival* Denver: The Denver Children's Museum, 1980

Bolton, Howard A. "How to Avoid Taxes," *Museum News*, 52 (September 1973), pp. 26-31.

Broughton, John G. "Keeping the Doors Open with State Money," *Museum News*, 52 (December 1973), pp. 26-27.

Brownrigg, W. Grant. *Corporate Fund Raising: A Practical Plan of Action.* New York: American Council for the Arts, 1978.

Coe, Linda, Denny, Rebecca and Roger, Ann. *Cultural Directory II: Federal Funds and Services for the Arts and Humanities.* Washington, D.C.: Smithsonian Institution, 1980.

Conrad, Daniel Lynn et al. *The Grants Planner: A Systems Approach to Grantsmanship.* San Francisco: Institute for Fund Raising, 1978.

Cultural Directory: Guide to Federal Funds and Services for Cultural Activities. New York: Associated Councils of the Arts, 1975.

Dermer, Joseph. *How to Get Your Fair Share of Foundation Grants.* New York: Public Service Materials Center, 1973.

_____. *How to Raise Funds from Foundations.* New York: Public Service Materials Center, 1975.

Des Marais. Philip. *How to Get Government Grants.* New York: Public Service Materials Center, 1975.

Faul, Roberta, "Licensing Programs: A Second Life for Museum Collections," *Museum News*, 54 (November/December 1975), pp. 26-33.

The Foundation Directory. New York: Russell Sage Foundation, 1960.

Foundation News, The Journal of Philanthropy. Published bi-monthly by the Council on Foundations, Inc., New York.

Grants Magazine. Quarterly publication by Plenum Press, New York.

Grantsmanship: Money and How to Get It. Chicago, Marquis Academic Media, 1978.

Gingold, Diane J. *The Challenge Grant Experience: Planning, Development and Fundraising.* Washington: National Endowment for the Arts, 1980.

Gross, Malvern J., and William H. Daughtrey, Jr. *Museum Accounting Handbook.* Washington, D.C.: American Association of Museums, 1977.

Hancock, Susan. *A Guide to Corporate Giving in the Arts.* New York: American Council for the Arts, 1978.

Hartman, Hedy A. *Funding Sources and Technical Assistance for Museums and Historical Agencies.* Nashville: American Association for State and Local History, 1979.

Hightower, Caroline. "Financing the Arts," *Museum News,* 54 (January/February 1976), pp. 44-47.

McC. Barron, Jean. *Marketing Strategies for Non-Profit Institutions: A Blueprint for Survival.* Denver: Children's Museum of Denver, 1980.

Museum Accounting Guidelines: Recommended Policies for Preparing Financial Statements at Museums, ed. Victor J. Danilov. Washington, D.C.: Association of Science-Technology Centers, 1976.

Museum News, 51 (February 1973). Entire issue on museum financing.

_____, *54 (May/June 1976).* Entire issue on government-museum relationships and funding.

_____, *55 (July/August 1977).* Articles on fund raising in the community.

Nelson, Charles A., and Frederick J. Turk. *Financial Management for the Arts: A Guidebook for Arts Organizations.* New York: American Council of the Arts, 1976.

Porter, Robert, Editor. *United Fundraising Manual.* New York: American Council for the Arts, 1980.

THE HANDICAPPED AND ACCESSIBILITY

Access to Cultural Opportunities: Museums and the Handicapped. Washington, D.C.: Association of Science-Technology Centers, 1980.

Arts and the Handicapped: An Issue of Access. New York: Educational Facilities Laboratories, 1975.

Beechel, Jacques. *Interpretation for Handicapped Persons: A Handbook for Outdoor Recreation Personnel.* Seattle: National Park Service, 1975.

Calhoun, S. N. "On the Edge of Vision," *Museum News,* 52 (April 1974), pp. 36-41.

Callow, K. B. "Museums and the Disabled," *Museum Journal,* 74 (September 1974), pp. 70-72.

Coon, N. *The Place of the Museum in the Education of the Blind.* New York: American Foundation for the Blind, 1953.

Futurai, Shiro. *How Can I Make What I Cannot See?* New York: Van Nostrand Reinhold, 1974. (Developing creative art experiences for nonsighted children.)

Hagemeyer, Alice. *Deaf Awareness: Handbook for Public Libraries.* Washington, D.C.: Public Library of the District of Columbia, 1975.

Isaacs-Deussen, Claire, ed. *Proceedings of the Conference on Art for the Deaf.* Los Angeles: Junior Art Center, 1974.

Kamien, Janet; Goldbas, Amy and Porter, Susan. *Is There Life After 504? A Guide to Building and Program Accessibility from the Children's Museum, Boston.* Boston: The Children's Museum, 1980.

_____. *What if I Couldn't. . . . ? A Book About Special Needs.* New York, Scribner's, 1979.

Kenney, Alice P. *Hospitable Heritage.: The Report of Museum Access.* Allentown, PA: Lehigh County Historical Society, 1979.

_____. "Museums from a Wheelchair," *Museum News,* 53 (December 1974), pp. 14-18.

_____. "A Test of Barrier-Free Design," *Museum News,* 55 (January).

Koberg, Don, and Jim Bagnall. *The Universal Traveler: A Soft Systems Guide to Creativity, Problem Solving and the Process of Reaching Goals.* Los Altos: Kaufman, 1974.

Kramer, Edith. *Art as Therapy with Children.* New York: Schocken Books, 1972.

Kresse, Frederick H. *Materials and Activities for Teachers and Children: A Project to Develop and Evaluate Multi-Media Kits for Elementary Schools.* Boston: The Children's Museum, 1968.

Levine, Les. *I Am Not Blind.* Hartford: Wadsworth Atheneum, 1976.

Molloy, Larry. "504 Regs: Learning to Live by the Rules," *Museum News,* 57, (September/October 1978), pp. 28-33.

_____. "The Case for Accessibility," *Museum News,* 55 (January/February 1977), pp. 15-17.

_____. "One Way to Comply with Section 504," *Museum News,* 57 (March/April 1979), pp. 24-29.

Museum News 55, (January/February, 1977). Entire issue on accessibility and handicapped.

National Arts and the Handicapped Information Service. *Annotated Bibliography.* New York: NA&HIS, 1978.

One Out of Ten: School Planning for the Handicapped. New York: Educational Facilities Laboratories, 1974.

Smith, Patricia Scherf. "Against Segregating the Blind," *Museum News*, 55 (January/February 1977), pp. 10-11.

Smithsonian Institution. *Museums and Handicapped Students, Guidelines for Educators*. Washington, D.C.: The Smithsonian Institution, 1977.

Snider, Harold. "The Inviting Air of an Accessible Space," *Museum News*, 55 (January/February 1977), pp. 18-20.

Steiner, Charles. *Museums and the Disabled*. New York City: Metropolitan Museum of Art, 1980.

———. *Museum Education for Retarded Adults, Reaching Out to a Neglected Audience*. New York: Metropolitan Museum of Art, 1979.

Sutherland, Mimi. "Total Communication," *Museum News*, 55 (January/February 1977), pp. 24-26.

Toll, Dove. "Making the Natural History Museum More Accessible to the Visually Handicapped." Unpublished report to the Women's Committee of the Smithsonian Institution, January 31, 1975.

Townsend, Sally O'C. "Touch and See—Architecture for the Blind," *Curator*, 18 (September 1975), pp. 200-205.

HISTORY RESOURCES

Banks, James. *Teaching Strategies for Ethnic Studies*. Boston: Allyn and Bacon, 1975.

Baum, Willa K. *Oral History for the Local Historical Society*. Nashville: American Association for State and Local History, 1974.

Beyer, Barry and Anthony Penna (Editors), *Concepts in the Social Studies*. National Council for the Social Studies, 1971.

Block, Jack. *Understanding Historical Research*. Glen Rock, New Jersey: Research Publications, 1968.

Cosby, Theo. *Architecture: City Sense*. New York: Reinhold, 1965.

Cox, Benjamin and Byron G. Massialas, *Social Studies in the United States: A Critical Appraisal*. New York: Harcourt, Brace and World, Inc., 1967.

Dunfee, Maxine and Helen Sagl. *Social Studies Through Problem Solving*. New York: Holt, Rinehart and Winston Inc., 1966.

Eriksen, Aase. *Architects-in-Schools: Planning Workbook*. Philadelphia: Educational Futures, 1976.

Felt, Thomas E. *Researching, Writing and Publishing Local History*. Nashville: American Association for State and Local History, 1976.

Fenton, Edwin. *The New Social Studies*. New York: Holt, Rinehart and Winston, 1967.

Fleming, E. McClung. "Early American Decorative Arts as Social Documents," *Mississippi Valley Historical Review*, 40 (September 1958), pp. 276-284.

Floyd, Candace. "Education at Old Economy, Programs Children can Understand." *History News*, 35, March, 1980.

Goldmark, Bernice, *Social Studies, A Method of Inquiry*. Belmont, California: Wadsworth Publishing Company, Inc., 1968.

Gross, Richard E. et. al., *Teaching the Social Studies, What, Why and How*. Scranton, Pennsylvania: International Textbook Co., 1969.

*Jenness, Aylette. *The Bakery Factory: Who Puts Bread on Your Table*. New York, Crowell, 1978.

*Kraska, Edie. *Toys and Tales from Grandmother's Attic: A Workbook and History of Fifteen Folk-art Toys, Crafts, Plays and Stories from the Collection of the Boston Children's Museum*. Boston, Houghton Mifflin, 1979.

Learning about Building the Environment. Arlington, Virginia: National Association of Elementary School Principals, 1975.

Martorella, Peter H., *Concept Learning in the Social Studies*. Scranton, Pennsylvania: Intext Educational Publishers, 1971.

Massialas, Byron G., and C. Benjamin Cox. *Inquiry in Social Studies*. New York: McGraw-Hill, 1966.

Metcalf, Lawrence E. (editor), *Values Education*. National Council for the Social Studies, 1971.

Museum Education Catalogue of Teaching Materials: Family Work Community. Sturbridge, MA: Old Sturbridge Village, 1979.

Nelson, Doreen. *City Building Educational Program: Manual—Architectural Consultant Edition*. Los Angeles: The Center for City Building Educational Programs, 1975.

Powell, Thomas F., ed. *Humanities and the Social Studies*. Washington, D.C.: National Council for the Social Studies, 1969.

One Hundred One Ideas from History News. Nashville, American Association for State and Local History, 1975.

Ronsheim, Robert D. "Is the Past Dead?" *Museum News*, 53 (November 1974), pp. 16-18, 62.

Social Studies Curriculum Guidelines. Washington, D.C.: National Council for the Social Studies, 1971.

Stewart, Donald. *A Short History of East Harlem.* New York: Museum of the City of New York, 1972.

Taba, Hilda, *Teacher's Handbook for Elementary Social Studies.* Palo Alto: Addison-Wesley Publishing Co., 1967.

Tilden, Freeman. *Interpreting Our Heritage.* Chapel Hill: University of North Carolina, 1967.

Trochtenberg, Alan, Peter Neill, and Peter C. Bunnell. *The City: American Experience.* New York: Oxford University Press, 1971.

Waserman, Manfred J. *Bibliography on Oral History.* Denton, Texas: Oral History Association, 1971.

Wiggington, Eliot. *Foxfire I.* Garden City: Doubleday, 1972.

———. *Foxfire II.* Garden City: Doubleday, 1973.

———. *Foxfire III.* Garden City: Doubleday, 1975.

MUSEUM EDUCATION: HISTORY, PHILOSOPHY, PROGRAMS AND TECHNIQUES

African Heritage, Teachers Manual. Washington, D.C.: Museum of African Art, [n.d.]

Alberty, Beth, and Bette Korman, eds. *Art and the Integrated Day.* New York: G.A.M.E., 1976.

Alderson, William T., and Shirley Payne Low. *Interpretation of Historic Sites.* Nashville: American Association for State and Local History, 1976.

Alexander, Edward. *Museums in Motion.* Nashville: American Association for State and Local History, 1979.

Allen, R. "New Roles for the University in Extra-Curricular Visual Arts Programs," *Curator,* V. 12, No. 1 (March 1969), pp. 57-59.

American Association of Museums. *Museums and the Environment: A Handbook for Education.* New York: Arkville Press, 1971.

———. *Museums: Their New Audience.* Washington: AAM, 1972.

Architecture: Discovery and Awareness Handbook. Washington, D.C.: Corcoran Gallery, 1976.

Art Education 33, (January, 1980). Entire issue on museum education.

Arth, Malcolm. "The People Center-Anthropology for the Layman," *Curator,* 18 (December 1975), pp. 315-325.

Arts and the Handicapped: An Issue of Access. New York: Educational Facilities Laboratories, 1975.

Association of Art Museum Directors. *Education in the Art Museum.* New York: American Association of Art Museum Directors, 1972.

Bach, Penny. "Rites of Passage: A City Celebrates Its Variety," *Museum News,* 55 (September/October 1976), pp. 36-42.

Baldi, Mary Lou. *Environmental Living Program.* Washington, D.C.: Government Printing Office, 1976.

Barnes, Frank. "Viewpoint: Living History, Clio or Cliopatria," *History News,* 29 (September 1974), pp. 202-203.

Bay, Ann. *Museum Programs for Young People.* Washington, D.C.: Smithsonian Institution, Office of Elementary and Secondary Education, 1973.

Beardsley, Don. "Helping Teachers to Use Museums," *Curator,* 18 (September 1975), pp. 192-199.

Benedict, Paul L. *Historic Site Interpretation, The Student Field Trip.* Nashville: American Association for State and Local History, 1971. Technical Leaflet 19.

Berrin, Kathleen. "Activating the Art Museum Experience," *Museum News,* 56, (March/April 1978), pp. 42-45.

Bertram, Susan, and Sidford, Holly. *Final Report on the Cultural Voucher Program.* ERIC no. ED 163 841. New York: Museums Collaborative, 1977.

Black, Patricia. *The Live-In at Old Economy.* Ambridge, Pennsylvania: The Harmonie Associates, 1972.

Botein, Stephen and Warren Leon. *Experiments in History Teaching.* Cambridge, Mass.: Harvard-Danforth Center for Teaching and Learning, 1978.

Bowman, Ruth. "Plugging into the Primary Audience," *Museum News* 56 (May/June 1978), pp. 49-59.

Bremer, John, and Michael von Moschzinsker. *The School Without Walls: Philadelphia's Parkway Program.* Chicago: Holt, Rinehart and Winston, 1971.

Brooking, Dolo. *The Extended Hand, a Portfolio of Experience for the Hand.* Lawrence: University of Kansas Art Museum, 1974.

———. "Play, in all Seriousness," *Museum News,* 56 (May/June 1978), pp. 21-24.

———. *Treasures and Pleasures, Exploring Art.* Lawrence: The University of Kansas Museum of Art, 1977.

Burch, Glenn E., and Linda M. Ulland. "Learning by Living," *Museum News,* 55 (September/October 1976), pp. 23-31.

Caston, Ellie. "An Interdisciplinary Approach to Education," *Museum News* 57 (March/April 1979), pp. 50-53.

Centre St. Boston, The Children's Museum, 1975.

Charles Carroll of Carrollton, His Family and His Maryland. Baltimore: Baltimore Museum of Art, 1975.

Chase, Richard A. "Museums as Learning Environments," *Museum News*, 54 (September/October 1975), pp. 37-43.

Children's Museum of Boston. *Citygames.* Reading, Mass.: Addison-Wesley Publishing Company, 1975.

Ciniglio, Ada V. "Pioneers in American Museums: Paul J. Sachs," *Museum News*, 55 (September/October 1976), pp. 48-52.

Coen, Leigh Hayford. "The Interpretive Function in Museum Work," *Curator*, 18, (December 1975), pp. 281-286.

Cohen, Lizabeth. "How to Teach Family History by Using an Historic House," *Social Education*, 39 (November-December 1975), pp. 466-469.

Coleman, Lawrence Vail. *The Museum in America.* Three vols. Washington, D.C.: American Association of Museums, 1939.

Coles, Robert. "The Art Museum and the Pressures of Society," *Art News*, 74 (January 1975), pp. 23-33.

Communicating with the Museum Visitor: Guidelines for Planning. Toronto: Royal Ontario Museum, 1976.

Condit, Louise. "A New Junior Museum," *Curator*, 2, no. 1 (1959), pp. 11-20.

Cook, Peter. "The Craft of Demonstrations," *Museum News*, 53 (November 1974), pp. 10-15.

Danilov, Victor J. "Science Museums as Educational Centers," *Curator*, 18 (June 1975), pp. 87-108.

_____. "Science Technology Museums Come of Age," *Curator*, 16 (September 1973), pp. 183-219.

_____. "Under the Microscope," *Museum News*, 52 (March 1974), pp. 37-44.

Dennis, Emily. "Seminar on Neighborhood Museums," *Museum News*, 48 (January 1970), pp. 13-19.

Dobbs, Stephen Mark. "Dana and Kent and Early Museum Education," *Museum News*, 50, (October 1971), pp. 38-41.

Draper, Linda. *The Explainer Program Report.* San Francisco: The Exploratorium, 1978.

_____ ed. *The Visitor and the Museum.* Berkeley: Lowie Museum of Anthropology, 1977.

Dunn, John R. "Museum Interpretation/education: The Need for Definition," *Gazette*, 10, No. 1 (Winter 1977), pp. 12-17.

Eason, Laurie, and Alan Friedman. *Star Games: The Pains and Pleasures of Formative Evaluation.* Berkeley: Lawrence Hall of Science, 1976. Unpublished manuscript.

"Educational Role of Science Museums Sparks Debate at ASTC Conference," *ASTC Newsletter*, 4 (January 1977), p. 1 ff.

Endter, Ellen. "Museum Learning and the Performing Arts," *Museum News*, 53 (June 1975), pp. 34-37.

Evans, Mary R. "Susan Sollins, Improvisational Tours for Art Galleries," *Gazette*, Fall 1976.

Falk, John. "Outdoor Biology Instructional Strategies: A Report from Anne Arundel County," *Roundtable Reports* (Summer 1976), pp. 6-7.

Fernbank Science Center School Programs Curriculum Outline. Atlanta: Fernbank Science Center, 1976.

Finlay, Ian. *Priceless Heritage: The Future of Museums.* London: Faber and Faber, 1977.

Floyd, Candace. "Education at Old Economy, Programs Children can Understand." *History News*, 35, March, 1980.

Franco, Barbara. "Exhibiting Archival Material: A Method of Interpretation," *Museum News*, 58, (September/October, 1979), pp. 55-59.

Friedman, Alan. *Participatory Planetarium Shows.* Chadds Ford, Pennsylvania: Spitz Space Systems, 1975. In *Planetarium Director's Handbook.*

_____, and Lowery, Lawrence. *Planetarium Educator's Workshop Guide.* Alexandria, VA.: International planetarium Society, 1980.

Gabianelli, Vincent J., and Edward Munyer. "A Place to Learn," *Museum News*, 53 (December 1974), pp. 28-33.

Gaffney, Maureen. *More Films Kids Like.* Chicago: American Library Association, 1977.

_____, and Gerry Laybourne. *What To Do When the Lights Go On: A Comprehensive Guide to 16mm Films and Related Activities for Children.* Phoenix AZ: The Oryx Press, 1980.

_____. "What's Going On: Evaluating Children's Media." *Educational Media Yearbook 1980.* Littleton, CO: Libraries Unlimited, 1980.

Gaines, William. "Virginia Museums: Two Pioneer Programs," *Museum News*, 50 (October 1971), pp. 22-25.

Gans, Susan. "Three Successful Programs do not a Museum Make," *Museum News*, 52 (April 1974), pp. 14-19.

Garrity, Nancy. *Idea Sheets—The Eye and Something About Light and Color.* San Francisco: Exploratorium, 1976.

Geise, Gregory B. *Zoo Animals and You.* Providence: Roger Williams Park Zoo, 1976.

Goldwater, Daniel L. "Games People Play—On Computers," *Museum News*, 51 (April 1973), pp. 30-34.

Graburn, Nelson H. H. *Ethnic and Tourist Arts.* Berkeley: University of California, 1976.

Grater, Russell K. *The Interpreter's Handbook.* Globe, Arizona, Southwest Parks and Monuments Assn., 1976.

Griesemer, Allan D. *Handbook of Programs for Museum Educators: Mountain-Plains Museum Conference.* Lincoln: University of Nebraska State Museums, 1977.

Grinell, Sheila, ed. *A Stage for Science: Dramatic Techniques at Science-Technology Centers.* Washington, D.C.: Association of Science and Technology Centers, 1979.

————. *Light, Sight, Sound, Hearing.* San Francisco: Exploratorium, 1974.

Grochau, Karen. *To "See" a Museum, a Guide to the Western Reserve Historical Society.* Cleveland: Western Reserve Historical Society, 1975.

————. *The Significance of Museum Education.* Cleveland: Western Reserve Historical Society, 1976.

Grove, Richard. *The Museum Community: New Roles and Possibilities for Art Education.* New York: Institute for the Study of Art in Education, 1969.

Haley, Frances, and Regina McCormick. *Directory of Social Studies/Social Science Service Organizations.* Boulder: ERIC Clearinghouse for Social Studies/Social Science Education and Social Science Education Consortium, 1975.

Hands-On-Museums: Partners in Learning. New York: Educational Facilities Laboratories, 1975.

Hands On: Setting Up a Discovery Room in Your Museum or School. Toronto: Royal Ontario Museum, 1979.

Harrison, Deborah and Samuelsen, Peter. *Zoo Animals and You, Teacher's Edition.* Providence: Roger Williams Park Zoo, 1976.

Heine, Aalbert. *Museums and the Student.* Corpus Christi, Texas: Corpus Christi Museum, 1976. Occasional Papers No. 2.

————. *Museums and the Teacher.* Corpus Christi, Texas: Corpus Christi Museum, 1977. Occasional Papers No. 3.

The Historian as Detective. St. Louis: CEMREL, Inc., 1975.

Holroyd, R.N. "Weaving Classes in an Art Gallery," *Handweaver*, 22 (Fall 1971), pp. 12-15.

Howard, James, and Sylvia Marchant. "Electragraphics," *Museum News*, 52 (January/February 1974), pp. 41-44.

Irwin, Howard S. "Grocery Store Botany," *Curator*, 20 (March 1977), pp. 5-14.

Jenness, Aylette. *Along the Niger River: An African Way of Life.* New York, Crowell, 1974.

————. *Creating a Partnership: Museums and Schools.* Boston: The Cultural Education Collaborative, 1980.

Johnson, Brooks. *Video References.* Oakland: Western Association of Art Museums, 1976.

Kennet, Frances, and Terry Measham. *Looking at Paintings.* New York: Van Nostrand and Reinhold Co., 1978.

Kenny, David H. *Fifty Years Young, The Children's Museum.* Princeton: Newcomen Society in America, Princeton University Press, 1975.

King, David. *Half Modelling.* Bath, Maine: Bath Marine Museum, [n.d.]

Krulick, Janet. *Beaumont, U.S.A. Our Build Environment, A Handbook for Students, Teachers and Docents.* Beaumont, Texas: Beaumont Art Museum, 1979.

Larrabee, Eric, ed. *Museums and Education.* Washington, D.C.: Smithsonian Institution, 1968. (Available only from ERIC-see Resource Section)

Lee, Byung-Hoon. *A Study of Science Museums with Special Reference to their Educational Programs.* Washington: Office of Museum Programs, Smithsonian Institution, 1974.

Lee, Sherman E. *On Understanding Art Museums.* Englewood Cliffs, New Jersey, Prentice-Hall, 1975.

Lesser, Gerald S. *Children and Television; Lessons from Sesame Street.* New York: Random House, 1974.

Levinson, Bonnie. "Playing with Film: An Approach to Museum Education." *Young Viewers*, 3. (Spring 1980). Available from the Media Center for children, Young Viewers is a quarterly magazine on using children's media.

Loar, Peggy A. "The Arts and the Three Rs," *Museum News*, 55 (September/October 1976), pp. 43-47.

Low, Theodore L. *The Educational Philosophy and Practice of Art Museums in the United States.* New York, Teachers College, Columbia University, 1948.

————. *The Museum as a Social Instrument.* New York, Metropolitan Museum of Art, 1942.

———. "The Museum as a Social Instrument: Twenty Years After," *Museum News*, v. 46 (March 1968), pp. 11-18.

Lynn, Robin. "On the Road: A Brief Guide to Traveling Exhibition Sources," *Museum News*, 53 (September/October 1975), pp. 64-68.

Madden, Joan. "The AAM Education Committee: "Who, What, When, Where, Why?" *Roundtable Reports* (January 1976), pp. 1-4.

Marcouse, Renee. *Using Objects, Visual Learning, and Visual Awareness in the Museum and Classroom.* New York: Van Nostrand-Reinhold, 1974.

Marcus, Stephen. *Designing Programs and Looking Ahead.* Boston: The Cultural Education Collaborative, 1978.

———. *Cultural Organizations in Career Education*, Boston: Cultural Education Collaborative, 1978.

Matelic, Candice; Compiler. *Handbook for Interpreters.* Des Moines: Living History Farms, 1979.

———. "Through the Historical Looking Glass," *Museum News*, 58 (March/April, 1980) pp. 34-45.

Matthai, Robert A., and Neil E. Deaver. "Child-Centered Learning," *Museum News*, 54 (March/April 1976), pp. 15-19.

McGlathery, Glenn, and Martha Hartmann. "Here Come the Touch Carts," *Curator*, 19 (September 1976), pp. 193-197.

———. "Museums as a Teaching Resource: an Inquiry Approach," *Science and Children*, 11 (November 1973), pp. 11-13.

McHugh, Alice. "Strategic Planning for Museums," *Museum News*, 58 (July/August, 1980) pp. 23-30.

Melcher, Victoria, and Dianne Deckert, eds. *The Dragon's Gate, Exploring Oriental Art.* Kansas City: William Nelson Gallery of Art, 1976.

Montgomery, Robert W. *History for Young People: Organizing a Junior Society.* Nashville: American Association for State and Local History, 1972. Technical Leaflet no. 44.

Moore, Donald. "In Search of the Past: A Travelling Exhibition for Schools," *Museums Journal*, 76, (September 1976), pp. 60-62.

Moore, Eleanor *Youth in Museums.* Philadelphia: University of Pennsylvania, 1941.

Morgan, Monica J. and Sebolt, Alberta. "Integrating the Family," *Museum News* 56 (May/June 1978), pp. 29-31.

Museum Education Catalogue of Teaching Materials. Sturbridge: Old Sturbridge Village, 1979.

Museum Education Roundtable. *Roundtable Reports.* Order through: Department of Education, National Portrait Gallery, Smithsonian Institution, Washington, D.C. 20560.

Museum News, 52 (April 1974). Entire issue devoted to museum education.

———, 55 (January/February 1977). Entire issue devoted to museums and the handicapped.

———, 56 (January/February, 1978). Entire issue on natural history museums and education programs.

———, 56 (May/June 1978). Entire issue on museum education.

———, 58 (March/April 1980). Entire issue on children and museums.

———, 58 (May/June 1980). Entire issue on the future of museums.

———, 59 (January/February, 1981). Several articles on museums use of computers, television and videodisks.

Museum Techniques in Fundamental Education. Paris: Unesco, 1956.

"Museums and Education," *Museum*, 1, nos. 3-4 (1948). UNESCO Publication No. 244.

Museums, Imagination and Education. Paris: UNESCO, 1973. Available from UNIPUB and from ERIC (ED 077 828)

Museums: Their New Audience: a Report to the Department of Housing and Urban Development by a Special Committee of the American Association of Museums. Washington, D.C.: American Association of Museums, 1972.

National Zoological Parks. *Zoo Animals: A Closer Look, A Science Program for Fourth Graders.* Washington, D.C.: National Zoological Park, 1978.

Newson, Barbara, and Adele Z. Silver, eds. *Art Museum as Educator.* Berkeley: University of California, 1977.

19th Century Michigan: A Guide for Teachers. Dearborn: Greenfield Village and Henry Ford Museum.

Noble, Grant. *Children in Front of the Small Screen.* Beverly Hills, CA: Sage Publications, 1975.

O' Connell, Peter S. and Mary Alexander. "Reaching the High School Audience," *Museum News*, 58 (September/October, 1979), pp. 50-56.

Olofsson, Ulla Keding, Editor. *Museums and Children.* Paris: UNESCO 1979.

Oppenheimer, Frank. "The Arts: A Decent Respect for Taste" in *National Elementary Principal*, Vol. 57, No. 1 (1977).

———. "Everybody is You or Me" in *Technology Review*, Vol. 78, No. 7 (1976), pp. 30-35.

_____. "The Exploratorium and Other Ways of Teaching Physics" in *Physics Today*, September 1975. (Letter)

_____. "A Rationale for a Science Museum" in *Curator*, Vol. 11, No. 3 (November 1968), pp. 206-210.

Parr, Albert E. "Marketing the Message," *Curator*, 12 (June 1969), pp. 77-82.

_____. "Museums: Enriching the Urban Milieu," *Museum News*, 56 (March/April 1978). pp. 46-51.

_____. "Theater or Playground," *Curator*, 16 (June 1973), pp. 103-106.

Perrin, Richard W. *Outdoor Museums*. Milwaukee, Wisconsin: Milwaukee Public Museum, 1975.

Pessino, Catherine. "City Ecology for City Children," *Curator*, 18 (March 1975), pp. 47-54.

Pitman, Bonnie. *Teacher Workbook, Museum Experience-Ancient and Colonial Latin America*. New Orleans: New Orleans Museum of Art, 1975.

_____. *Watermelon*. New Orleans: New Orleans Museum of Art, 1973.

Ponty, Maurice Merleau. "Eye and Mind." In *The Primacy of Perception*. Evanston, Illinois: Northwestern University Press, 1964.

Press, Nancy. *Museum in the School*. Ithaca: Herbert F. Johnson Museum of Art, 1979.

Reque, Barbara. "From Object to Idea," *Museum News*, 56, (January/February, 1978) pp. 45-47.

Ringling Museum's School Programs Developed for Kindergarten through Grade 6. Sarasota: Ringling Museum, 1980.

Ripley, Dillon. "Museums and Education," *Curator*, 10, no. 3 (1968), pp. 183-9.

_____. *The Sacred Grove, Essays on Museums*. New York: Simon & Schuster, 1969.

Riznik, Barnes. "Don't Tread on Me: Running the Obstacle Course of Community Education," *Social Education*, 39 (November/December 1975), pp. 458-460.

Rothman, Ellen. "The Worcester Source Book," *Museum News*, 56, (March/April 1978), pp. 31-39.

Russell, Charles. *Museums and Our Children: a Handbook and Guide for Teachers in Museums and Schools and for All Who Are Interested in Programs and Activities for Children*. New York: Central Book Company, 1956.

Sadkowski, J. *Methodology for Interpretive Planning in Historic Parks*. Toronto: Parks Canada, 1974.

Schlereth, Thomas. *Historic Houses as Learning Laboratories, Seven Teaching Strategies*. Nashville: American Association for State and Local History, 1978. Technical Leaflet 105.

School Services Division of New York Botanical Garden. *An Elementary Teacher's Handbook to the New York Botanical Garden*. New York: New York Botanical Garden, 1975.

Sebolt, Alberta. "Bicentennial Feature: Using the Community to Explore 200 Years of History," *Social Education*, 39 (November/December 1975), pp. 454-455.

_____. *Collaborative Programs: Museums and Schools*. Sturbridge MA.: Old Sturbridge Village, 1980.

_____. *A Guide for the Development of a Curriculum Model*. Sturbridge: Old Sturbridge Village, 1980.

Serrell, Beverly. "Survey of Visitor Attitude and Awareness at an Aquarium," *Curator*, 20 (March 1977), pp. 48-52.

Sharpe, Grant W. *Interpreting the Environment*. New York: Wiley, 1976.

Simons, Robin. *Recyclopedia: Games, Science Equipment and Crafts from Recycled Material*. Boston, Houghton Mifflin, 1976.

Sollins, Susan. "Games Children Play in Museums," *Art Journal*, 31 (Spring 1972), pp. 271-275.

Starkey, Don. *Mobile Museum, Information Workshop*. Topeka: Kansas State Historical Society, 1974.

Steiner, Charles. *Museums and the Disabled*. New York City: Metropolitan Museum of Art, 1980.

_____. *Museum Education for Retarded Adults, Reaching Out to a Neglected Audience*. New York: Metropolitan Museum of Art, 1979.

Supplee, Carol. "Museums on Wheels," *Museum News*, 53 (October 1974), pp. 26-35.

Taylor, Anne P. "Children and Artifacts—A Replacement for Textbook Learning," *Curator*, 16 (March 1973), pp. 25-29.

The Museum Educator's Manual. Brockton, Massachusetts: The Brockton Art Center-Fuller Memorial, 1979.

Tilden, Freeman. *Interpreting Our Heritage*. Chapel Hill: The University of North Carolina, 1967.

Tomkins, Calvin. *Merchants and Masterpieces. The Story of the Metropolitan Museum of Art*. New York: E.P. Dutton, 1970.

Vanderway, Richard. *Planning Museum Tours: For School Groups*. Nashville: American Association for State and Local History, 1977.

Vigtel, Gudmund. "Child's Work," *Museum News*, 55 (September/October 1976), pp. 32-35.

Walsh, Kathleen. *Handbook of Museum-Based Lesson Plans.* St. Louis: St. Louis Museum of Art, 1979.

Washburn, Wilcomb E. "Do Museums Educate?" *Curator,* 18 (September 1975), pp. 211-218.

Williams, Patterson B. "Find Out Who Donny Is," *Museum News,* 52 (April 1974), pp. 42-45.

———. "Perception Games and Body Language: The Philadelphia Museum of Art Museum Games," *Art Teacher,* 5 (Fall 1975), pp. 4-6.

———. "Teaching or Touring," *Roundtable Reports,* (Summer 1976), pp. 1-3.

Wilson, Ellen. "Indians and Africans, A School Van Program," *Curator,* 20 (March 1977), pp. 58-64.

Winn, Marie. *The Plug-In Drug: Television, Children and the Family.* New York: The Viking Press, 1977.

Wittlin, Alma S. "Junior Museums at the Crossroads: Forward to a New Era of Creativity or Backward to Obsoleteness?" *Curator,* 6, no. 1 (1963), pp. 58-63.

———. *Museums: In Search of a Usable Future.* Cambridge: Massachusetts Institute of Technology, 1971.

Wohler, J. Patrick. *The History Museum as an Effective Educational Institution.* Ottawa, National Museums of Canada, 1976.

Zubrowski, Bernie. *Ball Point Pens: A Children's Museum Activity Book.* Boston, Little, Brown, 1979. (paper)

———. *Bubbles: A Children's Museum Activity Book.* Boston, Little, Brown, 1979.

———. *Milk Carton Blocks: A Children's Museum Activity Book.* Boston, Little, Brown, 1979. (paper)

SCIENCE RESOURCES

Adams, Richard. *Nature Through the Seasons.* New York: Simon and Schuster, 1975.

Asimov, Isaac. *ABC's of the Ocean.* New York: Walker and Co., 1970.

Burton, Virginia Lee. *Life Story.* Boston: Houghton Mifflin, 1962.

Carlton, R. Milton. *Gardening Fun: Year Round Projects for Children.* Chicago: Reilly and Lee Brooks, 1970.

Cobb, Vicki. *Science Experiments You Can Eat.* Philadelphia: Lippincott, 1972.

Eames, Charles, and Ray Eames. *A Computer Perspective.* Cambridge: Harvard, 1973.

Friedman, Alan J., Lowery, Laurence, et. al. *Planetarium Educator's Workshop Guide.* Alexandria, VA: International Planetarium Society, 1980.

Gallob, Edward. *City Leaves, City Trees.* New York: Scribner, 1972.

———. *City Rocks, City Blocks and the Moon.* New York: Scribner, 1973.

Goldberg, Lazer. *Children and Science.* New York: Charles Scribner's Sons, 1970.

*Gottlieb, Leonard. *Factory Made: How Things are Made.* Boston, Houghton Mifflin, 1978. $7.95

Graf, Rudolf F. *Safe and Simple Electrical Experiments.* New York: Dover, 1973.

Grinell, Sheila. *Exploratorium: Light, Sight, Sound and Hearing.* San Francisco: The Exploratorium, 1974.

Heimer, Ralph, Cecil Trueblook. *Strategies for Teaching Children Mathematics.* Addison Wesley Publishing Co., 1977.

Hewitt, Paul. *Conceptual Physics,* Boston: Little, Brown-Co., 1974.

Horticulture in the Classroom. New York: New York Botanical Garden, 1975.

Hylander, Clarence J. *Wildlife Communities.* Boston: Houghton Mifflin Co., 1966.

Kaplan, Abraham, *The Conduct of Inquiry: Methodology for Behavioral Science.* San Francisco: Chandler Publishing Company, 1964.

Matre, Steve Van. *Acclimatization.* Martinsville, Indiana: American Camping Association, 1972.

Russell, Helen Ross. *Earth, The Great Recycler.* New York: Thomas Nelson, 1974.

Schmidt, V.E., and V.N. Rockastle. *Teaching Science with Everyday Things.* New York: McGraw-Hill, 1968.

Zaslavsky, Claudia. *Preparing Young Children for Math. A Book of Games.* New York: Schocken Books, 1979.

VOLUNTEERS

Alderson, W.T. and Low, S.P. *Interpretation of Historic Sites.* American Association for State and Local History, Nashville, TN 1976.

Bay, Ann. "Getting Decent Docents," *Museum News,* 52 (April 1974), pp. 25-29.

Black, Patricia F. "Teenage Docents at Old Economy," *Historic Preservation,* 24 (April-June 1972), pp. 19-21.

Bradshaw, Mary Claire. *Volunteer Docent Programs: A Pragmatic Approach to Museum Interpretation.* Nashville: American Association for State and Local History, 1973. Technical Leaflet 65.

Carter, Barbara. *Organizing School Volunteer Programs.* New York: Citation Press, 1974.

Center for Museum Education. *Volunteers in Museum Education. Source Book #2.* Washington D.C. The George Washington University, 1979.

Compton, Mildred. "A Training Program for Museum Volunteers," *Curator,* 8 (December 1965), pp. 294-98.

Covington, Joseph. *The Docent Programs of the Huntsville Museum of Art.* Huntsville: Huntsville Museum of Art, 1978.

Duff, James H. "An Untapped Resource," *Museum News,* 50 (May 1972), pp. 25-27.

Flanders, Ned A. *Analyzing Teaching Behavior.* Reading, Massachusetts: Addison-Wesley, 1970.

_____, and Mary P. Flanders. Evaluating Docent Performance," *Curator,* 19 (September 1976), pp. 198-225.

_____. *Interaction Analysis: A Minicourse.* Paul S. Amidon & Associates, 4329 Nicollet Avenue S., Minneapolis, MN 55409.

Fort Worth Museum of Science and History. *Docent Handbook.* Fort Worth: Fort Worth Museum of Science and History, 1973.

Hall, Nancy Johnston and Karla McGray. *How to Make a Museum Volunteer Out of Anyone.* Volunteer Administration, X, No. 3 (Fall 1977).

Heine, Aalbert. "The Care and Feeding of Volunteer Staff Members," *Curator,* 8, no. 3 (1965), pp. 287-90.

Henderson, A.K. "You Can be a Docent." *Retired Living,* December 1974.

"The Museum Docent," *Roundtable Reports* (Spring 1977), pp. 1-6.

Museum News, 56, September/October 1977. Entire issue on museum volunteerism.

Naylor, Harriet H. *Volunteers Today.* Dryden Associates, P.O. Box 363, Dryden, NY 13053.

Newsom, Barbara Y., and Silver, Adel Z. *The Art Museum as Educator.* Berkeley: University of California Press, 1978.

Panzer, Nora. *Information for Docents, National Collection of Fine Arts.* Washington, D.C.: Smithsonian Institution Press, 1976.

Payson, Huldah Smith. "Volunteers—Priceless Personnel for the Small Museum," *Museum News,* 45 (February 1967), p. 18.

Pell, Arthur R. *Recruiting, Training and Motivating Volunteer Workers.* Pilot Books, 347 Fifth Avenue, New York, NY 10016, 1972.

Pitman-Gelles, Bonnie. *Watermelon.* New Orleans: Museum of Art, 1972.

"Recruiting Low-Income Volunteers: Experiences of Five Voluntary Action Centers." Washington D.C.: National Center for Voluntary Action.

Recruiting Volunteers: Views, Techniques and Comments. The National Center for Voluntary Action, 1785 Massachusetts Avenue, N.W., Washington, D.C. 20036

Riebel, Daniel B. "The Use of Volunteers in Museums and Historical Societies," *Curator,* 17 (March 1974), pp. 16-26.

_____. "The Volunteer: Nuisance or Savior," *Museum News,* 49 (March 1971), p. 28.

Smith, David Horton. *Evaluating Voluntary Action.* Center for a Voluntary Society, 1507 M. Street, N.W., Washington, D.C. 20052, 1972.

Stagg, Brian L. "Getting Young People Involved," *Historic Preservation,* 24 (April-June 1972), pp. 16-18.

Swauger, James L. "Is There Life After Retirement?" *Museum News,* 52 (November 1973), pp. 31-33.

Training Student Volunteers. Washington, D.C. National Student Volunteer Program, ACTION.

Williams, Patterson. "Teaching or Touring?" *Roundtable Reports.* Summer 1976.

Wilson, Marlene. *The Effective Management of Volunteer Programs.* Boulder: Johnson, 1976.

You and Your Volunteers: A Partnership that Works, ed. State Department of Social Services, Carolyn F. Viall, 1450 Western Avenue, Albany, NY 12203.

ABOUT AAYM

The American Association of Youth Museums is a nonprofit organization of children's museums and museums that present programs primarily for young people. Organized to promote and improve youth museums and communications within the field, AAYM holds an annual meeting, offers technical assistance, and responds to inquiries regarding youth education in museums. For more information, contact any member of the AAYM Editorial Committee.

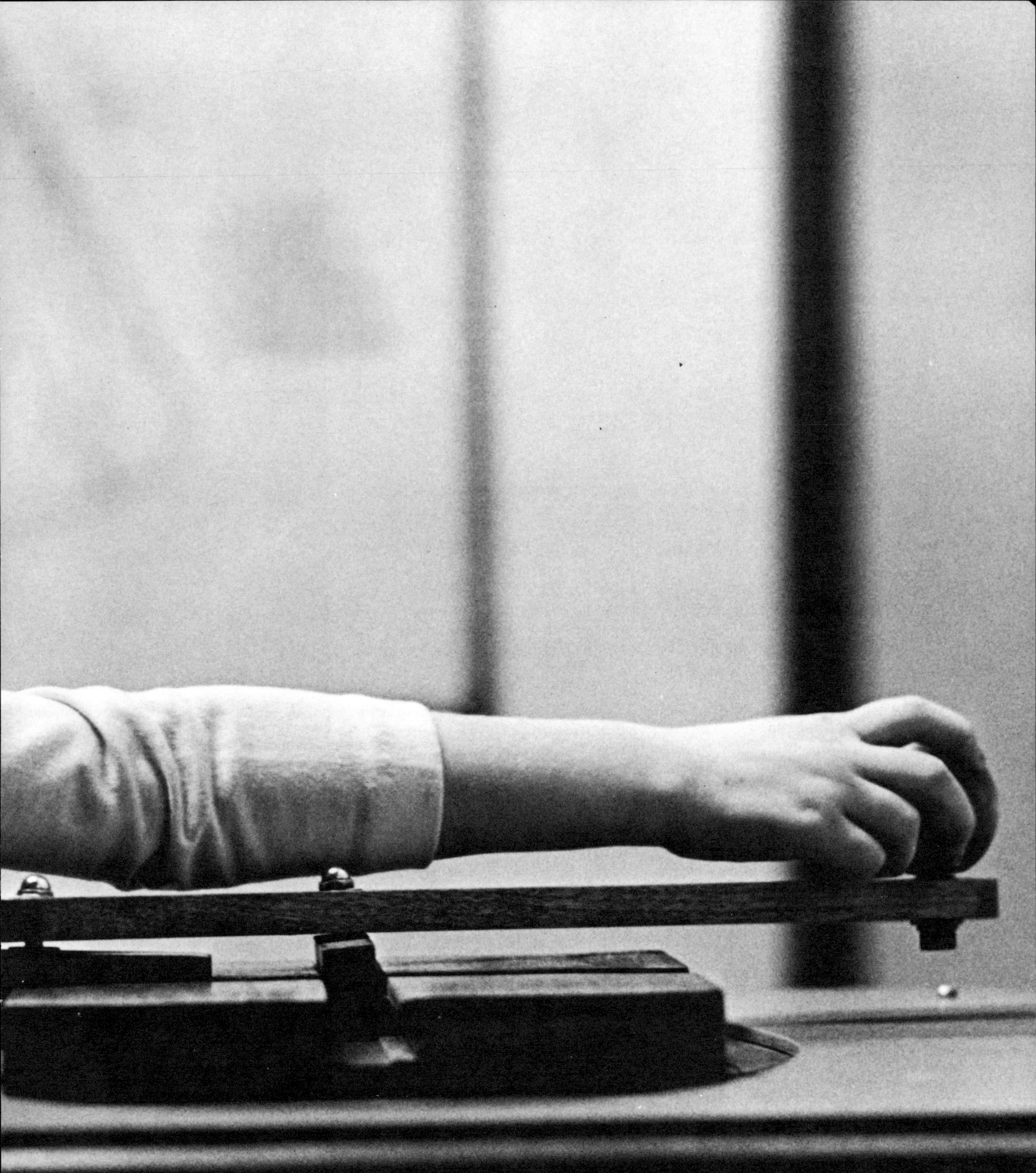

ABOUT ASTC

The Association of Science-Technology Centers (ASTC) is a not-for-profit organization of science museums dedicated to furthering the public understanding and appreciation of science and technology. Through its programs and services, ASTC works with its members to share information and to improve the operations and practices of science centers and museums.

Science-technology centers are science museums that are committed to increasing the public understanding of science through exhibits and education programs that actively involve the visitor. Although their subject fields may range from natural history and health to the physical sciences and astronomy, they share an interest in using participatory techniques in education and exhibitions. Current ASTC membership includes science-technology centers, nature centers, an aquarium, space theaters, and natural history, general, science, and children's museums.

Since its founding in 1973, ASTC has more than tripled its membership. It now represents and serves 170 science, technology, industrial, and health museums and related organizations. Its members are located in major metropolitan areas and smaller communities throughout North America and in 14 foreign countries. ASTC seeks to improve the operations of contemporary science and technology museums, sometimes called science-technology centers to describe their emphasis on participatory science education and exhibition techniques. The association serves as a vehicle for sharing resources among its members and to advance the role of science museums in our society.

ASTC serves as a clearinghouse for information, conducts surveys on science museum development, operations, and programs, and encourages or arranges cooperative projects involving science-technology centers.

For more information about ASTC and its programs, contact the Association of Science-Technology Centers, 1413 K St., NW, Tenth Floor, Washington, DC 20005.

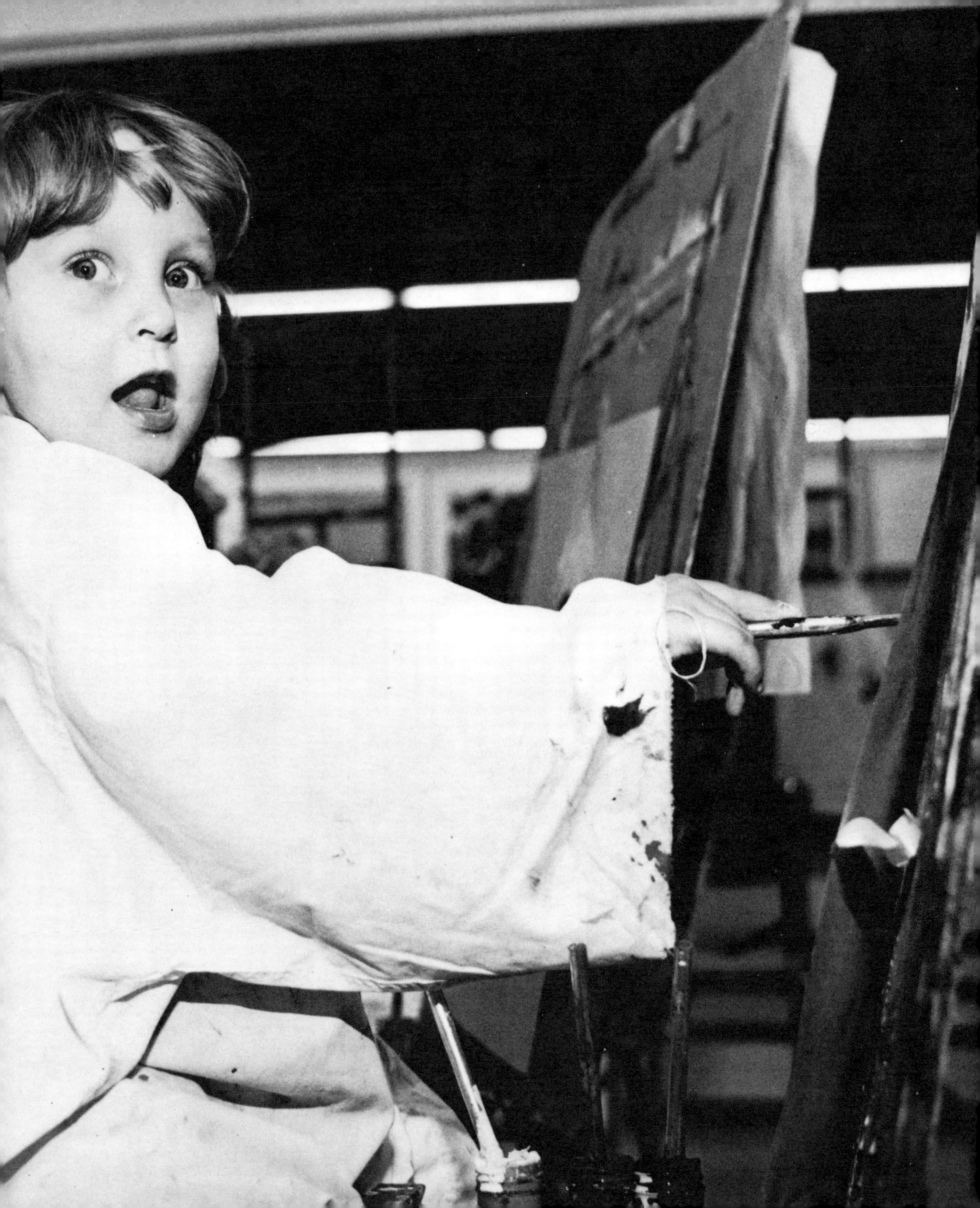